Software Engineering Methods, Management, and CASE Tools

Software Engineering Methods, Management, and CASE Tools

Jag Sodhi

TAB Professional and Reference Books

Division of TAB BOOKS
Blue Ridge Summit, PA

The author and publisher make no warranty of any kind, expressed or implied, with regard to the programs or documentation contained in this book. The author and publisher are not liable for damages in connection with, or arising from, the furnishing, performance, or use of these programs.

FIRST EDITION
FIRST PRINTING

© 1991 by **TAB Professional and Reference Books,** an imprint of TAB Books.
TAB Books is a division of McGraw-Hill, Inc.
The TAB Professional and Reference Books logo, consisting of the letters ''TPR''
within a large ''T,'' is a registered trademark of TAB Books.

Printed in the United States of America. All rights reserved. The publisher takes no
responsibility for the use of any of the materials or methods described in this book,
nor for the products thereof.

Library of Congress Cataloging-in-Publication Data

Sodhi, Jag.
    Software engineering : methods, management, and CASE tools / by
Jag Sodhi.
      p. cm.
    Includes index.
    ISBN 0-8306-3442-8 (h)
    1. Software engineering I. Title.
QA76.758.S644 1991   91-7473
005.1—dc20   CIP

TAB Books offers software for sale. For information and a catalog, please contact TAB
Software Department, Blue Ridge Summit, PA 17294-0850.

Questions regarding the content of this book should be addressed to:

Reader Inquiry Branch
TAB Books
Blue Ridge Summit, PA 17294-0850

Vice President and Editorial Director: Larry Hager
Production: Katherine G. Brown
Book Design: Jaclyn J. Boone

This book is dedicated to
Friends,
Students,
and Colleagues.

Contents

Acknowledgments xv

Preface xvii

Introduction xix

Section: I

Software engineering and methodology

1 Software engineering taxonomy   3

Importance of software engineering   3
   Structured methods   3
   Procedures   3
   Tools   4
Software engineering objectives   5
Software engineering characteristics   5
Software engineering systems classification   6
   Batch systems   7
   Reactive systems   7
   Concurrent systems   7
Properties of good software engineering   7

2 Software development processes   9

Software development process components   9
   Study process   10
   Design process   13
   Implementation process   16
   Maintenance process   16

3 Software life-cycle paradigms   17

Software life-cycle issues   17
Modeling concepts   20
   Software life-cycle model   21
   Waterfall model   21
   Incremental model   23
   Prototyping/simulation model   23

Assembling reusable components model   24
Spiral model   24
Operational model   26
Transformational model   26

4   Software engineering standards   27

Characteristics of a good standard   27
IEEE software engineering standards   28
U.S. Department of Defense standards   28
Tailoring standards   35
    Factors for tailoring   36
    Guidelines for tailoring   36
    Software development files   36
    Firmware   37
    System engineering   37
    Data-item tasking   37
    Nondeliverable software   37

5   Software development approaches concepts   39

Types of software development approaches   39
Structured approach   39
    Structured analysis   40
    Structured design   40
    Structured programming design language   45
    Structured programming   45
Object-oriented approach   46
Entity relationship approach   48
Event-oriented approach   48
Stepwise refinement approach   48
Strengths and weaknesses of the approaches   49

6   Software engineering methodology concepts   51

What is a software engineering methodology   51
Necessity of a software engineering methodology   52
    Enhancement of quality   54
    Cost effectiveness   54
    Requirements constraint   54
Properties of a good methodology   54
Modern technology impacts   55
Selection criteria of a suitable methodology   55
    Technical description   56
    Management aspects   56
    Productivity   58
    Ease of adoptability   59
    Vendor's support   59

Section: II

Software engineering practices

7 Structured analysis, design, and implementation of information systems　　　**63**

Overview 63
Technical description 67
Management aspects 69
Ease of adoptability 69
A case study 70
　　Structured analysis 70
　　Structured design 82

8 Structured analysis methods　　　**83**

Structured analysis and design technique 83
Structured system analysis 87
User-centered requirements analysis 88
Software engineering requirements analysis 90

9 Structured design methods　　　**97**

Structured design 97
Refinement method 100
Software engineering design 101
A case study 106

10 Structured methodology　　　**109**

Software cost reduction 109
The box structure methodology for information systems development 111
Essential systems development/essential systems analysis 113

11 Real-time systems methods　　　**117**

Software through pictures 117
Ward/Mellor real-time method 121
STATEMATE 122
Design approach for real-time systems 123
Strategies for system development 125
PROTOB 127
Overview 127
A case study 127

12 Software engineering methods　　　**149**

ProMod 149
Software requirements engineering methodology 153

13 Data/entity-oriented methodologies 161

Jackson structured programming 161
Warnier-Orr methodology 163
Entity diagram 166
Bachman diagram 167
Jackson system development 167

14 Data-based methods 171

Problem statement language/problem statement analyzer 171
Vienna development method 175
    VDM specification language 175
    Abstraction 175
    VDM modeling techniques 176
    VDM data models and database management systems 177
    VDM stepwise development 178

Section: III

Evolving software engineering practices

15 Technology for the automated generation of systems 181

Overview 181
    Input/output requirements language 182
    Storage and retrieval 184
    Configuration management 185
    Diagnostic analyzer 188
    Simulation compiler 189
    Analysis library 191
    Document processor 193
    Code generator 194
Technical description 194
Management aspects 196
Ease of adoptability 197
TAGS: Example-1 198
TAGS: Example-2 201
Greatest common denominator 213

16 Language-dependent methods 223

Program design language 223
Byron 225
Fourth-generation languages 229
Fifth-generation languages 230

17   Object-oriented design methods   231

Object-oriented programming   231
  OOP method   231
  OOP strength   232
  OOP vs. conventional approach   232
Object-oriented design   233
  OOD concept   233
  OOD principles   234
  OOD method   236
  OOD notation   238
  OOD and the software development life cycle   243

18   More object-oriented design methods   245

Object-oriented structured design   245
  OOSD goals   245
  OOSD concepts   245
  OOSD approach   246
  OOSD notation   247
  OOSD benefits   250
  OOSD application   250
Hierarchical object-oriented design   256
  HOOD concepts   257
  HOOD method   258
  HOOD notation   258

19   Object-oriented software methodologies   259

ObjectOry   259
  System development   259
  System analysis   261
  System design   265
ObjectOry methodology discussion   267
Advantages of ObjectOry   270

20   Object-oriented methodology   271

Object-oriented methodology for software engineering   271
  OOM goals   271
  OOM concepts   272
  OOM and DOD-STD-2167A   280
  OOM benefits   281
  OOM weaknesses   281

Section: IV

CASE tools

21 CASE technology   **285**

Definition of CASE tools   285
Characteristics of a good CASE tool   287
    Project management   288
    System requirements analysis phase   288
    Software requirements analysis phase   289
    Preliminary design phase   289
    Detailed design phase   290
    Coding and unit testing phase   291
    Software component integration and testing phase   291
    Software configuration-item testing phase   292
    System integration and testing phase   292
Types of CASE tools   293
    Forward software engineering   293
    Reverse software engineering   293
    Resoftware engineering   293
CASE tools evaluation guidelines   294
    Ease of use   294
    Capability   295
    Robustness   295
    Functionality   295
    Ease of insertion   296
    Quality of support   296
Assessing CASE tools for selection   297
    Perform needs and requirements analysis   297
    Perform analysis of the existing environment   297
    Develop a list of candidate CASE tools   298
    Apply assessment criteria and select a tool for use   298
Use CASE tools effectively   298

22 Existing CASE tools   **299**

CASE tools for information systems by McDonnell Douglas   299
Software through Pictures by Interactive Development
Environments   309
ProMod by Promod Inc.   313
Problem Statement Language/Problem Statement Analyzer by Meta
Systems   314
CASE tools for TAGS by Teledyne Brown Engineering   316
Artifex by ARTIS   320
Teamwork by Cadre Technologies   323
AISLE by Software System Design   328

23   Emerging CASE tools   **333**

Object Plus by EasySpec   333
CASEWORKS Tool Set by CASEWorks   336
Digital CASE Environment by Digital   338

24   CASE future trends   **345**

Intelligent CASE tools   345
Software prototyping/simulation tools   346
Supporting CASE tools   347

Appendices

A   List of acronyms and abbreviations   **349**

**B   List of vendors CASE tools and software engineering
      methodologies**   **353**

C   List of software development standards   **369**

Bibliography   **371**

Index   **377**

Acknowledgments

I thank all my friends, students, and colleagues who contributed in different ways toward the completion of this book. Identification of all the people who have contributed to the development of this project is not easy.

I express my appreciation to the reviewer of the first three chapters, Robert Stinson. My special thanks to Lee Whitley, Gary Meek, Rick Bucher, and Lyman Lackey of TELOS Federal Systems. I thank wholeheartedly Dr. Don Phillips, Tom Russell, Chairman Department of Technology, and Feridoon Moinian, Department of Mathematics Computer Sciences, Cameron University, Lawton, Oklahoma; Dr. William Wood, Software Engineering Institute, Carnegie-Mellon University, Pittsburgh, Pennsylvania; Dr. Cliff Layton, Roger State College, Claremore, Oklahoma; Donna Behnke, Director of Software Development, VSSI Claremore, Oklahoma; Victor Ward, Dowell Schlumberger, Inc., Tulsa, Oklahoma; Dr. K.M. George, Computer Science Department, Oklahoma State University, Stillwater, Oklahoma; Fred Ramos, Oklahoma City University, Oklahoma; Albert Rodrigues; Lois Nihen; and Jorge Diaz-Herrera, Computer Science, George Mason University, Virginia.

I owe a great debt to my friends who have contributed to the development of this book: Richard Hesselgren, Helaine Kinsey, and Lois Marie, Digital Equipment Corporation; Gerry Gotvald, Teledyne Brown Engineering, Huntsville, Alabama; Jeannette Baum, CASEWorks, Atlanta, Georgia; Diane Bicket, and Michelle Jackson, McDonnell Douglas, Hazelwood, Missouri; Anthony Wasserman, and Bill Baumler, Interactive Development Environments, Dallas, Texas; Marco Balsassari, ARTIS, Torino, Italy; Dan McGillivary, Intermetrics, Cambridge, MA; Sharon Van Sickle, Cadre Technologies; Lars Wilktorin, Objective Systems, Kista, Sweden; Anthony Lekkos, EasySpec, Houston, Texas; Promod Inc., Lake Forest, California; Information Systems Institute, Vero Beach, Florida; Tom Radi, Software Systems Design, Claremont, California; and Craig Dembeck, Meta Systems, Ann Arbor, Michigan.

I thank all the people at the publishing company who were involved in the editing and production of the text. My special thanks to Orlando Petrocelli, Larry Hager, and Jane Stark.

Finally, I commend my wife, Lynda, who diligently supported me in finishing this project successfully. Without the love and support of her and my children I would not have completed such a project.

Preface

Software Engineering: Methods, Management, and CASE Tools presents a variety of selected methods, methodologies, and CASE tools. I attempt to provide comprehensive information that will be beneficial to you. By learning these techniques and tools, you can produce cost-effective software of high quality.

Software engineering is a rapidly developing field, along with new methods, methodologies, and CASE tools that are cropping up every day. The main goal of this book is to present high-quality information results. This book covers a wide range of selected subject areas, such as structured methods/methodologies; data/entity-oriented, event-oriented, real-time, stepwise refinement, and object-oriented methodologies; and CASE tools. This material can certainly help you to understand and select a suitable method, methodology, and CASE tool for your requirements.

This book is intended for both beginners and experienced computer professionals—analysts, designers, programmers, engineers, and managers. The focus throughout the book is on practical software technology. This book can be an asset to university courses in computer sciences, software engineering, and other branches of computer curriculum.

This book presents state-of-the-art material; you can be assured it reflects what's currently happening in the software engineering field. Use of the book's appendices is encouraged. You can consult respective vendors for further discussion.

The information and data contained here has been compiled from various sources and is intended to be used for reference purposes. Neither the publisher nor the author warrants the accuracy of the information and data.

Introduction

This book consists of four sections. Section I reviews software engineering, standards, software development processes, life cycle, concepts for software development approaches, and methodologies. *Methodology* and *method* are interchangeable words throughout the book.

Chapter 1 defines the importance of software engineering, its objectives, characteristics, and main properties.

Chapter 2 deals with software development components: the study process, the design process, the implementation process, and the maintenance process. The software development process is viewed as an abstract object that evolves from an initial statement of requirements needed to finish a software engineering product. By the utilization of proper methods and CASE tools, software engineering builds and maintains high-quality software products.

Chapter 3 covers models of software evolution and their role in structuring software development. The life cycle organizes the activities of a developing software. It also identifies techniques and evaluates the practical utility of a given model of software evolution for development projects in various kinds of organizational settings.

Chapter 4 discusses many available standards and the techniques used to tailor them.

Chapter 5 presents various software development approaches. An approach includes the choice of environments and methods used for software development.

Chapter 6 covers the necessity of a software engineering methodology and the selection criteria of a suitable methodology.

Section II presents a variety of methods and methodologies for software engineering practices. Chapter 7 covers the structured methodology for the entire project by McDonnell Douglas Corporation. STRADIS begins with the development of an information systems transition plan that covers the organization's information systems requirements. The case study is a walk-through that explains the methodology.

Chapter 8 includes four structured analysis methods. Customer requirements need to be analyzed thoroughly and understood before system design is started. The Structured Analysis and Design Technique (SADT) uses a formalism of block diagrams that represent a structured analysis of the requirements. The Structured System Analysis (SSA) builds a system model much like SADT. The User-Centered Requirements Analysis (UCRA) is a method used in the development of detailed requirements specifications for a software application. This method combines concepts from Yourdon/DeMarco and Gane/Sarson process modeling and is based on data flow diagrams with requirements verifiability of military standards. The Software Engineering Requirements Analysis

(SERA) method primarily focuses on understanding and analyzing a customer's requirements for system software engineering. SERA is explained and an example is included.

Chapter 9 covers three structured design methods, which are methods that translate requirements specifications into another phase(s) of the software engineering life cycle. Structured Design (SD) provides techniques that address the activities of preliminary design and detailed design. It also defines the architectural (structural) design of the system that is being developed. The Refinement Method (RM) addresses the activities of design, coding, prototyping, and documentation. It provides ways that a design can be gradually completed. A top-down approach is followed, as are the principles of object-oriented programming and information hiding. The Software Engineering Design (SED) provides techniques and addresses the activities of preliminary design and detailed design. SED is explained and a case study is included.

Chapter 10 includes three software engineering methodologies. Software Cost Reduction (SCR) associates the concepts of information hiding and modularization by separation of concerns and examples of templates for functions, data items, and modes. The Box Structure methodology for Information System Development is described as a complete, mathematically based theory that extends software engineering principles to systems. The Essential System Development/Essential System Analysis (ESD/ESA) provides a framework for system development.

Chapter 11 discusses six real-time system methods. The realities of real-time systems are accuracy, reliability, and immediate response. Software through Picture (StP), by Interactive Development Environments, models real-time systems with data flow diagrams, data stores, and control flows. The Ward/Mellor Real-Time method adds control and behavioral specification aspects to the original structured analysis, with emphasis on function and data flow. STATEMATE, by i-Logic, is a comprehensive tool for specification, design, and analysis of real-time systems. Design Approach for Real-Time Systems (DARTS), by Dr. Hassan Gommas, extends SA/SD as a real-time problem domain that provides design criteria for multitasking. Strategies for System Development (SSD), by Hatley & Pirbhai, tailors the structured analysis techniques and then fits in real-time systems. PROTOB, by Marco Baldassari & Giorgio Bruno of Italy, uses PROT nets (Petri nets) and provides a graphical model for discrete event dynamics real-time systems.

Chapter 12 provides two more software engineering methods. ProMod, by Promod Inc., uses an integrated set of automated tools that support all technical phases of software development. The Software Requirements Engineering Methodology (SREM), by TRW, covers techniques and procedures for requirements decomposition and for management of the requirements development process.

Chapter 13 briefly presents five data/entity-oriented methodologies. Jackson Structured Programming (JSP) is a program design method concerned with smaller sequential problems. The Warnier-Orr Methodology uses a similar philosophy as JSP with more textual representation. Entity Diagram focuses on the information of a system as opposed to the function. Bachman diagrams use entity diagrams and relation class ratios that help with computer implementation. Jackson System Development (JSD) extends the philosophy used in JSP with a larger domain of application.

Chapter 14 describes two data-based methods. The Problem Statement Language/ Problem Statement Analyzer (PSL/PSA), by Meta Systems, is a computer-aided structured technique for analysis and documentation of requirements. The Vienna

Development Method (VDM) is a formal mathematically oriented method used in the specification and development of software.

Section III covers evolving software engineering methods and methodologies. Chapter 15 describes Technology for the Automated Generation of Systems (TAGS), by Teledyne Brown Engineering. TAGS is a computer automated systems engineering environment that provides automated definition, design, documentation, testing, and maintenance of complex systems. This chapter also presents a few examples that explain TAGS.

Chapter 16 starts with the Program Design language, a method that commonly uses structured English in the detailed design phase. Next, the Byron method for Ada language is presented. The fourth-generation languages are briefly explained. Finally, the fifth-generation language is briefly discussed.

Chapter 17 presents object-oriented software development methods that are receiving wide acceptance as a standard technology within the software industry. Object-Oriented Programming (OOP) changes from writing instructions to interconnecting reusable software components. The Object-Oriented Design (OOD) focuses on the design and implementation aspects of the software process.

Chapter 18 discusses two more object-oriented methods. The Object-Oriented Structured Design (OOSD), by IDE, builds on ideas from Constantine's structured design and Booch's object-oriented design. A case study is discussed and explains the OOSD. The Hierarchical Object-Oriented Design (HOOD) is an architectural design method that is used in the development of Ada projects.

Chapter 19 covers ObjectOry methodology, by Objective Systems, Sweden. ObjectOry is an object-oriented software development methodology. It covers the analysis, design, and test phases of the software development life cycle. It supports object-oriented features such as objects, classes, and inheritance during both analysis and design.

Chapter 20 discusses an Object-Oriented Methodology (OOM). The OOM is the combination of an object-oriented approach, a data structure approach with entity relationship modeling, and a functional process approach.

Section IV presents CASE tools and CASE technology. Chapter 21 contains the CASE tools concept, major components, characteristics, and various types of CASE tools, which are assessed for selection.

Chapter 22 discusses eight CASE tools. CASE Tools for Information System, by McDonnell Douglas, is called ProKit*WORKBENCH. StP, by Interactive Development Environments, supports many analysis and design methodologies with a family of graphical editors, template-driven Object Annotation Editor, and Document Preparation system. ProMod, by Promod Inc., has a central database as a project library. PSL/PSA, by Meta System, automates and assists in the description, analysis, and design of information processing systems. TAGS tightly connects all system representation, that is, data flow, control flow, functional flow, and timing in the database. Artifex is the CASE environment that ARTIS created for the production of event-driven systems, which includes: analysis, simulation, design, prototyping, and implementation; Teamwork, by Cadre Technologies, consists of six CASE tools; the Teamwork approach to software design provides consistency and early detection of errors. AISLE, by Software System Design, is the Ada/ADADL integrated software life-cycle environment.

Chapter 23 covers three emerging CASE tools. Object Plus, by EasySpec, supports the object-oriented approach and is a window-based integrated CASE tool set. The CASEWORK Tool Set, by CASEWorks, is an integrated tool set and consists of CASE:W for Microsoft windows and CASE:PM for OS/2 Presentation Manager. The Digital CASE Environment (DCE), by Digital, is a comprehensive solution to the problem of creating and maintaining timely quality software in today's diverse computing environment. DCE ties together tools that support the entire software life cycle, as well as tools that coordinate your development team. DCE includes tools that are developed by independent software vendors and by the Digital.

Chapter 23 also provides future trends of CASE tools; CASE tools hold promise for the future by addressing many of today's software engineering needs. Some of these needs will be the establishment of a uniform standard, creation of a generic template, and plain understandable English instructions. The proper use of CASE tools will help in controlling costs, reducing development time, and achieving quality products.

The numbers in square brackets, [ ], throughout the book refer to the references that are listed in the bibliography. All abbreviations and acronyms used in the book are also defined at the end of the book.

I

Software Engineering
and
Methodology

1

Software engineering taxonomy

Software development is now seen as a crucial issue facing computer users in industry. The demand for more complex, high-quality software is growing at an unprecedented rate. There is always a need to engineer system software that will meet user requirements and expectations within available resources and that can accommodate change throughout the software life cycle.

Software engineering can be defined as the disciplined application of engineering, scientific, and mathematical principles and methods in the economical production of quality software. Software engineering was first defined by Fritz Bauer in 1968 at a conference sponsored by the Science Committee of the North Atlantic Treaty Organization (NATO). Bauer used the term to mean the application of systems engineering principles to software development and maintenance.

IMPORTANCE OF SOFTWARE ENGINEERING

The importance of software engineering is its systematic approach to software development, implementation, and maintenance throughout the life cycle of the computer system. Software engineering consists of a set of structured methods, procedures, and tools used to engineer quality and cost-effective software, as illustrated in FIG. 1-1.

Structured methods

Structured methods are the manners in which software engineering tasks are performed. These technical approaches assist in the development of software. Some of the structured methods are planning, analysis, design, coding, testing, integration, and maintenance.

Procedures

Procedures are the management harnesses supporting the methods. Procedures include project tracking, project control, quality assurance, and configuration management.

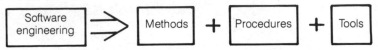

Fig. 1-1. Software engineering structure

Tools

Tools are support environments necessary to automate the software engineering practices. These environments are explained as follows.

- Project management
  - Planning
  - Estimating
  - Scheduling

- Modeling
  - Prototyping
  - Simulation

- Structured analysis
- Structured design
- Structured coding
  - Reuse code
  - Code generation

- Documentation
- Structured testing
- Software components and system integration and testing
- Database schema
- Quality controls
- Configuration management
- Data management

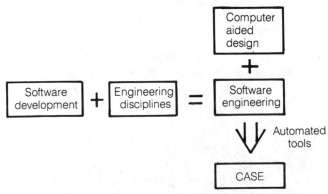

Fig. 1-2. Computer-aided software engineering overview

Computer-Aided Software Engineering (CASE) tools, as illustrated in FIG. 1-2, automate methods and procedures. CASE tools enable efficient implementation of disciplined software engineering objectives. CASE tools are considered a major breakthrough in software development and maintenance. The CASE tool reduces time and cost, and improves the quality of software engineering. CASE tools will be discussed in detail in later chapters.

SOFTWARE ENGINEERING OBJECTIVES

Software engineering objectives include the following main features:

- Software is reliable.
- Software works to original specifications.
- Software engineering is cost effective.
- Software is engineered within the resources.
- Software is engineered in time.
- Software engineering is a quality product.
- Software engineering meets user requirements.
- Software can accommodate change throughout the life cycle.
- Software is reusable on different systems.

Software engineering is a disciplined approach consisting of a set of principles and goals that are applied during various phases of software development. The goals and objectives of software engineering are synonymous in this book, and they are to achieve reliability, modifiability, maintainability, understandability, adaptability, reusability, efficiency, portability, and traceability.

Software engineering principles are techniques used in attaining software goals. The main principles are abstraction, information hiding, completeness, confirmability, modularity, localization, error handling, and uniformity. These principles are established during the software engineering life cycle.

SOFTWARE ENGINEERING CHARACTERISTICS

Software engineering characteristics such as uniqueness of size, complexity, and phase (i.e., concept exploration, proof of software engineering goals and principles, full-scale development, or post-development software support are coarse categories that influence the software process applied to the system. Certain explicit requirements categories include reliability, fault tolerance, performance, and compatability. Existing systems also warrant explicit attention in decisions as to appropriate life-cycle processes, both technical and managerial.

Management planning must consider in a sophisticated technical way all the technical considerations that are required for each particular system project:

- System characteristics
  - Size
  - Complexity
  - Newness

- Requirements characteristics
  - Nature
  - Degree of definition

- Training needs
- Project cost
- Schedule
- Available suitable methodologies/methods
- Modern CASE tools
- Effective project management techniques

Software engineering is the product of human professionals. Therefore, process models should consider incentives, margin for error, and self-correction schemes. Applied life-cycle models and processes should include any variation within them as a system evolves. Adaptable, flexible, fault-tolerant processes are needed.

These characteristics influence or determine such things as nature of risk, process models used, development technology needed, funding and procurement strategy, standards applicability, and organizational responsibility. Some of these characteristics are illustrated in FIG. 1-3. Correct choices in these areas will depend on correct categorization of the system characteristics by understanding the implications of each characteristic and accurately weighing the implications in the decision for the software development processes.

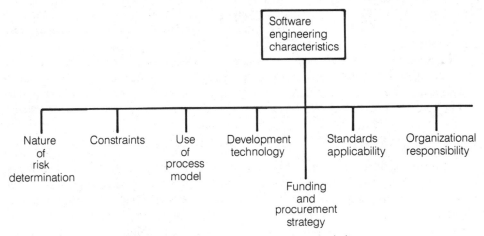

Fig. 1-3. Software engineering characteristics

SOFTWARE ENGINEERING SYSTEMS CLASSIFICATION

Problems that are to be solved with software engineering are often grouped on the basis of similar characteristics. These are called *problem domains*. Such a domain might encompass very broad areas such as data processing systems, real-time systems, or tightly defined compilers. A general scheme for the classification of systems is:

- Batch systems
- Reactive systems
- Concurrent systems

Batch systems

The main feature of a batch system is that all of its operating characteristics are essentially determined when it begins processing one or more data streams. Changes that occur to these characteristics are caused by the contents of sequential flows of stream data. Such a system should perform operations that are deterministic and repeatable.

Reactive systems

A reactive system is event driven, which is the principal characteristic of the system. The event is almost always asynchronous and nondeterministic. In addition, the specifications of the required responses to events often include quite explicit requirements about timing.

Concurrent systems

Concurrent systems are characterized by the use of multiple threads of execution that utilize one or more processors. They generally require that the design process consider such issues as scheduling overhead, mutual exclusion, and synchronization of processes in the system.

Many problems will lead to software engineering systems that are a combination of more than one of these classifications. They should not be considered as being mutually exclusive. Real time and embedded systems are generally classified this way but involve additional constraints on size, performance, and structure.

PROPERTIES OF GOOD SOFTWARE ENGINEERING

The principal properties of a good software engineering system are that a final product has achieved the software engineering objectives that meet the requirements and satisfy the customer. Software engineering that has inherited the maximum possible software engineering goals and principles also includes the following properties:

- Functionality—Correctness, reliability, etc.
- Performance—Response time, throughput, speed, etc.
- Economy—Cost-effectiveness
- Thorough analysis of requirements
- Robustness—Reuse of pretested components
- Use of a suitable matured methodology for its architecture

- Sound life cycle—Software development phases and activities
- Proper documentation—Operational and maintainable
- Ability to survive system evolution—Model well
- Use of effective CASE tools
- Establishment of retrace requirements
- Well-defined external interfaces
- Ability to keep track of requirements in various software development phases
- User-friendliness

Good software engineering should gear toward developing zero defect software. Software engineering incorporates some of the new technologies such as prototyping, reuse, and new software methods into the life cycle. Some of the benefits of reusing components are shown in FIG. 1-4.

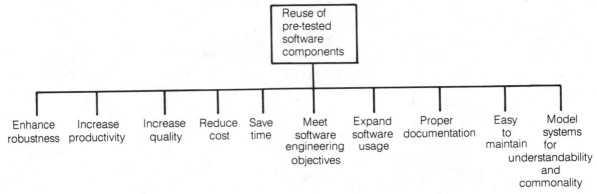

Fig. 1-4. Benefits for reusing pretested software components

2

Software development processes

The software development process is viewed as an abstract object that evolves from an initial statement of requirements needed to finish a software engineering product. By utilizing proper methods and CASE tools, software engineering builds and maintains high quality software products. Software productivity encompasses more than just the programming of software products. In this chapter, the improved software development processes, where software is created, that leads to better quality software and to better control is discussed. The major goal is not only to reduce the increasing cost of software development, but also the cost of maintenance to the software after the original development.

SOFTWARE DEVELOPMENT PROCESS COMPONENTS

Software development processes consist of components characterized by differences in their purpose and in the nature of constituent activities used to achieve these purposes, which is the *taxonomy* of the activities. Taxonomy specifies definition, development, maintenance, and subactivities for each of these main processes. The processes are not the same as software engineering development phases. These phases are discussed in following chapters. The software development processes are described as follows:

1. Study process
   - Requirements determination
   - Requirements specification
   - Requirements analysis

2. Design process
   - Principles of design

3. Implementation process
   - Coding
   - Testing

4. Maintenance process

Study process

The primary function of the study process is to determine requirements for the system software engineering. The developer creates requirements specifications before analyzing the requirements. Each of these topics will be discussed as follows.

Requirements determination   The requirements determination process determines what is desired. The emphasis is on understandability and facility of communication. Determining what is desired involves two subprocesses:

- The customer establishes the requirements.
- The developer learns of these requirements through communication with the customer.

The customer performs cost-benefit analysis to determine what he wants. This analysis stresses benefits because the customer lacks detailed knowledge of the development costs. Moreover, the analysis involves knowledge, experience, and mental scenarios, often at a subconscious level, to weigh the desirability of each requirement. This scenario sample is illustrated in FIG. 2-1.

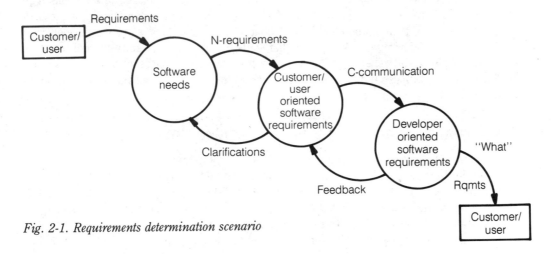

Fig. 2-1. Requirements determination scenario

In the communication subprocess, the developer learns the application and attributes of the product for delivery to the customer. The medium of communication is commonly one of meetings and phone conversations between the customer and the developer. The documents they generate supplement graphic diagrams of various sorts: prototype models, data flow diagrams, structured analysis/design diagrams, object orientation, flow diagrams, state diagrams, etc.

Requirements determine what the developer will have to deliver, and form the basis for acceptability of the product. Thus, the requirements serve to establish the intrinsic cost and benefits of the project.

Requirements specification   Requirements need to be stated rigorously before proceeding to other processes. Requirements specification puts requirements into a precise form, from which the corresponding system is derived. The emphasis is placed on exactitude and full elaboration of meaning. Total quality monitoring provides assurance that the necessary requirements are stated, stated correctly, and interpreted correctly as presented:

- Develop total quality assurance plan
- Develop quality metrics
- Perform reviews at transition points
- Collect and analyze quality metric data
- Analyze cause of defects
- Check compliance with standards
- Perform analysis of user's view of system quality
  - Correctness
  - Completeness
  - Consistency
  - Feasibility
  - Testability

- Identify organizational quality improvement needs

Requirements specification consists of establishing an extended representation of the requirements. Extensions are characterized by testability, and employ objective forms of reference without making use of intention.

Requirements specification is the first example of a more general process that applies to each step in an analysis and design *decomposition*. In decomposing the design, each step must meet requirements arising from and specified by the previous step. The specification maps back to the customer's intent as documented by the requirements. The requirements specification provides a check on the information produced by the requirements determination process. Specification also plays valuable roles in achieving software engineering objectives such as reusability and maintainability.

Requirements analysis Requirements are first analyzed and understood before proceeding to other software engineering processes. Graphic representation of the requirements analysis is encouraged to avoid ambiguity between the customer and the developer. Requirements for exceptional fault tolerance, performance, or robustness demand rigorous approaches, methods, and tools, and will be discussed in following chapters. Sometimes extensive simulation and prototyping is required to analyze requirements.

Software requirements analysis include evaluation for completeness, understandability, validity, consistency, and adequacy of content in the areas of performance, reliability, maintainability, supportability, and security. As mission needs change and affect system requirements, additional analysis is necessary to determine the effect on software requirements. One aspect of requirements analysis is task analysis as depicted in FIG. 2-2, which studies the system requirements concerned with human interaction.

The requirements for engineering a new system are specified in a formal requirement specification document, contract, or proposal. Requirement tracing and compliance reporting provides the tracking and communication mechanisms between the requesting organization and the software developing organization. Many standards utilize

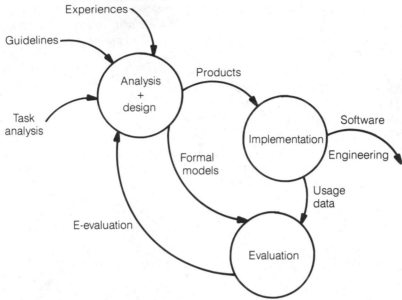

Fig. 2-2. Requirements/task analysis

good software engineering practices and require complete tracing of requirements from the initial requirements documents to the final documents created during analysis and the following processes.

The principal steps in requirements analysis are frequently iterated until all issues are resolved. These principal steps are shown:

Assessment of potential problems
Classification of requirements
Evaluation of feasibility and risks

Assessment of potential problems   The *assessment of potential problems* scrutinizes the requirements for feasibility, ambiguity, incompleteness, and inconsistency. Software requirements for embedded software must be verified to ensure consistency with system requirements.

Classification of requirements   Requirements should be classified into priority categories such as mandatory, desirable, and nonessential. *Mandatory* means the software will not be acceptable to the customer unless the requirements are provided in an agreed manner.

Assessing requirements regarding stability is frequently useful. A stable requirement addresses a need that is not expected to change during the life of the software. Knowing a requirement might change facilitates developing a software design that isolates the potential impact of the change.

Evaluation of feasibility and risks   Assessment of feasibility involves technical feasibility (can the requirements be met with current technology?), operational feasibility (can the software be used by the existing staff in its planned environment?), and economic feasibility (are the costs of system implementation and use acceptable to the customer?) [Ross].

The result of analysis is to formulate the various types of requirements as shown in:

- Functional requirements
- Nonfunctional requirements
- Design and implementation constraints

A *functional requirement* is a function that a system software component must be capable of performing.

Nonfunctional requirements relate to performance, reliability, security, maintainability, availability, accuracy, error handling, capacity, ability to be used by a specific class of users, anticipated changes to be accommodated, acceptable level of training, or support. In real-time systems, performance requirements might be of critical importance and functional requirements might be sacrificed in order to achieve minimally acceptable performance.

Design and implementation constraints are boundary conditions on how the required software is to be constructed and implemented. Examples of design constraints include the database system that the software must utilize, that either the software must fit into the memory of a 640K machine, or that certain techniques or tools are to be used.

The main objectives of requirements products are to achieve agreement on the requirements, provide a basis for software design, and provide a reference point for software validation. Many systems have been developed, tested, and made operational but were soon discarded because the actual requirements were not met. Although these systems were designed in accordance with the state requirements, you must define, analyze, understand, and document the real requirements before going to the next software development process.

Design process

Design is an important process and exerts a major influence on the other software development processes. The purpose of a design is to specify a solution to a given problem. The design postulates a solution, models the solution, evaluates it against the original requirements, and after some iteration of these operations produces a design specification to be used in the implementation process.

Design overview   The design process is concerned with how a system can be built to behave in the manner described by the requirements product. Figure 2-3 shows a simplified representation of the design process, without the inevitable iteration details. During the design process, further documents are generated that provide inputs to the implementation process.

Thus the design process is a form of the problem solving process that involves making extensive use of abstraction, which includes separation of logical aspects of the design from the physical aspects. Abstraction allows the designer to model logical structures as well as physical structures. Design choices often involve tradeoffs between the different qualities the designer is seeking to achieve in his solution. The ultimate criterion must be that of "fitness for purpose." The solution should not only exhibit the best possible structure, but must do the required job as well as possible. In practice, there

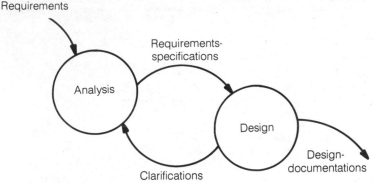

Fig. 2-3. Iteration (analysis and design)

will almost always be a set of constraints restricting architectural and other characteristics of the solution produced. The major constraints include:

- A set of company design practices
- Imply software development standards
- Standard hardware configurations
- Existing file structures
- Real-time
- Implementation language features
- Future changes

The software design process translates requirements specifications into a blueprint of the system. Designs are blueprints of components and their interconnections. The design process allocates the functional requirements to a design structure, presenting the form or design structure along with an indication where the various functions are to be performed. The structure and allocation should allow the performance and analytic requirements to be factored in and verified as constraints.

Principles of design   Software design is the process of synthesizing a specified abstraction from lower-level software components. Designs involve exploration to satisfy desirable characteristics, such as quality of the product and constraints on the software engineering process, as shown in FIG. 2-4.

Identifying certain properties expected of a good design is possible to some degree. Identifiable features that a design should exhibit include those related to the functioning of the system.

Fitness for purpose   The system must work, and work correctly. It should perform the required tasks in a specified manner and within the constraints of the specified resources.

Robustness   The design should be stable against changes to such features as file and data structures, user interface, etc.

Simplicity   The design should be as simple as possible.

Separation of concerns   The different concepts and components should be separated.

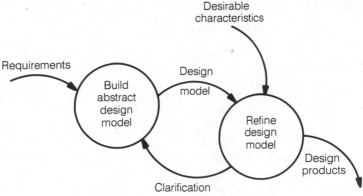

Fig. 2-4. Principles of design process

Information hiding   Information about the detailed form of objects such as data structures and device interfaces should be kept local to a unit and should not be directly visible outside that unit.

Retained state information   Avoid having too much retained state information spread around the system.

Interfaces   Avoid using interfaces that are too complex.

Control structures   Don't use excessively complex control structures.

Constructional issues   Distinguish between constructional issues that are essentially concerned with packaging and dependency.

Consider runtime issue   Runtime issues involve making decisions about such features as concurrency and the calling of hierarchy procedures.

The design step introduces artifacts (data types, variables, functions, etc.) that enrich the higher language to produce the representation in the lower language. The representation in the lower language must be shown to satisfy the requirements of the higher representation. Descent from higher to lower language adds detail from which quality attributes are more easily recognized. Design is thus seen as a significant information-generating activity. This information might have considerable impact on feasibility of solution, desirable requirements, cost, and schedule.

Software engineers in this process cite problems and errors, especially in the following areas:

- Ambiguities
- Inconsistencies
- Incompleteness
- Potential trouble areas
- Requirements with disproportionate cost/schedule impact

The output of the design process is a design product, which is the input to the implementation process.

Implementation process

The implementation process consists of the following subprocesses:

- Coding
- Testing
- Maintenance

Coding   *Coding* is the process of creating a representation of a software artifact that can be converted mechanically by a compiler to an acceptable machine-executable representation. Coding without adequate design is a common failure in software engineering. Coding standards are established according to each project.

Testing   *Testing* is the ultimate verification/validation step of the development process. Testing is called validation when performed against the original requirements and verification when performed against specification.

The primary categories of testing are the lowest level independent software components and the integration of related software components in a system. If the test results are consistent with the expected result, then the software components are deemed correct within the context of the test.

Maintenance process

The software maintenance process consists of fixing bugs and making revisions. Revisions are spurred either by corrections to the original requirements or by changes in response to user needs or technology developments.

Maintenance is regarded as a distinct elemental software development process. For example, the Japanese regard development to be a subset of maintenance. Clearly, maintenance differs from other activities in terms of when it is performed, who performs the maintenance, and with what starting materials. Maintenance might seem to involve processes different from other software engineering processes because of a lack of visibility into actual software maintenance activities and a lack of appropriate documentation.

It is estimated that more than 60 percent of the effort required for maintenance is expended in reconstructing the analysis and design information. Software maintenance would greatly benefit from the documentation of design description and design decisions. Design can be achieved by recording intermediate design specifications and the rationale for the refinement steps. Maintainability is a symptom and the result of the quality of earlier processes. Maintainability is critically dependent on design.

3

Software life-cycle paradigms

This chapter presents concepts and approaches for organizing software engineering activities throughout the life of software systems, and covers models of systems software evolution and their role in structuring software development. The life cycle organizes the activities of developing software. A system's software life cycle also identifies techniques for evaluating the practical utility for a given model of software evolution in development projects within various organizational settings.

SOFTWARE LIFE-CYCLE ISSUES

Software evolution represents the cycle of activities involved in the development, use, and maintenance of software systems. Software systems come and go through a series of passages that account for their inception, initial development, productive operation, upkeep, and retirement from one generation (version) to another.

Models of software evolution date back to the earliest projects where large software systems were developed. The apparent purpose of these models was to provide an abstract scheme to account for the "natural" or engineered development of software systems. The scheme could then serve as a basis for planning, organizing, staffing, coordinating, budgeting, and directing software development activities. An example is shown in FIG. 3-1. The activities are discussed as follows.

Activity 1: System initiation/adoption The system initiation/adoption activity identifies a system's origination. Many new systems are replaced or supplement existing processing mechanisms.

Activity 2: Requirement analysis and specification The requirement analysis and specification activity identifies the problems that must be solved. The software engineering process determines what must be produced. This activity involves requirements identification, analysis, representation, communication, and development of acceptance criteria and procedures.

Activity 3: Functional specification/prototyping/simulation The functional specification/prototyping/simulation activity identifies and potentially formalizes subactivities such as the objects of computation, attributes and relationships of the objects, the operations that transform these objects, and the constraints that restrict system behavior.

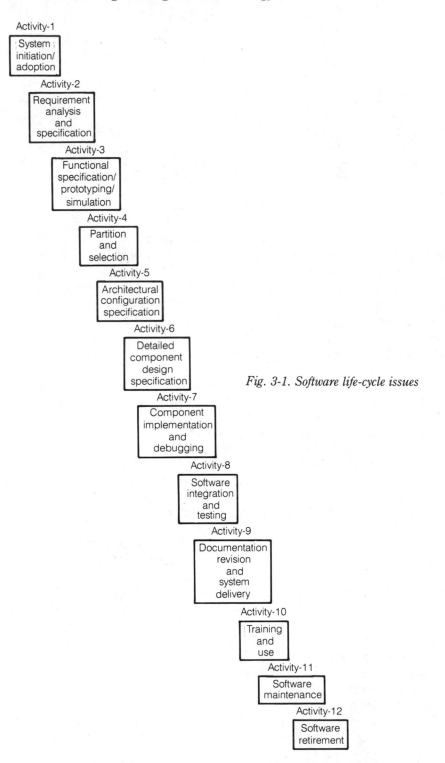

Fig. 3-1. Software life-cycle issues

Activity 4: Partition and selection   The partition and selection activity for the given requirements and functional specifications divides the system into manageable pieces that denote logical subsystems. Then you must determine whether new, existing, or reusable software systems correspond to the needed pieces.

Activity 5: Architectural configuration specification   The architectural configuration specification activity defines the interconnection and resource interfaces among system modules in ways suitable for their detailed design and overall configuration management.

Activity 6: Detailed component design specification   The detailed components design specification activity defines the procedural methods by which each module's data resources are transformed from required inputs to provided outputs.

Activity 7: Component implementation and debugging   The component implementation and debugging activity codifies the preceding specifications into source code and validates their basic operation.

Activity 8: Software integration and testing   The software integration and testing activity affirms and sustains the overall integrity of the software configuration by verifying the consistency and completeness of implemented modules, verifying the resource interfaces and interconnections with the specifications, and validating the performance of the system and subsystems with the requirements.

Activity 9: Documentation revision and system delivery   The documentation revision and system delivery activity packages and rationalizes recorded system development description into systematic documents and user guides. These documents are in a form suitable for dissemination and system support.

Activity 10: Training and use   The training and use activity provides system users with instructional aids and guidance for understanding the system's capabilities and limits in order to effectively use the system.

Activity 11: Software maintenance   The software maintenance activity sustains the useful operation of a system in its target environment by providing requested enhancements, repairs, performance improvements, and conversions. Maintenance represents ongoing incremental iterations through the life cycle activities that precede it. Maintenance activities are explained in FIG. 3-2.

Activity 12: Software retirement   The software retirement activity is not very common. Most retired system software is considered useless and therefore not in existence. Retired systems were once created for a special purpose, with a special language, and for a special computer. But with the advent of Ada, C++, object-oriented, and the Common Hardware Software (CHS) concept, some of the software components from the retired system can be reused. These software components, which have already been tested, are more economical to use than creating new ones.

You should understand and identify the reusability and viability of software components for new systems. The model of a new system can be compared with the existing model of the retired system to identify the suitable software components. Reusing pretested software components will save time and cost, and the quality of the software products will increase.

The model concept, taken at a high level of abstraction and applied to software development, is called the software life cycle. The life-cycle notion exists beyond the design and programming stages of development. The concept implies that software exists even in the conceptual stages of problem definition, that it needs to be maintained after formal development has been completed, and that it functions until retirement, as shown in FIG. 3-3.

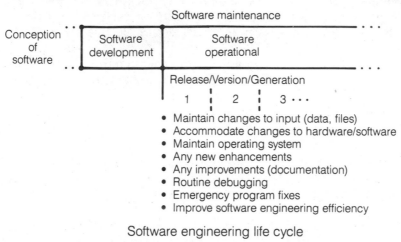

Fig. 3-2. Software maintenance activity

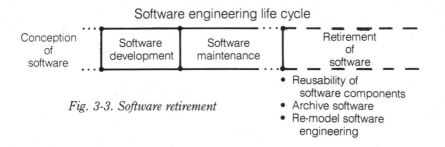

Fig. 3-3. Software retirement

MODELING CONCEPTS

Models are abstractions that assist the concepts of the software development process. A software model represents the components of the development process. The finite phases of a model are not realistic. Models are constructed with the builder's ideas of what is important. This idea must determine the greater visibility to a certain set of concerns. Some of these concerns are not clearly defined. A model can be a software development process, software, or a software management process. Models are drawn to assure that the software product matches the customer's intent. Assurances correlate to other considerations such as the:

- Type of system to be developed
- Technical orientation of people involved in the development effort
- Tools used in the effort

A customer can validate the system. A model can incorporate the concept in a structured manner that ties requirements to the end product.

Models exhibit various ways to view the software development process. The viewpoint contributes to the formulation of other models. Models can assist in managing software, testing, maintenance, and retirement. Some of the popular models are briefly discussed.

Software life-cycle model

The software life-cycle model encompasses many concepts throughout software engineering. These concepts vary from project management through system design and software coding to maintenance. Software requirements might change with time. With the advent of modern technology, the software has to be rewritten. Thus the life cycle provides a way of looking at various phases of software development for a system, and assists in explaining various aspects of software development in a common language, which can include graphics, so that the effects of changes to the development process can be determined. A software life-cycle model is either a *prescriptive* or *descriptive* characterization of software evolution.

A prescriptive characterization means the level of detail supplied by the method to provide direction for accomplishing various activities. A prescriptive life-cycle model is easier to develop. Many software development details can be ignored, glossed over, or generalized. Of course, a concern should be raised for the validity and robustness of life-cycle models when developing different kinds of application systems in different kinds of development settings.

A descriptive life-cycle model characterizes how software systems are actually developed. These models are less common and more difficult to articulate for one obvious reason: you must observe or collect data throughout the development of a software system. This development period is an elapsed time usually measured in years. Also, descriptive models are specific to the systems observed and only generalizable with systematic analysis.

Waterfall model

The class Waterfall model was first introduced by W. Royce in 1970. This software evolution proceeds in an orderly sequence of transition from one phase to the next in linear order. The model divides the software process into phases, as illustrated in FIG. 3-4.

Each phase is conceived in terms of input, process, and output. The software process proceeds through a sequence of steps with iterative interaction between the phases that are confined to successive steps. Deliverable software is usually produced and used as input into the next phase.

In reality, software development is never so clean. As shown in FIG. 3-5, feedback loops exist between phases. Because of these feedback loops, the deliverable products at each phase need reviews and changes before acceptance. The design phase can be subdivided into many phases with increased detail.

The model derives its strength from steps to be taken successively, and provides a structured template for software engineering. The weakness of this model is that more

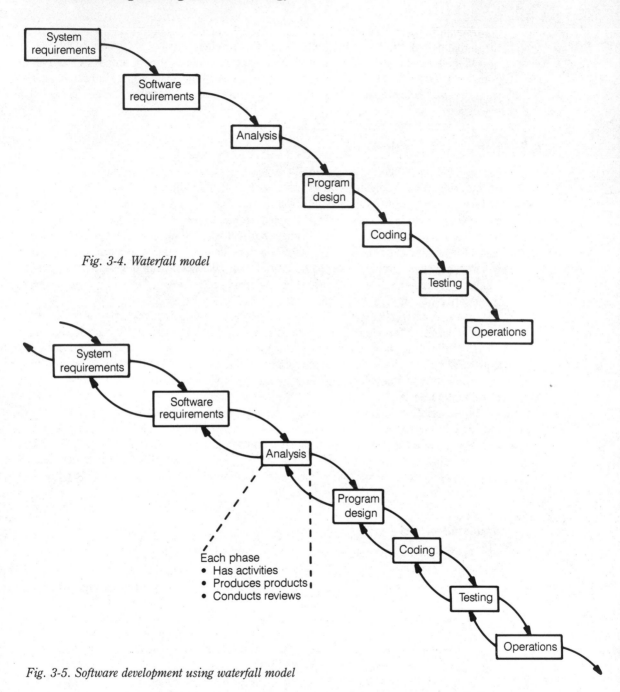

Fig. 3-4. Waterfall model

Each phase
• Has activities
• Produces products
• Conducts reviews

Fig. 3-5. Software development using waterfall model

interaction between nonsuccessive steps is necessary. The model has been most useful when helping to structure and manage large software development projects in organizational settings.

Incremental model

In the incremental model, an initial subset of the system is fully developed. Then in successive steps, more elaborate versions are built on the previous steps. The architectural design of the total system is envisioned in the first step, but the system is implemented by successive elaborations. The software is developed in increments, as shown in FIG. 3-6, which represent degrees of functional capability. Software is built in small manageable increments. Each increment adds a new function to the system.

The strength of incremental development is that the increments of functional capability are easier to understand and test. Use of the successive increments provides a way to incorporate user experience into a refined product in a less expensive way.

This model combines the classic software life cycle with iterative enhancement at the level of system development organization. It also provides a way to periodically distribute software maintenance updates and services to dispersed users. This model is popular for software evolution used in the computer industry.

Prototyping/simulation model

The prototyping model advocates the early development of components representing the eventual system. These components often represent the user interface to the system. A skeletal implementation of this interface is developed with the intent of providing an opportunity for feedback from the user before the final system is specified and designed. Although the clarification of the user interface is one goal, prototyping can also

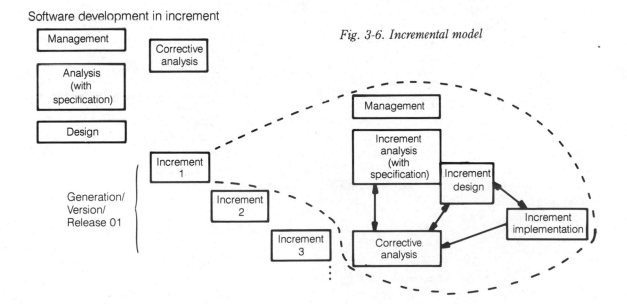

Software development in increment

Fig. 3-6. Incremental model

be employed as a concept within the context of another model. In this case, the second model of the software process might regard prototyping as one component of the process used to clarify the behavior of the system at an early point in the development.

Prototyping usually accepts some form of software-functional specifications such as input, which in turn is simulated, analyzed, or executed. These technologies allow software design activities to initially be skipped or glossed over. These technologies can then allow developers to rapidly construct primitive versions of software systems that users can evaluate. User evaluations are incorporated as feedback to refine the emerging system specifications and designs. Depending on the prototyping technology, the complete working system can be developed with a continuing process of refinement with the input specifications. This model has the advantage of always providing a working version of the developing system.

Assembling reusable components model

The basic approach of reusability is to configure and specialize preexisting software components into viable application systems, as shown in FIG. 3-7. However, the characteristics of the components depends on their size, complexity, and functional capability.

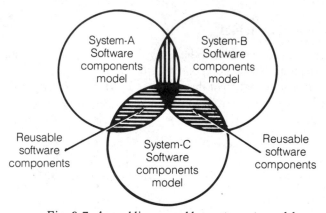

Fig. 3-7. Assembling reusable components model

Most approaches attempt to utilize components similar to the common data structure with algorithms as their manipulation. Other approaches attempt to utilize components resembling functionally complete systems or subsystems that are user interface management systems. There are many ways to utilize reusable software components to evolve software systems. Cited studies suggest that initial use of the reusable components during architectural or component design specification is a way to speed implementation. These components can also be used for prototyping purposes if a suitable software prototyping technology is available.

Spiral model

The Spiral model was developed at TRW by B. Boehm in 1988. The model involves multiple iterations through cycles that analyze the results of prior phases by determining risk estimates for future phases. This model is shown in FIG. 3-8. At each phase, alternatives are evaluated with respect to the objectives and constraints that form the basis for the next cycle of the spiral. Each cycle is completed with a review involving vested interested parties. Boehm states, "The model reflects the underlying concept that each cycle involves a progression that addresses the same sequence of steps for each portion of the product and for each of its levels of elaboration from an overall concept-of-operation document down to the coding of each individual program." [Boehm]

The radial dimension represents the incremental costs incurred in completing the developmental steps. The angular dimension represents the progress made in completing each cycle of the spiral. The basic premise of the model is that a certain sequence of

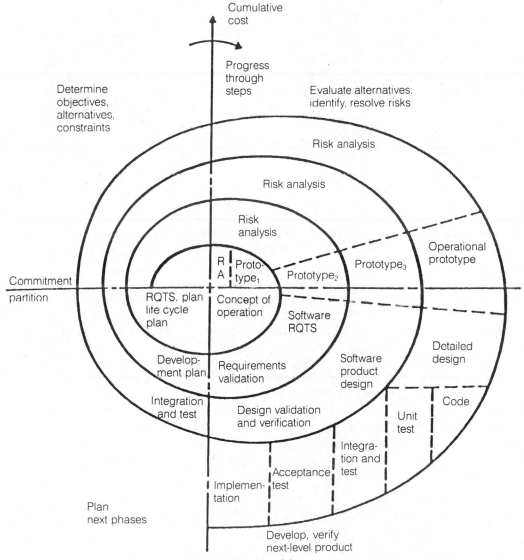

Fig. 3-8. Spiral model

steps is repeated while developing or maintaining the software. The steps are first done with a high level of abstraction. Each loop of the spiral represents a repeat of the steps at successively lower levels of abstraction.

The strength of the model lies in its flexibility for managing a software engineering life cycle. You can plan an examination of risk at each major abstraction. The model accommodates any mixture of specification-oriented, process-oriented, object-oriented, or other approaches to software development.

The weakness of the model is a lack of matching with any existing standards. The model relies on identifying and managing sources at risk to the project. The model needs more uniformity and consistency.

Operational model

Behaviors particular to the problem domain are modeled and simulated in the beginning stages of the operational model in order to explore with the software customer the way and order that events happen. This exploration is made possible with the construction of an operational specification of the system. Concern at the specification level with how the system behaves is in contrast to other models whose specifications define the system in terms of a black box mapping of the inputs and outputs.

Although the behavior of the problem domain is emulated in the specification, the software structures that will eventually be used in the system producing this behavior are determined later in the development process.

Transformational model

The Transformational model starts with a program specification and ends with a program. The Transformational model progresses with an automated series of transformations.

H. Partsch and R. Steinbrueggen say, "Transformation rules are partial mappings from one program scheme to another so that an element of the domain and its image under the mapping constitute a correct transformation. . . ." Transformational programming is a software process of program construction where successive applications of transformation rule. Usually, this process starts with a specification of a formal statement and its problem or solution, and ends with an executable program.

The benefits associated with the Transformational model are the reduction of labor in software production because of the automated transformation. This model assists in preserving correctness by applying formal transformations, and replaces the final product testing by verifying the program specifications. One of the abilities of this model is to produce desired transformations with a combination of small units from a specialized programming knowledge.

4

Software engineering standards

Standards for software development are variations of the classic model. These standards outline the software development life-cycle activities and the content of required documents. Standards also define software quality assurance, configuration management, and independent verification and validation as needed for embedded systems.

Software development standards are necessary so that any one of the computer systems can interoperate among the others. Standards establish uniform software engineering techniques that are applicable throughout the system life cycle. These standards incorporate practices which will be cost effective from a software life-cycle perspective.

Standards are intended to be dynamic and responsive to the rapidly evolving software engineering field. Standards should be selectively applied and tailored to fit the unique characteristics of a software engineering program.

Data Item Descriptions (DIDs) applicable to the standards are available to provide a set of complete and concise documents for recording and communicating information generated from the specified requirements.

CHARACTERISTICS OF A GOOD STANDARD

A good standard is tightly composed and concentrates on software engineering goals and principles. A standard should stress formal testing and contain evaluation criteria for each product of the software development process. Some characteristics of a good standard:

- Proper structure: represents clear thinking and a standardized means to communicate
- Establishes uniformity
- Fits in accordance with software engineering discipline
- Rigorous: follows the processes, standards, and procedures precisely
- Can be used along with other standards
- Provides guidelines, references, roadmaps, and checkpoints
- Involves quantitative feedback reviews and audits
- Produces quality products

- Includes reasonable documentations
- Provides quality activities and evaluations
- Provides visibility into software development status
- Provides a template model to introduce a suitable methodology
- Encourages tailoring aspects
- Establishes tests for the software engineering environment
- Standardizes software development and management processes
- Provides means to develop systems that are efficient and cost effective

There are many standards in existence for software development. Each organizational environment has established its own specific standards. However, most standards are not well documented. The two major sources of standards are the American National Standard Institute/ Institute of Electrical and Electronics Engineers (ANSI/IEEE) and the United States Department of Defense.

IEEE SOFTWARE ENGINEERING STANDARDS

The Institute of Electrical and Electronics Engineers (IEEE) composed professional software engineering practices into standards. The standard book consists of 17 standards, as is explained in Appendix C. Each IEEE software engineering standard is prepared with two goals (as mentioned in *Software Engineering Standards*, third edition).

1. The standard must fit with all other IEEE software engineering standards; that is, it must be compatible with and not contradict any other existing standards.
2. The standard must be capable of use without other IEEE standards. Because all IEEE standards are ''voluntary use'' in nature, the compliance with one standard does not require or imply compliance with any other.

The main motivation behind the creation of the IEEE standards is to provide recommendations reflecting state-of-the-art engineering principles to the development and maintenance of software.

U.S. DEPARTMENT OF DEFENSE STANDARDS

The Department of Defense has developed standards to meet the requirements of costly, complex systems' quality, performance, and reliability. These systems are long lived and sufficiently flexible to undergo continuous changes, and they need continuous maintenance for reliability and quality. Standards are developed to increase the compatibility and reliability of computer systems that are *mission critical* to our nation's defense. These systems use automatic data processing equipment or services. Their function and operation involve intelligence, cryptology, command and control of military forces, and others. The equipment, which is an integral part of a weapon system, directs fulfillment of defense systems.

DOD-STD-2167A   DOD-STD-2167A is a tightly composed standard that concentrates on software engineering. This standard stresses formal testing and contains evaluation criteria for each product of the software development process. The standard is applied to all phases of the acquisition process, concept exploration, demonstration/ validation, full-scale development, and production/deployment. Tailoring of the standard is essential if the optimum balance of system operational and support requirements is to be achieved.

The software development process includes major activities. These activities can overlap and can be applied iteratively or recursively:

- System requirements analysis/design
- Software requirements analysis
- Preliminary design
- Detailed design
- Coding and computer software unit (CSU) testing
- Computer software component (CSC) integration and testing
- Computer software configuration item (CSCI) testing
- System integration

The concerns for DOD-STD-2167A   Although the standard provides standardization for many aspects of software engineering, applying the standards within the framework of the acquisition process might have certain risks. The following list contains some suggestions for working around or solutions to minimize risks.

- The term Commercial-off-the-shelf (COTS) software is usually considered to be nondevelopment software.
- The detailed data required for internal interface elements in the software requirements specification (SRS) might be excessive and are more appropriate for SDD. Therefore, tailoring might be more appropriate.
- The DID for software product specification (SPS) does not include object listings. If these listings are desired, the contract data requirements list (CDRL) must be tailored accordingly.
- The use of the software development files (SDF's) is formalized in the standard as illustrated in FIG. 4-1. SDF's are stressed throughout the life cycle and maintained for CSU's, CSC's, and CSCI's. The files must contain informal test procedures, test results, and results of the formal qualification test (FQT) dry runs.
- The standard does not include instructions to document, manage, or control software in a hardware configuration item (HWCI) or software not delivered as a CSCI. The standard tasks the contractor to describe his methodology for the development of this software in the SDP, which the Government must evaluate and approve or disapprove.
- Delivery requirements for each CSCI include the source and object code and must be covered in the contract schedule as a separate contract line item number (CLIN), a sub-CLIN, or an integral part of a system or subsystem that has been defined as a CLIN. The specific media requirement for both source and object code will be defined in the SRS. The associated design documentation includes listings applicable to the CSCI and the SPS. Including the SRS and SPS on contract data requirements list (CDRL), which is attached to the contract, will satisfy the media requirements of the Federal Acquisition Regulation (FAR) and its associated supplements for listing the requirements on the CDRL.

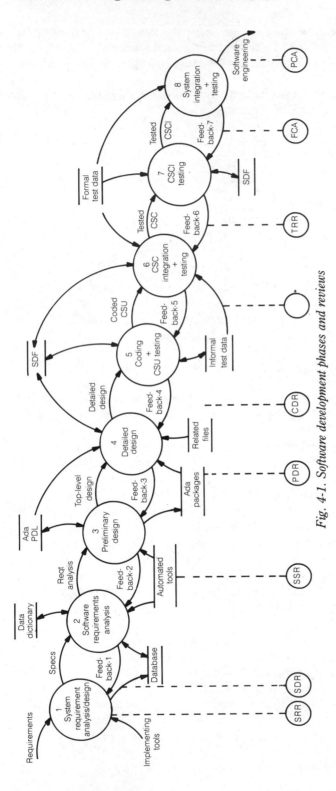

Fig. 4-1. Software development phases and reviews

- In some instances CSCI selection will occur after contract award. Make sure the contract schedule covers delivery requirements for all CSCI's. An example of a software delivery schedule for a four-year project in accordance with DOD-STD-2167A is presented in FIG. 4-2.

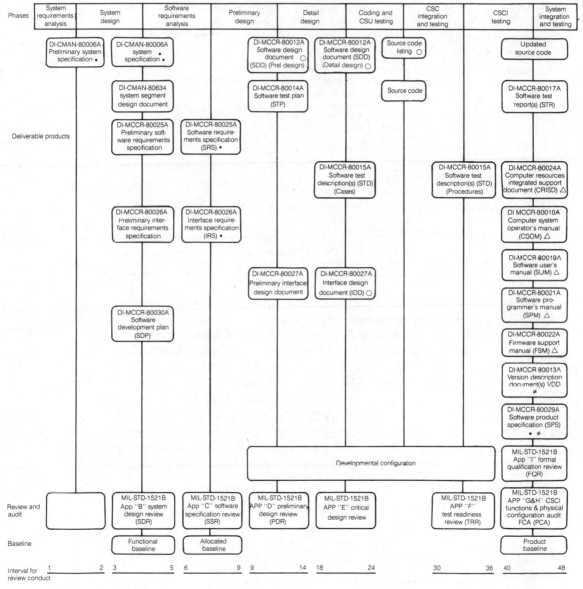

Above is example of a software delivery schedule for a four-year project.

Note:

- Incorporate into baseline
- ○ Incorporate into development configuration
- △ Support document

- May be a:
  1. System segment specification
  2. Prime item specification
  3. Critical item specification
- ≠ May be deferred until after system integration and testing

Fig. 4-2. Four year project delivery schedule chart (example)

Data item description (DIDs)   The software DIDs associated with DOD-STD-2167A fall into four categories: management, software engineering, test, and operational and support, as shown in TABLE 4-1.

Table 4-1. DOD-STD-2167A Appendices

Category	DIDs
Management	Software Development Plan (SDP)
Software Engineering	System/Segment Specification (SSS)
	System/Segment Design Document (SSDD)
	System Design Document (SDD)
	Version Description Document (VDD)
	Software Requirements Specification (SRS)
	Interface Requirements Specification (IRS)
	Interface Design Document (IDD)
	Software Product Specification (SPS)
Test	Software Test Plan (STP)
	Software Test Description (STD)
	Software Test Report (STR)
Operational and Support	Computer Systems Operator's Manual (CSOM)
	Software User's Manual (SUM)
	Software Programmer's Manual (SPM)
	Firmware Support Manual (FSM)
	Computer Resources Integrated Support Document (CRISD)

The system/segment specification (SSS) specifies the requirements for a system or a segment of a system. After government approval and authentication, the SSS becomes the *functional baseline* for the system or segment. The SSS provides a general overview of the system or segment that can be used by training personnel, support personnel, or users of the system.

The system/segment design document (SSDD) describes the design of a system/segment and its operational and support environments. It describes the organization of a system or segment composed of HWCI's, CSCI's, and manual operations. The SSDD contains the highest level design information for the system/segment. This information is produced by the system/segment contractor. It is used to document the system or segment design for review at the system design review (SDR). The DID for the SSDD requires three types of information:

1. Information that is appropriately defined by a contractor, and the definition that is consistent with the schedule (system design).
2. Information that must originate with the government but is consistent with the schedule (operational concepts).
3. Information that is not appropriate for the SSDD.

The SDD describes the complete design of a CSCI that is composed of CSCs and CSUs. The static logical structure is shown in FIG. 4-3. This document evolves throughout the life cycle and is to be submitted at:

- PDR containing the preliminary design
- CDR with the detailed design
- FCA/PCA when incorporated into SPS.

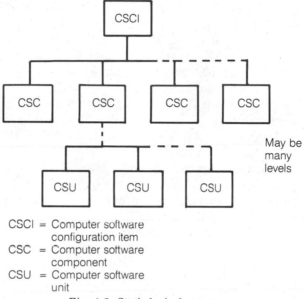

CSCI = Computer software
configuration item
CSC = Computer software
component
CSU = Computer software
unit

Fig. 4-3. Static logical structure

The SDD also provides requirements traceability for tracing the requirements to the design and the design to the requirements.

The version description document (VDD) identifies and describes a version of a CSCI.

The software test plan (STP) describes the formal qualification test plans for one or more CSCI. The STP identifies the software test environment resources required for formal qualification testing (FQT). The standard requires thorough planning of the CSCI test including documentation, installation, and testing of the test environment.

The software test description (STD) contains the test cases and procedures needed to perform formal qualification testing of a CSCI identified in the plan. The 2167A STD is to be prepared and delivered incrementally with the test cases being submitted at CDR and test procedures at TRR.

The software test report (STR) is a record of the formal qualification testing performed on a CSCI. This DID requires the reporting of the FQT test results for each test case defined in the STD.

The computer system operator's manual (CSOM) provides detailed procedures for initiating, operating, monitoring, and shutting down a computer system. The CSOM is also used for identifying a malfunctioning component in a computer system. This DID will not apply if the required information is provided in a commercially available document. The CSOM describes the general flow and operation of the computer system. This DID also contains all the information necessary for the day-to-day operation of the system. The CSOM references other commercially available documents where applicable and is organized to facilitate easy access of operational information.

The software user's manual (SUM) provides user personnel with instructions to execute one or more related CSCI. There might be some duplication of material if CSOM and SUM are delivered.

The software programmer's manual (SPM) provides information needed by a programmer to understand the instruction set architecture of the specified host and target computers. The SPM provides information that can be used to interpret, check out, troubleshoot, or modify existing software.

The firmware support manual (FSM) provides the information necessary to load software or data into firmware components of a system. The FSM applies to read-only memory (ROM), programmable ROM (PROM), erasable PROM (EPROM), and other firmware devices.

The computer resources integrated support document (CRISD) provides the information for planning for life-cycle support of deliverable software. The CRISD documents the contractor's plans for transitioning support of deliverable software to the support agency.

The software requirements specification (SRS) specifies the engineering and qualification requirements for a CSCI. The SRS identifies and describes the CSCI external interfaces.

The interface requirements specification (IRS) specifies the requirements for one or more interfaces among CSCI's and other configuration items. These interfaces will be documented in the SRS.

The interface design document (IDD) specifies the detailed design for one or more interfaces among CSCI's and other configuration items. The requirements for these interfaces are described in the companion IRS.

The software product specification (SPS) consists of the SDD and source code listings, as well as specification of the compiler assembler and measured resource utilization for a CSCI. The SPS becomes the product baseline when authenticated. The DID does not call for inclusion of the object listing.

The software development plan (SDP) contains information on software development management, software engineering, FQT, software product evaluation, and software configuration management. The DID describes a contractor's plans for conducting software development. Each item of nondevelopmental software must be described in the SDP along with the rationale for its use.

MIL-STD-483A   The MIL-STD-483A delineates uniform configuration control requirements and provides instruction for preparing and submitting proposed engineering changes and related information. The requirements include baseline management, system software engineering, interface control, engineering changes, and specification maintenance. These activities and documentation constitute the configuration management (CM) practices for software engineering.

MIL-STD-490A   The MIL-STD-490A sets forth practices for the preparation, interpretation, changes, and revision of program-peculiar specifications prepared by or for the agencies of the Department of Defense. This standard establishes a uniform format and contents of specifications for program-peculiar configuration items, processes, and materials. This standard ensures the inclusion of essential requirements and aids in the use and analysis of specific content. The software-related requirements of MIL-STD-490 consist of the directions to prepare types A, B5, and C5 specifications in accordance with the provisions in the standard. The remainder of MIL-STD-490 consists of directions to prepare types B1-B4, C1-C4, D, and E specifications, and format and word usage requirements.

MIL-STD-1521B The MIL-STD-1521B has been designed to take advantage of current technological advancements and management procedures for conducting reviews and audits. This standard prescribes the requirements for the conduct of technical reviews and audits on systems, equipment, and computer software. Specifically for software, this standard addresses all requirement, design, test, operation, and support documents that are invoked by DOD-STD-2167A. These reviews and audits occur at different points along the system development life cycle.

TAILORING STANDARDS

Tailoring standards for an individual application is essential. Tailoring means the selection of only those products, activities, and reviews that fit the characteristics of and are essential to a particular project. The purpose of tailoring is to evaluate requirements in a standard, save money, prevent duplication, and preserve the schedule of a project. The software developer/customer can recommend tailoring the standards, but ultimately the customer makes the final decision. The tailoring scheme is illustrated in FIG. 4-4.

The result of the tailoring process is reflected in the statement of work (SOW) that prescribes the tasks and reviews. The contract data requirements list (CDRL) contains

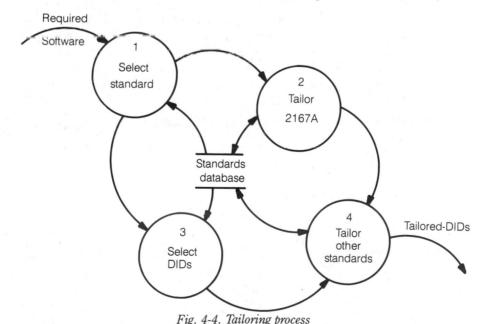

Fig. 4-4. Tailoring process

all the deliverable documentations. Sometimes a clarification is necessary rather than a deletion of the requirements. In these cases, the DID for a product can be modified, making it unique to the project. When tasks are being added, they may be included in the SOW, which leaves the DID unchanged.

Factors for tailoring

The following list shows some of the factors that should be considered when tailoring a standard.

- The software development process to be used
- Software characteristics and intended end use
- Acquisition strategy and type of project management
- Acceptable risk
- Schedule
- Budget
- Development visibility required
- Software maintenance concept

Tailoring of software engineering standards also depends on the class of software. Software classifications include operational, support, system, diagnostic, and automatic test equipment (ATE). The tailoring factor changes for the software being developed, modified, reused. Commercial off-the-shelf (COTS) software or nondevelopmental software (NDS) also affect the tailoring factor.

Guidelines for tailoring

The tailoring process is performed many times throughout the life cycle of a system. Many different events trigger the need to tailor the standards and DID's. First and foremost, tailoring should take place every time the system enters a new phase in the life cycle. Phases include: concept exploration, demonstration and validation, full scale development, and production and deployment. The levels and types of documentation needed for each phase vary and should be reflected in the tailoring process. The suggested guidelines for tailoring a software engineering standard are:

- Classify the required software by development/nondevelopment category
- Select activities and reviews in accordance with the applicable standards and DID's
- Select deliverable products
- Tailor the DID's

Software development files

DOD-STD-2167A requires a contractor to establish software development files (SDF's) at all three levels: CSU, CSC, and CSCI. However, these files do not need to be maintained separately. As CSU's are completed and integrated into a CSC, the CSUs development files should also be integrated into the CSC's development file. Similarly, as the CSCs are integrated into a CSCI, the SDF components should also be incorporated into the SDF of the CSCI. Guidance for consolidation of SDF's should be provided in the SOW.

Firmware

DOD-STD-2167A addresses firmware but does not provide direction for applying the standard to the life cycle of software that is to be stored on a hardware device, i.e., firmware. A good software engineering practice distinguishes between the firmware being developed within the software development environment and firmware that is part of the hardware specifications and baseline. The former is treated as software throughout the life cycle. After software is embedded in firmware, it appears as hardware on hardware drawings. Any changes or proposed changes to this type of software will be treated like changes to any other application software requiring configuration control of code and documentation.

System engineering

DOD-STD-2167A requires the contractor to perform system engineering tasks. MIL-STD-499 contains a similar requirement. In order to preclude dual performance of the same work, the SOW should contain a statement that the 2167A work will be performed as a subset of the tasks performed under MIL-STD-499.

Data-item tasking

Sections four and five of DOD-STD-2167A require the contractor to prepare various data items such as the CRISD, SUM, SDP, SRS, etc. If any of the items tasked in these two sections are not procured on a project, then they must be tailored out. Careful coordination of the CDRL and the content of sections four and five will be required.

Nondeliverable software

Nondeliverable software is not addressed by the standard. However, any nondeliverable software of concern to the government is a part of the software engineering environment or the software test environment.

5

Software development approaches concepts

Software development approaches cover a range of abstraction. An approach includes the choice of environments and methods to be used for software development. The strategy includes techniques that develop software efficiently. The principal software development approaches are structured, object-oriented, entity related, and stepwise refined. An overview of each principal approach is discussed. The selection of a suitable approach for the software development further depends upon your system requirements and environments.

TYPES OF SOFTWARE DEVELOPMENT APPROACHES

There are a few principal approaches available in the computer industry for software development. Some of the approaches available are either a variation of the basic approaches or are emerging in research environments. Constraints like requirements specifications and standards are necessary to enforce the right approach for the right software development. The principal approaches for software development are:

- Structured approach
- Object-oriented approach
- Entity related approach
- Event-oriented approach
- Stepwise refined approach

STRUCTURED APPROACH

The structured approach has been proposed for the software engineering life cycle. In the analysis phase, hierarchical and functional relationships between objects and activities are identified. At each level in the decomposition, components of the system are characterized in terms of the parent component, input, output, control, activity, and mechanism supporting the component. The following list depicts the various activities of the structured approach.

- Structured analysis
- Structured design
- Structured programming design language
- Structured programming

Structured analysis

Structured analysis was based on the use of data flow diagrams introduced by Tom DeMarco [DeMarco 78]. Data flow diagrams model the process with data flows and transformations; they form a network showing data entering as input, proceeding through a functional transformation process with or without other data, and then becoming output. Additionally, data flow diagrams provide a distinct representation of the external entities involved in the system, as shown in FIG. 5-1.

Structured design

Structured design maps the flow of data from its problem domain into its software structure. The steps of structured design involve characterization of the data flow through graphical representation, identification of the various transform elements, assembling these elements in an hierarchical program structure, and refining and optimizing the elements. The steps are shown in FIG. 5-2. Structured design uses many terms explained in the following sections.

Afferent   An *afferent* is the flow of information into a system just like an input. An afferent module obtains information from a subordinate module. It can perform a transformation on that data, and then pass the information to another superordinate module.

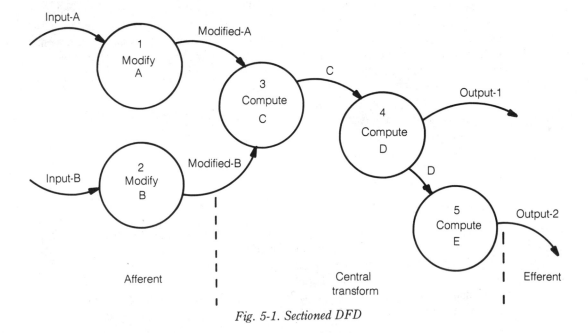

Fig. 5-1. Sectioned DFD

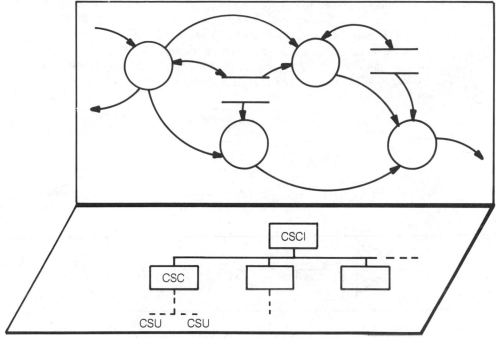

Fig. 5-2. Structured design software structure concept

Efferent *Efferent* is the flow of information out of a system like the output flow. Efferent modules take information from superordinates, possibly perform some data transformation, and then pass the information onto another subordinate module. The primary purpose of afferent and efferent modules is to pass information into and out of the software system. As afferent modules pass information into the system, the information becomes less and less recognizable as input data, which is more abstract. As the efferent flow is traced backward into the system, it becomes less recognizable as output data.

Points of highest abstraction of input and output data are furthest removed from the physical inputs and outputs. These points still constitute as inputs to and outputs from the system. The points of highest abstraction for the major input and output streams define the afferent, efferent, and central transformation portions of a software hierarchy.

Structured design does not provide precise guidelines for determining the points of highest abstraction. It relies on designer intuition and experience to make these determinations.

Central transform *Central transforms* are modules whose primary function is to transform information from one form into another, and perform the primary work of the system. Transform flow moves data from the invoking module to the subordinate module if the subordinate module has performed some transformation, and then back to the invoking module.

Structure chart The data flow diagram is used to develop a structure chart by performing top-down decomposition of the central transforms. The structure charts present the partitioning, hierarchy and organization, and communication among software modules, shown in FIG. 5-3. A *module* is defined as a set of one or more program statements that is invoked by other parts of the system. The structure chart is used to develop the data structure. All results are used to reinterpret the functional requirements of each computer program described in the software requirements specifications. A module is equivalent to a computer software unit or computer software component.

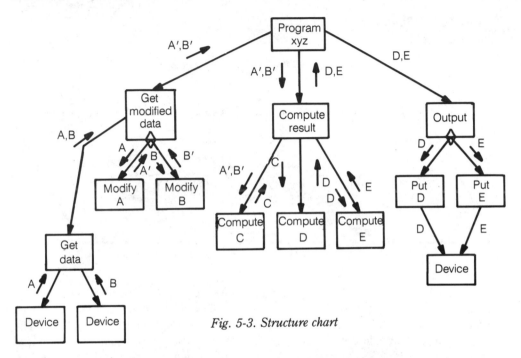

Fig. 5-3. Structure chart

A rectangle represents a process with a module name in a structure chart. Process modules are connected by single-headed arrows that form a hierarchy. The topmost module is the main procedure. Subordinate modules are invoked by the main procedure. A looped arrow on the bottom of a module process that crosses a straight arrow means the subordinate module is invoked more than once, depending on some decision process within the invoking module. A diamond (decision symbol) with two or more lines coming out means the invoking module process picks only one subordinate module at a time.

Fan-out can be defined as the number of subordinate modules that a module possesses. A high fan-out can lead to a flat system which has no intermediate levels in its structure. Whereas, a *fan-in* is defined as the number of invoking modules which a module possesses. A fan-in means duplicated code was avoided.

A small circle with an arrow indicates data is moving in the direction of the arrowhead. A solid circle means control is moving in the direction of the arrowhead.

Coupling   *Coupling* is a measure of relationships among modules and is used to evaluate various program organizations. It is a measure of the strength of interconnection when the strength of coupling and intermodule dependence are directly related. W. Stevens, G. Myers, and L. Constantine stated, "Coupling is the measure of the strength of association established by a connection from one module to another. Strong coupling complicates a system because a module is harder to understand, change, or correct by itself if it is highly interrelated with other modules. Complexity can be reduced by designing modules with the weakest coupling possible between modules.'' [Stevens 74] The premise is that the more independent a module is the easier it is to understand and the fewer the paths along which changes and errors can propagate.

Structured design defines five basic levels of coupling among modules. These levels are not precisely defined or discrete. The implication is that simple module interfaces improve reliability, allow commonly used functions to be more readily shared, and reduce the system sensitivity to change. The levels of coupling are listed in descending order of preference and are further discussed as follows.

1. Data
2. Control
3. Common data
4. External
5. Content

Data coupling The interface level where data elements needed only as input are passed to a module as explicit parameters. Data coupling is the minimum degree of communication necessary between two modules.

Control coupling The interface level where a control field is established. The use of a variable to indicate the type of processing required is an example of control coupling. This level requires the sending module to set a value in the control field. The receiving module must then test the value. The information passed between modules may consist of both data and control.

Common data coupling The interface level where the required data is a part of a larger data collection. The use of common data structure (global) are examples of this level of interface.

External coupling The interface level where a module receives its input by inspecting and using data variables that have been defined and reside in another module. For example, an Input/Output (I/O) module is coupled to a specific hardware device.

Content coupling The interface level where you must understand the mechanics of other modules. One example is knowing internal switch settings. Another example of the content coupling is when one module enters into the middle of another module or a module has multiple entry points.

Cohesion Cohesion is a measure of the strength of association of elements within a module. Modules with a high degree of cohesiveness are not only understandable but are excellent candidates for reuse. The proponents of structured design contend that optimal modular designs require programs to be partitioned into discrete functional modules. A measurement of cohesion enables designers to recognize functional and nonfunctional modules. A scale of cohesiveness proceeding from the best to the worst case has been tabulated and defined:

1. Functional
2. Sequential
3. Communicational

4. Temporal
5. Logical
6. Coincidental

Functional cohesion   A functionally cohesive module performs a single, discrete, logical transformation. All elements of a functionally bound module contribute to the execution of one and only one task. For example, a sine function performs only one task.

Sequential cohesion   Sequential cohesion occurs when a program is modularized on the basis of the control structure organization. In a sequentially bound module, the output of one processing element serves as input to the next element, such as editing transactions and updating a master file.

Communicational cohesion   Communicational cohesion in a program is modularized by grouping input and output activities within the module. All elements in a communicationally bound module operate on the same input data set and/or produce the same output data. A module that performs all I/O functions on a specific file is an example of communicational cohesion.

Temporal cohesion   Temporal cohesion creates separate modules to handle time-oriented activities. A temporally bound module is one whose elements are all related in time, such as initialization and termination routines.

Logical cohesion   Logical cohesion modularizes a program by logically grouping activities. An example is printing a number of different error messages originating in various segments. A *logical* module usually requires a control data element to be passed to determine what kind of processing must be performed.

Coincidental cohesion   Coincidental cohesion occurs when there is little or no relationship among the elements of a module. This cohesion sometimes results from attempts to modularize a program by arbitrarily segmenting the statements.

Structured design asserts that coupling and cohesion are related. Of the two, however, cohesion is a more important concept. Lower-level cohesiveness (e.g., coincidental) can be expected to increase coupling (e.g., content) as flags and switches are introduced into the code.

Heuristic design   In addition to coupling and cohesion, structured design discusses a heuristic design that is used to organize modules and decisions. It is used as a check or indicator by which a structure can be examined for potential improvement. A heuristic design uses two terms:

1. Scope of control
2. Scope of effect

Scope of control   The scope of control of a module is the set of modules that are ultimately subordinate to the module and the module itself.

Scope of effect   The scope of effect of a decision is the set of modules that contain some code whose execution is based on the outcome of the decision.

For any decision, structured design asserts that the scope of effect should be a subset of the scope of control of the module where the decision is located. If the scope of effect is a subset of the scope of control, then all modules affected by the decision are logically organized together, which minimizes the length of data paths and reduces the strength of coupling.

Additional heuristic designs for developing and examining program organization are explained in the following sections.

Module size   Modules should be small enough to be understandable.

Span of control   The number of modules immediately subordinate to a given module should be from 2 to 9. Spans of control beyond this range usually indicate that the module's function is too complex.

Levels of highly cohesive modules   A maximum number of single function modules should be utilized.

When assessing the wide popularity of structured design, L. Peters stated, "Structured design has gained wide popularity for two primary reasons. One is that it allows the software designer to express his perception of the design problem in terms he can identify with: data flows and transformations. The notation with which he expresses these flows is simple, easy to use, and understandable by management, customer, and implementor.

"The other primary reason for this method's popularity is that it provides the designer with a means of evaluating his (and others') design. This serves as a benchmark against which to measure his success or progress. The method is unique in this regard. If the design evaluation concepts consisted of nothing more than coupling and cohesion, structured design would still be a significant contribution to the software fields." [Peters 81]

Structured programming design language

The structured Programming Design Language (PDL) describes the control structure and general organization of computer software in a structured and logical design language notation. PDL uses the vocabulary of the English language and the overall syntax of another structured programming language. Thus, PDL is easier to read and understand than programming language code. In some programming language compilers, PDL can be compiled.

PDL is also a tool that supports the software development design of the structured approach for documentation and maintenance. It supplements pictorial representations such as flowcharts. A good PDL assists in translating design into a structured programming code.

Structured programming

Structured programming is an efficient approach for developing computer program codes. This approach is based on the mathematically proven structure theorem that states that any proper program (i.e., a program with one entry and one exit) is equivalent to a program that contains only the three logic structures given in the following list. [Bohm, Jacopini]

- Sequence of two or more operations
- Conditional branch to one of two operations and return (IF a THEN b ELSE c)
- Repetition of an operation while a condition is true (DO-WHILE p)

Figure 5-4 presents three logical illustrations that represent a proper program. A large and complex program can then be developed with appropriate sequencing and nesting of these three basic figures. The logic flow always proceeds from the beginning to the end without arbitrary branching. When these structures are used properly in programming, there are no unconditional branches or statement labels.

One advantage of structured programming is that it reduces the arrangement of the program logic. This process is similar to that found in engineering where logic circuits are constructed from a basic set of figures. Structured programming represents a standard based on a solid theoretical foundation.

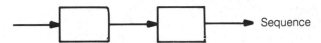

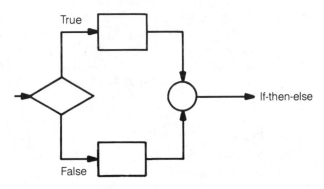

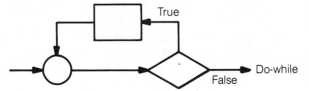

Fig. 5-4. Basic logic structures in structured programming

OBJECT-ORIENTED APPROACH

In the object-oriented approach to the software process, models of entities are constructed as self-contained components. This system is defined by the interactions and behavior of the components. An important aspect of the design process patterns the behavior of the model so that it is visible only when interactions are expected with other entities.

In this approach, a model inherits or extends the characteristics of other models. Further, program entities can refer to objects of more than one class. A characteristic known as *polymorphism* is shown in FIG. 5-5.

Object-oriented design is presented as a method for modeling a problem by taking a balanced view of objects and the operations performed on them along the lines suggested by Booch [Booch 86, 87]. The following list provides the basic design steps.

1. Define an informal strategy for the problem solution.
2. Identify the objects used in the informal strategy.
3. Identify the operations on the objects used in the informal strategy.
4. Define the software systems architecture and interfaces to the operations.
5. Iterate the above process as needed.

A system's behavior is patterned on the behavior of objects manipulated by the system, not the function of the system. You should address what the system acts on, rather than what the system does. G. Booch says, ''. . . object-oriented development requires certain facilities of the implementation language. We must have some mechanism to build new classes of objects and ideally, a typing mechanism that serves to enforce our

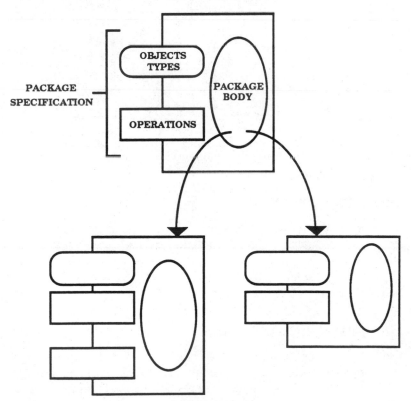

Fig. 5-5. OOD sample

abstraction. Also, the object-oriented development is only a partial-life-cycle method and so must be coupled with compatible requirements and specification methods.'' [Booch 86]

ENTITY RELATIONSHIP APPROACH

The entity relationship approach uses the Entity Relationship (ER) model [Chen 76] to categorize information from the real world problem domain. It recognizes that the database, as well as the code, needs to be considered at the logical and physical level. This information is conveyed by defining the entities in the domain, the interrelationships of those entities, and attributes possessed by the entities. These concepts must ultimately be mapped into a plan that can be implemented on a database management system.

The early development stages of a system involves underlying the database structure. The ER model is often used as a means to conceptualize information at a high level, shown in FIG. 5-6. C. Davis gives a perspective on the origins and use of the ER approach, as well as some reasons for its increased popularity since 1975. [Davis 83]

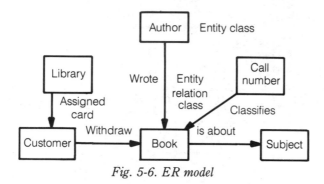

Fig. 5-6. ER model

EVENT-ORIENTED APPROACH

The event-oriented approach is characterized by the concept of a stimulus response, where events are the stimuli to the system, and responses are composed of actions taken by the system and the resultant outputs. Event orientation builds the system based on the kinds of events the system is likely to encounter. This approach is shown in FIG. 5-7.

STEPWISE REFINEMENT APPROACH

In a seminal paper published in 1971, N. Wirth proposed the concept of stepwise refinement, a top-down design strategy. The process starts at a high level of abstraction and incorporates details through a sequence of elaborations. This method of program decomposition parallels the process of partitioning and refinement that is frequently used in the analysis of requirements.

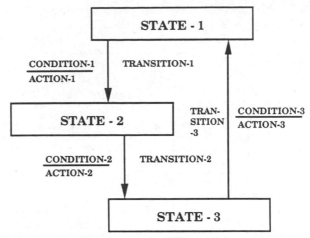

Fig. 5-7. Event (STD) model

Wirth summarized the refinement steps, "In each step, one or several instructions of the given program are decomposed into more detailed instructions. This successive decomposition or refinement of specifications terminates when all instructions are expressed in terms of an underlying computer or programming language, and therefore must be guided by the facilities available on that computer or language. The result of the execution of a program is expressed in terms of data. It might be necessary to introduce further data for communication between the obtained subtasks or instructions. As tasks are refined, decomposed, or structured, it is natural to 'refine program and data specifications in parallel'." [Wirth 71]

During the refinement process, a notation natural to the problem should be used as long as possible. Ultimately, the implementation language will determine the direction the notation must evolve. Wirth further states that each refinement step involves incorporating design decisions, such as efficiency, clarity, and regularity of structure. Various aspects of design alternatives must be weighed. At times early decisions must be revoked and restarting at an earlier step must be done. If done carefully, stepwise refinement can provide a modularity that facilitates later change.

STRENGTHS AND WEAKNESSES OF THE APPROACHES

The major strengths and weaknesses of each software development technique are discussed in TABLE 5-1.

Table 5-1. Types of Software Development Approaches

Technique	Strengths	Weaknesses
Structured	1. Graphics and easy to understand 2. DFD input directly to the design 3. Well documented 4. Supported by a number of software tools 5. Functional decomposition 6. Widely used 7. Concentrates on functionality and data 8. Top-down analysis	1. Heuristic approach 2. Emphasize on data flow than upon the encapsulation of data structures 3. Steps involved stronger transform analysis and transaction analysis than locating the central transform
Object oriented	1. Well matched to current developments in ada, Modula-2, C++	1. Depend upon the initial informal strategy 2. Hard to identify objects 3. Not matured yet 4. Not easy to understand 5. Difficult to present 6. Need analysis method
Entity relationship	1. Prescriptive 2. Use abstraction 3. Concentrates of information 4. Identifies entities and their relationships	1. Complex for larger systems 2. Difficult to describe data structure and its relationship
Event oriented	1. Widely used in real-time interactive systems 2. Identify external events 3. Establish a system boundary early in analysis 4. Highly visible response constraints 5. Easy to construct acceptance tests	1. Need requirements analysis 2. Need prototyping/ simulation 3. Time constraints
Stepwise refinement	1. Flexible 2. Easily amalgamated with other approaches	1. Need analysis method 2. Need design method

6

Software engineering
methodology concepts

Software engineering methodology is a set of integrated approaches, rules, procedures, methods, tools, and environment. A good methodology provides a series of steps that directs the engineering effort from start to finish. There are many methodologies available on the market. Selecting the best methodology to suit the requirements of a system is not an easy job. A good methodology results in well structured, reliable, and maintainable software engineering.

This chapter will define a software engineering methodology, why a methodology is needed, and what the properties of a good methodology are. Finally, the selection criteria of a good methodology is discussed.

WHAT IS A SOFTWARE ENGINEERING METHODOLOGY

A software engineering methodology is a set of integrated approaches, rules, procedures, methods, tools, environments, etc. A methodology is a disciplined approach to engineer system software. A methodology is also a set of guidelines that provide a road map with checkpoints for the development effort. A software engineering methodology concept is illustrated in FIG. 6-1.

Following the steps of development does not guarantee success. This concept is parallel to the travel concept, as it is illustrated in FIG. 6-2. When you start from a source with a desired destination, you normally observe the following steps:

- Understand the requirements
- Think
- Plan
- Select the best approach from many alternative routes depending upon:
  - Budget
  - Resources
  - Time schedule
  - State-of-the-art techniques, methods, and tools to be used
  - Environment
  - Availability of road map and checkpoints
  - Availability of experienced direction

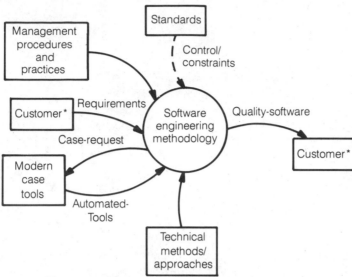

Fig. 6-1. Software engineering methodology concept

A methodology does not solve the problem for software engineering, but provides a means of tackling the problem. Selecting a methodology to reach the desired destination only helps to provide the convenience of traveling. You still have to experience traveling from start to finish. There might be many hazards and rough conditions to face while testing new methods and tools in the environment, but as the saying goes, "Well begun is half done." Good planning and a good methodology with modern tools definitely lead to success.

NECESSITY OF A SOFTWARE ENGINEERING METHODOLOGY

There are many methods available on the market, but there are only a few standard methods. However, many more are emerging every day.

Why are there so many methodologies? The only feasible answer is that there are varieties of systems. No one methodology is suitable for every system in software engineering. You have to select a suitable methodology to fit the needs of the system.

The question is often asked, "Why do we need a methodology in the modern trend of software engineering?" The simple answer is: no discipline is necessary at all if it is not required. Do you remember the good old days in the 50's, 60's, and 70's in the computer industry, when a programmer used to code in accordance with his/her own method. There was very little discipline available to follow. The software developed in those days has been hard and costly to maintain without any proper methodology to follow. The present systems are complex and need proper methodology to engineer the software. Some of the following factors listed are necessary for applying a methodology.

- Enhancement of quality
- Cost effectiveness
- Requirements constraint

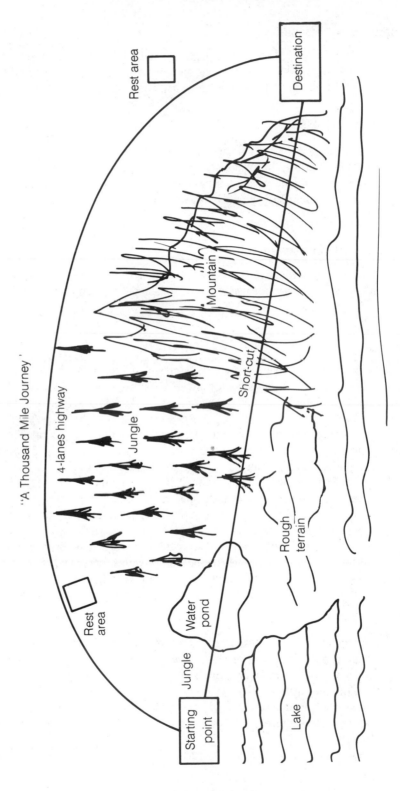

Fig. 6-2. Visiting a place methodology

Enhancement of quality

By applying a good methodology, higher-quality software is achieved that fulfills the requirements. Reduced costs for testing and maintenance can be reflected by increased effort to prevent and detect errors in the early phases of development.

Cost effectiveness

The cost of developing software is increasing every year, as is software maintenance. A good, matured methodology reduces the cost of development. Reusing pretested software components assists in controlling the cost. Proper documentation, in accordance with a standard, produces quality and cost-effective products during future maintenance.

Requirements constraint

Most companies require personnel to follow a software development standard. All U.S. military systems are mandated to follow standards such as DOD-STD-2167A for software development.

PROPERTIES OF A GOOD METHODOLOGY

Good software engineering methodologies result in well-structured, reliable, and maintainable software. A methodology is well structured if it is systematically organized, simple, easy to understand, and follows other methodologies (not only by the orginators).

A methodology should cover the entire development process, simplifying transitions between project phases, which means that the methodology should consist of well-proven methods integrated for each phase of software engineering. Moreover, these methods should smoothly move from one phase to another. The methodology should enhance communication among all participating personnel at all stages of development.

The methodology defines how the required software engineering activities are performed, what software development methods are used, and how these methods are related to each other and the required activities. Modern structured methods are well-defined and widely used. The analysis method provides mapping to the other phases of software engineering. These methods are compatible and must cover all of the required activities. Some of the properties of a good software engineering methodology can be compiled as follows:

- Improve effectiveness and productivity of software development activities
- Result in the creation of reliable software
- Fit together to form an integrated set of methods
- Promote automation
- Support software validation and verification through development process
- Facilitate the capture of analysis, design, implementation, and performance constraints
- Support software development organization

- Support the evolution of a system throughout its existence
- Make the evolving software product visible and controllable at all stages of development
- Be teachable and transferable
- Be open-ended
- Fit in the established standard

MODERN TECHNOLOGY IMPACTS

The methodology should survive the impact of modern technology, which can be due to modern generation languages, methodologies, CASE tools, and any other constraints. Some of these impacts are:

- Programming language
  - C^{++}
  - Object oriented
  - Ada
  - 4GL, 5GL, natural languages

- Real-time concept
- Artificial intelligence
  - Knowledge-based systems
  - Neural networks

- Emerging methodologies
- Emerging CASE tools
- Automated management aspects

SELECTION CRITERIA OF A SUITABLE METHODOLOGY

The selection of a suitable methodology primarily depends on the requirement. Quality, reliable, and well-documented products are desirable. Some of the factors for selecting a methodology are:

- Availability of experienced and trained personnel for the particular methodology
- Composition of the development team
- Environment provided for development
- Organizational structure used to manage the project
- Nature of the problem domain
- Time frame associated with development
- Availability of a suitable CASE tool

Quality methods are available for software development. The term methodology that names some of these methods is a misnomer. In a report on the assessment of methods, W. Wood and associates at the Software Engineering Institute made a similar assertion that states, ''There is no such thing as an overall best method for developing all software, only the method that will work best to help develop a system with particular characteristics and will blend with an organization's software development practices.'' [Wood 88]

The selection criteria for a suitable software engineering method depends on robustness, expressiveness, analyzability, stability, correctiveness, effectiveness, manageability, productivity, and ease of adoption. The criteria for selecting a suitable methodology is grouped in the following:

- Technical description
- Management aspects
- Productivity
- Ease of adoption
- Vendor support

Technical description

A technical description explains an overview and technical detail including robustness, expressiveness, analyzability, stability, correctiveness, and effectiveness of a methodology. *Robustness* is the number of problem domains to which the methodology applies. Associated with this criteria is the type of application and the size of application the methodology is intended for. Additional related characteristics include the amount of use of the methodology, and how suitable the methodology is to the programming language where the software system is being developed.

Expressiveness refers to the facilities provided by the methodology that represents the evolving system. Related to this criteria is the mode of representation used by the methodology along with the support provided by the methodology for communication among the development team, customer, and management.

Analyzing and *stability* include features that assist the software engineers to design complex systems. The criteria also includes features that assist the development team in contending with the inevitable changes that will occur during the development of a large system. You can expect that there will be changes in requirements and design decisions. Analyzability is the criterion that addresses the support provided for the activities of analysis and design. Stability involves the capability to continue to utilize the method despite changed requirements or design modifications.

Correctness involves the reliability of the software product using the methodology, and the conformity of the product to the customer's requirements. The *effectiveness* criterion involves the total quality of the resultant product. In addition to reliability, effectiveness is associated with how well the product software system is structured and the quality of the documentation for the system. In essence, an effective method will produce reliable and maintainable software.

Management aspects

Management aspects include project management, communication channel, quality assurance, and proper documentation. The project management refers to the support provided by the methodology relative to planning, controlling, and monitoring the software development process. The selected methodology describes the tasks that must be managed in a project. The methodology also specifies the resources that must be managed to get those tasks done by specifying what roles each activity is responsible for.

The tools and methods in detail have been discussed in my book, *Managing Ada Projects using Software Engineering.* Topics suitable for the project control and communication in relation to a methodology are briefly discussed.

The selected methodology should consist of more than one procedure for conducting activities associated with project management. The methodology should also consist of methods that recommend allocation of people to different activities. One of these activities involves writing a general project plan to establish goals for the project. The methodology should facilitate reviewing the plan often, and revising significant changes that have an impact on cost and the completion date. The method should provide estimation of the man-hours and elapsed time required to accomplish each goal. The project manager should ensure that the proper information is monitored and that it is getting to the right person.

Management needs the mechanism to help detect communication breakdowns. The selected methodology should have a provision to communicate within the development team by the use of walk-throughs, technical reviews, and the data dictionary.

A *structured walk-through* is a formal or informal review of a development product by a small group of competent professionals. The purpose is to review the product in a friendly, relaxed atmosphere to see the features such as completeness, correctness, consistency, relevancy, and feasibility. The principal objective of a walk-through is to use a fresh look at the product to find as many errors as possible. These errors can be corrected before more work is done on a potentially error-prone document. The earlier in the development process an error can be found, the cheaper it is to fix.

In a formal walk-through, a recorder writes down important points that arise. A moderator is also present to control the walk-through and resolve any disagreements. A representative from quality assurance verifies the quality of the product and the established standards.

After the product has been satisfactorily subjected to walk-throughs, a technical review is necessary. The technical review is performed by members of the project team. The technical review provides an overall perspective to evaluate the assembled pieces of the deliverable product for completeness, consistency, and overall correctness. Technical reviews also confirm the traceability of the implementation of the user's requirements.

Management reviews can be considered to satisfy the customer with the product. These reviews are also conducted to conform with applicable standards, and are conducted throughout the software life cycle. These reviews guarantee go or no-go management decisions to the next phase of the project. Management decisions of this nature are only made after the project has been reviewed by peer groups in the walk-throughs and after a technical review. Management must consider in the review if the estimated cost for completing the next phase is within the authorized general project plan budget. The review also confirms the customer's commitment and participation.

Quality is the assurance provided by those who are involved in the software engineering. The project manager establishes a quality assurance section to ensure that the established standards and quality principles are enforced in software engineering. A quality assurance section provides confirmation that the necessary requirements are stated, stated correctly, and interpreted correctly. The manager of the quality assurance section reports directly to the project manager. Project management monitors the quality of the product delivered to the customer. Quality assurance considers the following factors for quality:

- Software development plan
- Quality metrics
- Performing reviews at transition points in the software life cycle
- Performing code inspections and tests
- Collecting and analyzing quality metric data
- Analyzing causes of defects
- Checking compliance with standards
- Performing analysis of users view of system quality
- Identifying organizational quality improvement needs

The primary system evaluation criteria includes correctness, completeness, consistency, feasibility, and testability. Assistance for the various aspects of project management provides a basis to judge this criterion. The features of the methodology that assist in the preparation of required documentation for the system are a related concern.

Productivity

Productivity refers to the aspects of a methodology that facilitate software engineering. The metrics of software engineering deal with the measurement of the product and the process that develops the product. The effective management of a software development process requires quantification, measurement, and modeling. The metrics provide a quantitative basis for the development and validation of models in the software development process. Metrics can be used to improve software productivity and quality.

You often hear in the computer industry that the software produced has been of poor quality and without proper documentation. The lack of quality and documentation is a software crisis in the computer industry. As a result, there is a need for software engineering metrics to resolve this crisis.

Good metrics should facilitate the development of models that are capable of predicting process or product parameters, not just describing them. Thus, ideal metrics should be simple and precisely defined, so that the metric can be evaluated clearly. The metrics should be objective to the greatest extent possible, and be easily obtained at a reasonable cost. They should be valid, that is, the metric should measure what it is intended to measure. Metrics should be robust and relatively insensitive to insignificant changes in the software development process or product. Software engineering metrics can be classified in two ways:

- Product metrics
- Process metrics

Product metrics describe the attributes of the software system or components of a system and the related documentation, tests, and system control information. Size, usability, maintainability, number of defects, and performance are attributes of a software system. The product metrics are measures of the software engineering product at any stage of its development, from the requirements stage to the installation stage. Product metrics measure the complexity of the software design, the size of the final program (either source or object code), or the number of pages of documentation.

Process metrics are measures of the software engineering development process, such as overall development time, type of methodology, CASE tools used, or the average level of experience of the software engineering staff.

Ease of adoptability

The ease of adoption addresses the aspects associated with the introduction of a methodology into a development organization: ease of setup and learning time of the methodology. Descriptive characteristics related to this criterion include available training, hardware and software configuration needed to support the method, and cost of acquisition. Additionally, you should know what type of education and experience is required of the development team in order to gain proficiency in the use of the methodology.

Vendor's support

Vendor's support includes both technical and policy support. Technical support scores are based on the quality of service actually received by the users, which includes the availability of technicians ready to respond to problems the vendor might have. Policy support relies on product usability warranties, guarantees, a toll-free telephone line, and corporate extended support.

II

Software
Engineering Practices

7

Structured analysis, design, and implementation of information systems

(STRADIS) is a deliverable, driven approach to managing the entire information systems environment with rigorous software engineering concepts. STRADIS begins with the development of an information systems transition plan that maps the organization's information needs to an information system strategy for the following 3 to 7 years. The information system process uses structured analysis to define the logical model of the system. During the design phase, the analytical strategy used in the model is factored and allocated to the appropriate physical environment, and is ready for implementation with programming techniques. STRADIS relies on accurate models of the system at all phases. Each model is supported by a detailed object-oriented repository. STRADIS was developed by C. Gane, P. Sarson, and McDonnell Douglas personnel. This developer states that, ''STRADIS was the first method developed around the use of the tools and techniques of structured analysis and design.''

OVERVIEW

The STRADIS activity overview diagram is shown in FIG. 7-1. It illustrates a simplified overview of the activities and major deliverables in STRADIS. Activities are shown by rounded rectangles, and major deliverable products are shown by thick black lines with a summary of their contents in the blow up panels.

STRADIS starts with a *requestor* (top left hand corner of the chart). The requestor is typically a manager asking for service from the information systems function. The response to a request for service requires an application analyst to do an initial study. This study is a quick and dirty (2 to 10 day) look at the problem to establish the potential benefit from either building a new system or changing the existing information system. The product of an initial study, as shown by the thick black arrow, is an *initial study report*.

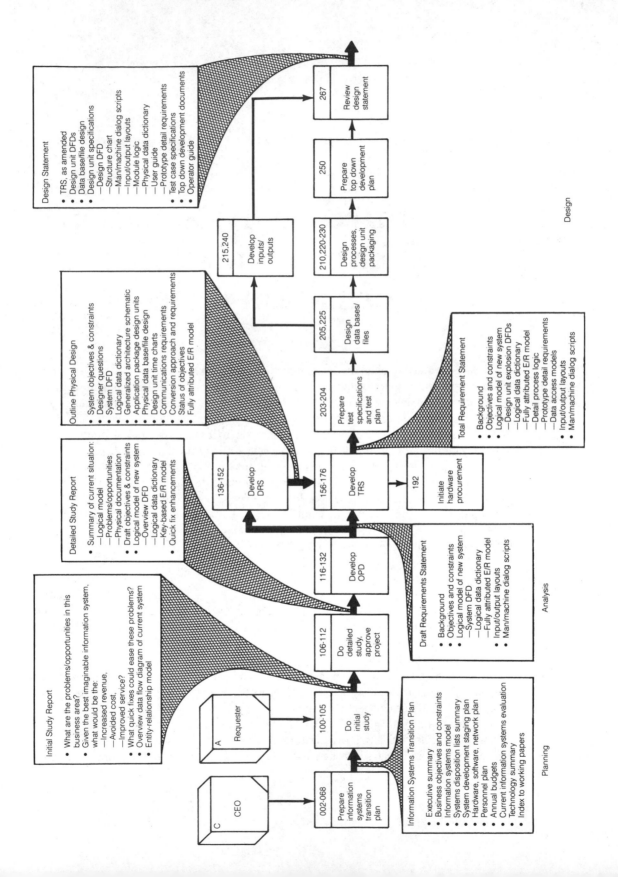

Initial Study Report

- What are the problems/opportunities in this business area?
- Given the best imaginable information system, what would be the:
  —Increased revenue,
  —Avoided cost,
  —Improved service?
- What quick fixes could ease these problems?
- Overview data flow diagram of current system
- Entity-relationship model

Detailed Study Report

- Summary of current situation:
  —Logical model
  —Problems/opportunities
  —Physical documentation
- Draft objectives & constraints
- Logical model of new system
  —Overview DFD
  —Logical data dictionary
  —Key-based E/R model
- Quick fix enhancements

Outline Physical Design

- System objectives & constraints
- Designer questions
- System DFD
- Logical data dictionary
- Generalized architecture schematic
- Application package design units
- Physical data base/file design
- Design unit time charts
- Communications requirements
- Conversion approach and requirements
- Status of objectives
- Fully attributed E/R model

Design Statement

- TRS, as amended
- Design unit DFDs
- Data base/file design
- Design unit specifications
  —Design DFD
  —Structure chart
  —Man/machine dialog scripts
  —Input/output layouts
  —Module logic
  —Physical data dictionary
  —User guide
  —Prototype detail requirements
- Test case specifications
- Top down development documents
- Operator guide

Total Requirement Statement

- Background
- Objectives and constraints
- Logical model of new system
  —Design unit explosion DFDs
  —Logical data dictionary
  —Fully attributed E/R model
  —Detail process logic
  —Prototype detail requirements
  —Data access models
- Input/output layouts
- Man/machine dialog scripts

Draft Requirements Statement

- Background
- Objectives and constraints
- Logical model of new system
  —System DFD
  —Logical data dictionary
  —Fully attributed E/R model
- Input/output layouts
- Man/machine dialog scripts

Information Systems Transition Plan

- Executive summary
- Business objectives and constraints
- Information systems model
- Systems disposition lists summary
- System development staging plan
- Hardware, software, network plan
- Personnel plan
- Annual budgets
- Current information systems evaluation
- Technology summary
- Index to working papers

Requester — A

CEO — C

| 002-068 Prepare information systems transition plan |
| 100-105 Do initial study |
| 106-112 Do detailed study, approve project |
| 116-132 Develop OPD |
| 136-152 Develop DRS |
| 156-176 Develop TRS |
| 192 Initiate hardware procurement |
| 203-204 Prepare test specifications and test plan |
| 205,225 Design data bases/files |
| 210,220,230 Design processes, design unit packaging |
| 215,240 Develop inputs/outputs |
| 250 Prepare top down development plan |
| 267 Review design statement |

Planning   Analysis   Design

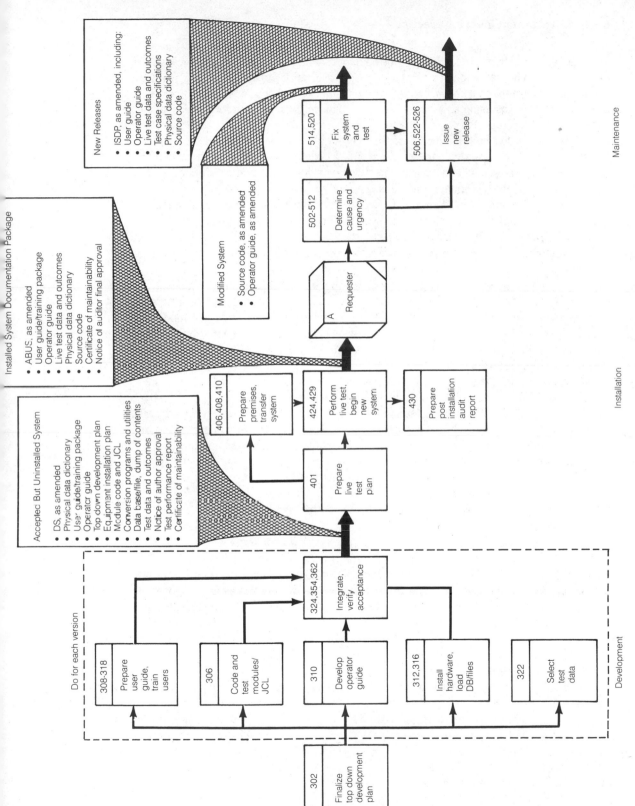

Fig. 7-1. Stradis activity overview diagram

Installed System Documentation Package

- ABUS, as amended
  - User guide/training package
  - Operator guide
  - Live test data and outcomes
  - Physical data dictionary
  - Source code
  - Certificate of maintainability
  - Notice of auditor final approval

Accepted But Uninstalled System

- DS, as amended
  - Physical data dictionary
  - User guide/training package
  - Operator guide
  - Top down development plan
  - Equipment installation plan
  - Module code and JCL
  - Conversion programs and utilities
  - Data base/file, dump of contents
  - Test data and outcomes
  - Notice of author approval
  - Test performance report
  - Certificate of maintainability

New Releases

- ISDP, as amended, including:
  - User guide
  - Operator guide
  - Live test data and outcomes
  - Test case specifications
  - Physical data dictionary
  - Source code

Modified System

- Source code, as amended
- Operator guide, as amended

Do for each version

| 308-318 Prepare user guide, train users |
| 306 Code and test modules/JCL |
| 310 Develop operator guide |
| 312,316 Install hardware, load DB/files |
| 322 Select test data |

324,354,362 Integrate, verify, acceptance

302 Finalize top down development plan

Development

401 Prepare live test plan

406,408,410 Prepare premises, transfer system

424,429 Perform live test, begin new system

430 Prepare post installation audit report

Installation

A Requester

502-512 Determine cause and urgency

514,520 Fix system and test

506,522-526 Issue new release

Maintenance

The initial study report, which includes a firm cost and time estimate, is reviewed by management, who has enough information to put a priority on the project. If justified, management authorizes a *detailed study*. If any action can be taken which is a quick fix to the problem, such as using a fourth generation language to create a report, it is specified in the initial study report.

A detailed study builds a model of the current system in the business area, automated or manual, to investigate the problem and to collect data that must be carried into the new system. Business and system objectives (that a new system must meet) and an overview of the new system are drafted in the study.

An initial *General Project Plan* (GPP) is developed, including a gross estimate of the cost and time to develop and operate the system. The detailed study report and the initial GPP are reviewed by management, who then makes another decision to: proceed with development of a *draft requirements statement*, alter project scope, or cancel the project.

The draft requirements statement refines the new system's logical models and objectives, establishes the constraints on any physical designs, and performs a rigorous test of checks and balances that validate the system model. The analytical model can then be given to a systems designer who reviews what the new system is required to do and produces an *outline physical design* that will achieve the objectives cost effectively and within the given constraints.

After generating the outline physical design, the system model is further refined. Explosions are developed, detailed business logic is written to show the logic of the business processes, and the system data models are completed. All this work creates a *total requirements statement* which contains enough information for a system designer to complete the scope of work within the cost and time estimate for the *design phase*.

The design phase consists essentially of three parallel streams of activity: the design of the computer processes (structure charts), the design of the physical data (files and databases), and the design of the human procedures, the *Human Subsystem* (HSS). These three streams of design affect one another. A top-down development plan is also drafted as part of design activities.

The various streams of work come together in the *design statement*, which is the subject of a formal review containing enough information for the development group. A commitment for completing the scope of work within the cost and time estimate of programming and testing is made. The project can be shelved at this point on economic grounds. The design statement is still a valuable tool and could stand alone for later use.

The *development phase* incorporates the top-down development approach. Each activity is repeated for each version of the system to ensure that all interfaces (including the man/machine interfaces) are working smoothly before additional investment is made on more development.

The software and procedures are tested and certified to meet the functional requirements. Then the system is installed and made to work as part of the business. This involves, of course, installing hardware, training users of the system, making sure the software does not interfere with other systems, tuning the system to give acceptable response time, converting files, and testing the system (often in conjunction with the old system) until the users and auditors are comfortable. Afterwards, the old system can be discontinued and the new system goes into maintenance status.

The maintenance phase identifies activities that control the flow for maintenance problems, changes control requests deferred from earlier phases, enhances requests coming from the detailed studies, and maintains requests from initial studies. STRADIS maintenance provides that all nonurgent software changes are grouped and incorporated in a controlled new release of the system. Reported problems are evaluated. If problems are found urgent, the system is patched immediately.

TECHNICAL DESCRIPTION

The application life cycle consists of 5 general phases as illustrated in FIG. 7-2. The activities of each phase recommend tools and techniques founded on several approaches of development which are shown in the following list.

- Entity Relationship Modeling (ERM)
- Data Flow Diagrams (DFD) synchronized to the ERM
- Translation of analytical models to physical design
- Continuity of requirements

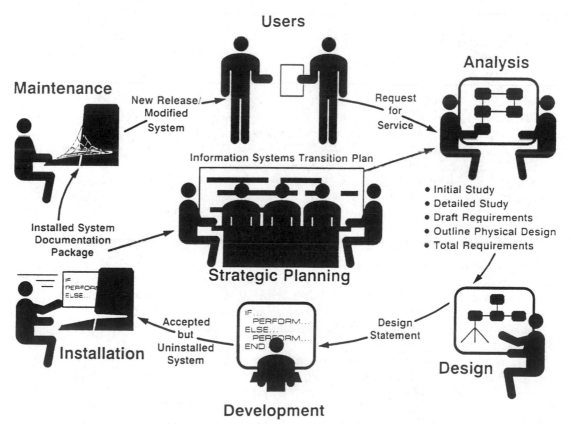

Fig. 7-2. Major phases of software development process

The concepts that are essential to the STRADIS method are:

- Stepwise refinement
- Modeling and abstraction
- Software engineering current practices
- Cross validation of models

Guidelines are provided by various types and sizes of projects to skip and/or combine work products throughout the life cycle. This method is well-suited to the Waterfall model. Effective use of the STRADIS method is not dependent on any particular paradigm of the software process.

STRADIS has been judged to be particularly well-suited for applications involving distributed processing or networks, data processing, and databases. McDonnell Douglas stated that the method has been used successfully on a wide variety of business applications for many industries including:

- Aerospace
- Banking
- Government: city and state
- Insurance
- Military
- Manufacturing
- Securities
- Telephone
- Utilities

This methodology is intended to be used on projects of all sizes. Implementation languages frequently used for coding systems developed with STRADIS are COBOL, Ada, C, and FORTRAN.

The methodology also advocates the use of a data dictionary, an object-oriented repository that maintains consistency within the developing system. Early detection of inconsistencies or errors is addressed by means of walk-throughs and user participation with the development team. Additionally, ProKit*Workbench can be used for detecting violations.

The hardware architecture is addressed by strategic design procedures that use knowledge about the user requirements reflected in the analytical models and data dictionary to determine the appropriate physical environment for each requirement. The methodology provides a template for each deliverable product, model, and repository guideline. Some recommended iconographical representations include DFD's and ERM's. Depending on the application, this template guides the project in the selection of appropriate tools and techniques.

Translating user requirements as represented in analytical models to a physical system is aided by rules prescribed for mapping data flow diagrams into structure charts. Work products similarly flow smoothly through the system life cycle. Traceability is provided from start to finish. Use of the CASE tool, ProKit*Workbench, assists in moving known facts from analysis to design via linkages established among the project phases.

The requirements are developed and defined in a modular fashion, which results in an independent but well integrated set of components that ease the impact of change. Reliance on a data dictionary guarantees that each system fact is stored in one place, which facilitates change via an automated tool environment. Change is first addressed in the highest level system model that affects and then flows through the remaining layers.

MANAGEMENT ASPECTS

STRADIS incorporates guidelines for project management, and recommends allocation of people to different roles, with each role performing some task in the activity. *General project plan* (GPP) establishes milestones for the project. Frequent reviews of the GPP and revisions should occur whenever events impact cost and/or completion date. There is also a provision for detailed estimation of the mantime and elapsed time required to accomplish each milestone.

Communication within the project team is facilitated by the use of walk-throughs, technical reviews, and the data dictionary. Management reviews oversee the entire development effort and management authorizations fund each phase, maintaining communication between the development team and management.

Between the development organization and the client, the method provides walk-throughs and roles that define the type and level of user participation and responsibility on the project team. The users are members of the project team with specific roles to play during the entire development life cycle. Also provided in this method are prototypes and extensive use of graphic models for process, data, and behavior (man/machine interaction).

STRADIS provides specific directions for test planning, integration testing, field testing, generation of test data, and regression testing at one or more points in the life cycle. One section of the project is the quality assurance plan. Review techniques utilized are design reviews, code walk-throughs, and *change control body* reviews.

STRADIS also provides directions for recording specification or design options, trade-off studies, rationales for decisions, personnel involved in making decisions, and changes related to specification or design decisions.

EASE OF ADOPTABILITY

One estimation says that a project team leader will need less than two years college-level technical education, one to two years of development experience, knowledge of one programming language, and experience with one software system in order to successfully use the STRADIS method. The major constructs necessary for understanding the method are:

- Data flow diagrams
- Data models
- Menu navigation diagrams (state transition)
- Decision table
- Structure charts

Available training includes overview presentations, classroom tutorials, on-site consulting by the vendor, a hot line service, user manuals, a user's support group, and periodic technical updates. The estimated learning time for a project manager to acquire an understanding of the major features and benefits of STRADIS is 5 days. An estimate of time for an experienced developer to learn the essentials is 10 days, and an expert user is 6 months. A user's level of competence can be gauged by the number of completed projects.

McDonnell Douglas provides ProKit, a CASE tool that gives support for the following:

- Data flow diagrams
- Entity-relationship diagrams
- Process-narrative capture
- Completeness/consistency checking
- Structure-chart creation
- Prototyping
- Complete documentation of project objects in a data dictionary
- Selected deliverable component generation

An IBM PC-XT or compatible or better PC configuration is appropriate for hosting tools associated with the methodology.

A CASE STUDY

This study will consider a simple business, Joe's Auto Parts (slogan: "If you want it, we'll get it"). Joe holds no inventory but takes orders for parts from his customers and promises future delivery. When he has enough orders for parts for a given car firm to earn a bulk discount, he sends that firm a bulk order. When the bulk order is received, Joe gives each customer what they want and charges them full retail price.

Structured analysis

The diagram in FIG. 7-3 shows a general picture of the flow of data in Joe's business. Customers send in orders and a single process handles them, using a store of data (in some form) for parts containing price, delivery, etc., and a store of data for customers (containing name, address, credit standing, etc.) Customer orders become orders to car firm suppliers. A return flow of invoices from suppliers to Joe and from Joe to his customers is also illustrated.

This basic data flow diagram uses 4 types of symbols:

1. An external entity symbol (square)—a source or destination of data outside the system
2. A data flow symbol (arrow)—a pathway that data moves into, around, and out of the system
3. A process symbol (rounded rectangle)—a function of the system which logically transforms data
4. A data store symbol (open-ended rectangle)—a place in the system where data is stored

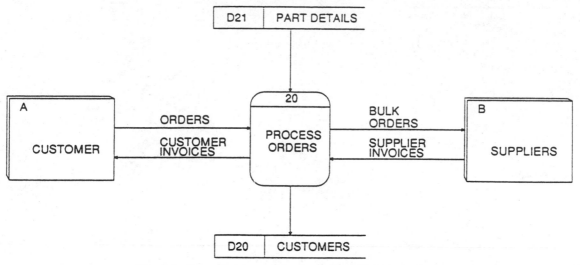

Fig. 7-3. General picture of the flow of data in Joe's business

These 4 simple symbols are the only symbols required to model the integration of a data flow diagram in any information system. A DFD can be used at any level of detail required. For example, the diagram in FIG. 7-3 is clearly a high level.

Figure 7-4 expands the Process Orders process. It shows orders coming from customers into a more detailed process called: Verify order is valid. This process needs data about parts (to check that the part exists and is available) and data about customers (to check credit). From the process comes valid orders.

In high-level DFD's, error paths and exception handling are omitted. The valid orders are kept in a data store of pending orders, which can be a spike on the traffic wall or a computerized database (we don't care at this stage). Note that there is a logical requirement to store valid orders until they can be batched to make a bulk order.

The lower stream of data in FIG. 7-4 shows the data describing the bulk shipment from the suppliers is verified (note that there are no error paths shown), assigned to individual orders, and delivered to customers. Clearly, there must be some financial flows. Customers must be billed and suppliers must be paid, as shown in FIG. 7-5.

The high-level logical data flow for transaction processing at Joe's Auto Parts has several interesting features:

- It is business oriented. It makes no distinction between manual processes, computer processes, tape files, disk files, or any such technicality.
- Because it is logical and uses a very simple set of symbols, the data flow is easily understood by nontechnical users such as Joe. When data flows are explained to managers, they commonly say, "That's the first thing you computer people have ever shown me that I have understood!" or, "Now I know what that system does!"
- It is precise enough, although abstract, to be criticized. "I see what happens to payments from my customers, but what happens if they don't pay?" Joe might ask.

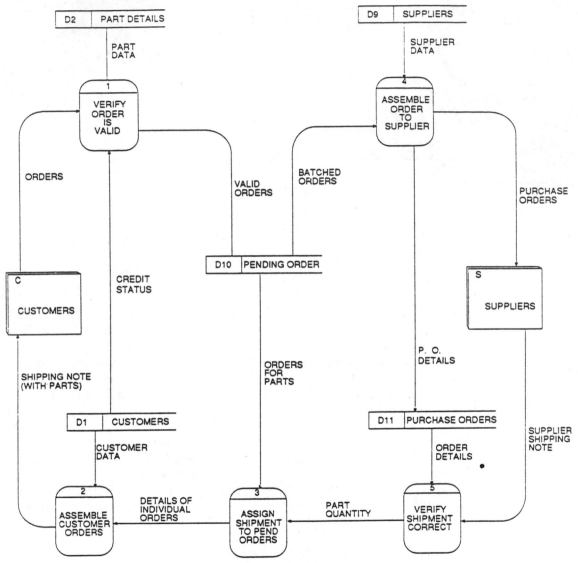

Fig. 7-4. Customers orders coming

Functions for analyzing accounts receivable for delinquency and for mailing billing letters to customers are missing. Of course, finding out that a desired function is missing early in the project, before designing and programming, is a bonus.

If more detail of a process is required, you can *explode* the process into a more specific lower-level DFD. The diagram in FIG. 7-6 is an explosion of the "Assemble Order to Supplier" process in FIG. 7-5.

On a broader scale, a DFD can cover the entire function of a company, as shown in FIG. 7-7.

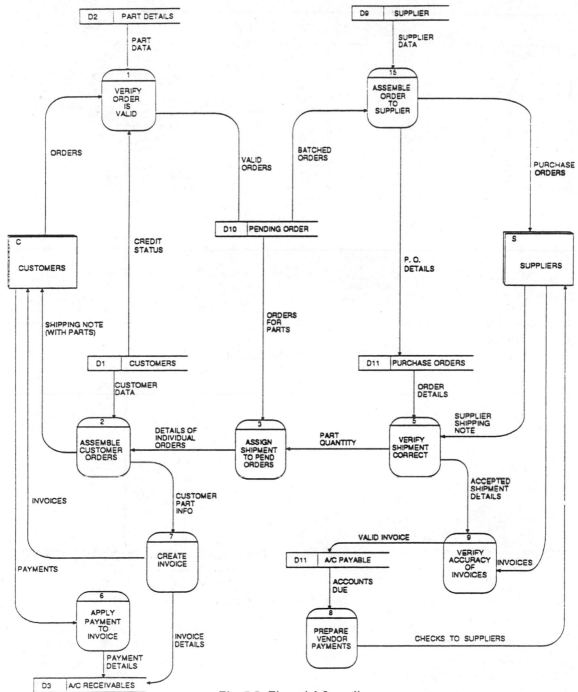

Fig. 7-5. Financial flows diagram

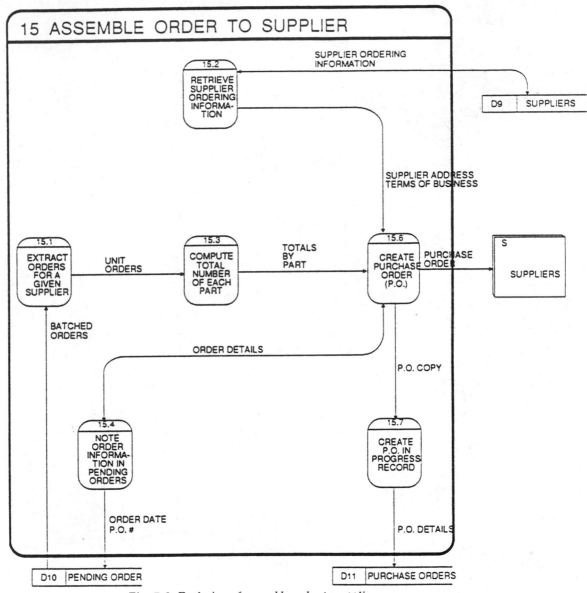

Fig. 7-6. Explosion of assemble order to supplier

If more detail of each data flow is required, you need to express its logical nature. For example, because the data structure in the orders data flow is hierarchical, you can give a series of more and more detailed answers to the question, "What do you mean by orders?" First, name the chief components:

- Order
  - Order identification
  - Customer details
  - Part details (iterated)

If this is not detailed enough, you can state the subcomponents of each component:

- Order
  - Order identification
    —Customer order number
    —Customer order date

  - Customer details
    —Customer name
    —Person authorizing
    —Phone
    —Ship to address

Express the data structure and data elements with honest, complete, and meaningful names. When you get down to the level of a data element (a piece of data that cannot be subdivided meaningfully), you must specify its logical (nonphysical) nature.

If all data structures are composed ultimately of data elements and if you can define each data element, state the way data elements are combined into data structures, state which data structures move along the various data flows, and state which structures are found at rest in the data stores of our DFD, then all the data objects have been provided required for a *logical* data dictionary. The logical data dictionary is the place where all detailed definitions of data objects are stored.

Now consider the definition of data stores. The contents of every data store must be defined (in terms of the data structures defined in the data dictionary). In addition, some data stores will have to show the immediate accesses that have to be made to it.

The definition of data store contents, in principle, is very simple: what comes out must go in—no more, no less. So look at the data flows coming into the data store, compare them with the data flows coming out, make sure that nothing is missing, see that nothing is redundant, and then derive the data store contents accordingly.

Suppose that all the detailed data flows for Joe's Auto Parts and that the complete data flows in and out of the Pending Orders data store are available, as shown in FIG. 7-8. Assume that the detailed contents of each flow have already been defined in the data dictionary. Some nonimmediate accesses to data (batched orders, orders for a given part) are necessary, as are some immediate accesses that might be online inquiries.

What must the contents of the Pending Orders data store be? Because it is fed by a stream of orders and a stream of orders come out, the data store must contain records of the data structure Orders, as defined in our previous list.

Is this information enough? An inspection shows that it would be. Of course, a more complex data store with 10 inflows and 20 outflows, the derivation of contents is far from being as easy, and the detailed logical components of each flow must be compared. You can reduce the contents of each data store to several tables or relations in *third normal form*, (the simplest useful form), which removes redundant data and makes the structures as simple as possible.

Because all the necessary and sufficient contents have been defined for the data store, you must now investigate the immediate accesses required. An immediate access can be defined as one that is required faster than it is possible to search or sort the entire

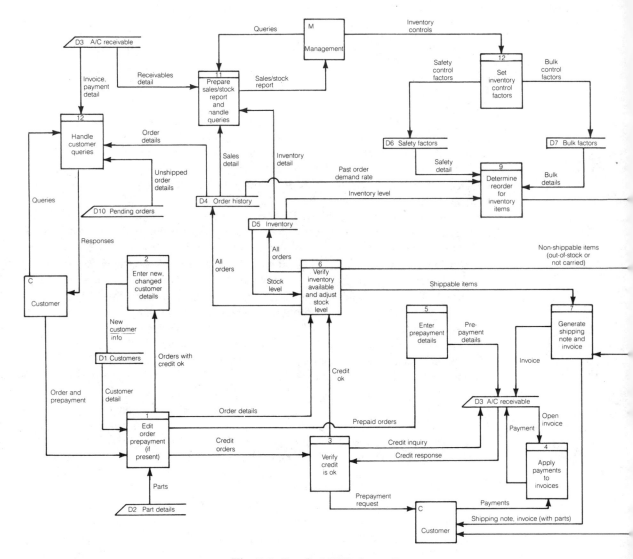

Fig. 7-7. Detailed DFD (control)

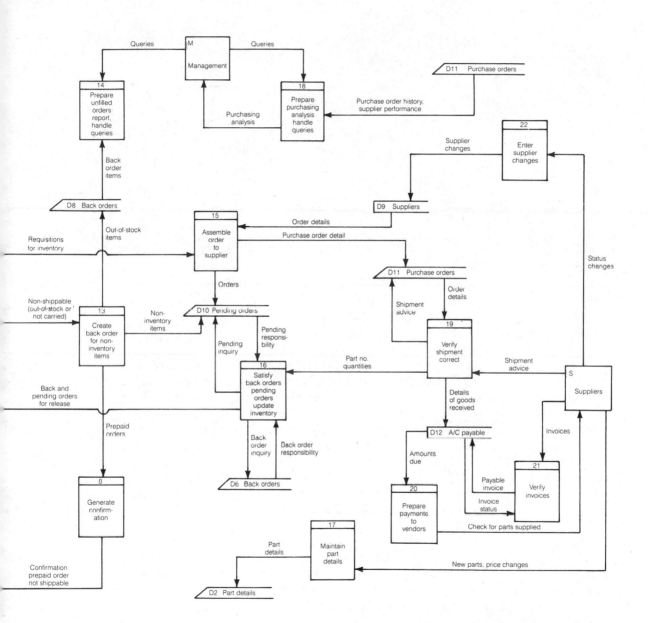

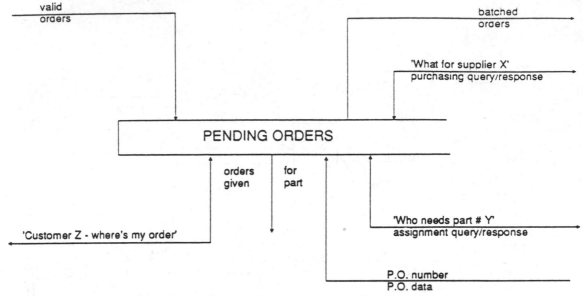

Fig 7-8. Complete data flows in and out of "Pending Orders"

data store. For example, because the supplier of each part is held as a data element in the data store, the question, "What orders do we have for Supplier X?" can always be answered while someone is on the phone. However, you must provide for some special secondary access path (an index, a logical pointer, or the equivalent).

You can use a simple access model, as shown in FIG. 7-9, to get a view of each of the various immediate accesses required by different members of the user community. The arrows connecting the rectangular symbols, data entities synchronical to a data store, are not data flows. These arrows represent access paths. Heavy arrows are immediate accesses and regular arrows are nonimmediate. Note that after you have access to a particular supplier record, you want to access the accounts payable records for the supplier.

When a composite access model (a consolidation of all simple access models) has been drawn up from tabulated volumes, file sizes, and frequency of access, then you can use both the fully attributed entity-relationship model and the composite access model as a database planning tool. After providing all the immediate accesses required, no technical problem exists and the accesses can be done at an acceptable cost.

However, if the cost of providing all the secondary access paths is unacceptable, then something has to go. The simple access models are very useful as a tool for helping users to put some value on the relative importance of immediate and nonimmediate accesses. Obviously, if an access is valuable to the business for pending orders by part number and only nice to have for customer name, then if necessary, the customer name access should be eliminated.

The last tool of structured analysis is the expression of detailed logic. A system level DFD exists for an entire application. Each of these system processes might be exploded into a detailed DFD. As a rule of thumb, the logic of these detailed processes should be expressed in one or two pages, but one or two pages of what? Normally you write logic in English, but suppose you exploded "Apply payment to invoice" in FIG. 7-5 and found

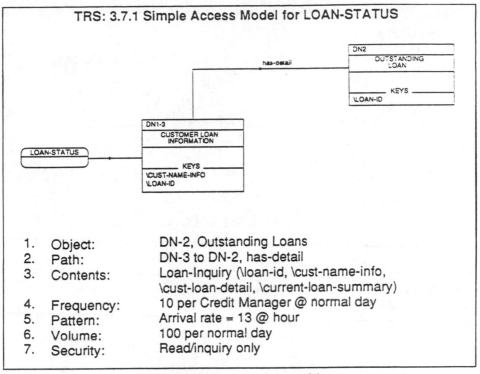

Fig. 7-9. A sample access model

one of the detailed processes was "Verify discount is correct." After inquiring about the detailed logic of this process, you are given the following memo:

". . . Trade discount (to car dealers) is 20%. For private customers, 5% discount is allowed on orders for 6 items or more, 10% on orders for 20 items or more, and 15% on orders for 50 items or more. Trade orders for 20 items and over receive the 10% discount over and above the trade discount."

This is fairly clear as memos go. But, however carefully it is written, you must read all of it to process any one case. For example, how long does it take to answer the question, "What is the discount for a trade customer with an item order of 21?"

A more reliable method of validating the structure of detailed logic is needed. Such a *decision tree* is shown in FIG. 7-10. The decision tree is an ideal tool for representing the detailed logic of processes that are mainly decisions. It also can lead to other questions that should be asked before any system is built. For example, are successive discounts cumulative or serial?

In many cases, however, when long sequences must be carried out, sometimes repeatedly, the decision tree cannot be used. You must use a second logic tool, *structured English*, as shown here:

Add the total number of items on the order:
IF   the order is from a trade customer

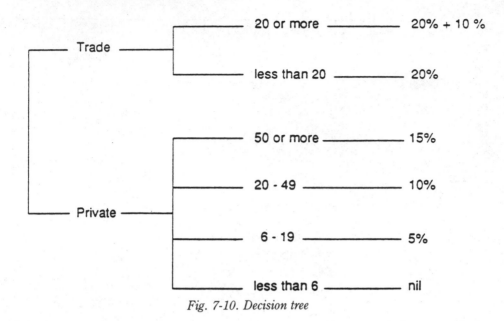

Fig. 7-10. Decision tree

and IF	the order calls for 20 or more	
THEN	discount is 30%	
ELSE	(order is for less than 20)	
SO	discount is 20%	
ELSE	(order is from a private customer)	
so-IF	order calls for 50 or more discount is 15%	
ELSE IF	order calls for 20 to 49 discount is 10%	
ELSE IF	order calls for 6 to 19 discount is 5%	
ELSE SO	(order is for less than 6) no discount is given	

Structured English is a variant of normal English narrative which uses sequence, decision, and repetition structures to express any detailed logic. It is at the same time perfectly general and very strict.

Figure 7-11 shows how these various tools fit together to make a logical model of either an existing or a proposed system. This logical model, with a statement of system

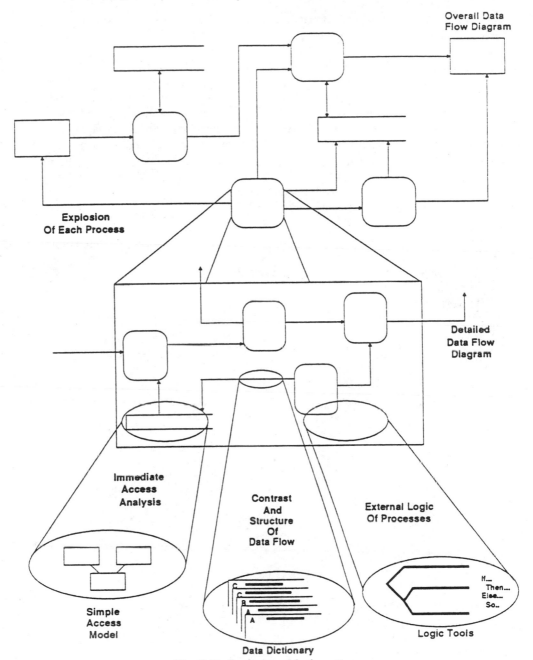

Overall Data
Flow Diagram

Explosion
Of Each Process

Detailed
Data Flow
Diagram

Immediate
Access
Analysis

Contrast
And
Structure
Of
Data Flow

External Logic
Of Processes

Simple
Access
Model

Data Dictionary

Logic Tools

Fig. 7-11. Logical model of a system

objectives and design constraints, forms a comprehensive requirements statement of what a new information system should do.

Structured design

After the logical model has been developed by the analyst and the user community agrees that it meets the system requirements, then system design can be started from a firm foundation. The first concern is strategic design, sometimes known as *design unit packaging*. What will the design units be? What parts of the system function will be automated and what parts will remain manual?

The development phase requires that each activity be repeated for each version of the system to ensure correctness of the interfaces.

The installation phase involves installation of

- Hardware
- Training
- Resolving software conflicts with preexisting systems
- Tuning for response
- Converting files and testing the system

This phase may be done in parallel with the old system. Additionally, a post-installation audit report is prescribed after users have had a chance to evaluate the new system. The report should be repeated every two years.

Maintenance involves responding to the requests for changes and enhancements in a prioritized way, and communicating with the users about new releases or urgent repairs.

8

Structured analysis methods

Customer requirements need to be analyzed thoroughly for understanding before starting system design. There are many methods available to analyze requirements. Many graphic tools are available to assist in requirements analysis. This chapter will discuss a few methods for structured analysis. The names method, methodology, technique, and approach have been mentioned interchangeably just to honor the recognized titles by developers. The methods discussed are:

- Structured Analysis and Design Technique
- Structured System Analysis
- User-Centered Requirements Analysis
- Software Engineering Requirements Analysis

STRUCTURED ANALYSIS AND DESIGN TECHNIQUE

Structured Analysis and Design (SADT) formalizes block diagrams that represent the structured analysis of the requirements. The system model consists of these diagrams in hierarchical arrangements. The method has been evolving since the 1960's. The Cell Model theory [Hori] provided the box notation that covers a small percentage of the current method. The first use of this method was in the production of a system in 1974. The method was first called *system blueprinting* for documenting the architecture of large and complex systems. In 1977, SofTech laid proprietary claim to the design technique. More recently, the SADT method has been interfaced with several other methods or techniques for detailed design and coding.

Structured analysis (part of SADT) covers requirements analysis. Whereas method design is a disciplined approach to system top-level design that makes use of the result of the structured analysis. This approach is a seasoned method and has undergone a number of variations used in a variety of systems analysis and design.

The SADT has been used primarily with models for analyzing requirements to understand present and future operations and for specifying and designing operational systems that involve hardware, software, and people. The method also is used for designing systems software by using models to define user requirements, to identify system components, to interfacing, and to develop a top-level design. The method assists in managing projects by making task assignments, defining procedures, analyzing communications, and processing simulations. Models help to analyze performance and man-machine interactions, and plan testing and integration of the system. The model used for developing the requirements and top-level design becomes the basis of the documentation.

The overall approach of SADT is data-flow oriented. It uses functional decomposition as well as the programming practices of stepwise refinement, process abstraction, and abstract data types. The hierarchical structure allows you to change levels of detail when necessary. Structured analysis of the SADT uses box and arrow diagrams to depict system components, as is shown in FIG. 8-1. The use of diagrams, as in FIG. 8-2, is similar to the use of a mathematical notation. Diagrams are also used to present an object or system whose properties are based on underlying assumptions. A collection of diagrams is called a model, shown in FIG. 8-3, and are suitable for describing systems with or without software subsystems.

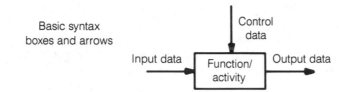

Fig. 8-1. Basic syntax of SADT: boxes and arrows

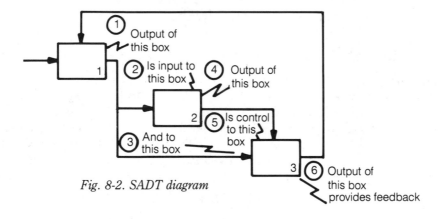

Fig. 8-2. SADT diagram

SADT is suitable for embedded, process control, scientific, engineering, artificial intelligence and expert, large scale simulation, distributed processing, and networking systems. The most frequently used languages include:

- Cobol
- Ada
- Fortran
- C

- PL/1
- Jovial
- Pascal

SADT addresses target constraints related to timing, space, concurrency, fault tolerance, security of access, and specific features of the hardware architecture and operating system. It provides a graphical representation of these constraints but does not contain specific syntax for each. The method assists in transporting end product systems to different target configurations through the separation of functional analysis modeling of a specific design targeted to different configurations. The aim of the method is to document all conspicuous aspects of a system in a clear and concise way.

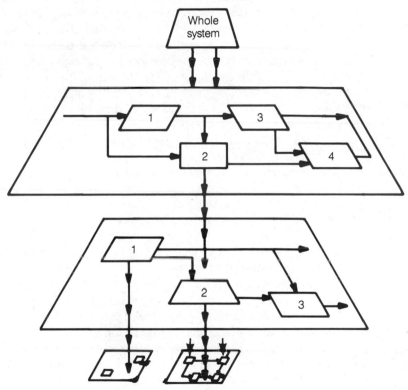

Fig. 8-3. SADT concept: model

SADT uses data and activity models to represent a system. The box and arrow diagrams of SADT are used in the early and middle periods of design. They show both data flow and control flow in the same diagram. They are supplemented with hierarchical representations, narrative overviews, and a formal specification language. Rules are prescribed for mapping between the data flow application and support system interfaces. These rules involve a special notation for intermodel ties.

SADT encourages the use of rapid prototyping, incremental development, simulation, dynamic animation, and executable specifications to clarify system requirements.

The method requires the use of data flow analysis, control flow analysis, and design reviews. SADT assists in reducing the effort needed to fully incorporate changes in the requirements by isolating aspects, bounding the context, and providing top-down decomposition levels. Also, the concise form of the graphics displays the scope of requirements. It assists in ensuring that consistency is maintained with specification design and code when changes are made through the required formal reviews cycle.

The method supports risk management and other project management activities. However, it does not include details of how to perform these activities. Specific directions and procedures for project planning are prescribed. SADT sets forth the goals for the system, makes recommendations for allocating people and resources to different activities, and shows specific personnel roles.

SADT provides coordinated communication among the development team and the relevant sectors of the development organization with the definition of formal review procedures. Design reviews and peer review sessions make up part of this process. Top-down decomposition provides communication at various levels of detail. Graphic diagrams define interfaces and data components more concisely and rigorously than text. Communication between management and the development team is facilitated by the use of levels of detail and support structures in graphic form and by the multiple viewpoints of management and systems applications. Communication between the client and the development organization is facilitated through the use of levels of top-down detail for requirements analysis models and high-level design, graphic chart formats, and interface definitions to client operational environments.

The method supports quality assurance activities, although it does not include details on how to perform them. It provides general guidelines for test planning and generation based on system requirements and automatically generates material suitable for inclusion in the quality assurance or test plan from the data produced in other steps of the development process. In order to ensure and assess conformity to specification, the method provides data flow analysis, control flow analysis and formal specification language. It assists development by ensuring that consistency is maintained among specification, design, and code when changes are made to any of these areas.

The method provides guidelines for configuration management. It gives specific directions for maintaining a traceable record of technical decision making that includes the design options considered, trade-offs studied, rationale for any decisions, personnel involved, and other related changes. The use of the method provides information in textual and graphical form suitable for inclusion in deliverable and internal project documentation. This information is automatically generated during the development process specified by the method.

The techniques required by SADT are incorporated in automated tools whose support goes beyond the method. The graphics tools support the diagrammetic aspects of the method. The hardware and software configuration required is dependent on the automated tools selected. Some of the hardware specified include IBM PC/AT, Apple, VAX, Apollo, Cyber, and IBM 43xx. (SofTech has copyrighted the training materials. Information regarding the various customer support tools and their vendors is available upon request from SofTech.)

STRUCTURED SYSTEM ANALYSIS

Structured System Analysis (SSA) is developed by Yourdon and DeMarco. This method builds a model much like SADT. DFD's are also known by other names such as *bubbles charts* or *diagrams*. The bubbles represent functions and activities that are linked by arrows showing data flow. The data is more precisely defined by a data dictionary. Data sinks and data sources are shown by rectangles that represent the external interfaces. A DFD sample is shown in FIG. 8-4.

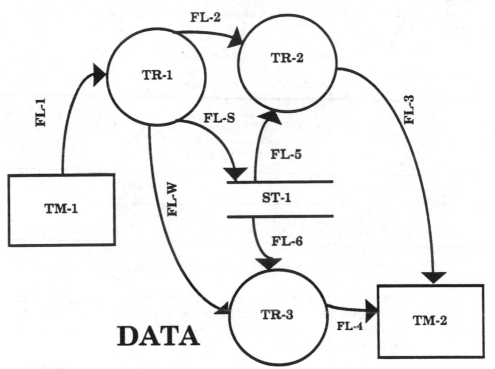

- **FLOWS (FL)**
- **TRANSFORMATION (TR) = PROCESSES**
- **STORES (ST) = FILES**
- **TERMINATOR (TM) = DATA SOURCE/ DATA SINK**

Fig. 8-4. DFD sample

SSA uses a structured top-down hierarchical technique. It also uses multilevel decomposition abstraction schema. Structuring and abstraction techniques assist in the understandability of system requirements. Hierarchical decomposition allows easy focusing on areas of interest which assist in some of the software engineering objectives, i.e., maintainability and traceability. SSA establishes modularity by following decomposition rules, and uses the formalism method of a data dictionary to tabulate data elements. The intuitive nature of diagrams aids review, which enhances the software engineering objectives of correctness and verifiability.

A data dictionary consists of a set of definitions of data items declared in the DFD's data flows and data stores. It is a repository of data about data. The data dictionary defines the specific meaning of data items, specifies the domain of the data elements by setting limits, and specifies whether data elements are discrete or continuous. The data dictionary is concise and nonredundant. It uses a specific set of logical operators to produce an accurate and concise description of data. TABLE 8-1 describes some of these operators.

Table 8-1. Data Dictionary Operators

Operator	Description
=	Consists of (comprises)
+	And (sequence)
{ }	Iteration (repetition)
[ ]	Choose only one (selection)
( )	Optional
* *	Comments

A Yourdon DFD is shown in FIG. 8-5, these diagrams are some of the most widely used structured analysis techniques. They have been popularized through several texts by many authors, especially Tom DeMarco. These DFD's are used to build hierarchical models much like SADT.

Another similar technique has been created by Gane and Sarson with slightly different graphics. For example, the Gane and Sarson technique uses square bubble rectangles with rounded corners, as is shown in FIG. 8-6. The Gane and Sarson technique uses a similar but less precise data dictionary.

USER-CENTERED REQUIREMENTS ANALYSIS

User-Centered Requirements Analysis (UCRA) is a method for developing detailed requirements specifications for a software application. The method combines concepts from Yourdon/DeMarco and Gane/Sarson process modeling based on data flow diagrams with requirements verifiability of military standards. The method was used and refined on 12 system definition projects in 1984 and 1985. The method also uses Bachman, Chen, and Martin data modeling techniques, which use entity-relationship diagrams.

UCRA employs a stepwise refinement process to define requirements for a software application in a manner that is intended for the end user in terms that can be understood and critiqued, instead of a vague user-defined requirements specification followed by a developer-defined system specification. The resulting specification is owned by the user and allows the developer to skip the traditional system specification step.

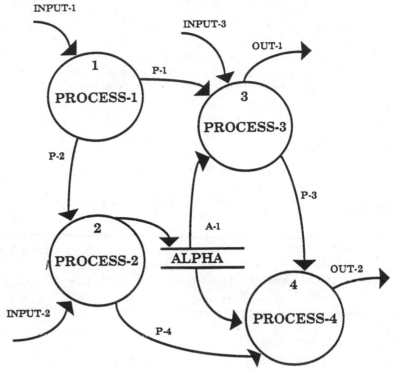

Fig. 8-5. A typical DFD

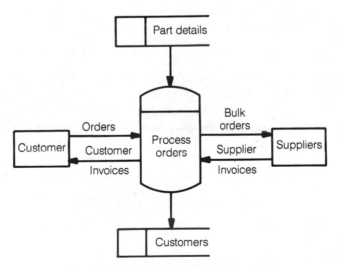

Fig. 8-6. Gane and Sarson DFD sample

The method starts with diagrams and then provides verifiable requirements detail. By treating processes and data equally, the UCRA models of functional processes and databases are parallel. The diagrams are supplemented with textual detail. UCRA prescribes a series of 13 ministeps for generating the requirements specification. The method covers many concerns when creating a requirements specification, which includes coordinating numbering systems, melding diagrams and text, creating performance requirements, and assessing the requirements to determine risk and feasibility.

The method is designed for applications with extensive user interaction and an integrated database. Thus, it is best suited for data processing or database applications. UCRA also can be used to support parts of scientific, engineering, or real-time applications that deal with a database and user interaction. For example, it could help describe the subsystems in a command and control system that displays status to users and accepts human decisions. The implementation languages most frequently associated with the method are fourth-generation DataBase Management System (DBMS) languages, C, Fortran, and Cobol.

The UCRA method focuses on defining requirements for target systems involving a large amount of user interaction and integrated database. The method prescribes steps for handling frequency and completing times of major processes, response times, and security of access. Concurrency issues are addressed indirectly by specifying the workload requirements. The method gives no specific guidelines for handling fault tolerance issues but allows them to be defined in a textual section customized for the application.

Because design techniques are better tailored to the target environment, you will need to tailor your own transition from requirements to the design technique you select for the environment.

The method requires narrative overviews of modules. It suggests a natural specification outline, but also accommodates prescribed formats such as DOD-STD-2167A. UCRA also encourages the use of structured English and decision tables. The diagramming basis for requirements is composed of user concept diagrams, data structure diagrams, and hierarchy charts.

The method assists in reducing the effort necessary to fully incorporate changes in the requirements and assists in the early detection of inconsistencies. The structure of the requirements specification simplifies locating the requirements to be changed and the process prescribed by the method eliminates redundancy. The diagrams utilized are designed to be effective at pointing out inconsistencies early in the requirements analysis.

UCRA prescribes specific directions and procedures for analyzing risk, project planning, and scheduling. It provides guidelines or a framework for estimating initial cost, projecting cost of completion, and other project management activities.

There are many CASE tools available to support UCRA. The hardware requirements depend on the automated tools selected.

SOFTWARE ENGINEERING REQUIREMENTS ANALYSIS

Software Engineering Requirements Analysis (SERA) primarily focuses on understanding and analyzing a customer's requirements for a system's software engineering.

A system needs analysis first, including prototype modeling, before starting the system's preliminary design and detailed design.

SERA uses structured techniques to graphically analyze customer requirements. The techniques separate the requirements into manageable, logical independent functions. The relationship of functions and objects are then established for use later by the Object-Oriented Design Method and Ada advanced features. SERA covers software engineering goals, principles, and various phases of the software engineering life-cycle development phases in accordance with DOD-STD-2167A, as shown in FIG. 8-7.

SERA is designed on the basis of the structured approach to understand customer requirements. It translates these requirements correctly to develop efficient and cost-effective software. The graphical model formed assists in testing and maintaining software engineering throughout the life cycle. Frequent changes are implemented by the user. A generic, real-time model is shown in FIG. 8-8. The method is a combination of concepts from Yourdon/DeMarco, and Mellor/Ward. The major components of the model are:

- Context diagram
- Functional-event list
- Logical data flow diagrams
- State-transition diagram
- Data dictionary
- Decision table
- Miniature specifications
- Structured English

The overall approach of SERA is data flow oriented and uses functional decomposition. The method uses state-transition approach for real-time systems. The method also includes stepwise refinement. SERA uses circles as dynamic transformation processes. Rectangles are used to show external interfaces for data sources and data destinations. The data flow shows a vector-curve flow instead of a straight line. This scheme, shown in FIG. 8-9, assists in drawing clearer models rather than a mesh model, as is shown in FIG. 8-10.

SERA documents dynamic transformation processes with the help of *miniature specifications* (mini-specs). Data in static files is tabulated in the data dictionary. The input/output data flows are also recorded in the data dictionary. These documents are used and enhanced in the following phases of software development.

The SERA method is suitable for analyzing requirements for any system, including embedded systems, real-time systems, commercial systems, scientific systems, and networking systems. SERA is practically independent of language and machine.

SERA supports managing systems effectively with the help of graphical models. It encourages the use of rapid prototyping, incremental development, and simulation. The method uses effective data flow analysis, control flow analysis, and reviews. A structured walk-through technique is used throughout modeling to catch errors in the very beginning of software development. With proper documentation of data elements, SERA ensures consistency in all phases of software engineering.

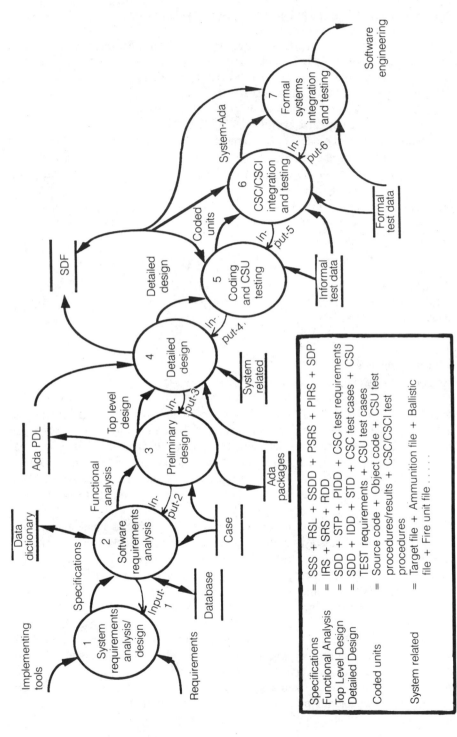

Fig. 8-7. DOD-STD-2167A: Software development phases

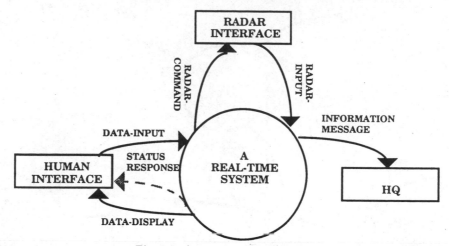

Fig. 8-8. A system context diagram

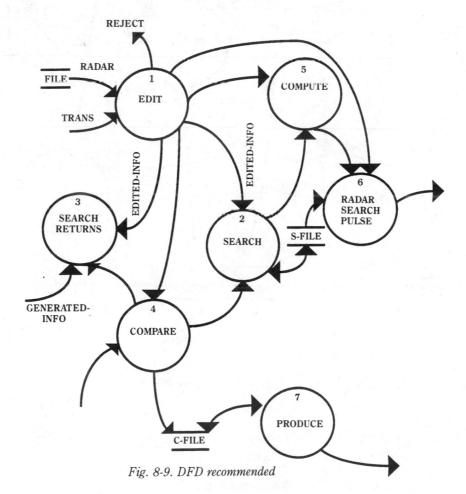

Fig. 8-9. DFD recommended

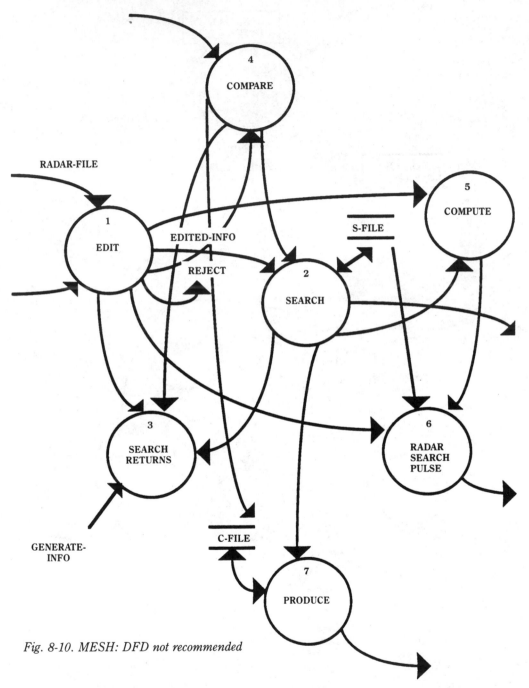

Fig. 8-10. MESH: DFD not recommended

SERA supports management techniques for planning, estimating, and scheduling. However, it does not include details to perform these techniques.

SERA provides effective communication within the members of the software engineering team. Top-down decomposition provides communication at various levels of detail. Graphic diagrams clarify interfaces better than narrative texts.

SERA can be taught within three to five days to experienced analysts, software engineers, system engineers, and programmers. Management can be taught a SERA overview in one day. I have developed this course and presented it successfully to hundreds of computer professionals for the last ten years.

There are many CASE tools available to support SERA. The graphic tools support the diagrammatic aspects of the method. The hardware/software configuration required is dependent on the automated tools selected.

9

Structured design methods

A structured design method translates requirements specifications into another phase of the software engineering life cycle. According to DOD-STD-2167A, a design phase consists of two major phases: preliminary design and detailed design. The purpose of this method is to provide insight to the major aspects of the design phase of the life cycle. Design is a blueprint of software components and their interconnections. The design process allocates the functional requirements to a design structure. The design methods to be discussed in this chapter are:

- Structured Design
- Refinement Method
- Software Engineering Design

STRUCTURED DESIGN

Structured Design (SD) provides techniques to address the activities of preliminary design and detailed design. It is used to define the architectural (structural) design of the system being developed, and carries out the functional analysis result to individual software components and their interconnections. SD uses structure charts and data flow diagrams.

Structured design was introduced by IBM in 1974 [Stevens]. Prior to that, the various concepts were referred to as modular design, logical design, composite design, or design of program structure [Peters]. Stevens, Myers, and Constantine described the concepts and techniques of structured design, including structure charts, based on Constantine's research. From DeMarco's work, data flow diagrams and structure charts were combined. Structured design was first used on a system in the early 1970's. Its use has been actively promoted by Yourdon, Inc.

The techniques of SD are used in the transition from user requirements to architectural design: the description resulting from structured analysis is refined to become the preliminary and detailed designs of functional modules. Structured design provides techniques to reduce the complexity of programs by dividing them into hierarchies called functional modules. The data flow diagram, shown in FIG. 9-1, was analyzed to produce structure charts that reflect the hierarchical modular structure. Structured design uses the structure chart shown in FIG. 9-2, a HIPO (Hierarchy, plus Input, Process, and Out-

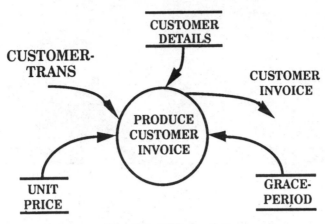

Fig. 9-1. DFD (partial)

put) chart as shown in FIG. 9-3, and narrative representations. Structure charts are used to specify the modular characteristics of the software being designed with additional notation showing control flow.

Structured design, as presented by Yourdon and Constantine [Yourdon], consists of the following four groups:

1. Documentation techniques are graphic and descriptive representations and include data flow diagrams and structure charts.
2. Evaluation criteria and heuristics are the guidelines for assessing a proposed structure, and include the concept of *coupling, cohesion, span of control, scope of effect/scope of control*, and *packaging*.
3. Design strategies are techniques for viewing the design requirements and include top-down design, transform-centered design, transaction analysis, and modular design [Parnas].
4. Implementation strategies are the plans for sequence of coding and implementation.

Structured design begins with a system specification generally in the form of data flow diagrams from structured analysis. From these diagrams that show the inherent data flows and transformations, the natural aggregates are identified and structure charts are derived. Structure charts are defined, evaluated, and redefined iteratively. The charts are based on the coupling between modules and functional cohesion within modules. The issues analyzed with coupling are:

- Interface complexity
- Type of connection
- Type of communication

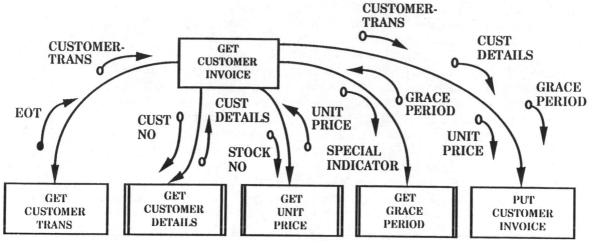

Fig. 9-2. Structure chart (partial)

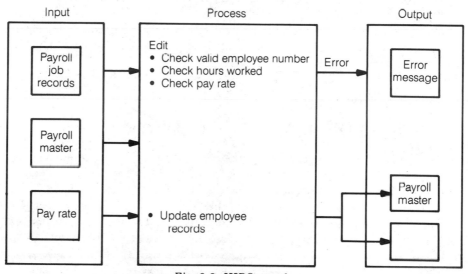

Fig. 9-3. HIPO sample

Finally, the system specification is reexamined and the process is selectively repeated.

Although the method is founded on functional decomposition, the data flow orientation differs from functional decomposition, where tree-like hierarchical structures are created with a top-down design. SD tends to retain the logical shape of the system, which is useful for identifying and organizing the physical design.

The structured design method is best suited for use in systems programming and business applications, but is appropriate for some other applications. The most frequently used languages are Cobol, Fortran, PL/1, APL, Assembler, and Basic.

The data flow orientation does not provide representation for the passage of time. This method simplifies the definition and user's review of transformations, input, and output. Other methods are built on structured design and have added techniques to model timing and other target constraints.

The method does provide specific directions and procedures for assessing complexity. The available evaluation checklists are designed to aid in managing and controlling the project. Data flow diagrams provide a representation that more closely resembles natural human values [Stevens]. The use of DFD's and structure charts provides documentation for further development and maintenance activities. A definition of interfaces provides for communication among developers working on separate modules of the system. Developers need to communicate only when the interface changes. Management can monitor progress on the project by monitoring progress on individual modules.

The SD method is intended to reduce original errors and simplify testing. It ensures the consistency of specification, design, and code by reducing complexity, defining interfaces, and using self-contained modules. SD provides for data flow and control flow analysis of dependencies. Formal definition of interfaces between modules is designed to cause early detection of inconsistencies and errors.

Many of the current CASE tools incorporate structured design and support activities. Hardware and software requirements depend on the CASE tool selected.

Many companies and consultants provide courses and assistance in implementing the techniques of structured design with a variety of perspectives and alterations. Many reference books and articles are also available.

REFINEMENT METHOD

The Refinement Method (RM) addresses the activities of design, coding, prototyping, and documentation. It provides ways for the design to be gradually completed with a top-down approach while following the principles of object-oriented programming and information hiding. This method results in programs that are structured as a hierarchy of layers. RM is based on ideas found in stepwise refinement and object-oriented design. It was developed by Vaclav Rajlich, who has published several articles on the refinement method. The method was first used with respect to a deliverable system in 1986. Since this time, several organizations have used close derivatives of RM to develop large systems.

RM specifically addresses system design and implementation activities. It is founded on the functional decomposition approach. The concepts of stepwise refinement and module coupling and cohesion are essential to RM. The method also incorporates object-oriented programming. RM is well suited for use within the context of an incremental software-process model. However, the most effective use of RM is not dependent on any one process model. The steps of design and coding are merged to form one step of development. RM uses Ada as both a program design language and a programming language. (Some organizations have used C and Pascal languages with this method.)

During development, the program can be thought of as two parts:

- The existing part
- The intended part

Development progresses as additions are made to the existing part and deletions are made to the intended part. All undefined entities used in the existing part, but are not yet defined, constitute the *backlog interface*. Development is a series of repeating steps that define all entities and remove them from the backlog interface. At this time, the development is finished. The resulting program is structured into a hierachy of layers.

The method prescribes rules for mapping backlog interfaces or data flow diagrams into skeletons of modules, which assists in translating from one mode of expression to another. Throughout phases of the software process, the refinement method guarantees consistency of specification and design with the code because specification and design are represented by certain layers of the code. Moreover, skeletons of the code are generated from backlog interfaces.

Specification, design, and code are overlapped with certain layers that are specification oriented and other layers that are design oriented. The only documents separate from the code are backlog interfaces, whose consistency with the code is checked automatically.

Rapid prototyping and incremental or evolutionary development are required to clarify system requirements.

SOFTWARE ENGINEERING DESIGN

Software Engineering Design (SED) provide techniques to address the activities of preliminary design and detailed design. It uses the result of the SERA method. SED is used to map the result of SERA by defining the structural design of the system that is being developed into individual computer software components and their interconnections. SED uses a system hierarchy chart by mapping data flow diagrams and structure charts to define the logic of software components and their interconnectivity. It refines the model by further decomposing the modular structure.

SED is a structured method composed of the Yourdon/Constantine and Ward/Mellor approaches. The major components of SED include:

- System hierarchy charts
- Structure charts
- Top-down design
- Heuristic design
- Concepts of coupling, cohesion, span of control, and packaging
- Transform-centered design
- Transaction analysis
- Modular design

SED starts with SERA specifications and DFD's, as shown in FIG. 9-4. A system hierarchy chart is designed to transform the analysis view of the system into the design blueprint shown in FIG. 9-5. From these diagrams, the inherent data flow and transformations show that natural aggregates are identified and structure charts are derived. Structure charts are defined, evaluated, redefined, and iteratively based on the coupling and the functional cohesion within CSC/CSU's. Finally, the system specification is reexamined and the process is selectively repeated. This graphic provides a comprehensive picture of one CSCI comprising a number of CSC/CSU's and their relationship.

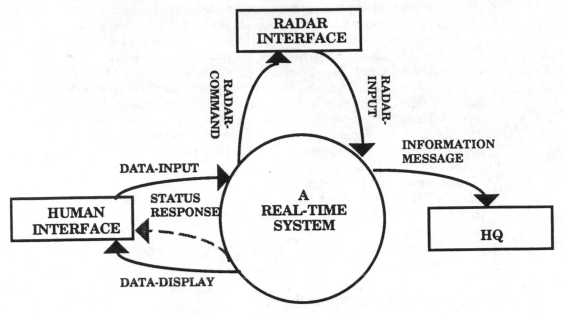

Fig. 9-4 (a). A system context diagram
(b). Functional requirements event list
(c). First level DFD

FUNCTIONAL REQUIREMENTS

EVENT LIST

1. **REQUIREMENT - A**

    1.1 **PROCESS - A1**

    1.2 **PROCESS - A2**

    1.3 **PROCESS - A3**

    1.4 **PROCESS - A4**

    1.5 **DATA-STORAGE - 1**

    1.6 **DATABASE - A**

2. **REQUIREMENT - B**

3. **DATABASE**

4. **REQUIREMENT - C**

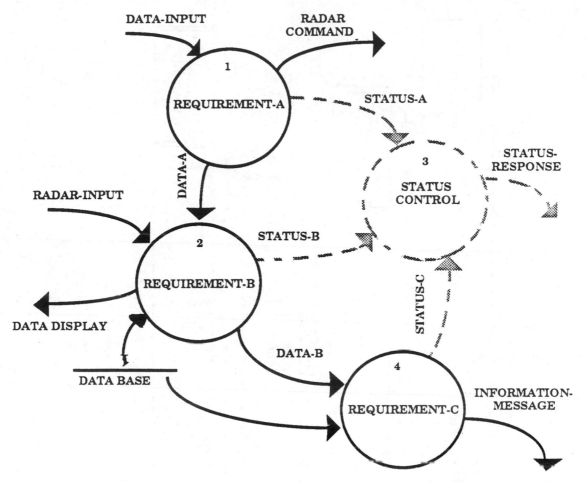

For real-time systems, a State Transition Diagram (STD) is drawn. An example is shown in FIG. 9-6. This shows the control flow of the DFD's. State transition diagrams are a supplement to DFD's.

This method is best suited for use in scientific, business, and embedded systems. SED is based on the following concepts:

- Stepwise refinement
- Information hiding
- Module coupling and cohesion

The use of DFD's and structure charts provides documents for further development and maintenance activities. Definitions of interfaces provide for communication between developers working on separate software components of the system. Members of the team need to communicate only when the interface changes. Management can monitor progress on the project by monitoring progress on individual software components.

SED reduces errors by introducing walk-throughs at all levels of software development. It ensures and simplifies testing of units and integrated software components.

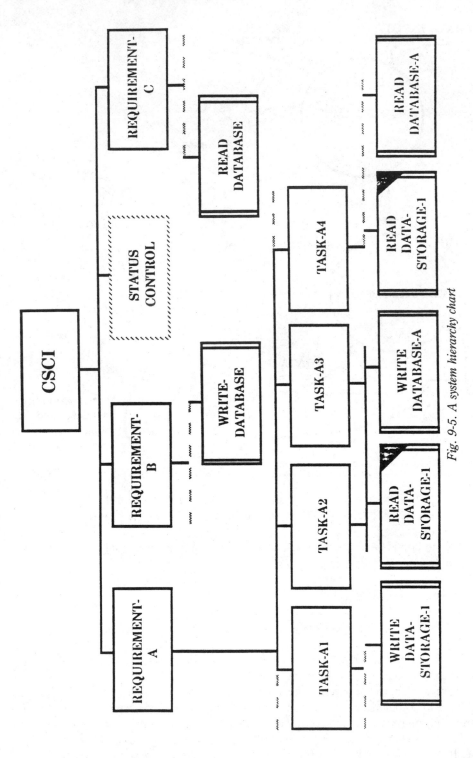

Fig. 9-5. A system hierarchy chart

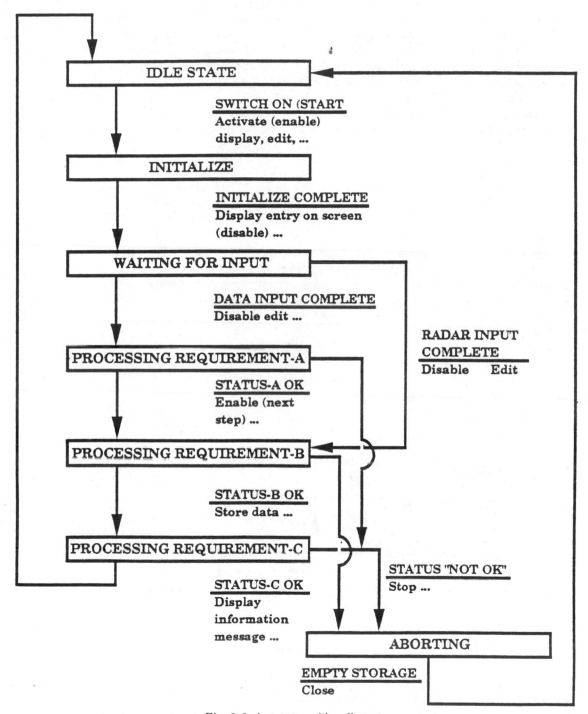

Fig. 9-6. A state transition diagram

STD also ensures the consistency of specification, design, and code by reducing complexity, defining interfaces, and using self-contained software components. Evaluation checklists are provided to confirm that the procedures have been correctly completed.

An experienced professional does not need much effort to learn SED. Classroom courses are available for this course that take from three to five days. For management, a one day overview course is available.

Many CASE tools incorporate SED and support its activities. The hardware and software requirements depend on the CASE tool selected.

A CASE STUDY

Suppose you must design a radar system. The requirements are that the system should initially set up the radar, detect, and track an object. The coordinates of the object should be computed and relayed to the authority. The operator monitors the functionality of the system at all times.

The requirements should be analyzed and understood before proceeding any further. Experience counts a lot to understand the requirements. Structure the context of the system as shown in FIG. 9-7. Study the requirements and interview the customer for clarification. A compiled functional requirement event list would be:

- Set up radar
- On-line control
- Send radar beam
- Track an object
- Information transmitting
- Operator display unit

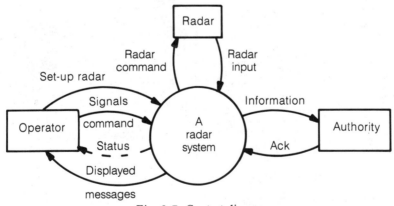

Fig. 9-7. Context diagram

These are the major functions so far identified. The first level of a logical DFD is given in FIG. 9-8. The selected names of data flows and files are tabulated in the data dictionary. The activities within the transformation processes are expanded in the miniature specifications and structured English. A decision table and decision tree are tabulated to enhance the explanation of these activities.

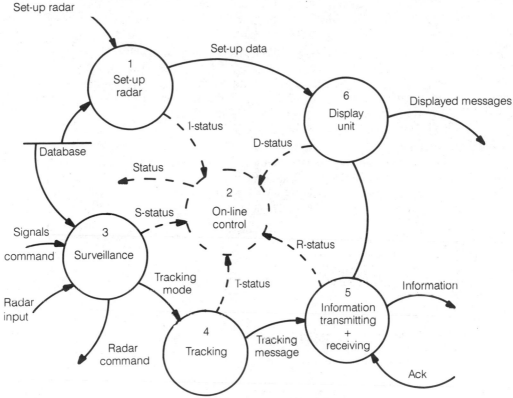

Fig. 9-8. First level DFD (partial)

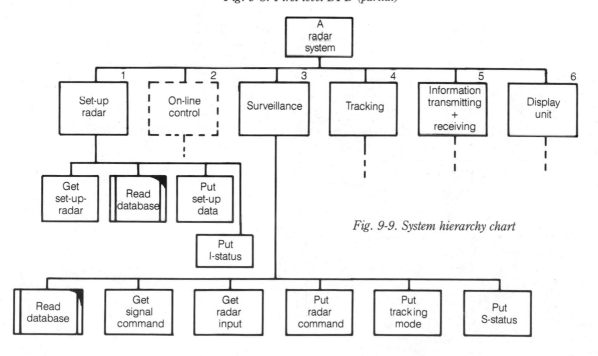

Fig. 9-9. System hierarchy chart

You can always subpartition the level 1 DFD into lower levels of DFD's to depict the smallest independent function. The details of drawing DFD's are explained in the SERA course [Sodhi]. This view of the model conforms with the customer's requirements. Thus the requirements are mutually understood by the customer and developers for proceeding with the design of the system.

You should utilize the knowledge of SED to further design the system by using the model created. Figure 9-9 presents the system hierarchy chart. Figure 9-10 provides another view of the system as a state transition diagram.

The model can be improved by refinement techniques as discussed in the structured design methods. The model assists in understanding the customer's requirements and identifying the software components and their logical relationships with each other. This model further helps in managing the system, development, testing, and maintenance phases. The software developed will be cost effective, efficient, and properly documented. (The study presented should be completed by the readers.)

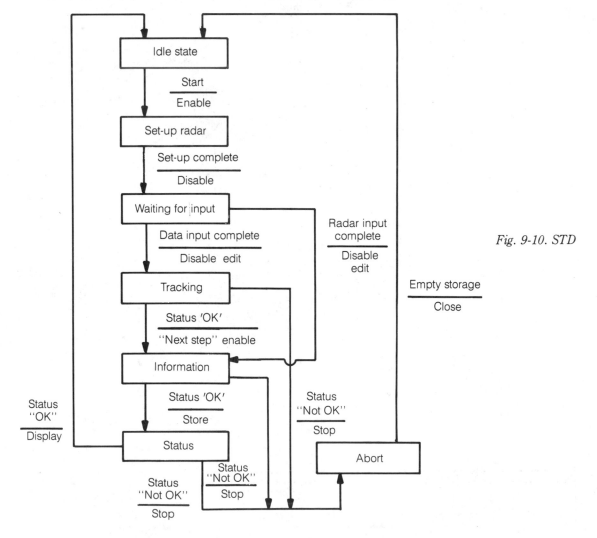

Fig. 9-10. STD

10

Structured methodology

A few selected software engineering methodologies will be addressed in this chapter. The concept throughout the book has been to include only material that is practical and well proven in the industry. The methodologies discussed in this chapter are:

- Software cost reduction
- The box structure methodology for information systems development
- Essential systems development/essential systems analysis

SOFTWARE COST REDUCTION

Software Cost Reduction (SCR) associates the concepts of information hiding and modularization by separating concerns and examples of templates for functions, data items, and modes. In this methodology, inputs and outputs are independent of functions. There are any number of relationships that exist between functions and outputs. This scheme creates many small functions. SCR uses templates for additional formalism and uses precisely defined concepts of modes and events. Modes are used to simplify function descriptions.

The customer's requirements are split into relatively independent parts to localize changes. Similarly in system design, possible changes are encapsulated in one module or a small number of related modules to make change easy. The basic principles of SCR are:

- Separation of concerns
- Formalism
- Additional design-related principles

SCR is a product of research effort in software engineering at the U.S. Naval Research Laboratory. The methodology has been developed over the past decade by a group of people that includes David Parnas, Paul Clements, Kathryn Britton, Stuart Faulk, and Bruce Labaw. SCR will reduce life-cycle maintenance costs.

SCR is considered well suited for use with several software process paradigms including: waterfall, spiral, rapid prototyping, and incremental.

The requirements of the target system in the SCR methodology are not prescribed in specific steps. However, a template for documentation and an example that serves as a model is provided. All timing requirements are defined in a specific chapter of the requirements document, and are given in terms of mathematical functions for the system outputs.

Functions can be periodic or on demand. A timing constraint is associated with each function in terms of its period or deadline in real time.

Specific features of the target hardware architecture and target operating system are given as part of the description of system inputs and outputs because this is relevant to the software. Typically, this identifies all the essential characteristics such as timing, representation, and instruction sequences for accessing particular devices. The concepts of SCR are:

- Stepwise refinement
- Information hiding
- Process abstraction
- Abstract data types
- Structured programming

The SCR methodology not only provides a set of basic principles, but also provides an example for proceeding through the design process step by step and organizing the documentation of the design. The first two levels of a high-level design decomposition are reusable for all embedded applications. The first step in the design of the high-level modular decomposition is documented in the software module guide. This guide is the only design document that all implementors or maintainers should read. Most of the process or tasking structure of the system is documented in the function driver and shared services module specification, where the stimulus behavior of the system is documented.

The abstract interface specifications describe the interface to the computer, to all peripheral devices, and to certain other modules that implement software decisions (i.e., the database module). These decisions are not derived from the functional specification.

The specification of concurrency issues is nonalgorithmic by design. SCR does not specify an order among actions except when one action is explicitly required and preserves the maximum concurrency. Fault tolerance issues are treated like any other system requirements; they must be expressed as constraints on the system outputs. The traceability of customer requirements is recorded throughout the design description.

SCR's preliminary design phase documentations are:

- Requirements specifications
- Module decomposition
- Module dependency
- Process structure
- Resource allocation
- Module interface
- Module design
- Test plan

The SCR methodology is suited for use on the following systems:

- Embedded systems
- Process control
- Time critical systems
- Real-time systems
- Systems programming
- Distributed processing/networks

In general, the methodology is architecture and language independent. It can be tailored to specific features of target architecture, operating system, and implementation language. The system is developed as a hierarchy of abstract machines. The abstract machine at any given level hides the target configuration. By redeveloping the implementation of the abstract machine, such as a compiler, the system can be ported to a new configuration.

The SCR methodology encourages the use of finite state diagrams, functions, and state tables to convey the representation graphically. The set of documents produced in this methodology contains all significant design decisions throughout the life cycle. As such, you can determine from the completeness of various documents how the development stands at a given time, which facilitates communication between the development team and management.

THE BOX STRUCTURE METHODOLOGY
FOR INFORMATION SYSTEMS DEVELOPMENT

The Box Structure Methodology for Information System Development is described as a mathematically based theory that extends software engineering principles to information systems. Each part of the system under development is viewed at three different levels of detail:

1. Black box
2. State box
3. Clear box

The black box view provides a description of external behavior from defined data abstraction with stimulus response. The initiation of a black box with an entry and any required data is described as the stimulus. Completion of the black box with an exit and the data that might be produced is described as the response. This stimulus response description is seen as a mathematical function from the stimulus history of the black box to the next response from the black box.

Expansion of the black box into a state box requires that the stimulus history of the black box is transformed into a state description, described as a mathematical function where the stimulus and state histories correspond to the new response and state.

The clear box view describes behavior in terms of four procedural structures necessary to derive the state and black box views. The procedural structures are sequence, alternation, iteration, and concurrency. These structures are used for replacement of the internal data abstraction defined in the state box.

Creative invention is required to go from a black box to a state box, and from a state box to a clear box. However, analysis and mathematical derivation techniques allow you to go from a clear box to the corresponding state box, and from a state box to the corresponding black box. These box structures are the integrating concept in the complete system and software development process.

Four principles assist in the effective use of box structures for development of information systems. These four principles are:

1. Referential transparency
2. Transaction closure
3. State migration
4. Common services

The box structure methodology for information systems development is an extension of data abstractions, objects, hierarchies of data abstractions, and mathematical verification of programs and systems. The evolution of the methodology occurred at the IBM Federal Systems Division. The principal architects are H. Mills, R. Linger, and A. Hevner. The methodology specifically addresses the following activities:

- Requirements definition
- System specification
- System design
- Implementation
- Software quality assurance

The methodology uses stepwise refinement and verification to produce a system design. The design is composed of small steps that allow immediate verification using mathematical derivation techniques that map one step to another. The design process of the method is founded on three principles, [Mills,88]:

1. All data defined and stored in the system is hidden in data abstractions.
2. All processing is defined by sequential and concurrent use of data abstractions.
3. Each use of data abstraction in the system occupies a distinct place in the usage hierarchy.

Mills rated the methodology as best suited for all applications. Cobol, C, and Pascal are the main languages that have been used in developing systems with this methodology.

Hierarchy charts are a required iconographical mode. Finite state diagrams and entity-relationship diagrams are strongly encouraged. All of these iconographical modes are provided with automated support. Textual modes of expression required for the method are:

- Structured English
- Program design language
- Formal specification language
- Mathematical notation

Mills states that the underlying mathematics are based on theory and representation, and allow precise technical communication and management control. Between the customer and the developer, box structure graphics provide a visual means of communication. Box structures are used during analysis and design to review the customer's requirements. The methodology requires test planning at precise points in the software process, and provides guidelines for prescriptive checking of interfaces. The methodology requires quality assurance or a test plan document. Producing documents requires a tailorable format. Documents are generated automatically from data produced in other steps of the methodology.

ESSENTIAL SYSTEMS DEVELOPMENT/ESSENTIAL SYSTEM ANALYSIS

Essential Systems Development (E-DEV) provides a framework for system development. Strategies are designed for integrating requirements definition techniques and tools that are based on framework developed as part of essential system analysis (ESA). ESA addresses the activities of requirements definition and specification as well as preliminary design. E-DEV expands on ESA's treatment of design, yielding the design technique essential systems design (ESD) and adds a data modeling front end called quintessential system analysis (QSA). QSA, ESA, and ESD are all submethods of essential systems development.

Essential systems analysis is derived on DeMarco's structured analysis. Essential systems development incorporates techniques of information that models a logical database design. Two examples are Yourdon/Constantine's structured design and IBM's structured joint application development.

QSA provides strategies for developing data models, ESA provides strategies for developing logical process models, and ESD provides strategies for integrating logical data and process requirements with implementation technology. E-DEV strategies are organized with the waterfall and spiral development process paradigms.

By taking a waterfall view, the E-DEV technical strategy presents logical systems development and requirements definition. First, the data model is developed using QSA. The output of QSA is transformed into a logical process model with the ESA application. Both logical process and data requirements are then integrated with technology through ESD.

From a spiral view, the E-DEV managerial strategy begins a project with the development of a first-cut data model, logical-process model, and implementation model by using parts of QSA, ESA, and ESD. The resulting models form the basis of a system prototype. They are also the basis for estimating the complexity of detailed requirements definition and for precise establishment of the project scope. During the detailed requirements definition, various models and prototypes are updated as additional requirements are identified. The final system is either a fully evolved prototype or one coded from the combined detailed passive requirements model and prototype.

ESA views the system being developed as two different types of system models: essential model and incarnation model. The essential model focuses on analysis of major activities of the system from a logical view, i.e., what the system must do.

The incarnation model is an extensive implementation environment requirements model. It provides a physical view of the system and its environment, i.e., how the system will be built.

The ESD process consists technically of two activities: specifying the implementation environment and mapping essential requirements to the implementation environment model. Data flow diagrams and entity-relationship diagrams are redefined, as well as state-transition diagrams that show the allocation of the essential model to processors. From this allocation, decisions are related to the concurrency requirements of each processor, and the system support environment is modeled for the application.

Next, the code organization phase incorporates the techniques of structured design to perform initial design and detailed design. An object-oriented design is also used to convert fragments of the essential model to program designs. As in SD, the lower-level data flow diagrams are created with successive refinement that produces hierarchical sets of diagrams at increasing levels of detail.

Structure charts are used to define the physical structure of program units of the system. Structure charts show the calling hierarchy—what program units call or are called by other units. Created by transform analysis from data flow diagrams, they are refined based on coupling, cohesion, complexity, and reusability of individual models. The process is also divided into an external and an internal design stage. As part of the internal design, database and program design are integrated.

ESA and ESD have been used in hundreds of projects of all sizes. The languages most frequently used have been Cobol and C.

In addition to addressing portability issues, separating concerns between the essential model and the incarnation model is intended should reduce the effort required to adapt end produce systems for new applications.

The E-DEV managerial strategy is an expansion of ESA's leveled systems development concept. The techniques for analysis of business and technological problems provide a means for analyzing risk, assessing cost and complexity, tracking project progress, planning the project, scheduling and allocating personnel, and doing other development resources. The techniques of function point analysis [Albrecht] have been used for assessing complexity of projects under development.

E-DEV and ESA provide a medium for communicating the system requirements to management and users within the development team. Visual representations of the existing system or the proposed system with data flow diagrams use processes and information meaningful to the user [McMenamin]. Utilization of other visual representations such as structured English and a data dictionary provides coordinated communication within the development team.

Essential systems development uses blitz meetings, one-on-one interviews, and client walk-throughs to involve the client in the development process. Throughout the project, client walk-throughs of models and prototypes are held. These walk-throughs ensure quality and conformance to actual needs. A list of events coordinates sessions of blitz meetings and walk-throughs. A work group in a blitz meeting establishes requirements for a given event. The review group in a walk-through reviews the specified requirements.

Event orientation facilitates communication between management and the technical team. At each stage of the requirements definition, requirements can be partitioned into an event-based unit. These units are the basis for requirements complexity estimation, team and team member productivity estimation, team and team member work assignments, and an overall project plan.

This methodology requires testing activities and maintaining records by technical decision making. E-DEV supports the early detection of inconsistencies and errors through its leveled systems development approach. Each method within E-DEV has a blitzing strategy as previously described. Involving the user in group workshops helps find inconsistencies that would not be found during a one-on-one interview. Additionally, passive models from information modeling, structured analysis, and structured design, that are combined with active models from prototyping, make finding inconsistencies easier.

The textual and graphical information required by this methodology also provides a basis for internal documentation of the system when it is proposed, while it evolves, and after it is finalized. Some of the system models, especially the higher-level diagrams, are suitable for insertion in the documentation.

11

Real-time systems methods

The important aspects of real-time systems are accuracy, reliability, and immediate response. Real-time systems must supply correct results within specified time limits. Any information that is accurate but late has no value. Real-time systems should have predictable timing characteristics and should be robust under stress. There is a need for an analytical basis to predict when a system will be able to meet its deadlines. The analytical approach should deal with transient overload, task blocking due to synchronization requirements, and aperiodic events.

Many computer languages, such as Ada, meet demands by utilizing multitasking. Ada tasks are executed concurrently by helping describe many situations where several threads of control execute in an interrelated fashion.

Currently, most software engineering methodologies have addressed issues of logical correctness. In this chapter, only those methodologies that address timing and composition correctness for real-time systems are discussed. These methodologies also address the aspects of control devices and managing concurrency.

SOFTWARE THROUGH PICTURES

Software through Pictures (StP) was developed at Interactive Development Environments (IDE) by A. Wasserman and P. Pircher. Real-time systems are modeled not only with data flows and data stores, as used in structured analysis, but also with *control flows*. A control flow is shown in FIG. 11-1. Control flows are signals or events that cause processes to be activated and other control flows to be generated. In more complex systems, several concurrent control flows are possible that make specifying the results of these activations necessary.

Real-time systems are complex. Many systems include combinations of control signals that cause the activation of several different processes. These different processes can be activated in a predetermined order or as independent tasks. The activation of a process might generate a control signal, which in turn might lead to an indefinite number of other activations. Therefore, the final system has thousands of possible results. All results must be completely and correctly specified by the analysis process.

State transition diagrams and control specification tables are used to model a real-time system. StP utilizes the following seven control specifications:

1. State transition tables
2. State event matrices
3. Decision tables
4. Process activation tables
5. Process activation matrices
6. Event logic tables
7. Action logic tables

Combination systems are described with decision tables, process activation tables and matrices, event logic tables, and action logic tables. Decision table rows show all

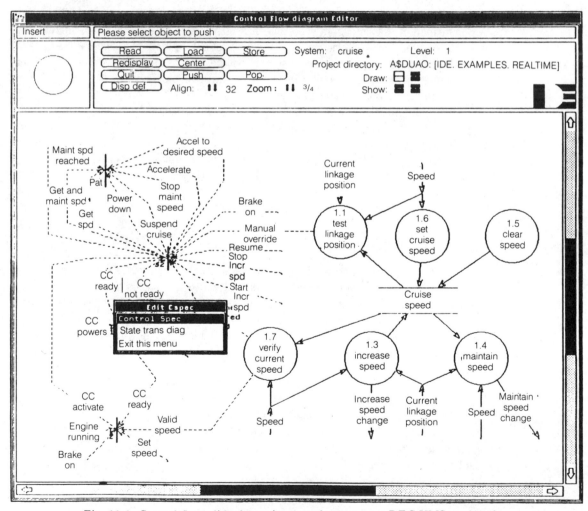

Fig. 11-1. Control flow editor for cruise control system on a DEC VMS workstation

possible combinations of input signal values with the corresponding output signal values. Process activation tables and matrices show input signal values and the processes each signal activates. Event logic tables show input signal values and their corresponding events. Finally, action logic tables show actions, corresponding output signal values, and activated processes.

Sequential systems are described with notations that show the possible states of the system with the events and actions that cause transitions from one state to another. Available notations include: state transition diagram, state transition table, or state event matrix. An example of a state transition diagram is shown in FIG. 11-2.

For a sequential system, the completed analysis report includes data flow diagrams, state transition diagrams, event logic tables, action logic tables, and data dictionary reports.

The method provides an integrated graphical environment targeted to support the analysis and design phases of software development. This method allows the user to customize the environment, to use a variety of well-known methods, and to generate comprehensive template-driven documentation automatically. StP provides complete integration of information through a multiuser data dictionary built on a relational database management system. StP incorporates concepts associated with the methods of DeMarco, Yourdon, Constantine, Gane, Sarson, Hatley, Pirbhai, Jackson, and Chen.

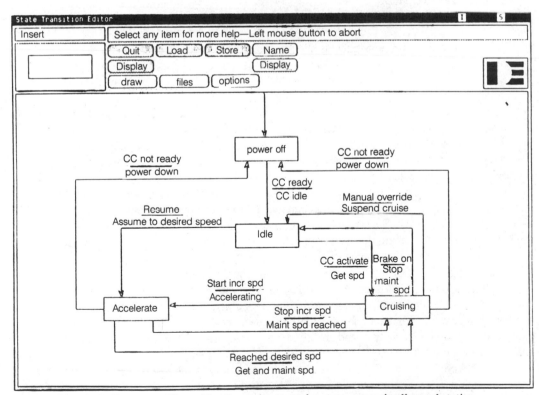

Fig. 11-2. State transition editor for cruise control system on an Apollo workstation

StP addresses requirements definition, system specification, and system design. It is founded on data flow, control-oriented approaches, and entity-relationship modeling. StP is not linked to any particular paradigm of the software process. It allows you to model software systems using any of the following techniques:

- Data flow diagrams
- Structure charts
- Entity relationship diagrams
- Data structure
- Real-time representations
- Rapid prototyping

Structured analysis for a real-time systems environment includes a family of graphical editors, an StP data dictionary, comprehensive checking programs, an object-annotation editor, and a document preparation system. Graphical editors include:

- Dataflow diagram editor
- Control-flow editor
- State transition editor
- Control specification editor
- Data structure editor
- Entity-relationship editor

The dataflow diagram editor allows the user to view a system from a functional perspective with decomposition techniques that divide the system into individual processes. The data structure editor and entity-relationship editor allow the user to view a system from a data perspective.

The control-flow editor is built as an extension to the dataflow diagram editor, and allows the user to switch between data flow and control flow modeling. The control flow editor lets you select the type(s) of flow to be displayed. The basic data flow diagram notation is extended with dashed arrows to represent control flow, and with solid bars to represent control specifications.

The state transition editor allows the user to draw state transition diagrams to enter states, symbolized by rectangles, and to connect them with arcs. Transitions are then associated with the arcs. Each transition, represented by a horizontal bar, can contain the name of an event causing the transition (above the bar) and the name of an action that occurs during the transition (below the bar).

The control specification editor is a seven-in-one table editor that supports the seven different table types used in the strategies for system development method (discussed later in this chapter). One or more table types may be associated with a single control specification. For example, sequential systems can be described with an event logic table, a state event matrix, and an action logic table. An example of a decision table and a process activation table is shown in FIG. 11-3.

StP is based on open architecture and provides customized file formats and data dictionary formats. Open architecture allows you to integrate StP with other available tools

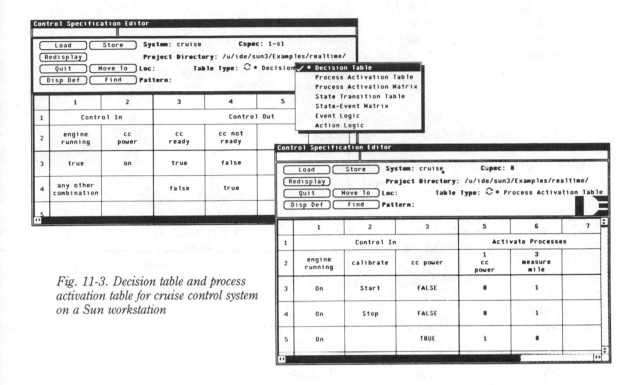

Fig. 11-3. Decision table and process activation table for cruise control system on a Sun workstation

in their environments. StP provides support in software development for the following tools:

- PICture: an object-oriented drawing tool
- Troll/USE: a relational database that contains the data dictionary
- Document Preparation System: supports the generation of documents
- Tools for the object-management library, including typesetting support, general utility routines, and multiuser project support with diagram locking and version control

The StP method encourages specific documentation templates, narrative overviews of modules, structured English, PDL, and decision tables. Encouraged iconographical modes include finite state diagrams, data flow diagrams, control flow diagrams, and entity-relationship diagrams. Automated facilities for all modes are provided with this method.

WARD/MELLOR REAL-TIME METHOD

The Ward/Mellor Real-Time method is one of the most popular real-time extension approaches. The method primarily adds control and behavioral specification aspects to the original structure analysis emphasizing functions and data flows. The method addresses specification, preliminary design, and detailed design. The method also provides simulation and prototyping capabilities through execution of data, control, and timing information.

This method provides one of several real-time extensions to Yourdon's SA/SD. The method is primarily based on DeMarco's structured analysis (SA) and Yourdon/Constantine's structured design (SD).

Ward/Mellor's technique *transformation schema* extends the data flow diagram as described by DeMarco for SA, by Gane and Sarson for STRADIS, and by Ross and Brackett for SADT. The idea for the method's dynamic execution capability is based loosely on a version of Petri net execution.

With this method, you must understand the world in which the system operates. The environment is viewed as events that the system must respond, and as an information model, a description of objects, relationships between objects, and its attributes.

The method utilizes an extension of the data flow diagrams, called transformation schema, to build a comprehensive system model representing the data, control, and timing aspects of systems. The transformation schema is heavily dependent on the objects defined in the information model and the results of its execution provide a behavior pattern model.

The transformation schema permits the creation and evaluation of two different types of system models: essential model and implementation model. The same types of models are created in ESA. The essential model shows the system as a virtual machine with infinite resources. Whereas, the implementation model assumes a real machine with constraining resources. The method uses multiple simultaneous views to model a system with data transformations and control transformations.

To reduce the complexity of modeling a large system, Ward/Mellor applies a hierarchical presentation scheme to both transformations and flows, which creates a multi-leveled set of schemes. Most modeling activities are carried out concurrently with continuous interaction among activities during successive refinement.

This method provides simulation and prototyping capabilities through transformation schema execution. Execution rules utilize tokens to indicate actual or potential activity such as transformations, flows, and buffers that is depicted in the schema notation. The types of actions taking place depend on the type of element with the token. Execution rules can be incorporated into an execution plan where a table is used to show a series of interactions. Each series occurs at a point in time.

STATEMATE

STATEMATE was developed at i-Logic Inc., by Drs. Pnueli and Harel. The method is a comprehensive tool for specification, design and analysis of real-time systems. Specifications are designed with visual languages called *statechart*, *activity chart*, and *module chart* languages. Along with editing, analysis, and management support tools, STATEMATE has a simulation capability available for testing a design, which supports rapid prototyping of the target system. The method extends the state/event paradigm and involves the use of state transition diagrams. It also extends concepts related to data flow analysis and finite state machines.

Some of the development activities of the STATEMATE method are:

- Requirements definition
- System specification
- Software quality assurance
- Validation of specification
- Design through simulations
- Executions
- Dynamic testing
- Rapid prototyping

A conceptual model is used by the method to deal with notions, entities, and procedures relevant to system development. Three visual languages are included in the support of software tools. By using icons to represent these visual languages in an interactive setting, a software developer establishes a specification for the behavioral, functional, and structural aspects of the system.

Statecharts extend the concept of finite state machines by using and/or logic to support the decomposition of states. The results are a visual representation that overcomes the limitations of state transition diagrams. Statecharts are capable of addressing issues such as:

- specifying behavior hierarchically
- concurrency: synchronous and asynchronous
- basing the current system behavior on its past behavior

The activity chart is used to specify the function of the system. The activity chart is similar to a data flow diagram.

The module chart language is used to specify the structure of the system. The module chart shows the physical structure of the system. Mapping rules are prescribed to go from control activities within the activity chart to statecharts, from activities to modules, and from modules to activity charts.

The STATEMATE method assists in the early detection of inconsistencies and errors with a model of the system that is syntactically analyzed, executed, dynamically tested, prototyped, and debugged. Consistency is maintained at different phases of development through test scenarios and test results that are defined and achieved. The method also encourages the identification of units that can be reused.

The STATEMATE method provides procedures for conducting test planning at one or more points in the software process, generating tests, prescribing checks for interfaces, and dynamic testing of specifications. These procedures have automated support. The method also provides a specific and automated level of configuration management.

DESIGN APPROACH FOR REAL-TIME SYSTEMS

Design approach for real-time systems (DARTS) extends SA/SD into a real-time problem domain by providing design criteria for multitasking. Dr. Hassan Gommaa of

George Mason University, developed the DARTS method. He considered the characteristics of real-time systems that typically consist of several concurrent tasks or processes.

The steps of this method provide structural criteria for identifying concurrent tasks and guidelines for defining task interfaces. These steps occur after a structured system specification has been developed and before each task is designed. DARTS is founded on the following kinds of approaches:

- Data flow oriented
- Control oriented
- Event oriented

The essential concepts of DARTS are:

- Information hiding
- Abstract data type
- Structured programming
- Module coupling

There are four major steps to the DARTS method.

1. Develop structured system specification with real-time structured analysis.
2. Structure the system into concurrent tasks with task structuring criteria.
3. Define task interfaces.
4. Design each task that represents a sequential program by using the structured design method.

The task-structuring criteria guides the designer in decomposing a real-time system into concurrent tasks. The main consideration for identifying tasks is the asynchronous nature of the functions within the system. A task might exhibit more than one of the task structuring criteria. The event-dependency criteria include device I/O dependency, user-interface dependency, periodic dependency, periodic I/O, and entity modeling. The task cohesion criteria include sequential cohesion and functional cohesion. The task priority criteria are the time critical and computationally intensive criteria. DARTS is largely based on timing criteria:

- I/O dependency—An I/O device will set the pace for the transform that immediately interfaces the device. Such a transform becomes a separate task.
- Priority—Time-critical transforms are separated from low-priority background transforms in different tasks.
- Periodic execution—A transform that is executed periodically can be made into a separate task activated at regular intervals.

DARTS allows you to combine transforms into tasks based on functional or temporal cohesion, i.e., functionally related or simultaneously executed transforms can be grouped together in one task. Finally, each data store can be equipped with a guardian or server task that serializes the accesses by other tasks. Tasks primarily communicate via messages. DARTS provides for tight coupling (where two tasks must be synchronized to exchange messages) and loose coupling (where the communication takes place via a message queue).

When defining a task interface, a data flow between the two tasks is designed as a message. Either loosely coupled or tightly coupled message communication is supported. Event signals are used for synchronizing the two tasks when there is a need for communicating. Data stores are encapsulated into information hiding modules, which defines the data structures and the access procedures. The access procedures also synchronize access to the data.

DARTS prescribes steps for handling several requirements of the target system. Concurrency issues are central to the method. Timing constraints are addressed with the use of event-sequence diagrams that trace critical external events through the system.

The method requires structured English as a textual mode of representation. Required iconographical modes include finite state diagrams, data flow diagrams, control flow diagrams, and structured design charts. The method prescribes mapping rules for translating from data flow diagrams to task structure diagrams, and from task structure diagrams to module hierarchies.

STRATEGIES FOR SYSTEM DEVELOPMENT

Strategies for system development (SSD) have been developed by Derek Hatley and Imtiaz Pirbhai. They have tailored the structured analysis techniques to fit in real-time systems. The method focuses on the definition of requirements and specification for the total system, not just the software component of the system. This goal is attained by building two models of the system:

- System requirements model
- System architecture model

In the system requirements model, a statement of the problem is formulated that is independent of technology. Thus, a thorough understanding of the problem can be gained without deciding on a solution. A data flow diagram is used to construct a process model that provides a decomposition of the system's functional requirements. In this model, related functions are grouped together, unrelated functions are separate, and each function is specified as nonredundant. A DFD is nonprocedural, and the processes within a DFD are nonhierarchical. In this idealized DFD model of the system, a process is assumed to operate instantaneously. After a process is started, sufficient data is available to do its task.

The next step requires the construction of a control model so the control flow can be defined with the system's functions and finite state behavior processing. The finite state projection provides information for the processing of discrete signals, which trigger different modes of behavior for the system. Data and control are kept separate by the creation of control flow diagrams that are parallel to the DFD's. State transition tables, decision tables, and activation tables are also used to further clarify the requirements.

The requirements dictionary is the principal tool for ensuring a formal and rigorous approach to this strategy. The requirements dictionary contains an alphabetical list of data and control flow names with a definition of its components and structure. The dictionary must contain every data flow name and data store name. Group names must be decomposed into precise components. Every entry in the dictionary must be broken down to primitive physical entities. The dictionary may contain attributes for those primitive entities including units, range, or accuracy.

A technologically dependent solution in the system architecture model specifies how the problem should be solved with the available technology. From the requirements model, a system architect model is constructed, and includes:

- The physical components of the system
- Tasks to be performed by each physical component
- The way physical components communicate with each other
- The communications among these physical components

The three steps taken to create the architecture model are:

1. Enhance the requirements model by using a specified template.
2. Define the processes concerned with user interface, input/output, maintenance, and self-test.
3. Allocate the requirements model to architecture modules.

During each of these activities, an evaluation of the allocation is made and a trade-off is decided.

The major components of the system architecture model are explained as follows:

- Architecture context diagrams that are used to show the communication between the system and entities in the system environment.
- Architecture flow diagrams that map a group of data and control flows and processes from the requirements model to architecture modules.
- Architecture interconnect diagrams that represent communication channels for the modules.
- Architecture module specifications that describe the functions of individual modules and establish traceability between the requirements model and the architecture model.
- Architecture interconnect specifications that establish the characteristics of the interconnect channels among modules.
- The architecture dictionary that establishes the allocation of data and control flows from the requirements model to the architecture model.

This process of defining system requirements and architecture can be repeated at a lower level to model the system hardware components and the software components.

The SSD method supports two different kinds of real-time systems: combinational systems and sequential systems. In a combinational system, the input signal combinations completely determine the values of output signals. In a sequential system, the output signals are determined not only by the combination of input signals, but also by the past values of inputs, internal elements, and outputs. In other words, sequential systems have memory, but combinational systems do not.

PROTOB

PROTOB consists of PROT nets to provide a conceptual graphical model for discrete event dynamics systems. PROTOB object-oriented formalism is the common language that integrates the activities of the simulation. It builds a model of the whole system. The behavior of the modeled system and each system component can be simulated, analyzed, and fed back to the specification, design, and implementation phases. PROTOB was developed by Giorgio Bruno and Marco Baldassari. It is based on the mathematical theory of Petri nets.

Overview

PROTOB is based on the object-oriented and control-oriented approaches. The design and coding steps traditionally associated with the development process can be skipped because the system allows executable tasks to be generated from the PROTOB's model according to a given configuration. Each task implements a portion of the model. PROTOB provides both visual and textual information in a model which can be used for simulation and automatic-generating code. The symbols used in the visual model are circles, rectangles, and squares. The circles hold data structures called tokens. Text associated with each token provides name and type information of the data. Transitions, shown as rectangles, have four attributes associated with them:

1. A predicate provides the condition to be evaluated on the contents of the tokens present in the input. Tokens satisfying this predicate enable the transition to *fire*, or take place.
2. Actions are the operations performed on selected tokens during firing.
3. Delay is the period of time to wait before delivering tokens to outputs. The default is immediate movement of tokens from input to output during firing.
4. Priority is a nonnegative integer specifying the relative importance of the firing transition when more than one transition is enabled. Default priority is zero.

Squares represent subobjects that are the object-oriented decomposition of a PROTnet.

The method is well suited for real-time systems, distributed systems, communication protocol systems, and automation systems.

Case Study

PROTOB formalism   PROTOB was designed to support the construction of models according to the object-oriented paradigm. The system is decomposed in interacting objects to improve its comprehensibility and to simplify the modification and reuse of system components. Objects can be composed of objects to form a hierarchy; the internal behavior of terminal objects is defined by PROT nets. Most information on each object is conveyed visually by a formal graphical representation called graph; textual information can also be provided in a script file.

An *object* is a model of a real-world entity, which groups data and operations on that data. It is the building block of a PROTOB model. An object captures the notion of autonomous entity or activity characterized by a life cycle, depending on time and the interactions with other objects. Examples of objects are: a machining center, a production control module, a protocol level. Objects are known by their external properties and by the way they interact with other objects. The internal structure of an object is hidden to the user. An object is an abstraction of a set of real world things having the same characteristics and conforming to the same rules. It represents a class of individuals sharing the same behavior.

An individual belonging to a given class is called an *instance* of that class. Instances have separate existence and are graphically represented by squares within squares; they are labelled with the name of the instance followed by the name of its class object. An object class per se has no graphical representation. Objects may have parameters that allow instances to be properly characterized. Defining a class and then instantiating any number of individuals conceptually simplifies both the definition and modification of a model.

An object may contain, and therefore be composed of, instances of other objects. If an object has no interaction with the outside, it is called a *closed object*. The closed object models the part of the universe that is involved in our problem. It is the model of our problem.

The closed object can contain any number of instances of open objects, and each open object can contain several other instances of open objects to form a hierarchy. Open objects send and receive information to and from the outside. An open object is like the model of the ''software chip'' that Cox desires, with input and output *pins* called I/O ports. The set of I/O ports of an object make up its interface. Figure 11-4 is the graphical representation of an instance of an object.

The communications between instances of objects are defined graphically with lines. A directed line between two instances virtualizes the asynchronous sending of messages, i.e., information tokens from the output ports of one instance to the input ports of the other. I/O ports are represented by particular symbols: input ports are graphically represented by a circle within a circle; output ports by an upside-down triangle within a circle. They are labelled with the name of the port followed by the name of the type of the exchanged information token.

An object is active if it has an internal state and control activity that cause its response to external stimuli to be asynchronous and delayed. Otherwise, an object is passive. An active object receives an asynchronous trigger/controlflow and reaction to this request/stimulus might be delayed according to the internal state of the object. In a passive object, the required service is performed immediately and the control is returned. A PROT net is an active object because the processing of the input tokens depends on the state of the net. A stack is an example of a passive object, while a timer is a typical active object. Active objects can use other objects freely, but passive objects can use only passive objects.

Hidden inside the instance is the body at a conceptually lower but more detailed level that implements the object's behavior. The body of a compound object contains instances of other objects, while that of a simple object does not. Simple objects are the

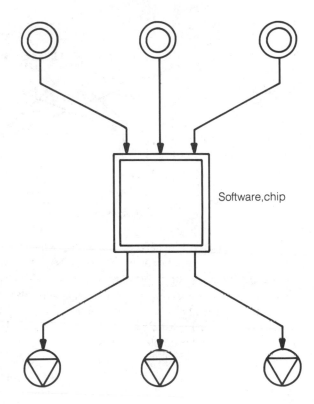

Software,chip

Fig. 11-4. The "software chip": an instance of a PROTOB object

terminal or leaf objects at the lowest level in the hierarchy, while compound objects permit the hierarchical decomposition of systems into subsystems that are still modeled with objects.

Objects can be structured and interconnected in two types of hierarchies:

- Composition (parent/child) relationship—Parent objects can be decomposed into several instances of child objects. The composition relationship is represented by drawing the children inside the parent. Two instances that are children of the same parent are called *peer* instances.
- Usage (senior/junior) relationship—Senior instances use services provided by junior instances. The usage relationship is represented by drawing a directed line from the senior to the junior instance. The senior instance sends a message to the junior to request its service. The junior might send back an acknowledge message immediately or a reply at completion.

The difference between composition and usage should be clear in FIG. 11-5. It shows users requesting services from devices. *System* is a closed object composed of two *device* and three *user* instances. The first identifier is the name of the instance, the second is the name of the object class. Each *user* instance uses two *device* instances.

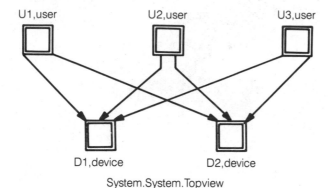

Fig. 11-5. Closed object: users that use devices

In PROTOB, an object does not know which object will provide the services it requires. The usage relationships are specified in the definition of the parent object that includes the instances of the senior and junior objects. The parent object is free to connect a senior instance to any instance of any junior object that provides the required services, without having to change the definition of the senior object.

Characterization of PROT nets   The internal behavior of an object is defined in its body. The body of a simple object is a PROT net, a graphical formalism that integrates extended dataflows with Petri nets and high-level languages.

Introducing PROT nets, first see the concepts inherited from the Petri nets experience and, subsequently, their enhancement to model activities. Like a Petri net, a PROT net models a system's behavior in terms of two primitive concepts of state and state transition. Possible states are represented by circles called places. Transitions, represented by a rectangle, model actions associated with state transactions. A transition is caused by certain states and has the effect of activating other states. This is represented graphically with directed arcs going from cause-places to the transition and from the transition to the effect-places. A state transition occurs when all the cause-places are active. All the effect-places will be activated and the cause-places disactivated. A PROT net statically describes in a visual way the relationships of cause and effect among states (places) and actions (transitions). Names of places should be nouns that describe a state, while names of transitions should be verbs describing an action.

Marking the active states by putting a token in the corresponding places makes a PROT net a dynamic model. A transition will then activate its effect-places by moving the tokens from its cause-places to its effect-places when all its cause-places are active. In this sense, Petri nets are executable models.

Figure 11-6 is a simple PROT net modeling the actions of opening and closing a tap in order to fill a reservoir. When the water level is low, the closed tap will be open. The tap being open will fill the reservoir getting the water level from low to high. When the water level is high, the open tap will be closed. Note how events are considered to be atomic or discrete. The number inside places is the number of tokens they contain. The first identifier near a place is the place name, the second after a comma, is the name of the type of tokens it may contain. The optional number of tokens contained at the beginning of execution, called starting tokens, is written in the graph after the place name and type.

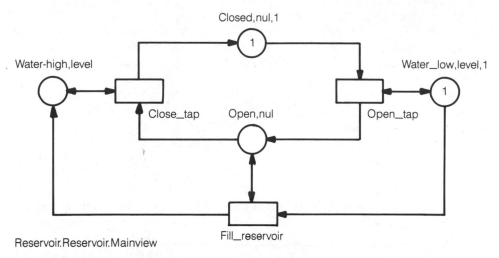

Fig. 11-6. A simple PROT net

The number of starting tokens in each place defines the initial marking of the net. The label in the bottom left corner RESERVOIR.RESERVOIR.MAINVIEW is formed by the names of the instance, of the object, and of the view. The graph of a large object may be decomposed in conceptual views as it will be explained later.

A transition of a PROT net, together with its cause and effect-places, may be considered a graphical if-then rule. Requirements naturally come in rules. Associating data with tokens and operations with transitions completes the formalism making it suitable for the specification of the object activity.

Places contain units of information called tokens. Tokens are *mobile information packets*. They are structured data whose type is defined in the script as a record type. Each place can contain several tokens at a time, all of the same type. Places are basically queues of tokens; when a token is put into a place it is added at the end of the queue. Tokens are usually taken from places in FIFO order, but they can also be retrieved according to a particular policy defined by the user. In the graph, the type of tokens to be contained in a place is written, separated by a comma, after the place name.

Transitions are the *processing units of the model*. They act only on the tokens of the places they are connected to. Cause-places and effect-places, also called input and output places of a transition, form the graphical context of a transition. A transition models a token-driven computation, where the activation of the computation and the propagation of the information is established unambiguously by its graphical context. In fact, the necessary condition for a transition to fire is that each of its input places is not empty. When a transition fires, it removes one token from each of its input places and adds one token to each of its output places.

Tokens removed from the input places are called input tokens of the transition, tokens delivered to output places are called output tokens of the transition. The default rule is that the transition removes the oldest token from each of its input places in a FIFO order. It is often necessary to specify a more flexible policy allowing tokens that satisfy a particular condition to be selected from the input places of the transition. To do so, the user specifies in the script an explicit condition, called *predicate*, which input tokens must satisfy with their contents to be selected. If there is a tuple of tokens (one token for each input place of the transition), which satisfies the predicate, its tokens are selected and removed from the input places, even if they are not the oldest ones. If more than one tuple satisfying the predicate exist, the user can specify the one to be selected by establishing in the script the order in which the input places of the transition are to be examined. If an input place of the transition is not involved in the predicate, the oldest token of its queue is selected. In general a transition may act on several sets of working tokens at the same time: it behaves like an infinite server facility.

The propagation of information takes place as follows: if there are exactly one input place and one output place of the same type, the token removed from the input place is added to the output place; in all other cases, tokens removed from the input places are destroyed and tokens added to the output places are created. The tokens managed by the transition during its firing, i.e., those propagated, those destroyed, and those created are called working tokens of the transition. When a transition fires, an action, specified in the script, can be executed: it is a piece of code having the visibility of the working tokens of the transition. Before the execution of the action, output tokens that are not propagated from input ones are created empty. After the execution of the action, input tokens that are not propagated are destroyed. The action can modify the contents of propagated tokens, initialize the contents of created tokens, and perform external operations as well. Predicates and actions can also manage local variables of the instance they belong to.

When two or more transitions have an input place in common, they are said to be in conflict because the firing of one of them might disable the others. When two or more transitions in conflict can fire, the choice of which might fire first depends on the priorities and on the predicates associated with them. The priority is a nonnegative integer number that allows transitions to be ordered according to their importance; the default is zero. When several transitions can fire at the same time, the one with the highest priority is chosen first and will fire if its predicate is satisfied.

Transitions are responsible for introducing timing constraints into the model. In fact, it is possible to associate a timing constraint with a transition in order to model the actual duration of the performed activity. With respect to the timing constraint, the firing of a transition can be given two different behaviors:

- Delayed release—When the transition fires, it fetches the tokens from its input places, performs the action, and holds the tokens in a private storage for a specified time. When the delay expires, it delivers the tokens to the output places.
- Delayed firing—When the transition can fire, it does not fetch tokens from its input places immediately, but waits for the firing delay to elapse. Then, if all the enabling tokens are still there, having been in the input places all that time and they satisfy the predicate, the transition takes them, performs the action, and delivers the working tokens to its output places; otherwise no action is taken.

Transitions characterized by the delayed firing are called *time-out transitions* and their name on the graph is followed by the letter T. The values of the delays associated to a transition are set by calling in the script two PROTOB primitives: xx_setdelay( ) to specify the release delay, xx_settimeout( ) for the firing delay. Time-out transitions may also have a release delay. An immediate transition is a transition with null release and firing delays. The delays of a transition can be varied by an action associated to any transition of the object. It might depend on the contents of the input tokens, and set to a value returned by any function or expression.

Figure 11-7 is the graph of a simple object that models a machine with a PROT net.

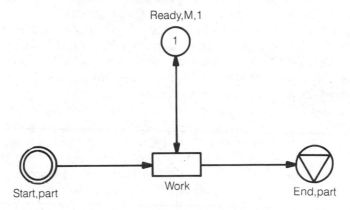

Machine.Machine.Mainview

Fig. 11-7. Graph of a simple object that models a machine with a PROT net

The interface to the outside world is defined by the two I/O ports *start* and *end*. The object receives from the outside a token of type *part*, modeling the part the machine is to work, in input place *start*. Transition *work* takes the token from *start* when a token is in place *ready*, i.e., when the machine is ready. Initially place *ready* will contain a token but the transition will fire and put the token back only after the release delay, modeling the device service time, has expired. It will also put the *part* token in output port *end*, which will cause the token to be sent out to some other connected port. The script file completes the information conveyed by the graph. It introduces a second level of detail where the action of the transition *work* is defined by an instruction in embedded C code. The embedded code is delimitated by the keyword '%%'. It increments the value of next_ operation_number that is a field of the working token contained in place *end*. The initial action sets the release delay of transition *work* to the value of *service_time* that is a parameter of the *machine object*. Parameter values of a child instance are set by their parent with function xx_setparameter ( ).

```
OBJECT machine IS
CMN communication_types_description_file_name;
PARAMETERS float service_time;
TRANSITION work IS
     ACTION %% END – >next_operation_number + + ; %%;
ENDTR work;
INITIALIZE %%
     xx_setdelay("work",MACHINE – >service_time);
     %%;
END machine.
```

PROT nets can be executed. Their execution can be supplemented by such activities as traceability and data collection, so as to lead to a real simulation of the system. This is a remarkable aspect because specification and simulation activities are usually carried out in unrelated environments, which precludes the rapid analysis of the consequences of a change in a specification.

Using PACKAGE objects   PROTOB allows the smooth transition from specification issues to the architectural and detailed design of the modeled system. PACKAGE objects allow PROTOB specifications to mix with design techniques and concepts.

PROT nets are a visual programming language. In fact, pieces of code written in the target language can be associated with the transitions of the net. Transitions may therefore carry out well-defined actions, while the overall control structure is visually established by the PROT net. The final program results from a translation phase that assembles these actions into the appropriate framework.

Predicates and actions can call functions and services that are not defined in the script associated to the object, but that are provided by PACKAGE objects. PACKAGE objects are objects that do not need a PROT net to define their internal behavior. They are represented by a small square on the left side of a large square. The ''A'' stands for Active and ''P'' for Passive. Their internal behavior is not defined by a PROT net, but by code structured with the pure HOOD methodology. The interface of a PACKAGE object is the list of provided and required services (i.e., entry points or routines) and exported data types. Their hierarchical composition is allowed too. They are useful to add architectural design details to the specification.

For example, predicates and transitions can call SQL statements to retrieve information from a relational database. During the model refinement, these statements are likely to grow in number and size. It would be better to group them in a separate PACKAGE object that implements the interface to the database.

This feature integrates PROTOB, the HOOD methodology, and other programming languages and environments. The documented and integrated reuse of already existing software libraries and modules is also enabled.

Therefore, PROTOB has two kinds of objects: PROT objects, containing PROT nets, are always active; PACKAGE objects can be either active or passive and are defined graphically and textually like an Ada package. The architecture of package objects may be modeled in greater detail according to the HOOD methodology.

A transition might need to use in its action a service provided by a PACKAGE object. Following is a fragment of two script files that show how two transitions of PROT object *example* use services provided by PACKAGE object *stack*. The script files complete the graph defining the actions each transition is to perform when it fires.

```
OBJECT example IS
    [. . .]
    TRANSITION store IS
        ACTION % % push (accepted.info);
                        push(coded.info); % %;
    ENDTR store;
    TRANSITION send IS
        ACTION % % out.data := process(pop,pop);
                % %;
    ENDTR send;
```

```
[. . .]
END example.

PACKAGE stack IS
     PROCEDURE push (x:item);
     FUNCTION pop RETURN item;
END stack;
PACKAGE BODY stack IS
     [. . .]
END stack.
```

Transition *Store* uses the *Push* and transition *Send* the *Pop* operations to be provided by a PACKAGE object. *Stack* is a PACKAGE object that provides procedure *Push* and function *Pop*. Which object is actually to provide the required operations will be defined in the graph of the parent object with a directed line from the senior to the junior object. This would correspond to the WITH and USE pragmas in an Ada implementation of the senior object.

Figure 11-8 adds two instances of a *Driver* PACKAGE object that groups the implementations of the services provided by a device driver. The services required by each *device* object will be provided by a different instance of the *driver* active PACKAGE object. The names of the provided services are not displayed by the representation of the instance but may be viewed by means of a pop-up display.

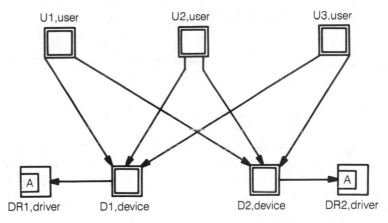

System.System.Topview
Fig. 11-8. Using PACKAGE objects

Of course, a PACKAGE object also may use the operations provided by another PACKAGE object.

Interconnections of instances   In general, the body of a PROT object is built by generating instances of child objects and by interconnecting them. The generation of an instance of a compound object forces all the instances making up that object to be automatically generated. The organization of a model is then a tree of instances, called *instance tree*, the root of which is the instance of the top-level object of the model. Obviously the top-level object has a single instance, which is assumed to have the same name of the object itself.

Instances of PROT objects communicate by message passing; sending tokens to one another. The communication between objects is defined graphically by lines.

Instances of PROT objects use other PROT instances by sending them tokens. A service might be requested to a junior instance by sending a token to the input port that is associated with that service. The junior instance might then reply by sending back another token. This is described graphically by connecting instances with an arrow pointing to the used instance, as in FIG. 11-5. The direction of the arrow is purely descriptive: the flow of tokens between instances goes in both directions.

There are two ways to connect instances of PROT objects: peer-to-peer and parent-child connections.

Peer-to-peer connection of two instances is carried out by establishing a link from an output port of an instance to an input port of another. Graphically, the link is a directed segment drawn between the icons of the two instances; it is labelled with the name of the source port, followed by an arrow (the symbol $->$) and by the name of the destination port. This is the default label, which can be overridden by a user-defined label. Links connecting peer instances are also called horizontal links. Figure 11-9 shows peer-to-peer connections between machines. The body of each machine is defined by the PROT net of FIG. 11-7. Input port *in* accepts tokens from the outside and passes them on to port *start* of the first machine, while output port *out* sends outside the tokens it receives from port *end* of the last machine.

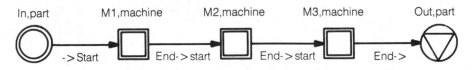

In,part   M1,machine   M2,machine   M3,machine   Out,part

-> Start   End-> start   End-> start   End->

Line.Line.Mainview

Fig. 11-9. Three machines connected with horizontal links

When objects have complex interfaces, many horizontal links are likely to exist between the same pair of instances. In order to simplify the graph, compound connections have been introduced. A compound connection, called *superlink*, stands for a set of horizontal links connecting instances with token flows in both directions. The lines of FIG. 11-5 are actually superlinks.

Superlinks are connections between *superports*. A superport is a named sequence of I/O ports associated with an object. When building an object, it is possible to associate several superports with it. When a superlink is established between two instances, it connects a superport of the first instance to a superport of the second instance. Graphically the superlink is a directed segment between a pair of instances. It is labelled with the name of the source superport, followed by an arrow and the name of the destination superport. This is the default label which, as in the case of links, can be overridden by a user-defined label. Superports that are connected by a superlink must be congruent, that is they must have the same number of components which are ordinately of the same type and of different I/O direction. For example, if A and B are two connected superports with n ports each, A_i and B_i must be of the same type, and if A_i is an input port B_i must be an output port and vice-versa.

A compound instance is sometimes not merely an envelope enclosing child instances, but has its own dynamics, characterized by places and transitions, in addition to the instances it includes. Therefore, there is the need for the PROT net of a compound instance to communicate with its child instances. This is the case of the parent-child connection. It can be achieved by using vertical links. A vertical link connects a place of the parent instance to the input port of a child instance (downward link) or the output port of a child instance to a place of the parent instance (upward link).

Graphically, the vertical link is a directed segment drawn between places and instances. It is labelled with an arrow followed by the name of the destination input port, if it is a downward link, or with the name of the source output port followed by an arrow, if it is an upward link.

Two places connected by a link must be of the same type since they handle the same tokens. A place that is or will be connected by a link is therefore called a *communication* port and the types of communication ports are called communication types that must be defined uniquely for all PROT nets using them.

All I/O ports are of course communication ports, but of a special kind as they define the interface of the object. Ports connected to instances with vertical links are internal communication ports. Figure 11-10 shows a closed compound object that contains a child instance and a PROT net. Note that *raw* and *finished* are internal communication ports, not I/O ports as they connect the PROT net to a child instance.

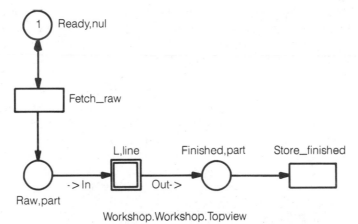

Workshop.Workshop.Topview

Fig. 11-10. Closed object: testing a line of machines

A port from which a link starts does not hold tokens, but it delivers them immediately to the port it is linked to. Output ports and internal ports that send tokens to a child instance therefore have no associated token queue and so they cannot be input places of a transition. Input ports and internal ports that accept tokens from child instances do have token queues and they can be input places of transitions.

Considering the token as a message, the link can be said to be a transmission line a PROT net may use to send a message to another PROT net. A token reaching a port from which a link starts is sent to the connected port of another net. Sending tokens makes the object-oriented connection of PROT nets possible. Connecting PROT nets by merging places might cause transitions of different PROT nets to be in conflict, and thus alter the original behavior of the nets, going against the object-oriented paradigm.

The information hiding mechanism needed to ensure the reusability of objects prevents you from being able to reach any place of a subobject. Only the I/O ports, i.e., the interface, of a child instance are visible from the body of the parent object. Links cannot be directly connected from outside the parent object to the I/O ports of a child instance. A vertical link would have to reach an I/O port of the parent object and that I/O port would have to be connected to the child instance with a vertical link in the parent object body.

Selective routing and broadcasting   Several links might originate from the same port. In this case, the question arises on which path a token should take. Consider for example the case of a device which provides several users with a service. A user requests the service by sending a request token through its output port *request_out* to the input place *request_in* of the device. Upon completion, the device answers back to the user that requested the service by sending a reply token through its output port *reply_out* to the input place *reply_in* of the user.

The output port *reply_out* of the device is linked to the input ports *reply_in* of several users. How is the device supposed to select the user to reply to? The device is built to serve any number of users that can be implemented in any way as long as they are interface compatible. The problem is solved in PROTOB by using a token exchange protocol which will be illustrated.

Each instance in the model has a unique identity that can be read by invoking a suitable PROTOB primitive, xx_myaddress( ), from an action specified in the script. Each token has a routing address that can contain the address of its destination instance. This hidden field can be set by using a suitable PROTOB primitive, xx_setaddress( ), to be called by a script action.

Now suppose that more than one device is available, say two. You are in the case of FIG. 11-5. Each user may then partition its service requests on the two devices. The user is built to receive service from any number of implemented devices. Before issuing any request, each user must receive the identity of all the connected devices to properly route requests. Therefore, each device must send a token containing its identity to all connected users to let them know of its existence, which is achieved by broadcasting the identity token to all connected users. Figures 11-11 and 11-12 show the PROT nets that define the body of the *user* and *device* objects of FIG. 11-5.

To maintain the PROTOB object-oriented structure, an object must be defined independently from the number and type of objects to which it will eventually be connected. Thus the object may not select "a priori" the instance to which the token is to be actually sent. Each instance first must receive the identity of all the reachable instances; it will then be able to send tokens selectively by mentioning the identity of the destination object.

In brief, PROTOB provides two ways of sending tokens:

- Selective Routing—Each token, after leaving an instance through a port, can be stamped by a transition with the address of the destination instance by using primitive xx_setaddress( ). The token is sent only to the connected instance whose identity matches the routing address. An instance might know its own address by reading it with function xx_myaddress( ) and store it in a variable of type XX_AD-DRESS. An instance can send its address to some other instance by writing it in a field of type XX_ADDRESS of a token.

- Broadcasting—If the routing address is undefined, the token is copied and sent to each connected place. Broadcasting is the sole protocol an object may use when the identities of the destination instances are unknown.

Linking a port to more than one place requires special care to design the objects involved and their communications. Ports that allow more than one link to start from them are called derouting ports.

The superlink of FIG. 11-5 that connects users to devices is made up of two links: *reply_out – > reply_in* and *request_in < – request_out*. Each device initially broadcasts

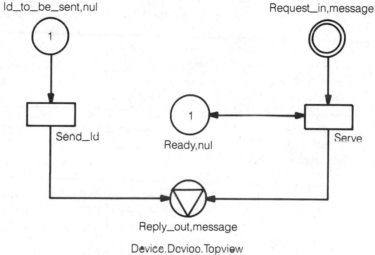

Fig. 11-11. Device object

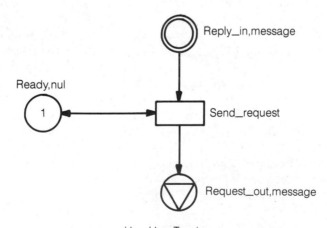

Fig. 11-12. User object

its address to all users with a token from port *reply_out*. Each user keeps the identities of the reachable devices in port *reply_in*. As soon as the user is ready, a service request message, modeled by the token of type *message*, is sent selectively to a device. When the device is ready, it serves the request. When it has finished, it sends a reply message to the user. This time the reply is not broadcast, but is routed selectively back to the user that had sent the request.

Views   When an object graph is so complex that it does not fit on the screen, it can be logically decomposed into several views. Views focus on logically related portions of the net. Places and instances are allowed to appear in more than one view. Duplicated places are represented with a boldface circle to mark the borderline with another view. Transitions and arcs cannot be duplicated because the graphical context of a transition must be defined completely in one view: transitions are like graphical if-then rules that connect causes to effects. Links and superlinks may not be duplicated either. Places and instances are the only elements that two views may have in common. Views may be represented in views: a rounded square stands for a view included in the body of another view. An included view may be connected with infolinks to places that are also contained in its body. Views and infolinks do not modify the PROT net, they are presentation features. An infolink connecting a place to a view must mirror the way the place is connected to the transitions contained in the body of the view.

Views are a very powerful and versatile way to decompose a PROTOB model for presentation purposes. They provide conceptual decomposition only: the underlying structure is not decomposed. Recursive inclusion is allowed, although only indirect recursion makes sense. Horizontal and hierarchical decomposition are allowed to exist at the same time and mix.

The developer might use the top-down functional decomposition approach and even divide the body of an object into two trees of views: one addressing the activities and the other the state transitions if he wishes to stick to that way of presenting information. The only rules are the ones previously mentioned.

Take a look back at the PROTOB model of FIG. 11-6. Extended dataflow diagram would look like FIG. 11-13. The two transitions *close_tap* and *open_tap* are actual state transitions of a state transition diagram which has two states: *open* and *closed*. The transition to state *open* is triggered by event *water_low*. State *open* is also a control that enables the activity of transition *fill_reservoir* that is a data and state transformation at the same time: *water_low* and *water_high* are dataflows, states and events at the same time. *Fill_reservoir* as a data transformation reads the low-level value and calculates the high-level value. *Level* is the type of the *water_low* and *water_high* dataflows. When the high level has been calculated, the ''water-level'' state is changed from *water_low* to *water_high*, which is the event that makes the ''tap'' state switch to *closed*.

Case study   You wish to design a part of an embedded automotive system for the measurement and display of the car speed. The system receives a pulse from a sensor every time the wheel completes a revolution. It must measure the period of the input pulses; filter it with a very simple low-pass digital filter: a fraction of the measured period is added to the complementary fraction of the current value of the filtered period to find its new value; it must drive a speedometer with a square wave the frequency of which is the estimated wheel rotation frequency, having been proportionately reduced. A hardware timer may be used to measure the flow of time and to request a one-shot interrupt to be generated after a settable amount of time.

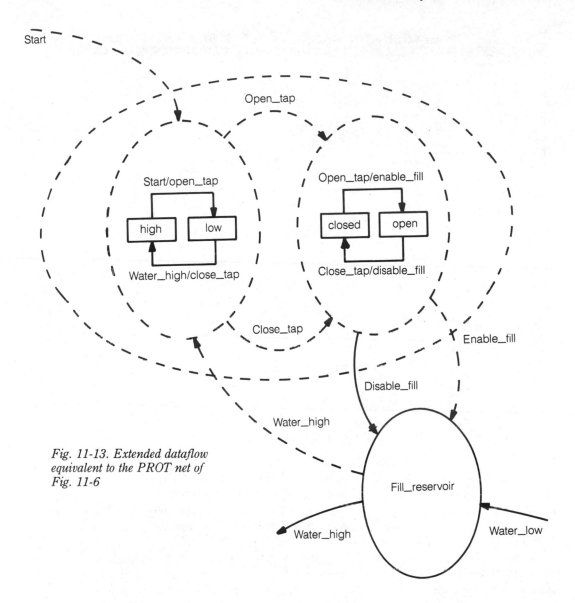

Fig. 11-13. Extended dataflow equivalent to the PROT net of Fig. 11-6

The measured periods whose values are above a certain threshold must be discarded. The system must be able to generate the output wave and to measure the input pulse periods independently. Initially, the estimated output period must be equal to the threshold value. The output square wave must be generated always, even if the measure of the last estimate is not over yet or if the measured input period drops below the threshold.

The model of the problem *Automtv*, of FIG. 11-14, is the closed object that models our problem. It groups all the objects having a physical or logical existence that are related to our problem: the system and the environment objects. *Control* is the model of the system that is to be developed. *Pulse_gen* is an environment object that models a wheel sensor that sends a pulse each time the wheel completes a revolution.

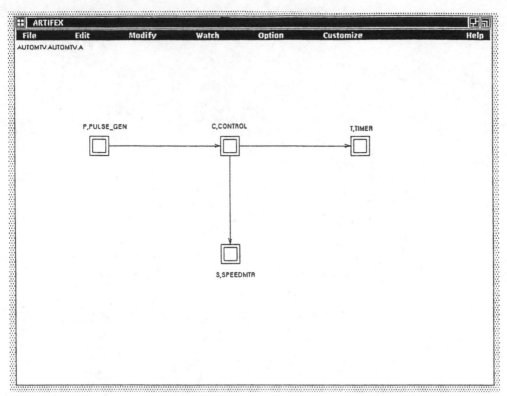

Fig. 11-14. Closed object "automtv" is the model of the problem

Speedmtr models a speedometer display control, which expects in input a square wave the frequency of which is proportional to the speed to be displayed. *Timer* is a model of a hardware timer that emits a one-shot interrupt after a settable amount of time. It starts counting when it receives the value of the time interval to the next interrupt. It also might be inquired to know the amount of time left to the next interrupt. *Timer* and *speedmtr* are environment objects too.

The environment objects   *Pulse_gen* of FIG. 11-15 models a sensor that sends a pulse each time the wheel has performed a complete revolution. This is quite easy to emulate with a transition, *emit_intr*, that reads from a file the time to the next pulse and sets its token release delay accordingly. Until the release delay is not over, the "pulse token" is not sent from output port *intr*, token *ready* is not put back, and the transition cannot fire a second time.

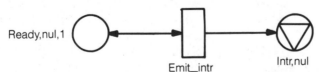

Fig. 11-15. The pulse generator

Speedmtr of FIG. 11-16 emulates the behavior of a speedometer display control that, receiving a square wave the period of which is proportional to the estimated wheel rotation period, calculates and displays the speed. The transition *display_speed* computes and displays the speed value. *Oldtime* is a datastore that contains the time when the last *level* token was received.

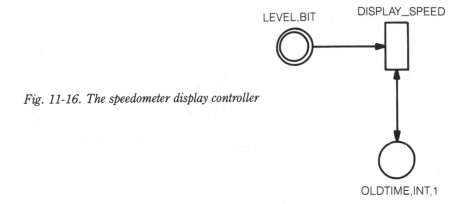

Fig. 11-16. The speedometer display controller

Timer of FIG. 11-17 models the hardware timer. The model is not detailed in the implementation aspects. It is a behavioral model, but not of a system to be developed. Its purpose is to emulate the environment to test the control system.

The timer starts when it receives in *value* a token with the value of the time interval to the next interrupt. Transition *set_counter* copies in place *counter* the current time and the number received in *value*. It also sets the timeout value of *emit_intr*. A time-out transition is used so that *counter* can be read in. Sending a token in *req* will cause *emit_time_to_intr* to reply with a token in *counter_out* containing the value of the actual time to the next interrupt. The transition computes the time to the next interrupt using the current time. It then sets the timeout of transition *emit_intr* to the current time to the next interrupt: because it retrieves the token from datastore *counter*, it must reset the timeout value when it puts the token back.

When the timeout expires, *emit_intr* puts a token in *intr* to send the interrupt. When the timer is not counting (no token in *counter*) *emit_zero* replies to the request of the current time to the next interrupt with the value zero.

Connecting objects   Having defined the environment object's bodies, now consider the communications between the system and the environment of FIG. 11-14. The communications are defined with superlinks with no labels, which makes the diagram tidier. A pop-up display permits the superlinks to be exploded so the underlying links are displayed graphically.

The superlink that connects *control* to the *timer* is an interface composed of four links. The timer is used in two ways: as a clock and as an interrupt generator. To start the timer, *control* sends a token through its output port *timer_out* to input port *value* with the time to the next interrupt. The timer will send back through port *intr* a token in *timer_intr* when that time has elapsed. Sending a token through port *timer_req* to *req* will cause the timer to reply with a token from port *counter_out* to *timer_in* containing the value of the actual time to the next interrupt.

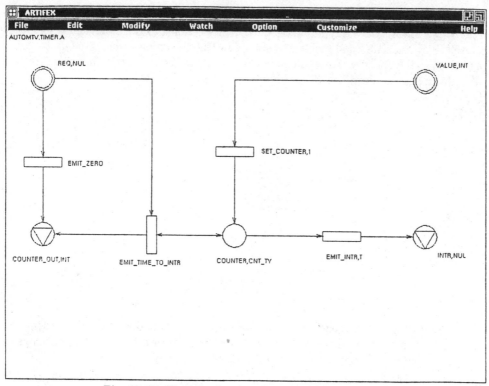

Fig. 11-17. The behavioral model of the hardware timer

The interface to the speedometer consists of the sending of a token with a bit value each time the output square wave changes level: it is a link from *level* to *level*.

The wheel sensor sends a pulse from *intr* to *pulse_intr* each time the wheel has accomplished a revolution.

Modeling the system behavior   *Control* is the object that models the system to be developed. It must perform three activities: receive pulses at each wheel complete revolution and calculate the input period (the time between two pulses); calculate the new period estimate as an average of the new measure and the old estimate; and generate a square wave (emit tokens at the square wave frequency). It uses a timer to measure the time interval between two pulses and to be interrupted when half a period of the output wave expires.

The three activities are quite independent and can be performed concurrently. The activities have been split in two different views: *compute_periods* and *manage_timer_intr*. The second view is incharged of generating the output wave.

In view *compute_periods* (see FIG. 11-18), the pulses are received in input port *pulse_intr*. The initial token in place *w_next_intr* enables transition *read_timer* that, when a pulse is received, sends to the timer a token through port *timer_req*. If you remember the connections, this causes the timer to reply with a token in place *timer_in* of type *int* with an integer value that is the current time to the next interrupt. The arrival of the token in *timer_in* causes transition *compute_in_p* to perform the calculation of the input period using the time value received from the timer.

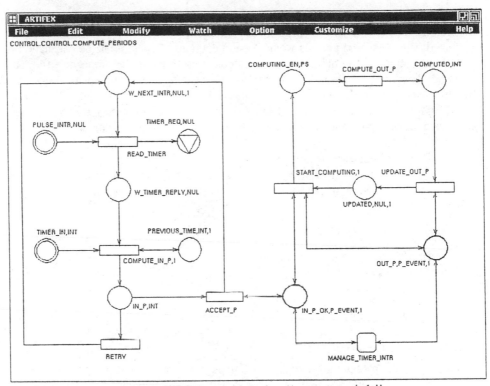

Fig. 11-18. Object control: view "compute-periods"

The input period is the time elapsed because the previous pulse was received. It is the time from the previous pulse to the first following timer interrupt (read from place *previous_time* that is used like a datastore) plus the time from the first timer interrupt following the previous pulse to the next timer interrupt (stored in *carry*) minus the actual time to the next timer interrupt (from the token in *timer_in*). *Carry* is a local variable to which the time to the next timer interrupt is added each time the timer is loaded. The value that has just been received from the timer is copied in *previous_time*. The release of the token in *in_p*, that contains the calculated input period value, is delayed to model the computation time. The computation is defined with C code associated to the transition:

```
TRANSITION compute_in_p IS
    ACTION % %
        IN_P – >value = PREVIOUS_TIME – >value +
CONTROL – >carry
                    – TIMER_IN – >value;
        PREVIOUS_TIME – >value = TIMER_IN – >value;
        CONTROL – >carry = 0; % %;
ENDTR compute_in_p;
```

If the value is above the threshold, it is discarded by *retry*, otherwise it is accepted by *accept_p* and copied in *in_p_ok* that is used like a datastore. A token is put back in state *w_next_intr* to start waiting for the next pulse.

A place like *in_p_ok*, that is connected in input and output to an immediate transition, models a datastore and requires a starting token. If the double connection had not been used, the calculated periods would have queued up in *in_p_ok* if the calculation of the filtered output period did not manage to consume them at the same rate they are produced. This might happen: in this case the old values should be skipped, hence the need to use a datastore.

In_p_ok is also an event flag signaling to transition *start_computing* that a new input value has been accepted and is available for computation. The event flag is set by transition *accept* with the assignment set = 1 (field set = = 1 means the value has not yet been consumed). If the predicate is satisfied, the transition consumes the *in_p_ok* event and resets the event (set = 0). It also fetches the values of the input and output period from the two datastores *in_p_ok* and *out_p* and copies them in place *computing_en* that enables *compute_out_p*.

```
TRANSITION start_computing IS
    TESTED_TOKENS IN_P_OK;
    PREDICATE % % (IN_P_OK – >set) % %;
    ACTION % %
        OUT_P – >set = 1;
        IN_P_OK – > set = 0;
        COMPUTING_EN – >in_p = IN_P_OK – >value;
        COMPUTING_EN – >out_p = OUT_P – >value; % %;
ENDTR start_computing;
```

Compute_out_p uses the two values to compute the new output period. The release of token *computed*, that contains the newly calculated value, is delayed to model the output period calculation time. The two delays of *compute_in_p* and *compute_out_p* are set by the initialize section to the values of two parameters. The identifier CONTROL – > decay used in the calculation is also a parameter. The computation of the period estimate is quite simple: it is an average of the measured period and of the previous estimate. The old estimate is multiplied for a factor between zero and one (parameter decay) and then added to the new measure that is first multiplied for (1-decay).

```
TRANSITION compute_out_p IS
    ACTION % %
        COMPUTED – >value = CONTROL – >decay *
(float)COMPUTING_EN – >out_p
                    + (1.0 – CONTROL – >decay) *
(float)COMPUTING_EN – >in_p;
    % %;
ENDTR compute_out_p;
```

When the calculation is over, *update_out_p* updates the value of datastore *out_p* and a new calculation can start. Note that if *compute_out_p*, that is a delayed release transition, had direct access to the two datastores, it would lock out all the other transitions, like *accept*, for the duration of the delay.

The two datastores *in_p_ok* and *out_p* are connected with infolinks to view *manage_timer_intr* to show the interaction with that view.

View *manage_timer_intr* (see FIG. 11-19) is quite simple: it only has to emit the token through *level*, that models the output square wave, every time it receives an inter-

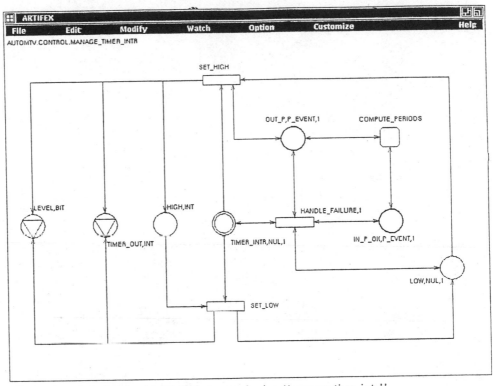

Fig. 11-19. Object control: view "manage-time-intr"

rupt from the timer. The interrupt token is accepted in *timer_intr* and either *set_high* or *set_low* fire depending on whether the state of the wave is *low* or *high*. When the interrupt is received, the timer must be reloaded with the time to the next interrupt. This is a multiple of half the output period that is read from datastore *out_p*. The value is copied in token *high* so that *set_low* can set the timer to the same value even if *out_p* has changed. The value to load the timer with must be put in output port *timer_out*.

Transition *handle_failure* was added to the net after a simulation revealed that a non-nominal behavior was not handled. If the sensor on the wheel breaks down and emits no more pulses, *out_p* would maintain the last calculated period, which is pure nonsense. Because the period of the output wave is k > 1 times that of the input pulses, if no pulse has been accepted between three successive timer interrupts a failure must have occurred. So give the datastore *in_p_ok* also the meaning of event *"no input period calculated in the meanwhile*: transition *set_high* sets the event flag set = 1 of *in_p* and *accept* reset it. If *out_p* has set = = 1, a failure is assumed to have occurred in the input period calculation. In this case, the threshold value is written in datastore *in_p_ok* and its event flag is set (set = 1) to start the output period calculation.

This enhancement only required a transition to be added and place *in_p_ok* to be duplicated in view *manage_timer_intr*. Due to the well-defined interface of transitions no other modification of the net was needed.

```
TRANSITION handle_failure IS
    TESTED_TOKENS OUT_P;
PREDICATE % % (!OUT_P – >set & &
                    ((float)OUT_P – >value < CONTROL – >maxtime) )
% %;
    ACTION % %
        IN_P_OK – >value = CONTROL – >maxtime * 1.005;
        IN_P_OK – >set = 1;
        OUT_P – >set = 1;
        xx_setcolor(1); (* turn the instance blue *)
    % %;
ENDTR compute_out_p;
```

Figure 11-20 is a snapshot of the animation of the nets performed by the supporting environment.

The pulse generator turns blue when it stops emitting pulses. The control system turns blue when it detects a failure in the measure of the pulse period. The pulse generator reads the time to the next pulse from file "tin.dat" and stops when it reads −1. The control objects write the calculated period estimates in file "tout.dat".

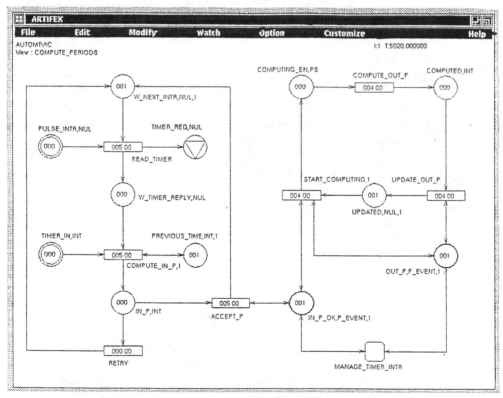

Fig. 11-20. Monitoring the execution: animation of "control"

12

Software engineering
methods

In this chapter two methods of software engineering are discussed. These methods are:

- ProMod
- Software Requirements Engineering Methodology

PROMOD

ProMod uses an integrated set of automated tools that are shown in FIG. 12-1. These tools support all technical phases of software development. This set of integrated tools is based on the following principles:

- Yourdon/DeMarco's method of structured analysis
- Real-time extensions to structured analysis
- D. L. Paranas' principles of information hiding and data abstraction
- Paranas/Booch/Buhr methods of modular design
- Caine, Farber, and Gordon techniques for pseudocode program specifications
- N. Wirth's technique of stepwise refinement for programming

The ProMod method was developed at GEI (Gesellschaft fuer Elektronicische Informations-verararbeitung in Germany) and is distributed by ProMod, Inc. The major components of ProMod are:

- Structured analysis
- Modular design
- ProSource
- ProCap

ProMod's structured analysis module implements the Yourdon/DeMarco methodology, as shown in FIG. 12-2. This method utilizes data flow diagrams. Corresponding to each DFD is a data dictionary entry. Each process node is described by a minispecifica-

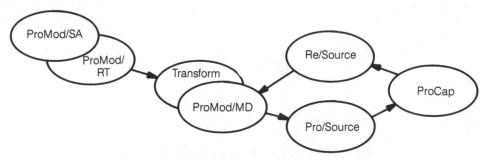

Fig. 12-1. ProMod automated tools

tion. During the creation of the analysis model, ProMod checks for consistency and completeness by performing global balancing checks to ensure full consistency between DFDs, minispecifications, and the data dictionary.

ProMod's analysis package includes real-time extensions that are shown in FIG. 12-3. These extensions provide visibility of control flows with control specifications and state transition diagrams (STD). Real-time systems require attention for critical control and timing requirements. ProMod/RT has extended traditional structured analysis with control flow diagrams (CFD), control specifications (CSP), state transition diagrams

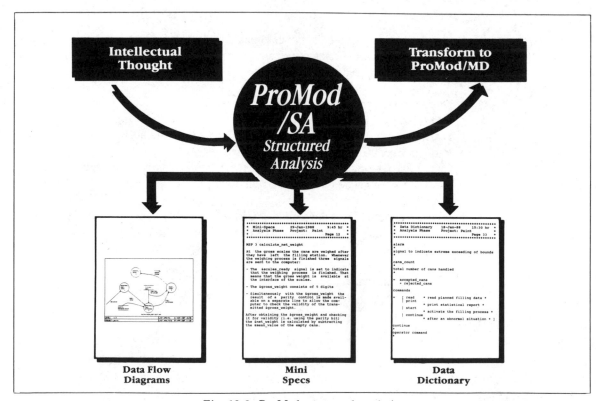

Fig. 12-2. ProMod structured analysis

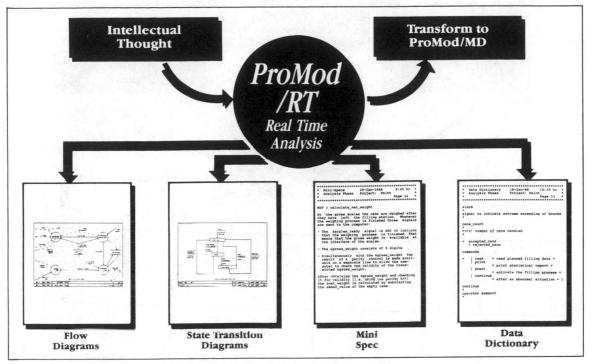

Fig. 12-3. Structured analysis for real time

(STD), and a requirements dictionary (RD). These elements allow real-time systems to recognize and make decisions on past events, current conditions, and anticipated future events.

The modular design transforms the analysis model into a hierarchical structure of subsystems, modules, functions, and data elements. The modular design structure is shown in FIG. 12-4. When a system model that has been defined with structured analysis is complete, then the modular design transforms the model into a suggested system solution for implementation.

This structure diagram is used as the basis for further stepwise refinement into a more detailed system structure, described in FIG. 12-5. A ProMod design chart can create and display a graphical representation of a software system at any time during the design phase. Design charts portray graphical pictures of the system at any level:

- Total system structure
- Individual modules
- Single functions

You can see at a glance where potential bottlenecks might be evolving in a design, or what areas are not yet complete. For example, you can see where a different packaging or partitioning might make the system more efficient. Development costs are drastically reduced by viewing potential pitfalls and unnecessary complexities before implementation begins.

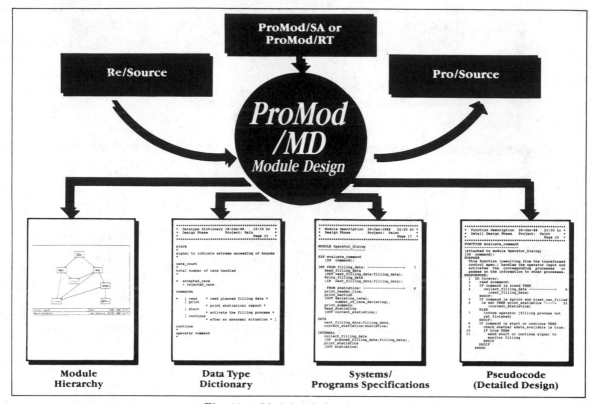

Fig. 12-4. Modular design

Part of the modular design is a pseudocode editor that allows language-independent code structures that define details of modules and functions. This method has a strong emphasis for information hiding, parameter passing, and interfaces.

The Pro/Source code generator translates pseudocode, which was developed during the design phase, into code constructs for the Ada or C. An example of this generator is shown in FIG. 12-6. Pro/Source automatically provides a template for the final programming. The design data collected in ProMod/Modular design contains all structures needed to create source code. Together ProCap and Pro/Source provide an automatic translation of design into syntactically correct code, while all of the design data is maintained.

ProCap is an interactive system for source code development in either Ada or C. ProCap maintains the code and the design abstractions in a multilevel file structure, shown in FIG. 12-7. ProCap improves productivity and reduces errors at the detailed coding and code maintenance level.

Automatic report documentation provides a wide variety of detail reports, including a special DOD-STD-2167A report generator for the software requirements specifications (SRS) document. An example of this generator is given in FIG. 12-8. ProMod covers the systems development life cycle from analysis to design and into coding. Each of these

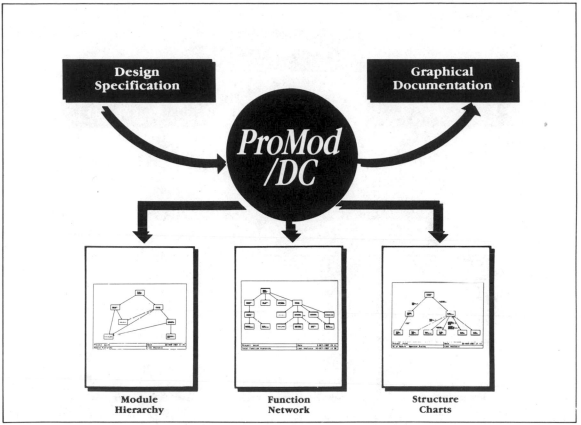

Fig. 12-5. Design charts

phases has distinct milestones given in DOD-STD-2167A. The development methodologies supported by ProMod provide consistent and complete models for analysis (logical model) and design (physical model).

ProMod's traceability matrix system (TMS) automatically traces requirements through the architectural and detailed phases. This tracing provides visibility of the selected items through all developments with increased control and considerable time savings. The report shows where each item is found, referenced, omitted, or duplicated in documents. Figure 12-9 gives an example of traceability.

SOFTWARE REQUIREMENTS ENGINEERING METHODOLOGY

Software Requirements Engineering Methodology (SREM) [Alford] was originally developed for performing requirements definition for large embedded systems with stringent performance requirements. With the addition of extensions for supporting distributed concurrent systems, the name was changed to distributed computer design system (DCDS). SREM was developed by TRW for the U.S. Army. SREM was developed

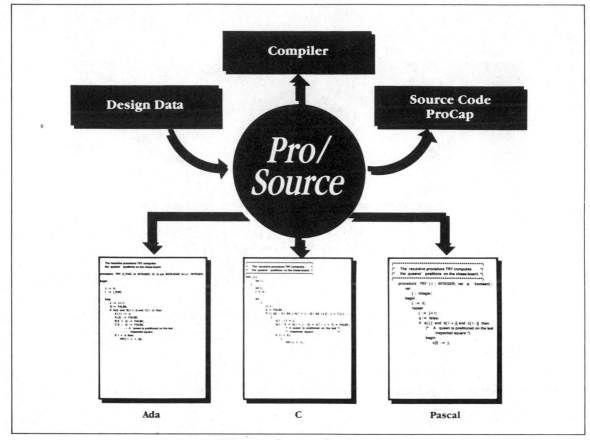

Fig. 12-6. Source code generators

for real-time systems. SREM covers techniques and procedures for requirements decomposition and for managing the requirements development process.

SREM starts with the translation and decomposition of system-level requirements, shown in FIG. 12-10. The other activities include allocation and analytical feasibility demonstration.

SREM includes the following set of software support tools:

- Requirements statement language (RSL)—A machine processable language for stating requirements
- Requirements engineering and validation system (REVS)—An integrated set of tools to support the development of requirements in RSL

This set of tools was implemented for automating many manual activities that were associated with requirements engineering.

All requirements in REVS are translated into a central relational database called the abstract system semantic model (ASSM), shown in FIG. 12-11. The RSL statements are not stored in the ASSM, but are translated into representations of the information con-

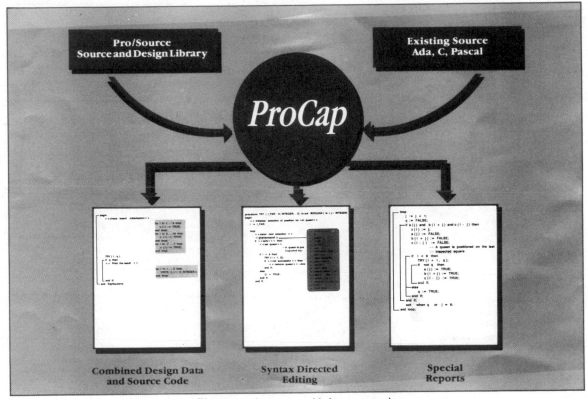

Fig. 12-7. Computer-aided programming

tent of the requirements statements. This method is efficient and flexible for maintaining a large specification of data in a relatively small computer database. Figure 12-12 shows REVS consisting of a computer program with a database. The requirements information that is written for a system will be stored in this database. The database can be corrected until all detected errors are removed. Tools are available for mechanically generating a simulation for the system, which also provides automatic documentation.

RSL expresses requirements in an unambiguous machine language, as opposed to free-form and free-content English. R-Net is a flow graph. The R-Net traces a stimulus/response network. R-Net provides a circuit-like description of the input stimulus to output response of the system. These flow graphs are expressed in RSL as structures. The flow graphs are the products of the mapping of a two-dimensional graph onto a one-dimensional stream that is suitable for computer input. Support is available for automatically processing the requirements and performing a wide range of important activities. An example is the identifying of syntax errors by using the RSL translator. R-Net notations are explained in FIG. 12-13. The principles of SREM are:

- Formalism
- Modularity
- Structuring

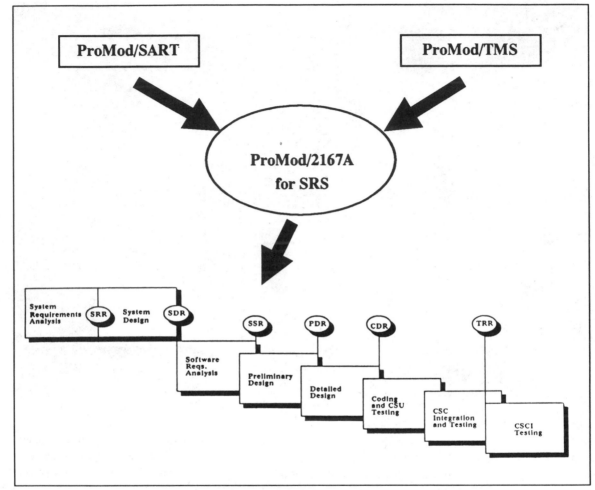

Fig. 12-8. DOD-STD-2167A: Report generator

- Separation of concerns
- Uniformity

Formalism is achieved by RSL and R-Nets. Modularity is achieved by subnets and RSL entities. Structuring is achieved by R-Nets syntax and RSL. The separation of concerns is gained by RSL entities and relationships and RSL/R-Net partitioning. The uniformity is enforced by automated checking. Some of the major goals of SREM include:

- Correctness
- Verifiability
- Testability
- Maintainability
- Modifiability
- Reliability
- Efficiency

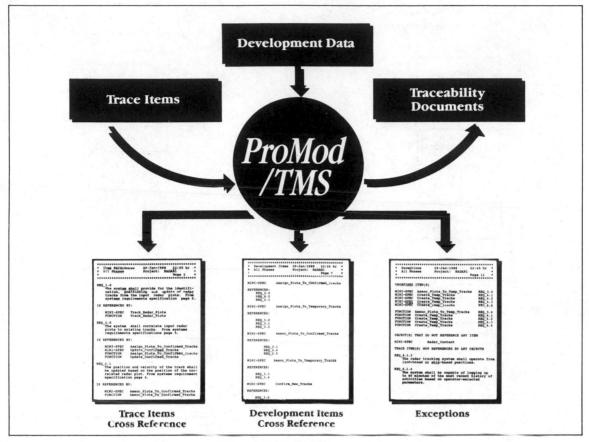

Fig. 12-9. Traceability

Correctness, verifiability, and testability are supported by formal language, consistency checking, and dynamic simulation capability. Maintainability and modifiability are aided by automated database and extensive reports. Reliability depends on consistency checking and simulation. The efficiency can begin with parallelism and tuning analysis.

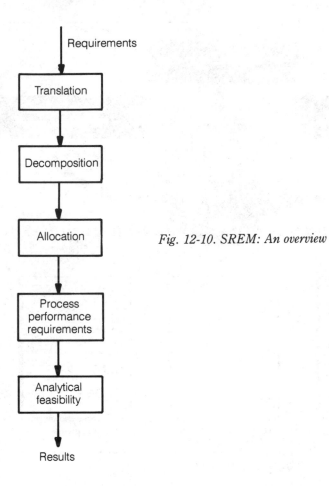

Fig. 12-10. SREM: An overview

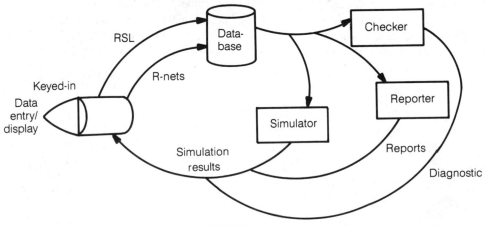

Fig. 12-11. SREM concepts

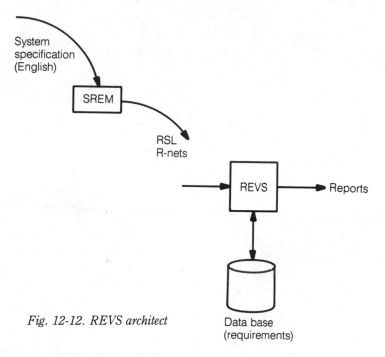

Fig. 12-12. *REVS architect*

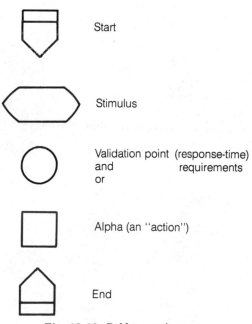

Fig. 12-13. *R-Net notations*

13

Data/entity-oriented methodologies

In this chapter, some of the methodologies dealing with data and entity, instead of functions, are discussed. The scope of this book does not permit a detailed discussion of these methodologies. There are many books available that cover these subjects. The methods outlined are:

- Jackson structured programming (JSP)
- Warnier-Orr methodology
- Entity diagram
- Bachman diagram
- Jackson system development (JSD)

JACKSON STRUCTURED PROGRAMMING

The Jackson Structured Program (JSP) method is a program design method concerned with small sequential problems. The JSP design reads and writes a set of serial data streams. The software is determined by the structure of the input and output data. The key concept of JSP is that the program structure should mirror the data structure, which mirrors the problem structure. The JSP notations are shown in FIG. 13-1. The main steps in JSP are:

- Describe data streams with structure diagrams.
- Merge data structure diagrams to create the program structure diagram.
- List operations and allocation of elements in the program structure.
- Convert the program to text without conditions.
- Add iteration and selection conditions.

In JSP, the input and output data are analyzed first and then produce a design that maps the input structure into the output structure as is shown in FIG. 13-2. When there are multiple input data streams, they can be organized and structured with different keys (an ordering clash). One stream might contain multiple record types, which can lead to

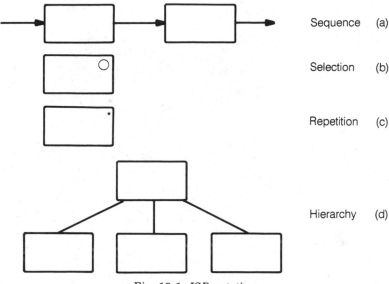

Fig. 13-1. JSP notations

an interleaving clash. When input and output structure do not match, intermediate files and program inversion must be used to resolve this structure clash. Program inversion means almost turning the input or output structure upside down.

The JSP method is used to design sequential programs. It has been used widely for the design of data processing systems, although techniques like program inversion make JSP possible for a wide range of program formats.

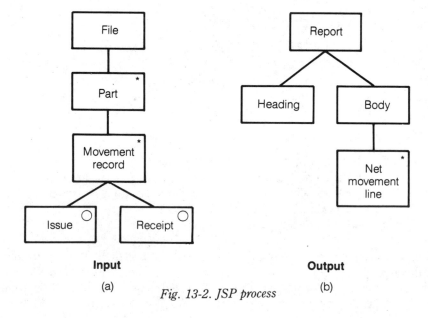

Fig. 13-2. JSP process

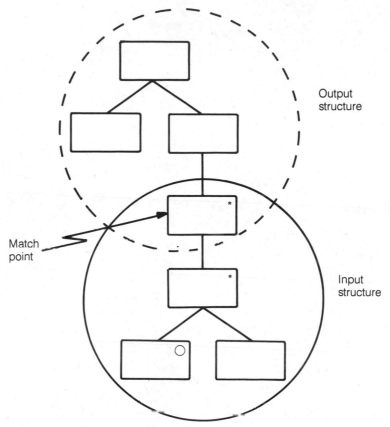

Fig. 13-2. Continued

The JSP method is highly prescriptive. Various designers that use JSP can produce a similar design. The method does become complex for large systems with many structure clashes.

WARNIER-ORR METHODOLOGY

The Warnier-Orr methodology was developed in France by Jean Warnier and popularized in the U.S.A. by Ken Orr. This methodology uses much the same philosophy as the JSP methodology, but with textual representation. Input and output are analyzed first and then produce a design that maps the input structure into the output structure. This methodology is shown in FIG. 13-3.

The principles of Warnier-Orr include:

- Structuring
- Modularity
- Uniformity
- Formalism

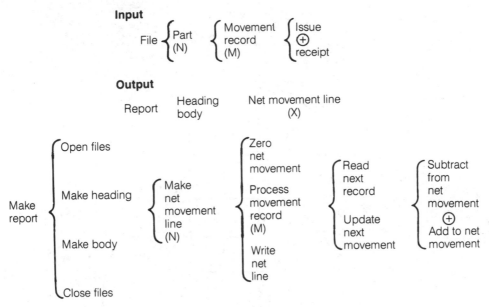

Fig. 13-3. Warnier-Orr

Structuring and modularity are derived from the data structure. Uniformity and formalism are a result of syntax and semantic rules for handling complex data structures. The notation conventions are detailed in FIG. 13-4.

Number
of
times
$$(0,1) = \text{zero or one time}$$
$$(0,n) = \text{zero or N times}$$
$$(1,n) = \text{one or N times}$$
$$(\text{blank or (1))} = \text{one time}$$

Connectives
⊕   = "OR"
+   = Concurrency
▢   = Arithmetic operator
blank   = "AND" or sequence
process = Not

Fig. 13-4. Warnier-Orr notations

An example of Warnier data structure is given in FIG. 13-5. An example of a Warnier-Orr diagram is presented in FIG. 13-6. In the example, the function computes a programmer's statistics. The problem statement is defined as follows:

"If employee is a female programmer, count as such. If nonprogrammer is a female, count as such. If employee is not female, count as such."

A suggested sample Warnier-Orr chart is shown in FIG. 13-7.

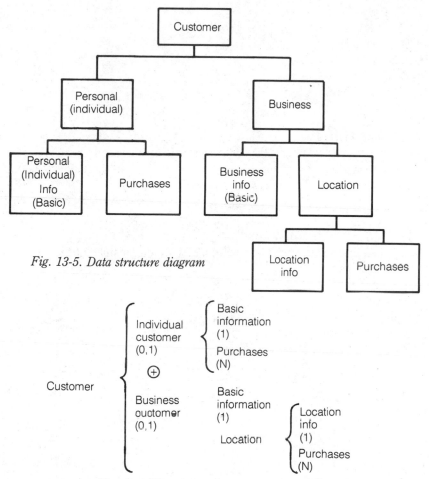

Fig. 13-5. Data structure diagram

Fig. 13-6. Warnier-Orr diagram (example)

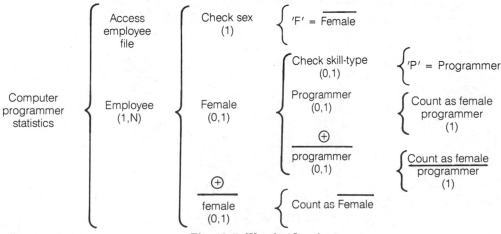

Fig. 13-7. Warnier-Orr chart

The goals of Warnier-Orr are:

- Understandability
- Traceability
- Productivity
- Maintainability
- Modifiability

Understandability and traceability are achieved from the program structure that relates directly to data structure. Productivity is an easy approach for data handling applications. Maintainability and modifiability relate to changes in the input or output map, which directly corresponds to program structure changes.

ENTITY DIAGRAM

Entity diagrams focus on the information of a system, instead of the functions. The method involved is:

- Identify entities
- Group entities into entity classes
- Identify relations
- Group relations into relation classes
- Draw entity diagram

The necessary notations used to draw an entity diagram are shown in FIG. 13-8.

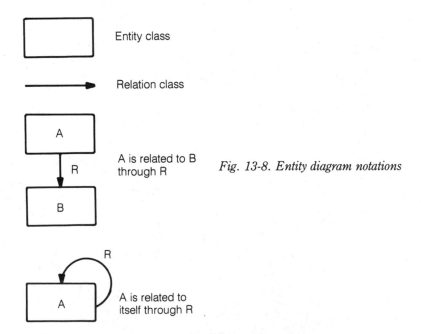

Entity class

Relation class

A is related to B through R

Fig. 13-8. Entity diagram notations

A is related to itself through R

The entity can be defined as selection of nouns in a sentence. Whereas, the relations can be defined as the selection of verbs in a sentence. The entity class can be defined as the collection of entities with similar properties, and the relation class can be defined as the collection of similar relations between entities.

BACHMAN DIAGRAM

Bachman diagrams help to implement entity diagrams into computer systems. A Bachman diagram uses entity diagrams and relation class ratio's to help with computer implementation. The Bachman diagram assesses the relation class ratio, which allows only 1:1 and 1:N ratio's, and converts the others to this type.

The notations used in Bachman diagrams are listed in FIG. 13-9. The Bachman diagram's method is:

- Label ratios
- Decide how to convert to Bachman diagram from Entity diagram
- Redraw Bachman diagram if necessary

A sample of a Bachman diagram is shown in FIG. 13-10.

JACKSON SYSTEM DEVELOPMENT

The Jackson System Development (JSD) method extends the philosophy used in JSP into a larger domain of application. JSD was developed by Michael Jackson. This methodology is widely used in Europe. Jackson's form of structure diagram is used for modeling the structure of design entities. The model is based on a set of disconnected processes, and provides information about the time ordering of actions performed by an entity. The main phases of JSD are as follows:

- Model
- Function
- Implementation

JSD employs a network of sequential processes that communicate with one another to address the process and data aspects of requirements. The development of a system uses composition, as opposed to decomposition. This method precisely defines each successive intermediate stage in the system.

The method utilizes object-oriented and event-oriented approaches to software development. Process abstraction and structured programming are essential to the method. This method conceptualizes problems facing a software developer as two separate matters:

1. The subject matter of the system reflects the real world entities and their behaviors.
2. The implementation environment consists of the machinery and associated software facilities for running the completed system.

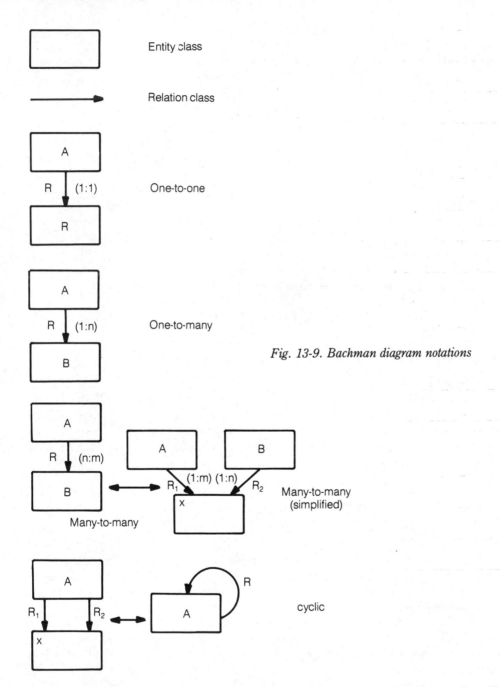

Entity class

Relation class

One-to-one

One-to-many

Fig. 13-9. Bachman diagram notations

Many-to-many

Many-to-many (simplified)

cyclic

When constructing a model of the subject matter, you should use events, their attributes, and their orderings for building a specification whose structure directly reflects the structure of the application domain. JSD views the internal structure of the system as part of the problem statement and not as a result of a particular implementation. The JSD model elaborates the necessary data, processes, and communication

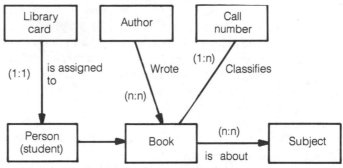

Fig. 13-10. Bachman diagram (example)

streams, which includes semantics for timing requirements that might constrain the implementation of the system. This model is described as a network of communication for sequential processes, and is represented as an explicit simulation of the system's subject matter.

The steps for constructing the system specification is:

- Entity/action and entity structures
- Initial model
- Interactive functions
- Information functions
- System timing

Entity/action and entity structures describe the real world at an abstract level with entities that perform and suffer actions. Time ordering is considered when there are constraints in the sequence of actions. Other structures are added when describing an entity of several sequential processes is necessary.

The initial model then takes these structures of the entity/action step and defines the set of sequential processes that are used for modeling the problem domain. This action is accomplished by viewing each structure as the definition of a process in the model. The addition of a data stream or state vector communications enables modeling of the connections among processes to reflect changes that correspond to the dynamics of the real world.

The interactive functions and information functions steps are executable operations and processes added to produce the outputs of the system. These outputs can be messages to an external system user.

The System Timing step specifies any constraints that might be necessary when implementing the software to ensure reasonable performance. These constraints include speed of execution and relative scheduling.

Implementation of the JSD model transforms the network of sequential processes into a smaller set of programs, which can be loaded and executed on the processors. Three of these techniques are:

1. Process scheduling
2. State vector separation
3. Process dismemberment

The procedure implementing a specification involves distributing the processes among the available processors. The set of processes assigned to a single processor must then be combined into a single program. The combination is done by a scheduler at the upper level with a hierarchical structure of inverted process texts. The scheduling algorithm for each processor must be defined, and a scheme must be devised for storing, accessing, and protecting the state vectors of the system, which might require the design of access logic to manipulate the data.

The JSD method recognizes that the structure of the specification (an executable object) should not be the same as the structure of the implemented system. The former reflects the requirements, whereas the latter reflects the implementation environment.

JSD is primarily intended for large systems including concurrent systems where time-ordering of events is important. Both data processing and process control systems are suggested as appropriate domains of application.

The JSD method is a relative prescription for the model-building analysis steps. It encourages the use of abstraction and makes good use of the object-oriented philosophy. The major weakness of the JSD method is that data structures and relationships cannot reasonably be described as histories of events.

14

Data-based methods

This chapter covers two methodologies: problem statement language/problem statement analyzer and Vienna development method.

PROBLEM STATEMENT LANGUAGE/PROBLEM STATEMENT ANALYZER

The Problem Statement Language/Problem Statement Analyzer (PSL/PSA) is a computer-aided structure technique for analysis and documentation of requirements. The methodology assists in preparing functional specifications for information processing systems. PSL/PSA was originally created by the U.S. Air Force, calling it URL/URA.

The methodology was developed by the Information System Design and Optimization System (ISDOS) project in 1968 at the University of Michigan, which was directed by Dr. Daniel Teicherow. The work was assisted by Hasan Sayani at the University of Maryland. ISDOS was separated from the University of Michigan in 1983 as a commercial venture, and it is now called Meta Systems.

PSL/PSA provides an automated approach to systems requirements definition. The concepts of the method are shown in FIG. 14-1. The use of PSL/PSA does not depend on a particular model of the software process and it can be customized to a variety of software development methods.

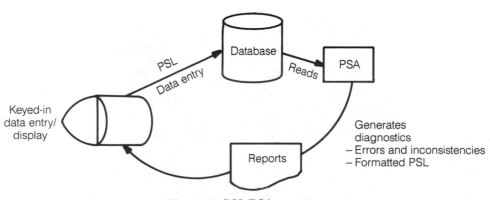

Fig. 14-1. PSL/PSA concepts

The system description language describes a system in its processible form. This language is nonprocedural, and is intended to represent system requirements. It provides a textual representation of logical system design.

PSL is founded on entity-relationship modeling, which views a system as a collection of objects and relationships. Objects have properties with values. Relationships are connections or interrelationships between objects. This method defines specific types of objects and relationships that are needed for capturing information for functional requirements and specification. PSL provides the following kinds of representations:

- System input/output flow
- System structure
- Data structure
- Data derivation
- System size and volume
- System dynamics
- System properties
- Project management

A sample PSL is given in FIG. 14-2. PSA records the description of the system in a database, modifies the information incrementally, performs analyses, and produces reports

Process		Hourly-employee-processing:
Generate	:	Pay-statement, error-listing, hourly-employee-report
Receives	:	Time-card;
Subparts are	:	Hourly-pay-check-validation, hourly-emp-update, Hourly-paycheck-production;
Part of	:	Payroll-processing;
Derives	:	Pay-statement
Using	:	Time-card, hourly-employee-record;
Derives	:	Hourly-employee-report;
Using	:	Time-card, hourly-employee-record;
Derives	:	Error-listing
Using	:	Time-card, hourly-employee-record;
Procedure	:	1. Compute gross pay from time card data.
		2. Compute tax from gross pay.
		3. Subtract tax from gross pay to obtain net pay.
		4. Update hourly employee record accordingly.
		5. Update department record accordingly.
		6. Generate paycheck.
Note :		If status code specifies that the employee did not work this week, no processing will be done for this employee;
Happens	:	Number-of-payments times-per pay-period;
Triggered by	:	Hourly-emp-processing-event;
Termination-causes:	:	New-employee-processing-event;
Security is	:	Company-only;

Fig. 14-2. A command language and analyzer

in a variety of forms. The analyzer is controlled by a command language, which is shown in FIG: 14-3. PSA capabilities include:

- Analyzing the similarity of input/output
- Detecting gaps in the information flow or unused data objects
- Showing the dynamic behavior of the system
- Showing the objects, properties, and relationships from various views
- Provide project management reports

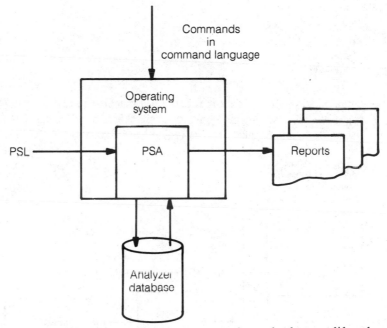

Fig. 14-3. PSL/PSA approach for a system software development life cycle

PSL/PSA supports and provides guidelines for the following activities of software development process:

- Requirements definition
- System specification
- System design
- Coding
- Documentation
- Reengineering
- Project management
- Quality assurance
- Maintenance

- Risk analysis
- Complexity assessment
- Cost estimation
- Integration
- Test planning and generation

PSL/PSA was created as an approach to improve the software development life cycle. The approach is shown in FIG. 14-4. The activities of logical system design are:

- Data collection
- Analysis
- Design
- Evaluation
- Improvements

In the data collection phase, data is recorded in machine-readable form. The intermediate outputs of PSA also provide convenient checklists for deciding what additional information is needed and checklists for recording the information.

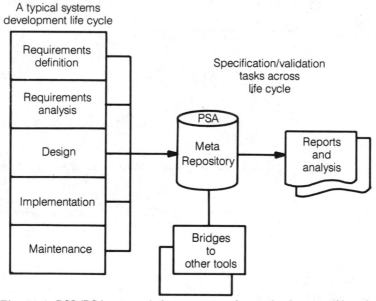

Fig. 14-4. PSL/PSA approach for a system software development life cycle.

A number of different kinds of analysis can be performed on demand by PSA, which means manual analysis is no longer necessary.

Design is essentially a creative process and cannot be automated. However, PSA can make more data available and allow you to manipulate it more extensively. The results of decisions are entered into the database.

In the evaluation phase, PSA provides some rudimentary facilities for computing work measures from the data in the problem statement.

Identification of possible improvements is a creative task. However, PSA output, particularly from the evaluation phase, can be useful to the analyst.

The PSL/PSA methodology is based on three primary premises:

1. More effort and attention should be devoted to front-end portions of the development process.
2. Make maximum use of automation with the large amount of information that must be handled.
3. Put automation in correct perspective, i.e., emphasize the need for documentation.

The major advantage of PSL/PSA is that it monitors the system's development process throughout the life cycle. PSL/PSA improves coordination and communication among project members by storing and retrieving information easily. PSL/PSA develops accurate, consistent, and easily modifiable specifications by detecting and resolving errors, omissions, and inconsistencies promptly.

VIENNA DEVELOPMENT METHOD

The Vienna Development Method (VDM) is a formal, mathematically-oriented method for specifying and developing software. This method is formal because it leads to a set of interrelated formal documents. A formal document is written in a formal language, which is a language with mathematically defined syntax and semantics. In addition, a formal document in development could prove correct with some prior formal document. A formal method includes a formal language, also called a specification language.

VDM specification language

The VDM specification language is called Meta-IV [Bjorner]. The name came from the first application of VDM. Meta-IV (and VDM) was first applied in the early 70s at the IBM Vienna Research Lab to give a formal semantic definition of a large PL/1 subset [Bekic]. A language that is used to define the semantics of another language is often referred to as a *metalanguage*. The IV is a play on the word metaphor.

Meta-IV is a *wide-spectrum* language because it allows you to write specifications at different levels of abstraction. It can be used as the single specification language throughout a number of steps in the development process. Abstraction is obtained through mathematical concepts (such as sets and functions), rather than through mechanisms offered by a particular implementation language. Meta-IV provides abstraction, and is not oriented toward any particular application area.

Meta-IV has a model-oriented view of a system. A model-oriented specification explicitly defines mathematical objects and operations used to describe a software system. The models are defined by using a number of type definitions (for the objects) and function definitions (for the operations).

Abstraction

Abstraction plays a central role in VDM. The principle is applied to both the definition of objects (data structures) and operations (functions applicable to data structure).

Following requirements analysis, the first abstract formal specification is developed. This specification describes the objects and the operations of the system. An abstract model traditionally contains three components:

1. Semantic domains that define the state of the system, and invariant predicates that define conditions that must be satisfied for each object belonging to a semantic domain.
2. Syntactic domains that define the information contents in the commands of the system, and well-formed predicates that define the conditions under which a given object belonging to a syntactic domain can be given a meaning by semantic functions.
3. Semantic functions that define the meaning of objects from the syntactic domains by using objects from the semantic domains.

VDM modeling techniques

VDM modeling techniques, that are similar to those used in describing high-level programming language concepts, are applicable to a wide class of problems outside formal programming language semantics. One reason for this is that most systems employ some language for a user to communicate with the system. Such languages often embody concepts that are found in traditional programming languages, such as TYPES. The TYPES language requires certain expressions that denote values that belong to certain data types. Keep in mind that the programming language concepts are not seen as a means of implementing a VDM model (in the final development step), but as concepts that are similar to those found in the system that is to be developed. These VDM concepts are explained in the following sections.

Types and values   A type identifies a set of values and introduces the concept into a system that partitions all values into subsets (integers, files, etc.) A type is also characterized by the operations that are applicable to the identified values. These operations are arithmetic for integers and file operations like ''open'' and ''read'' for files. Hence, expressions involving operators must respect the limitations of the operations. Expressing constraints is often referred to as *type checking*. In VDM this is expressed by the following 4 rules:

1. Syntactic domains define the classes of syntactically correct expressions and type definitions.
2. Semantic domains define the classes of descriptors for expressions and types (atomic as well as composite).
3. Functions define the descriptors corresponding to a given expression or type definition.
4. Functions define denotationally (by a Boolean result) whether a given expression or type definition (object belonging to a syntactic domain) is correct if it uses the defined descriptors in the semantic domains.

These four parts are always used in the formal description of programming languages that have types. VDM has a number of standards to define descriptors. These standards depend on the type equivalence rules of a language, such as name equivalence and structural equivalence.

Variables, storage, and locations   One basic concept of programming languages such as COBOL, FORTRAN, Pascal, and Ada, is that variables are assigned a value for storage (for the current values) and for location (for holding the values in storage). The values of variables can be changed at any time.

Blocks   Blocks in programming languages allow the local introduction of new entities and names for the entities, which means that entities are only used within the block. From a semantics point of view, capturing the visibility is most important of the declared names, including binding the declared entities. In VDM, binding is described with mappings. The effect of nesting blocks is described by passing mappings as parameters from one Meta-IV function to the subfunctions by utilizing the nested blocks.

Subprograms and macros   Nonlocal names referenced with subprograms, whether applicative or imperative, are bound at the point of definition within the subprogram, which is in contrast to macros where such names are bound at each point of call.

Calling a subprogram must generate a value because no side effects are possible. Because all global names are bound at the point of subprogram definition, a natural meaning of a subprogram in VDM is: a function, when given parameters (values), returns a value. This denotation associates the name of a subprogram in the VDM environment.

Macros, because of their name-binding rules, are described as functions from parameters, an environment (name bindings), storage to an optional value, and potentially changed storage (from side effects).

Flow of control   The flow of control in VDM directs the semantics style or the exit style. The exit style is preferred because it matches the intuition of most software engineers.

VDM data models and database management systems

A data model defines data objects and their operations. A database management system stores data objects and executes the operations. The functions of a database are divided into meta-functions that operate on descriptions of data (such as database schema operations) and on data objects (such as queries and general data manipulation). The data models are:

- Relational data models
- Hierarchical data models
- Network data models

In VDM, a relational data model is a collection of named relations. These relations are described with maps. A relation is a set of rows, and a row is a set of values or a mapping from row names to values. Because of this data model, the traditional relational database operations of select, project, join, and divide are easily defined. General predicate calculus query languages, such as SQL, also are easily described [Bjorner].

The basic concept in a hierarchical data model is records (of particular record types) which are arranged in tree structures. The hierarchy among record types is part of the schema of the data model. This hierarchy is described as a hierarchy-diagram type that is recursively defined as a mapping from record type identifiers to hierarchy-diagram types (the subhierarchies of the record type). Mapping is empty for the bottom elements of the hierarchy. The descriptors of the actual fields in the record types (at each level) must be added to the hierarchy so the complete schema of information is received. Throughout the formal description of the hierarchical data model, recursively defined mappings are used for capturing hierarchical tree structures, rather than using Meta-IV trees, which would lead to a fixed number of subhierarchies for each record type.

The basis for a VDM description of network data models is the formalization of Bachman's concept of data structure diagrams [Bachman]. These diagrams consist of boxes and arrows. A box denotes a set of records with descriptions in VDM. An arrow denotes a relation among records, and is described as a mapping from records to sets of records (a one-to-many relation).

The syntactic form of any data structure diagram can be seen as a set of unique box names and a set of unique arrow names (a mapping from arrow names to pairs of "from" and "to" box names). A model of data structure diagrams is created by combining this syntactic view with the semantic view and adding the necessary invariants. The model easily allows a description for navigating through the database.

VDM stepwise development

The idea behind a stepwise development process is that commitments should be made sequentially, instead of all at once. In VDM, most commitments comprise an object transformation (selecting new data representations) or an operation transformation (choosing more algorithmic definitions). Object transformations often necessitate operation transformations because the original operations used the characteristics of the corresponding data type. Also, most VDM specifications are compositional (i.e., isolating properties of a model) parts of a specification, which can be developed in isolation. The VDM is well suited for the following systems:

- Embedded systems
- Scientific/engineering systems
- Distributed processing

Tools that support VDM have been developed recently. Most of the tools are related to Meta-IV and the handling of formal specifications only. The tools do not provide direct support of the development process [Hansen]. These tools include:

- Editors for writing Meta-IV specifications
- Syntax analyzers
- Context condition checkers (type-checkers, etc.)
- Databases for formal specifications
- Output tools for screen and paper

VDM is a formal or mathematical method for developing software systems that consist of an orderly plan for using specific tools, techniques, and notational systems.

III

Evolving Software Engineering Practices

15

Technology for the automated generation of systems

Technology for the Automated Generation of Systems (TAGS) is a computer automated systems engineering environment that provides automated definition, design, documentation, testing, and maintenance of complex systems. TAGS consists of a universal, precise, and unambiguous system requirements and design language supported by a series of integrated software packages in a distributed workstation environment. TAGS gives systems and software engineer complete visibility and control of the system development process.

TAGS was developed at Teledyne Brown Engineering by a team headed by G. J. Gotvald, shown in FIG. 15-1. The TAGS system is composed of three elements:

1. An iconographic input/output requirements language
2. Computer-based tools supporting design of systems and software
3. A development method based on stepwise refinement

The requirements language records system design concepts emphasizing traceability between requirements and implementation. The language can be used to develop new systems and analyze existing systems. The tools that support the software process are:

- Validation and verification
- Configuration management
- Documentation generation
- Simulation of design behavior

OVERVIEW

TAGS is a system engineering methodology addressing the creation of complex systems, and is illustrated in FIG. 15-2. The TAGS methodology components are shown in FIG. 15-3. The major components are explained in the following sections.

Fig. 15-1. G. J. Gotvald, principal architect for TAGS

Input/output requirements language

Input/output requirements language (IORL) is a universally applicable graphical systems requirements and design language. It combines system specification, design, and documentation into a single creative cohesive process. IORL consists of graphical engineering symbols and mathematical expressions that allow clear and precise graphical representation of system requirements and design. The ambiguity of the English language never comes into play.

IORL provides a detailed graphic description of all input and output requirements for a particular system, shown in FIG. 15-4. Independent components are identified, interfaces are properly labeled, and each process is depicted. All data types and their values, timing constraints, parallel logic, and concurrent logic are properly defined.

System decomposition into distinct documents, sections, and pages allows the designer to work with essential system elements as related groups of information. A document is a set of related diagrams and parameter tables used to describe one system component. Sections are diagrams or parameter table, and are the building blocks of an IORL system design. A page, in the literal sense, is a single sheet of information.

Thus, an IORL system design is composed of one or more documents. Each document is comprised of several sections, and each section is composed of one or more pages. This tree structure prevents the system design from becoming a confusing arrangement of drawings and specifications and provides a clear top-down definition.

TAGS METHODOLOGY

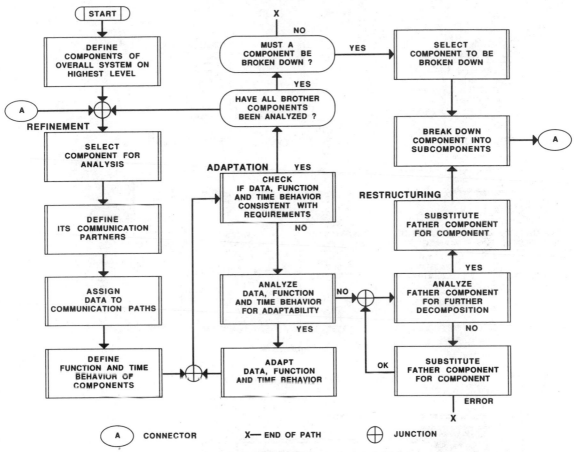

Fig. 15-2. TAGS methodology: An overview

Another important feature of IORL is the ability to successfully trace logic flow and data flow through a system design hierarchy. A low-level and highly detailed part of the design can be traced back to the highest generalized level with no ambiguity.

Each component and data interface is labeled with a unique name and number that is referenced by all associated diagrams and parameters tables within the appropriate document. Thus, the logical steps required for a system component and the data that travels between components can be followed.

Each IORL page is uniquely identified by system name, document ID, section name, and page number. Page identification not only establishes the distinct position of the page within the system hierarchy, but also allows related pages to be cross-referenced. For example, several diagram pages with the same document ID can be assembled and studied as a coherent group of logical processes.

IORL minimizes errors and enables the system designer to avoid crucial flaws and oversight by using rigorous procedures for structuring in a logical, consistent, and precise manner.

TAGS SOFTWARE APPLICATION PACKAGES

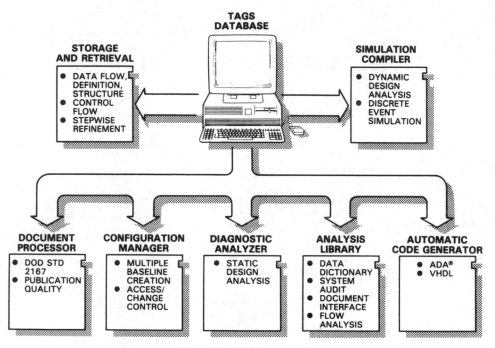

Fig. 15-3. TAGS components

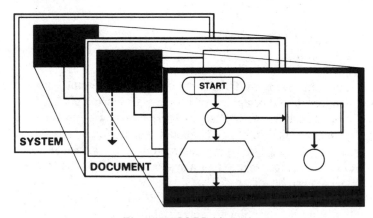

Fig. 15-4. IORL hierarchy

Storage and retrieval

Storage and retrieval allows IORL pages to be created, stored, retrieved, modified, and deleted from disk-resident files, as shown in FIG. 15-5. The entire IORL system design process occurs at the computer workstation. The designer is not limited to a few

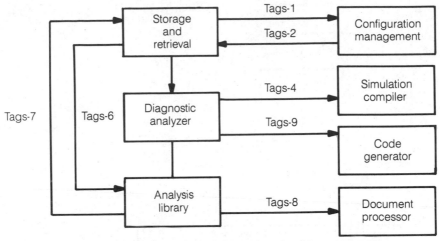

Fig. 15-5. Storage and retrieval features

specialized functions, but is provided with a variety of user-friendly screen displays, called *menus*. Menus present a broad range of functions that allow the user to construct and manipulate the diagrams and parameters tables required for an IORL system.

This multiuser applications software, which is icon driven, eliminates traditional physical design obstacles by allowing a design team to interactively generate a design specification in a multiple workstation environment. IORL systems are automatically displayed upon request. Pages of a document can be created, stored, retrieved, modified, hardcopied and/or deleted from disk resident files. Errors are easily corrected by deleting or modifying faulty symbols of text, which are shown in FIG. 15-6.

Configuration management

Configuration Management (CM) automates and maintains system documents, and keeps track of changes throughout the life cycle. CM is the menu-driven applications software package that automates change documentation to a system. Visibility and control are enhanced by a series of formal requests, which enables you to list the action status of specific system changes, to display user-defined cross sections of the system, and to implement approved changes that update the system.

CM forms provide a highly structured means to document the ongoing growth of a system. Well-defined formats enable the user to record extensive details regarding system problems and design changes. When a system problem occurs, all pertinent facts can be entered at the workstation quickly and easily, including items such as the level of urgency.

Because all necessary information is well organized and readily available, you are better prepared to make critical design decisions that will improve system reliability. Moreover, if several people are working on the same problem, then a complete and accurate record of essential details prevents confusion, improves communication, and helps increase productivity.

CM supports multiple revisions of individual IORL system design pages. Thus, design pages of different revision levels can be collected to form a distinct system design

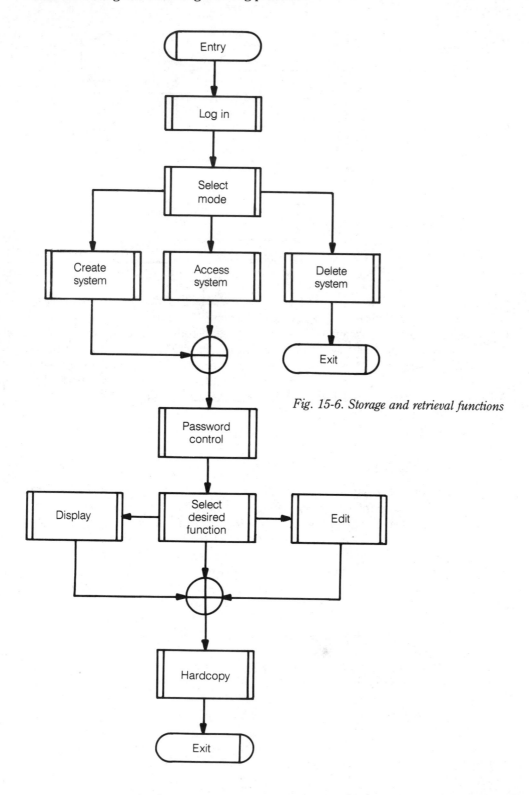

Fig. 15-6. Storage and retrieval functions

version called a *baseline*. Each baseline is established as a useful reference point in the development and growth of the system. An example of a baseline is shown in FIG. 15-7.

One crucial advantage of maintaining multiple revision levels is that testing system changes becomes more flexible and effective. Various combinations of proposed system changes can be tested separately, which will determine the optimum system design.

CM forms furnish a history of IORL system design changes. Every approved change and proposal is uniquely identified. Thus, every stage of system growth can be traced in a precise manner. Action dates, personnel involved, and design pages can be recorded for each system change. The user can indicate proposed changes to current status, as well as the reasons for approval or rejection of system changes.

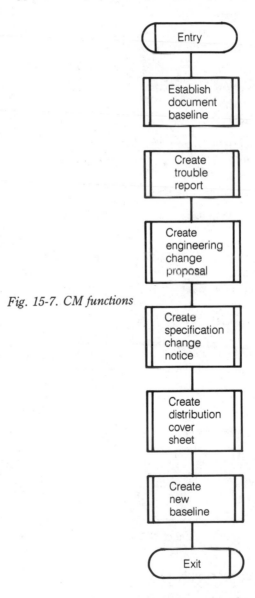

Fig. 15-7. CM functions

Diagnostic analyzer

A diagnostic analyzer provides thorough error analysis in the early stages of the system development life cycle. It searches for static errors that do not rely on variable values or control flow. Incorrect references are identified and invalid symbol constructions are located. Missing sections also are detected. Moreover, this process is computer automated to provide an efficient and reliable error analysis.

The diagnostic analyzer also assists when determining the completeness and correctness of the IORL system. Every system part is thoroughly checked for missing items. The following list is a sample of incomplete error types that are detected:

- Missing diagram/table
  - diagram has no associated parameters table
  - parameter table has no associated diagram

- Missing symbol
  - no START symbol
  - no ENTRY symbol
  - no EXIT symbol

- Missing symbol text
  - no component range
  - no interface label
  - no predefined process number

- Missing parameter information
  - no parameter name
  - no parameter description

- Closure errors
  - unconnected component
  - dangling connector
  - unmatched interface

The diagnostic analyzer checks the validity of all diagrams and parameter tables in an IORL system design. The following list gives examples of the validity errors that are identified:

- Semantic errors
  - invalid parameter name
  - illegal character
  - invalid symbol number
  - illegal data value

- Syntax errors
  - illegal symbol for type of diagram
  - symbols improperly connected

- Cross-reference errors
  - parameter referenced but not defined

- mismatched page connectors
- predefined process referenced by wrong number

- Consistency errors
  - parameter name not unique
  - two conflicting directions of data flow portrayed

- Control-flow errors
  - illegal combination of incoming and outgoing paths at a junction

- Type mismatches
  - comparison of two unlike items

Several diagnostic analyzer characteristics enhance the effectiveness of the analysis process. First, the diagnostic analyzer enforces a particular order of analysis, which prevents the user from bypassing the analysis of sections that function as prerequisites for other sections. Up-to-date analysis information also is maintained, so the results of analyzing one section are current and available when needed for analysis of related sections.

Secondly, the diagnostic analyzer preserves data integrity. Certain lockout functions prevent a data file from being accessed by more than one analysis process at a time.

Finally, the diagnostic analyzer provides an accurate and comprehensive record of analyses that have been performed. The user can avoid repeating analyses already completed because the data and descriptions of each analysis are retained.

The list of error conditions detected by the diagnostic analyzer is not simply a random record of problems. Each error is coded to convey the type of error, which uniquely identifies the specific error condition. The exact location of the error within the system design is also indicated, as can be seen in FIG. 15-8.

Additionally, each error condition functions as a useful diagnostic message, which is easy to understand. The user is assisted in determining the appropriate corrective action because each message is labeled according to one of the following diagnostic levels:

- Warning—identifies a question
- Severe—detects an invalid construct that prevents the analysis of related sections

Simulation compiler

A simulation compiler is a software package that produces an executable discrete-event simulation of a system designed with IORL, using Ada as a source code. The simulation executive controls execution of this code.

The model is specified and built in the TAGS network environment, where the TAGS database resides. The system model and the simulation controller are then exported via magnetic tape to a larger DEC VAX environment that has more computing power.

You can provide a wide range of simulation model inputs, collect data on the communication traces between components, and execute components internally in this environment. The output data collected can be post-processed, which produces a trace listing of the simulation execution. The simulation also performs dynamic error analysis that can locate problems such as timing and control faults—errors that cannot be found by static testing. Also, the trace listing assists the user to determine the optimum system and processing algorithm designs, as is shown in FIG. 15-9.

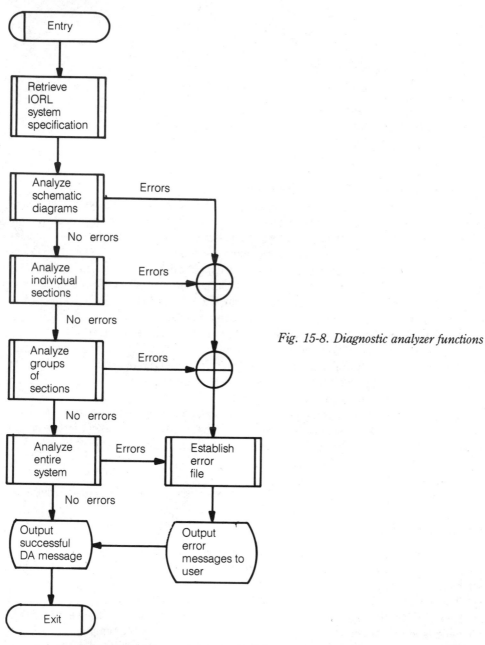

Fig. 15-8. Diagnostic analyzer functions

Another important feature of the simulation compiler is the use of functional input/ output macros for replacing the actual macros used in the system design. This capability provides input or receives output from a component-executing part of the simulation via a terminal or data file. This input or output replaces the communications the component normally would have with another component in the simulation. This feature allows special values of input to control the simulation or selected values of output to monitor the actual execution.

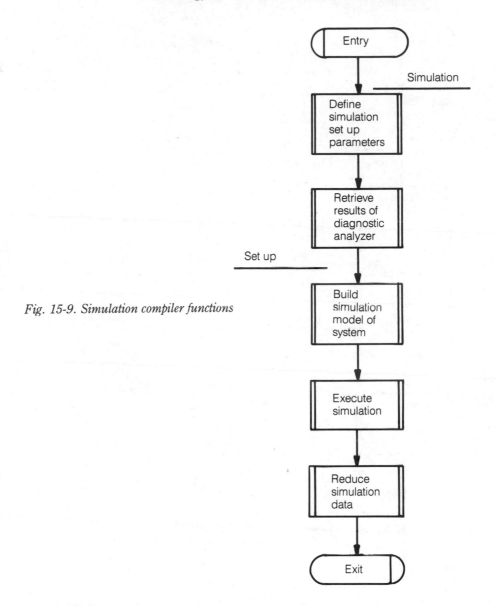

Fig. 15-9. Simulation compiler functions

Analysis library

An analysis library creates a data dictionary and maintains miniature specifications. The analysis library software package is a series of tools that extends insight into the system being developed, and provides you with the capability to examine and/or modify the IORL database. The functions of the analysis library are shown in FIG. 15-10.

The analysis library improves management visibility into the design database with the Audit tool, which provides a quantitative measure of the design progress. The Flow Analysis tool defines all of the system interfaces, and traces the system's hierarchical logic and component structure.

Other analysis library tools enhance the software engineer's effectiveness during

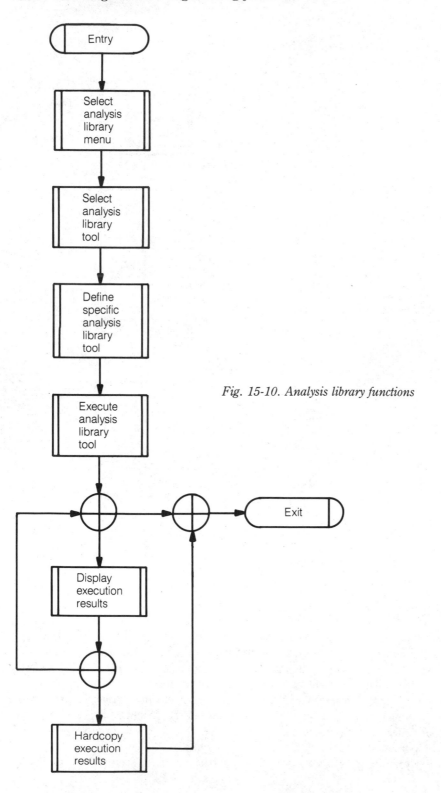

Fig. 15-10. Analysis library functions

the design process. The data dictionary tool provides an alphabetical list of variable definitions and associated references within a TAGS system. Entire systems, documents, or sections can be renamed, resequenced, copied, or merged from one system to another. Designs also can be moved between TAGS installations.

Document processor

A document processor produces and updates necessary technical documentations. The document processor allows you to develop standard publications in DOD-STD-2167A, NASA, and commercial formats. The functions of the document processor are shown in FIG. 15-11.

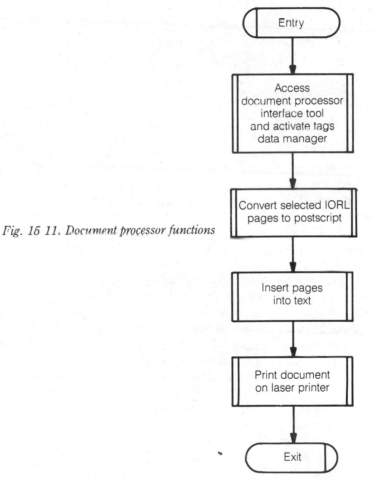

Fig. 15-11. Document processor functions

A TAGS document processor greatly reduces the time and effort to produce technical documentation of a system designed with IORL. Within a distributed workstation environment, you can create custom or standard format documents including text, illustrations, schematics, analysis displays, footnotes, references, table of contents, and index. As revisions to the design specification are made, the time-consuming task of updating the document is fully automated. The major components of the TAGS document processor include a text editor, graphics editor, and TAGS access.

At every stage of building a document, you can view the format, text, and graphics exactly as they will appear in the output.

Code generator

A code generator produces Ada source code and keeps track of IORL specifications to and from the code. Ada source code can be generated from any system that has successfully passed the TAGS diagnostic analyzer. The generator checks for syntax and construction errors in the design specification. Individual compilation units are produced for each IORL section in support of IORL's hierarchical design methodology. Code does not need to be produced for the entire system, but can be produced incrementally for each section to review implementation efficiency and optimization. An example of a code generator is shown in FIG. 15-12.

TECHNICAL DESCRIPTION

The entry point into the software process occurs during the development of an early specification. By using the IORL and the TAGS workstation, icons representing high-level components of a system can be assembled and interfaced with other icons that represent the environment of the system functions. These diagrams emphasize the identification of independent system components, their interfaces, and data flow, instead of control at this level. The system being developed is elaborated by stepwise refinement (functional decomposition). Predefined processes or stubs and control flow are incorporated into logic diagrams as the elaboration continues.

The assembled system model is treated as a prototype. The software tools supporting the TAGS system are used to make checks for syntactic and semantic correctness of the prototype. A static tool is used to check interfaces and proper use of the IORL language. A dynamic tool is used to simulate the behavior of the target system by exercising the prototype. A configuration management tool is also part of the support systems, as well as a natural language processing tool that catalogs requirements for traceability to the IORL design database. Finally, an automatic code generator is used to produce Ada code from the IORL model. Proceeding through the steps several times to make revisions as needed offers an opportunity to better understand the system being designed or maintained.

The method is well suited for the following applications:

- Embedded systems
- Process control
- Time-critical processing
- Real-time processing
- Scientific
- Engineering
- Distributed processing and networks
- Large-scale simulation and modeling

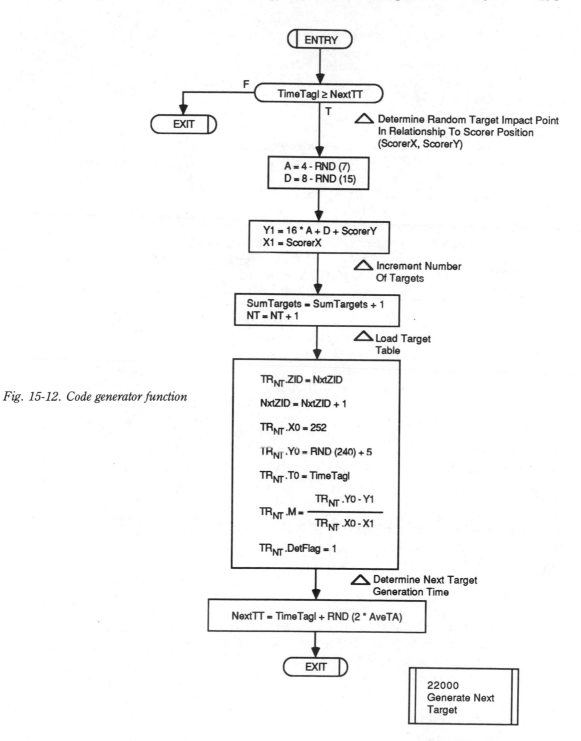

Fig. 15-12. Code generator function

ENTRY

TimeTagl ≥ NextTT   F

T

EXIT

△ Determine Random Target Impact Point
In Relationship To Scorer Position
(ScorerX, ScorerY)

$A = 4 - RND (7)$
$D = 8 - RND (15)$

$Y1 = 16 * A + D + ScorerY$
$X1 = ScorerX$

△ Increment Number
Of Targets

$SumTargets = SumTargets + 1$
$NT = NT + 1$

△ Load Target
Table

$TR_{NT}.ZID = NxtZID$

$NxtZID = NxtZID + 1$

$TR_{NT}.X0 = 252$

$TR_{NT}.Y0 = RND (240) + 5$

$TR_{NT}.T0 = TimeTagl$

$$TR_{NT}.M = \frac{TR_{NT}.Y0 - Y1}{TR_{NT}.X0 - X1}$$

$TR_{NT}.DetFlag = 1$

△ Determine Next Target
Generation Time

$NextTT = TimeTagl + RND (2 * AveTA)$

EXIT

22000
Generate Next
Target

Some of the examples of systems developed with the method are:

- Trident submarine program updates
- BM/C3 control centers for ballistic missile defense experiments
- E3 AWACS upgrade program
- Medical instrumentation systems

TAGS has been used in 21 to 50 organizations and has yielded 21 to 100 delivered systems. The method is intended for use on medium to large projects, but has been used on some small projects. Implementation languages most frequently used when coding systems developed with TAGS are Ada, C, and FORTRAN.

The method addresses timing constraints on the target system by embedding I/O definitions in each system component's control flow. Schematic block diagrams identify process parallelism, while controlled AND and OR constructs identify task concurrency. Probability of failure is specified on communications interfaces. Portability is assisted because TAGS formulates an implementation-independent design. With the generation of Ada, cross-compiling is accomplished for different target configurations.

Required textual modes of representation include a formal specification language and mathematical notation. Specified documentation templates are strongly encouraged. TAGS provides automated support for all of these modes. Data flow diagrams and control flow diagrams are required iconographical modes of representation.

The method has several rules for mapping one mode of representation to another. In particular, schematic block diagrams can be translated into hierarchical physical decomposition. Input/output relationships are mapped into hierarchical decomposition training diagrams and predefined process diagrams with recursion and reusability.

Transformation across phases of the software process is facilitated by decomposition and an elaborated system concept. All system functions are considered mathematical transformations with inputs and outputs. At the design level, these mathematical constructs are automatically inserted into Ada source code templates for simulation or target environments.

Rapid prototyping, simulation, and executable specifications essential to TAGS for clarifying system requirements and behavior. Required analysis and review techniques are data flow analysis, control flow analysis, facilitated application specification techniques, and change control board reviews.

The method assists with incorporating changes in the requirements by on-line requirements editing and analysis of subsequent ripple effects. Consistency is maintained among specification, design, or code by means of consistency checks with static and dynamic analysis tools. Ada code is automatically generated from the design.

TAGS predefined process diagrams can be placed into reusable libraries, which are at a higher level of design abstraction. Schematic block diagram and predefined process diagram trees identify recurrent logic areas.

MANAGEMENT ASPECTS

Through automation, configuration management transforms the formidable task of system management paperwork into a smooth and efficient operation of screen displays at the workstation. TAGS has specific procedures for addressing configuration management, which is provided with automated support. Automated support also exists for tracking a project's progress. Estimating initial cost, providing incremental data about expenditures, and tracking progress are all addressed as guidelines for accomplishing these activities.

The ability to manage IORL pages is another valuable storage and retrieval feature. With a combination of keyboard selection and cursor positioning, a multitude of functions can be performed.

Because of a hierarchical nature, system design is thoroughly manageable. The ability to maintain a constant management or system engineering overview, while manipulating smaller segments, is a powerful technique for implementating design modifications. Pages, sections, and even entire documents can be added or deleted without disrupting the overall system hierarchy. Thus, maintenance and revision capabilities are available for the entire system life cycle.

The inherent language traceability also provides excellent management. For example, the unique identification of each IORL page enables you to rapidly locate and arrange related diagrams and parameter tables.

Facilitation of communication within the development team is accomplished in several ways. First, interfaces are explicitly defined in one location between system components. Second, there is one universal unambiguous system design language that serves as a foundation for clear communication. Third, the actual design can be used for design walk-throughs and reviews. Finally, TAGS incorporates automated configuration management changes and revisions.

EASE OF ADOPTABILITY

Qualifications for a development team leader should be:

- Minimum of a Bachelor's degree
- Two years of development experience on one or more software systems
- Knowledge of one or more programming languages

TBE provides training assistance in many forms. Some of these are:

- Hands on demonstrations
- Overview presentations
- Classroom tutorials
- User manuals
- Toll-free telephone facilities
- On-site consultations
- Video tapes
- Seminars

TBE provides the presentations for learning TAGS: a one-day overview for management and a five-day overview for experienced developers.

At least $1^{1}/_{2}$ months is necessary for an experienced developer to reach the level of an expert TAGS user.

TAGS: EXAMPLE-1

A discrete Fourier Transform, shown in FIGS. 15-13, 15-14, and 15-15, where:

Nbr_of_sample is the total number of samples.
Samples n is the input (n = 1,2,. . .,512).
X k is the discrete frequency-domain
frequency (k = 1,2,. . .,256).
n = sample index (time index) (n = 1,2,. . .512)
k = freq bin index (freq index) (k = 1,2,. . .,256)

$= =$ See FIG. 15-13.

```
with TEXT_IO;
with OVER_OPS;
with BUILTINS;

package body AIR_PPT_PPD_420 is

    use TEXT_IO;
    use OVER_OPS;
    use BUILTINS;

    procedure AIR_PPD_420 is
    begin
            ASSIGN (c1, (2 * PI * (0.0, 1.0)) / nbr_of_samples);
            ASSIGN (c, e(c1));
            ASSIGN (k, 1);
            ASSIGN (x, zero_data);

    < <PAGE_1_SYMBOL_4> >
            if k > nbr_of_fr_bins then
                goto PAGE_1_SYMBOL_11;
            else
                goto PAGE_1_SYMBOL_10;
            end if;

    < <PAGE_1_SYMBOL_10> >
            ASSIGN (n,1);

    < <PAGE_1_SYMBOL_9> >
            if n > nbr_of_samples then
                goto PAGE_1_SYMBOL_8;
            else
                goto PAGE_1_SYMBOL_5;
            end if;

    < <PAGE_1_SYMBOL_5> >
            ASSIGN (x.value(k), x.value(k) + (c ** ((k − 1) * (n − 1)) *
            samples.value(n)));
            ASSIGN (n, n + 1);
            goto PAGE_1_SYMBOL_9;

    < <PAGE_1_SYMBOL_8> >
            ASSIGN (k, k + 1);
            goto PAGE_1_SYMBOL_4;

    < <PAGE_1_SYMBOL_11> >
            return;
    end AIR_PPD_420;

end AIR_PPT_PPD_420;
```

Ada CODE GENERATION ERROR LISTING
27-Apr-89 13:04:06.00

SYSTEM NAME: AIRASW

AREA OF CODE GENERATION: SINGLE SECTION
DOCUMENT NAME: AIR
SECTION NAME: PPD-420
MAP NAME: DEFAULT_MAP

LEVEL   MESSAGE

ERRORS FOUND IN

W   Unable to read SAT tree.

ERRORS FOUND IN AIR PPD-420

W   Identifier or Operator has no associated type. c1.
             PAGE: 1 SYMBOL: 1

W   Identifier or Operator has no associated type. nbr_of_samples.
             PAGE: 1 SYMBOL: 1

W   Identifier or Operator has no associated type. c.
             PAGE: 1 SYMBOL: 1

W   Identifier or Operator has no associated type. c1.
             PAGE: 1 SYMBOL: 1

W   Identifier or Operator has no associated type. k.
             PAGE: 1 SYMBOL: 1

W   Identifier or Operator has no associated type. x.
             PAGE: 1 SYMBOL: 1

W   Identifier or Operator has no associated type. zero_data.
             PAGE: 1 SYMBOL: 1

W   Identifier or Operator has no associated type. k.
             PAGE: 1 SYMBOL: 4

W   Identifier or Operator has no associated type. nbr_of_fr_bins.
             PAGE: 1 SYMBOL: 4

W   Identifier or Operator has no associated type. n.
             PAGE: 1 SYMBOL: 10

W   Identifier or Operator has no associated type. n.
             PAGE: 1 SYMBOL: 9

W   Identifier or Operator has no associated type. nbr_of_samples.
             PAGE: 1 SYMBOL: 9

W   Identifier or Operator has no associated type. x.
             PAGE: 1 SYMBOL: 5

W   Identifier or Operator has no associated type. value.
             PAGE: 1 SYMBOL: 5

W   Identifier or Operator has no associated type. k.
             PAGE: 1 SYMBOL: 5

W   Identifier or Operator has no associated type. x.
        PAGE: 1 SYMBOL: 5

W   Identifier or Operator has no associated type. value.
        PAGE: 1 SYMBOL: 5

W   Identifier or Operator has no associated type. k.
        PAGE: 1 SYMBOL: 5

W   Identifier or Operator has no associated type. c.
        PAGE: 1 SYMBOL: 5

W   Identifier or Operator has no associated type. k.
        PAGE: 1 SYMBOL: 5

W   Identifier or Operator has no associated type. n.
        PAGE: 1 SYMBOL: 5

W   Identifier or Operator has no associated type. samples.
        PAGE: 1 SYMBOL: 5

W   Identifier or Operator has no associated type. value.
        PAGE: 1 SYMBOL: 5

W   Identifier or Operator has no associated type. n.
        PAGE: 1 SYMBOL: 5

W   Identifier or Operator has no associated type. n.
        PAGE: 1 SYMBOL: 5

W   Identifier or Operator has no associated type. n.
        PAGE: 1 SYMBOL: 5

W   Identifier or Operator has no associated type. k.
        PAGE: 1 SYMBOL: 8

W   Identifier or Operator has no associated type. k.
        PAGE: 1 SYMBOL: 8

                     Ada CODE GENERATION COMPLETED SUCCESSFULLY
                         . = =See FIG. 15-14.

```
with TEXT_IO;
with OVER_OPS;
with BUILTINS;

package body AIR_PPT_PPD_491 is
    use TEXT_IO;
    use OVER_OPS;
    use BUILTINS;

    procedure AIR_PPD_491 is
    begin

            ASSIGN (k, 1);

    < <PAGE_1_SYMBOL_6> >
            if k >nbr_of_fr_bins then
                goto PAGE_1_SYMBOL_7;
            else
                goto PAGE_1_SYMBOL_9;
            end if;

    < <PAGE_1_SYMBOL_7> >
            return;
```

```
< <PAGE_1_SYMBOL_9> >
        ASSIGN (x, REAL(cartesian_data.value(k)));
        ASSIGN (y, IMAG(cartesian_data.value(k)));
        ASSIGN (polar_data.value(k).magnitude, NTH_ROOT(x * * 2 + y * * 2, 2));
        ASSIGN (polar_data.value(k).phase, ARCTAN(y / x));
        ASSIGN (k, k + 1);
        got PAGE_1_SYMBOL_6;

    end AIR_PPD_491;

end AIR_PPT_PPD_491;
```

= =See FIG. 15-15.

```
with TEXT_IO;
with OVER_OPS;
with BUILTINS;

package body AIR_PPT_PPD_490 is

    use TEXT_IO;
    use OVER_OPS;
    use BUILTINS;

    procedure AIR_PPD_490 is
    begin

        ASSIGN (j, 1);
        ASSIGN (k, 2);
    < <PAGE_1_SYMBOL_5> >
        if j > nbr_of_sp_lines − 1 then
          goto PAGE_1_SYMBOL_2;
        else
          goto PAGE_1_SYMBOL_11;
        end if;
    < <PAGE_1_SYMBOL_2> >
        return;
    < <PAGE_1_SYMBOL_11> >
        ASSIGN (spectro.value(j), spectro.value(k));
        ASSIGN (j, j + 1);
        ASSIGN (k, k + 1);
        goto PAGE_1_SYMBOL_5;

    end AIR_PPD_490;

end AIR_PPT_PPD_490;
```

TAGS: EXAMPLE-2

Greatest Common Denominator (GCD) is a small system composed of two components. Component 1, called "SYS," performs the calculations using a recursive approach (PPD-20). Component 2, called "USER_TERMINAL," is replaced by the user at the terminal providing input to the calculation component.

GCD_SYS demonstrates concurrency because this system calculates the greatest common denominators of two sets of numbers, not just one set of numbers. Using the "Fan-out AND" IORL construct (see PPD-10, Symbol 2), the calculations are done in parallel. Figures 15-16, 15-17, 15-18, 15-19, 15-20, 15-21, 15-22, and 15-23 are used for this GCD example.

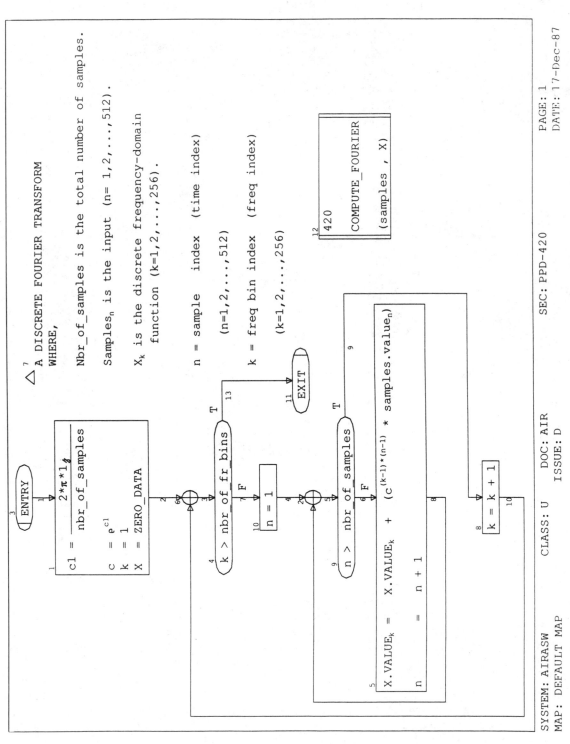

Fig. 15-13.

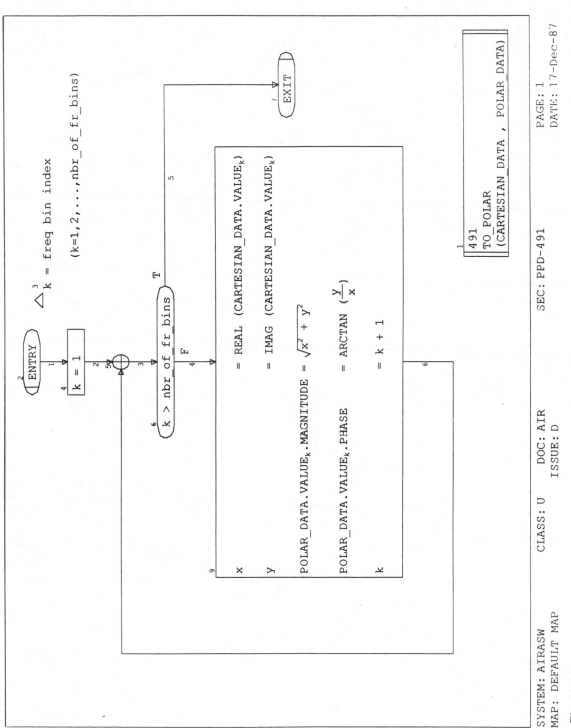

Fig. 15-14.

SYSTEM: AIRASW   CLASS: U   DOC: AIR   SEC: PPD-491   PAGE: 1
MAP: DEFAULT MAP   ISSUE: D   DATE: 17-Dec-87

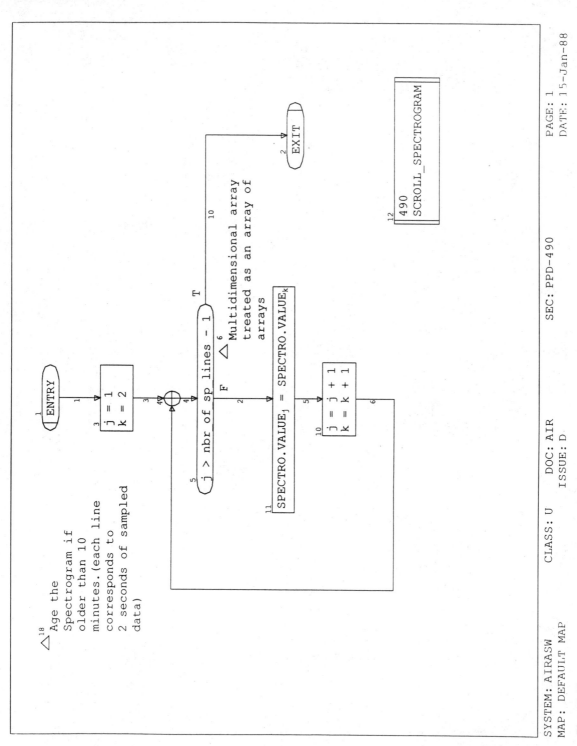

Fig. 15-15.

SYSTEM: AIRASW   CLASS: U   DOC: AIR   SEC: PPD-490   PAGE: 1
MAP: DEFAULT MAP   ISSUE: D   DATE: 15-Jan-88

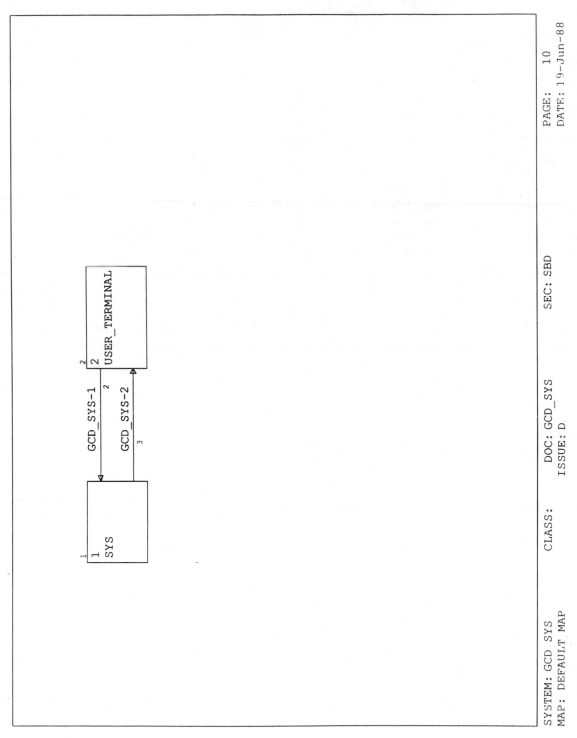

SYSTEM: GCD SYS   CLASS: DOC: GCD SYS   SEC: SBD   PAGE: 10
MAP: DEFAULT MAP   ISSUE: D   DATE: 19-Jun-88

Fig. 15-16.

GRP	PARAMETER DESCRIPTION (DIM)	NAME	VALUE RANGE	UNITS/VALUE MEANING
1	1 \<CONTROL GROUP\>	&XOFF	{TRUE , FALSE}	
2	2 \<GCD OPERANDS\>			
	3	A	I	
	4	B	I	
3	5 \<GCD OPERANDS\>			
	6	C	I	
	7	D	I	
4	8 \<CONTINUE SWITCH\>			
	9	&CONTINUE	{TRUE , FALSE}	
	10			

SYSTEM: GCD_SYS   CLASS: DOC: GCD_SYS   SEC: IOPT-1   PAGE: 10

MAP: DEFAULT MAP   ISSUE: D   DATE: 19-Jun-88

Fig. 15-17.

GRP	PARAMETER DESCRIPTION (DIM)	NAME	VALUE RANGE	UNITS/VALUE MEANING
1	1 <CONTROL GROUP>	&XOFF	{TRUE , FALSE}	
	2			
2	3 <GCD RESULT>	RESULT_1	I	
	4			
3	5 <GCD RESULT>	RESULT_2	I	
	6			
4	7 <QUERY 1>	$QUERY_1	"CONTINUE?"	
	8			

SYSTEM: GCD_SYS   CLASS: DOC: GCD_SYS   SEC: IOFT-2
MAP: DEFAULT_MAP   ISSUE: D

PAGE: 10
DATE: 19-Jun-88

Fig. 15-18.

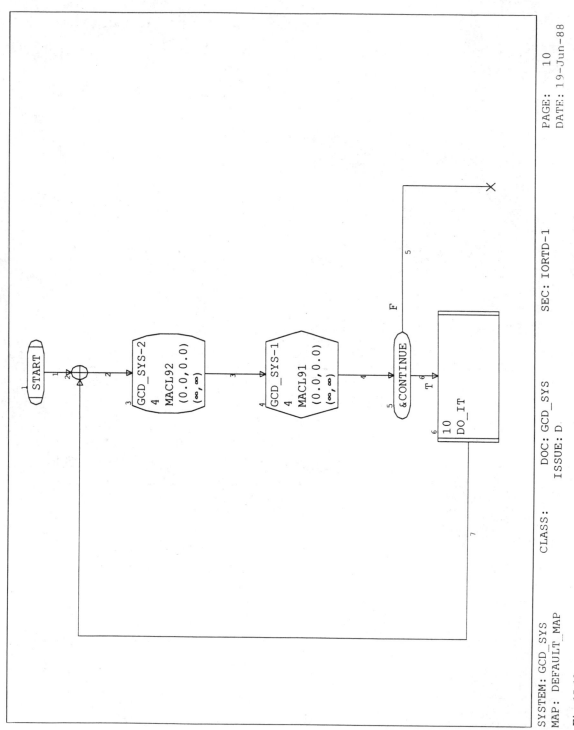

SYSTEM: GCD_SYS   CLASS: DOC: GCD_SYS   SEC: IORTD-1   PAGE: 10
MAP: DEFAULT_MAP   ISSUE: D.   DATE: 19-Jun-88

Fig. 15-19.

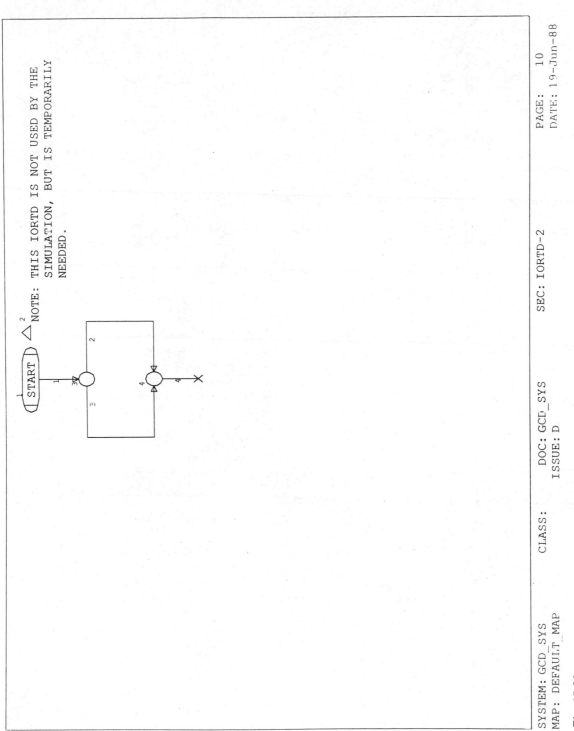

SYSTEM: GCD_SYS   CLASS: DOC: GCD_SYS   SEC: IORTD-2   PAGE: 10
MAP: DEFAULT_MAP   ISSUE: D   DATE: 19-Jun-88

Fig. 15-20.

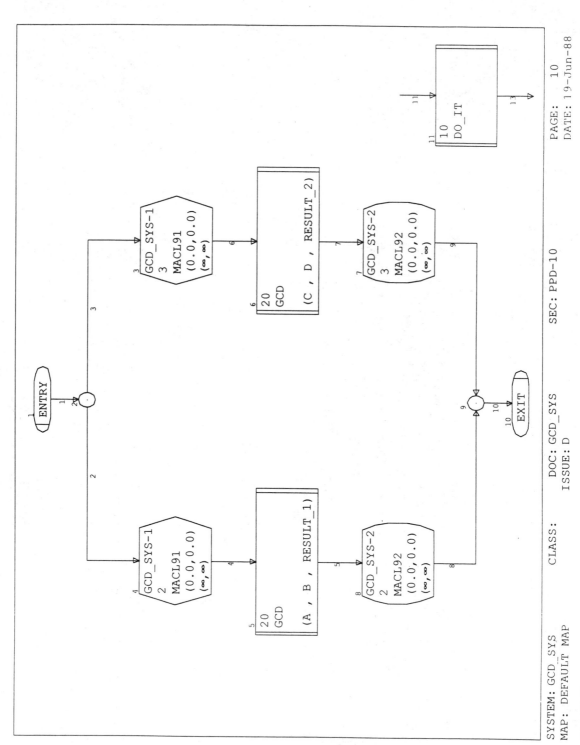

SYSTEM: GCD_SYS   CLASS: SEC: PPD-10   PAGE: 10
MAP: DEFAULT MAP   DOC: GCD_SYS   DATE: 19-Jun-88
                          ISSUE: D

Fig. 15-21.

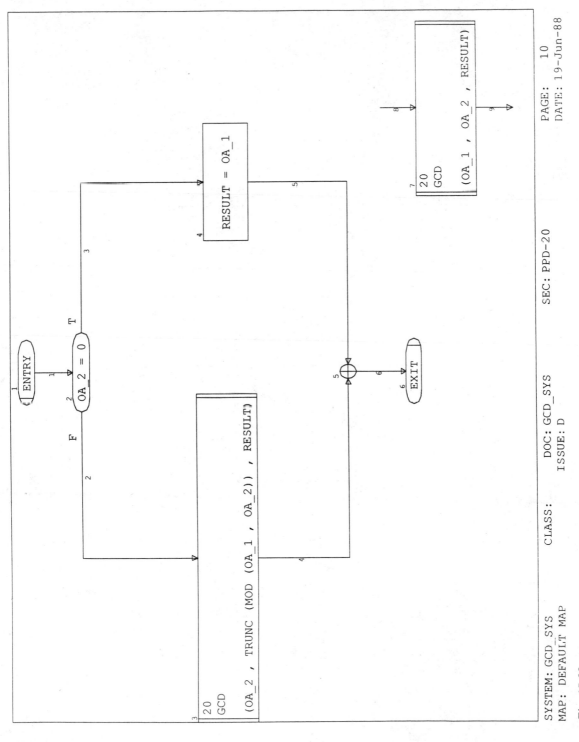

Fig. 15-22.

GRP	PARAMETER DESCRIPTION (DIM)	NAME	VALUE RANGE	UNITS/VALUE MEANING
1	OPERAND 1	OA_1	I	[INPUT]
2	OPERAND 2	OA_2	I	[INPUT]
3	RESULT	RESULT	I	[OUTPUT]

SYSTEM: GCD_SYS   CLASS: DOC: GCD_SYS   SEC: PPT-20   PAGE: 10
MAP: DEFAULT MAP   ISSUE: D   DATE: 19-Jun-88

Fig. 15-23.

Greatest common denominator

GCD_SYS is a small system composed of two components. Component 1, called "SYS," performs the calculations using a recursive approach (PPD-20). Component 2, called "USER_TERMINAL," is replaced by the user at the terminal providing input to the calculation component.

GCD_SYS demonstrates concurrency because this system calculates the greatest common denominator of two sets of numbers, not just of one set of numbers. Using the "Fan-out AND" IORL construct (see PPD-10, Symbol 2), the calculations are done in parallel.

IORL and the Simulation Compiler support recursive algorithms. GCD_SYS contains a recursive PPD which performs the calculations.

Two Functional Macros are resident in the TAGS Macro Library (MACL13 and MACL14). You can make inputs via the terminal screen for particular variables as the system is being simulated. You can also receive outputs via the terminal screen from the simulation program. In this way, you can monitor values interactively during the course of simulation. The following example demonstrates this capability:

* * USER IS QUERIED WHETHER OR NOT TO CONTINUE.

This program would seek to calculate indefinitely until you provide input to the simulation program to stop.

* * USER IS QUERIED TO INPUT TWO SETS OF NUMBERS.
* * RESULTS OF THE CALCULATIONS ARE OUTPUT TO THE TERMINAL.

```
with TEXT_IO;
with OVER_OPS;
with BUILTINS;
package body GCD_SYS_PPT_PPD_20 is
     use TEXT_IO;
     use OVER_OPS;
     use BUILTINS;
procedure GCD_SYS_PPD_20(oa_1_0          : in    LONG_INTEGER;
                         oa_2_0          :in     LONG_INTEGER;
                         result_0        :out    LONG_INTEGER) is
     begin

             if oa_2_0 = 0 then
                 goto PAGE_10_SYMBOL_4;
             else
                 goto PAGE_10_SYMBOL_3;
             end if;
     < <PAGE_10_SYMBOL_3> >
                 GCD_SYS_PPD_20(oa_2_0,   TRUNC(MODULO(oa_1_0,   oa_2_0)),
```

```
                        result_0);
        < <PAGE_10_SYMBOL_6> >
                    return;
        < <PAGE_10_SYMBOL_4> >
                    result_0 : = oa_1_0;
                    goto PAGE_10_SYMBOL_6;
        end GCD_SYS_PPD_20;
    end GCD_SYS_PPT_PPD_20;

    with DATA_TYPES;
    with INT_PKG;
    with GCD_SYS_IOPT_1, GCD_SYS_IOPT_2;
    package GCD_SYS_PPT_PPD_20 is
        use DATA_TYPES;
        use INT_PKG;
        use GCD_SYS_IOPT_1, GCD_SYS_IOPT_2;
    procedure GCD_SYS_PPD_20(oa_1_0          :in      LONG_INTEGER;
                             oa_2_0          :in      LONG_INTEGER;
                             result_0        :out     LONG_INTEGER);
    end GCD_SYS_PPT_PPD_20;

    with DATA_TYPES;
    with INT_PKG;
    with GCD_SYS_IOPT_1, GCD_SYS_IOPT_2;
    package GCD_SYS_PPT_PPD_10 is
        use DATA_TYPES;
        use INT_PKG;
        use GCD_SYS_IOPT_1, GCD_SYS_IOPT_2;
            procedure GCD_SYS_PPD_10;

    end GCD_SYS_PPT_PPD_10;

    with TEXT_IO;
    with OVER_OPS;
    with BUILTINS;
    with GCD_SYS_PPT_PPD_20;
    package body GCD_SYS_PPT_PPD_10 is
        use TEXT_IO;
        use OVER_OPS;
        use BUILTINS;
        use GCD_SYS_PPT_PPD_20;

    type TASK_PAGE_10_SYMBOL_2_CONNECTOR_2_NEXT_CALL_TYPE is
        (ACTIVE,
        START_TASKS_PAGE_10_SYMBOL_9_NEXT,
        TERM);
```

```
type TASK_PAGE_10_SYMBOL_2_CONNECTOR_3_NEXT_CALL_TYPE is
    (ACTIVE,
    START_TASKS_PAGE_10_SYMBOL_9_NEXT,
    TERM);
TASK_PAGE_10_SYMBOL_2_CONNECTOR_2_NEXT_CALL : TASK_PAGE
_10_SYMBOL_2_CONNECTOR_2_NEXT_CALL_TYPE : = ACTIVE;
    TASK_PAGE_10_SYMBOL_2_CONNECTOR_3_NEXT_CALL : TASK_
PAGE_10_SYMBOL_2_CONNECTOR_3_NEXT_CALL_TYPE : = ACTIVE;
task type TASK_PAGE_10_SYMBOL_2_CONNECTOR_2_TYPE is
    entry task entry;
end TASK_PAGE_10_SYMBOL_2_CONNECTOR_2_TYPE;
task type TASK_PAGE_10_SYMBOL_2_CONNECTOR_3_TYPE is
    entry task entry;
end TASK_PAGE_10_SYMBOL_2_CONNECTOR_3_TYPE;
task type TASK_PAGE_10_SYMBOL_9_CONNECTOR_10_TYPE is
    entry task entry;
end TASK_PAGE_10_SYMBOL_9_CONNECTOR_10_TYPE;
task body TASK_PAGE_10_SYMBOL_2_CONNECTOR_2_TYPE is
begin
        loop
            accept task_entry;
            - -GCD_SYS_MACL_91("GCD_SYS-1", 2, 0.0, 0.0, INFINITY,
            INFINITY);
            GCD_SYS_PPD_20 (a_0, b_0, result_1_0);
            - -GCD_SYS_MACL_92("GCD_SYS-2", 2, 0.0, 0.0, INFINITY,
            INFINITY);
            TASK PAGE_10_SYMBOL_2_CONNECTOR_2_NEXT_CALL : =
            START_TASKS_PAGE_10_SYMBOL_9_NEXT;
        end loop;
end TASK_PAGE_10_SYMBOL_2_CONNECTOR_2_TYPE;
task body TASK_PAGE_10_SYMBOL_2_CONNECTOR_3_TYPE is
begin
        loop
            accept task entry;
            - -GCD_SYS_MACL_91("GCD_SYS-1", 3, 0.0, 0.0, INFINITY,
            INFINITY);
            GCD_SYS_PPD_20(c_0, d_0, result_2_0);
            - -GCD_SYS_MACL_92("GCD_SYS-2", 3, 0.0, 0.0, INFINITY,
            INFINITY);
            TASK_PAGE_10_SYMBOL_2_CONNECTOR_3_NEXT_CALL : =
            START_TASKS_PAGE_10_SYMBOL_9_NEXT;
        end loop;
end TASK_PAGE_10_SYMBOL_2_CONNECTOR_3_TYPE;
task body TASK_PAGE_10_SYMBOL_9_CONNECTOR_10_TYPE is
begin
```

```
            loop
                accept task_entry;
            end loop;
    end TASK_PAGE_10_SYMBOL_9_CONNECTOR_10_TYPE;
    task GCD_SYS_PPD_10_TASK_CONTROL_PAGE_10_SYMBOL_2 is
        entry task entry;
    end GCD_SYS_PPD_10_TASK_CONTROL_PAGE_10_SYMBOL_2;
    task body GCD_SYS_PPD_10_TASK_CONTROL_PAGE_10_SYMBOL_2 is
    TASK_PAGE_10_SYMBOL_2_CONNECTOR_2 : TASK_PAGE_10_
SYMBOL_2_CONNECTOR_2_TYPE;
    TASK_PAGE_10_SYMBOL_2_CONNECTOR_3 : TASK_PAGE_10_
SYMBOL_2_CONNECTOR_3_TYPE;
    TASK_PAGE_10_SYMBOL_9_CONNECTOR_10 : TASK_PAGE_10_
SYMBOL_9_CONNECTOR_10_TYPE;
    begin
accept task entry;
TASK_PAGE_10_SYMBOL_2_CONNECTOR_2.task_entry;
TASK_PAGE_10_SYMBOL_2_CONNECTOR_3.task_entry;
loop
                exit  when  TASK_PAGE_10_SYMBOL_2_CONNECTOR_3_NEXT-
                        _CALL = TERM and
                        TASK_PAGE_10_SYMBOL_2_CONNECTOR_2_NEXT_CALL
                        = TERM;
                case  TASK_PAGE_10_SYMBOL_2_CONNECTOR_3_NEXT_CALL
                    is
                        when START_TASKS_PAGE_10_SYMBOL_9_NEXT = >
                            TASK_PAGE_10_SYMBOL_2_CONNECTOR_3_NEXT_CALL
                            : = TERM;
                            TASK_PAGE_10_SYMBOL_9_CONNECTOR_10.task_entry;
                        when ACTIVE | TERM = >
                            NULL;
                end case;
                case  TASK_PAGE_10_SYMBOL_2_CONNECTOR_2_NEXT_CALL
                    is
                        when START_TASKS_PAGE_10_SYMBOL_9_NEXT = >
                            TASK_PAGE_10_SYMBOL_2_CONNECTOR_2_NEXT_CALL
                            : = TERM;
                            TASK_PAGE_10_SYMBOL_9_CONNECTOR_10.task_entry;
                        when ACTIVE | TERM = >
                            NULL;
                end case;
            end loop;
    end GCD_SYS_PPD_10_TASK_CONTROL_PAGE_10_SYMBOL_2;
    procedure GCD_SYS_PPD_10 is
    begin
```

```
        G C D _ S Y S _ P P D _ 1 0 _ T A S K _ C O N T R O L _ P A G E _ 1 0 _ S Y M -
BOL_2.task_entry;
    end GCD_SYS_PPD_10;
end GCD_SYS_PPT_PPD_10;
    task body TASK_PAGE_10_SYMBOL_4_CONNECTOR_4_TYPE is
    begin
            loop
                accept task entry;
            end loop;
    end TASK_PAGE_10_SYMBOL_4_CONNECTOR_4_TYPE;
    task GCD_SYS_IORTD_2_TASK_CONTROL_PAGE_10_SYMBOL_3 is
        entry task entry;
    end GCD_SYS_IORTD_2_TASK_CONTROL_PAGE_10_SYMBOL_3;
    task body GCD_SYS_IORTD_2_TASK_CONTROL_PAGE_10_SYMBOL_3 is
    TASK_PAGE_10_SYMBOL_3_CONNECTOR_2 : TASK_PAGE_10_
SYMBOL_3_CONNECTOR_2_TYPE;
    TASK_PAGE_10_SYMBOL_3_CONNECTOR_3 : TASK_PAGE_10_
SYMBOL_3_CONNECTOR_3_TYPE;
    TASK_PAGE_10_SYMBOL_4_CONNECTOR_4 : TASK_PAGE_10_
SYMBOL_4_CONNECTOR_4_TYPE;
    begin
accept task entry;
TASK_PAGE_10_SYMBOL_3_CONNECTOR_2.task_entry;
TASK_PAGE_10_SYMBOL_3_CONNECTOR_3.task_entry;
            loop
                exit   when   TASK  PAGE_10_SYMBOL_3_CONNECTOR_3_NEXT-
                        _CALL = TERM and
                        TASK_PAGE_10_SYMBOL_3_CONNECTOR_2_NEXT_CALL
                        = TERM;
                case  TASK_PAGE_10_SYMBOL_3_CONNECTOR_3_NEXT_CALL
                    is
                    when START_TASKS_PAGE_10_SYMBOL_4_NEXT = >
                        TASK_PAGE_10_SYMBOL_3_CONNECTOR_3_NEXT_CALL
                        : = TERM;
                        TASK_PAGE_10_SYMBOL_4_CONNECTOR_4.task_entry;
                    when ACTIVE | TERM = >
                        NULL;
                end case;
                case  TASK_PAGE_10_SYMBOL_3_CONNECTOR_2_NEXT_CALL
                    is
                    when START_TASKS_PAGE_10_SYMBOL_4_NEXT = >
                        TASK_PAGE_10_SYMBOL_3_CONNECTOR_2_NEXT_CALL
                        : = TERM;
                        TASK_PAGE_10_SYMBOL_4_CONNECTOR_4.task_entry;
                    when ACTIVE | TERM = >
```

```
                              NULL;
              end case;
          end loop;
    end GCD_SYS_IORTD_2_TASK_CONTROL_PAGE_10_SYMBOL_3;
    procedure GCD_SYS_IORTD_2 is
    task TASK_GCD_SYS_IORTD_2 is
        entry task entry;
    end TASK_GCD_SYS_IORTD_2;
    task body TASK_GCD_SYS_IORTD_2 is
    begin

            accept task entry;
            GCD_SYS_IORTD_2_TASK_CONTROL_PAGE_10_SYMBOL_3.task_entry;
    end TASK_GCD_SYS_IORTD_2;
    begin
            TASK_GCD_SYS_IORTD_2.task_entry;
    end GCD_SYS_IORTD_2;
end GCD_SYS_IPT_IORTD_2;
with DATA_TYPES;
with INT_PKG;
with GCD_SYS_IOPT_1, GCD_SYS_IOPT_2;
package GCD_SYS_IPT_IORTD_2 is
    use DATA_TYPES;
    use INT_PKG;
    use GCD_SYS_IOPT_1, GCD_SYS_IOPT_2;
    procedure GCD_SYS_IORTD_2;
end GCD_SYS_IPT_IORTD_2;
with TEXT_IO;
with OVER_OPS;
with BUILTINS;
package body GCD_SYS_IPT_IORTD_2 is
    use TEXT_IO;
    use OVER_OPS;
    use BUILTINS;
    type TASK_PAGE_10_SYMBOL_3_CONNECTOR_2_NEXT_CALL_TYPE is
        (ACTIVE,
        START_TASKS_PAGE_10_SYMBOL_4_NEXT,
        TERM);
    type TASK_PAGE_10_SYMBOL_3_CONNECTOR_3_NEXT_CALL_TYPE is
        (ACTIVE,
        START_TASKS_PAGE_10_SYMBOL_4_NEXT,
        TERM);
    TASK_PAGE_10_SYMBOL_3_CONNECTOR_2_NEXT_CALL : TASK_PAGE
```

```
_10_SYMBOL_3_CONNECTOR_2_NEXT_CALL_TYPE : = ACTIVE;
    TASK_PAGE_10_SYMBOL_3_CONNECTOR_3_NEXT_CALL : TASK_PAGE
_10_SYMBOL_3_CONNECTOR_3_NEXT_CALL_TYPE : = ACTIVE;
    task type TASK_PAGE_10_SYMBOL_3_CONNECTOR_2_TYPE is
        entry task entry;
    end TASK_PAGE_10_SYMBOL_3_CONNECTOR_2_TYPE;
    task type TASK_PAGE_10_SYMBOL_3_CONNECTOR_3_TYPE is
        entry task entry;
    end TASK_PAGE_10_SYMBOL_3_CONNECTOR_3_TYPE;
    task type TASK_PAGE_10_SYMBOL_4_CONNECTOR_4_TYPE is
        entry task entry;
    end TASK_PAGE_10_SYMBOL_4_CONNECTOR_4_TYPE;
    task body TASK_PAGE_10_SYMBOL_3_CONNECTOR_2_TYPE is
    begin
            loop
                accept task entry;
                TASK_PAGE_10_SYMBOL_3_CONNECTOR_2_NEXT_CALL : =
                START_TASKS_PAGE_10_SYMBOL_4_NEXT;
            end loop;
    end TASK_PAGE_10_SYMBOL_3_CONNECTOR_2_TYPE;
    task body TASK_PAGE_10_SYMBOL_3_CONNECTOR_3_TYPE is
    begin
            loop
                accept task entry;
                TASK_PAGE_10_SYMBOL_3_CONNECTOR_3_NEXT_CALL : =
                START_TASKS_PAGE_10_SYMBOL_4_NEXT;
            end loop;
    end TASK_PAGE_10_SYMBOL_3_CONNECTOR_3_TYPE;
with DATA_TYPES;
with INT_PKG;
with GCD_SYS_IOPT_1, GCD_SYS_IOPT_2;
package GCD_SYS_IPT_IORTD_1 is
    use DATA_TYPES;
    use INT_PKG;
    use GCD_SYS_IOPT_1, GCD_SYS_IOPT_2;
    procedure GCD_SYS_IORTD_1;
end GCD_SYS_IPT_IORTD_1;
with TEXT_IO;
with OVER_OPS;
with BUILTINS;
with GCD_SYS_PPT_PPD_10;
package body GCD_SYS_IPT_IORTD_1 is
    use TEXT_IO;
    use OVER_OPS;
```

```
use BUILTINS;
use GCD_SYS_PPT_PPD_10;
procedure GCD_SYS_IORTD_1 is
task TASK_GCD_SYS_IORTD_1 is
    entry task entry;
end TASK_GCD_SYS_IORTD_1;
task body TASK_GCD_SYS_IORTD_1 is
begin
        accept task_entry;
< <PAGE_10_SYMBOL_3> >
        - -GCD_SYS_MACL_92("GCD_SYS-2", 4, 0.0, 0.0, INFINITY, INFIN-
        ITY);
        - -GCD_SYS_MACL_91("GCD_SYS-1", 4, 0.0, 0.0, INFINITY, INFIN-
        ITY);
            if Bcontinue then
                goto PAGE_10_SYMBOL_6;
            else
                goto TASK_TERMINATION;
            end if;
< <PAGE_10_SYMBOL_6> >
        GCD_SYS_PPD_10;
        goto PAGE_10_SYMBOL_3;
< <TASK_TERMINATION> >
        NULL;
end TASK_GCD_SYS_IORTD_1;
begin
        TASK_GCD_SYS_IORTD_1.task_entry;
end GCD_SYS_IORTD_1;
end GCD_SYS_IPT_IORTD_1;
with DATA_TYPES;
with INT_PKG;

package GCD_SYS_IOPT_2 is
    use DATA_TYPES;
    use INT_PKG;

    Squery_1: constant IORL_STRING := "CONTINUE?";
    Bxoff: BOOLEAN;
    result_1_0: LONG_INTEGER;
    result_2_0: LONG_INTEGER;
end GCD_SYS_IOPT_2;

with DATA_TYPES;
with INT_PKG;

package GCD_SYS_IOPT_1 is
```

```
        use DATA_TYPES;
        use INT_PKG;

        Bcontinue: BOOLEAN;
        Bxoff: BOOLEAN;
        a_0: LONG_INTEGER;
        b_0: LONG_INTEGER;
        c_0: LONG_INTEGER;
        d_0: LONG_INTEGER;
end GCD_SYS_IOPT_1;
```

16

Language-dependent methods

This chapter starts with Program Design Language, a method that commonly uses structured English in the detailed design phase. The method stresses development of a complete design before any code is written. Next, a commercially available Byron method for Ada is presented. Finally, fourth-generation and fifth-generation languages are discussed.

PROGRAM DESIGN LANGUAGE

A Program Design Language (PDL) is used during the detailed design phase of software engineering. PDL creates a structured design with commonly understood terms and concepts. It is accompanied by documenting the detail design.

The complete detail design defines all external and internal interfaces, error situations, global data, and control blocks. Detailed design also identifies all procedures and procedure calls. It specifies the processing algorithms of all procedures, which are:

- Interfaces
- Error situations
- Global data
- Control blocks
- Procedures
- Procedure calls
- Processing algorithms

PDL is a textual language that is precise enough to describe software, yet expressive enough for design. It provides a vehicle for communicating and supporting various activities of the software engineering life cycle. The main features of PDL are:

- Precise
- Analyzable

- Verifiable
- Supports various methodologies and methods
- Understandable

A PDL is also a design tool that supports many methods and methodologies. It encourages conceptualization at a high level and standardizes communication. PDL is based on the concept of pseudo-code and includes logical structured statements that are easily understandable to the software engineer. It is distinct from the implementation language, and it supplements detail design graphics like flow charts. Some standards for software engineering are mandatory to use PDL. The goals of PDL are to achieve formalism and uniformity for a programming language. It also follows modularity, structuring, and abstraction like a high-level language. PDL supports information hiding and separation of concerns. The fundamental advantages of PDL are:

- Increase in productivity
- Improve software quality
- Minimize risks while developing and maintaining software

PDL enhances productivity because most of the PDL's are readable by the computer. There are many automated tools available that can check a PDL for completeness, consistency, and conformance to standards. PDL is also defined as a common language, which enhances communications within a software engineering project.

PDL improves software quality by aiding communications and verifications. This scheme facilitates early detection and correction of errors. PDL generates a mechanism for verifying design and translation of the design notation.

PDL minimizes the risks that are involved during development, and maintains software by making design more visible. It increases communication among members of the software development team. PDL makes implementing a programming language easier for the programmers.

A PDL addresses the characteristics of the methodology, such as expressive power, human factors, and analyzability. It also addresses the relationship of the PDL and implementation language, the impact of using tools, and implementation considerations. PDL should not be considered as a coding tool, but is still a part of the design phase. PDL is still not compilable for many implementing languages.

Ada goes further than most high-level languages by structuring information in a useful and comprehensive fashion:

- Modularity and separate compilation
- Powerful data abstraction
- Information hiding
- Generics
- Exception handling

Ada is a design language as well as an implementation language. It focuses on providing information for implementing a program. The BYRON PDL focuses on providing information about a program unit's purpose.

BYRON

Byron is an Ada PDL and a document generator. It provides a means to make comments for Ada programs (following Ada commenting conventions), which provides more information that it is not expressible in Ada. This information is stored in a database with the source code. From the database, an unlimited variety of reports can be automatically generated, including documentations of DOD-STD-2167A. Several predefined document templates are provided and the Template Language is also provided for tailoring.

Byron is an extension of Ada (MIL-STD-1815A). It consists of a single source file that contains Ada source code and comments. A document generator is included with predefined templates and template language. It does extensive program library management, including revision control.

Byron improves design and engineering productivity. It is flexible and accommodates a variety of design methods. It aids configuration management, providing uniform means of expression. Byron reduces cost by reusing software. It utilizes automatic report production, including DOD standards and saves time maintaining documents.

Figure 16-1 shows the major components of Byron. Byron Analyzer checks Ada syntax and semantics, as well as Byron constructs. If no errors are detected, the analyzer stores an internal representation of the source file in a program library. The analyzer enforces the collection of information with keywords and phase checking. Phase checking is used to enforce the inclusion of comments at a given phase of program development. The phases are prototype, specification, design, implementation, test, and maintenance. When the source file is analyzed, a phase can be passed to the analyzer, which will determine if the Byron PDL directives required at that phase are present in the code. If there are no directives in that phase, then warning messages will be produced. The analyzer also assists in maintaining a standard style of documenting programs.

The Program Library stores the results of the analyzer, shown in FIG. 16-2. It facilitates the organization of information in a manner that keeps it close to the source code. The Program Library Manager supports configuration management by generating, building, and releasing software. The library tracks multiple versions of software. It can create any version, and ensures that changes are made to the appropriate version. The library also prevents multiple concurrent updates, and provides tracing of recompilation dependencies. The program library helps determine what needs to be retested after changes are made to the program.

The Byron Document Generator creates the user manual, data dictionary, dependency table, and CallTree reports. The user manual generates a report from Ada specifications that describes how to use a set of packages or procedures in the program library. The data dictionary describes types, objects, subprograms, packages, tasks, and entries or any combination in a selected set of program units. The dependency table generates a report that shows direct or indirect dependencies among library units. The dependency level can be set by the user. CallTree generates a report that shows the following calls of subprograms:

- Calls
- Called by
- Indirect calls
- Indirect called by

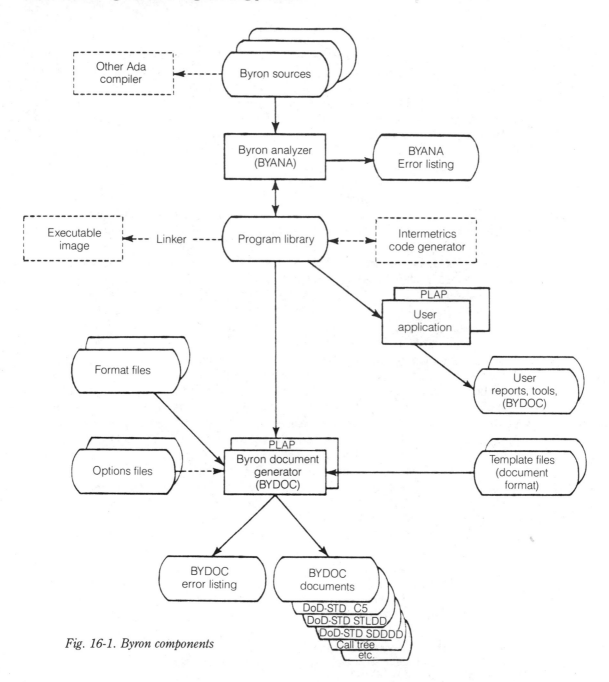

Fig. 16-1. Byron components

These calls are optional. CallTree includes subprograms, which are called at elaboration and run-time. The depth of lexically nested program units and the CallTree (Call Depth) can be specified by the user. Synopsis is used in this document, so each procedure and function will be described briefly in the CallTree. A sample CallTree is presented in FIG. 16-3.

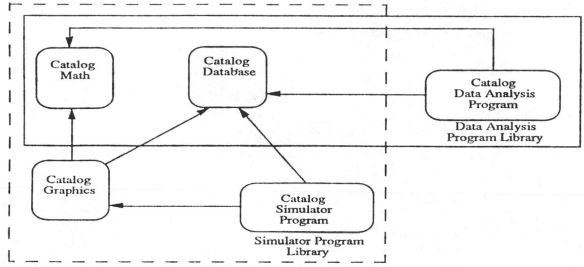

Fig. 16-2. Program library

Calls:
    AtLeastTwoElements (in Sort.QuickSort)
        Is section non-trivial? True if 2 or more elements
    SortSection (in Sort.QuickSort)
        Sort a section of the array.
        Recursive
    Split (in Sort.QuickSort)
        Divide section into two subsections.

Indirectly Calls:
    AtLeastTwoElements (in Sort.QuickSort)
        Is section non-trivial? True if 2 or more elements
    SortSection (in Sort.QuickSort)
        Sort a section of the array.
    Split (in Sort.QuickSort)
        Divide section into two subsections.

Fig. 16-3. Sample calltree

Called By:
    QuickSort (in Sort)
        QuickSort of an array.
    SortSection (in Sort.QuickSort)
        Sort a section of the array.
        Recursive

Indirectly Called By:
    QuickSort (in Sort)
        QuickSort of an array.
    SortSection (in Sort.QuickSort)

A general purpose document generator allows you to define your own document format, as well as provide templates for the DOD defined documents. It retrieves information from the program library in many useful forms.

```
procedure SortSection        − −   Sort a section of the array.
    Low,                     − −   Start of section.
    High: IndexType          − −   End of section.
) is

    − −   REQUIRES
    − −   Low must be less than High.

    − −   EFFECTS
    − −   SortSection sorts one section of the array.
    − −   from Low to High, into ascending order.

    − −   ERROR_HANDLING
    − −   Error handling for SortSection

    − −   DATA_CONVERSION
    − −   Data conversion for SortSection

    − −   UTILIZATION
    − −   Utilization for SortSection

    − −   LOGIC_FLOW
    − −   Logic flow for SortSection

Middle:          − −   New median of this section.

                 − −   REPRESENTATION
                 − −   Positive

                 − −   SIZE
                 − −   2 Words

                 − −   MEASURE
                 5 msecs

                 IndexType;

begin

    − − Divide this section into subsections.             —
    Split (Low, High, Middle);
                                                          —
    − − Sort the left subsection (if not trivally sorted);  —
    if AtLeastTwoElements (Low, Middle) then
        SortSection (Low, Middle − 1);                    —
    end if;
                                                          —
    − − Sort the right subsection (if not trivally sorted).  —
    if AtLeastTwoElements (Middle, High) then
        SortSection (Middle + 1, High);                   —
    end if;

end SortSection;
```

Fig. 16-4. Byron PDL input sample

A sample Byron PDL input is presented in FIG. 16-4. The method can be easily automated and incorporated in an integrated environment, or it can provide a framework for customizing the software development process with the use of other methods and tools.

FOURTH-GENERATION LANGUAGES

Fourth-generation languages (4GL) are advanced languages that make prototyping possible. These languages are used for creating the design phase directly, instead of going through all the other phases of software engineering. The 4GL enable the development of programs in a short time rather than the typical high-level languages, such as COBOL, Basic, and FORTRAN. 4GL have been in existence in the computer industry for the last decade. The evolvement of nonprocedural languages is shown in FIG. 16-5.

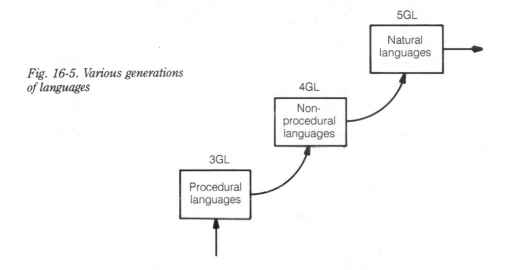

Fig. 16-5. Various generations of languages

This generation of languages can be used by application professionals as well as end users. File definitions are not written, nor are other rules of syntax that are required by procedural languages. Thus, a few lines can be written in a 4GL that are very flexible. A 4GL increases productivity in software engineering.

Many third-generation languages inaugurated the use of English-like language and syntax for programming computers. This use resulted in an improved man-to-computer relationship.

A single statement in a 3GL results in many machine code commands. A 3GL is procedural and requires logic and sequence of commands.

A 4GL enhances the interface from the design phase of software development, which provides a new tool for professionals to design, compile, install, and maintain complex applications. 4GL's are more natural and conducive to human thoughts.

A 4GL uses procedural words and terms to control the execution of a program and the system's interaction with inputs and outputs. 4GL are commonly used for data definition languages, data dictionaries, complete database management systems, and query languages. Their significance is a friendlier, more human-like interface with the user. A natural human language is used for describing, executing, or requesting the process of specific data.

A 4GL presents characteristics of portability, flexibility, and maintainability. These characteristics are the key attributes that let 4GL transcend the need for regulatory standards. 4GL also foster applications that can be ported across various hardware platforms by supporting multiple distributed processing systems and other design systems that access enormous numbers of data elements and relationships.

Portability brings an application or database across a different processing environment, which creates data access, processing cycles and times, and training. Standardizing open architectures in systems development and design is necessary to allow for the portability of 4GL and database management systems (DBMS).

Flexibility provides easy integration with new or existing applications, databases and hardware platforms. Products are available that are database independent, which allows the database to be accessed for specific or unique inquiries, regardless of the DBMS. A 4GL can be employed to manipulate, query, and build on system needs.

Maintainability is possible in 4GL because of the natural ability that software engineers, programmers, systems managers, and database managers have to work with these languages. 4GL maintain their information base, prevent loss of data, enhance data access, and enhance definition, which ensures its survival across varying environments.

A 4GL provides a new way to look at logical programming. It enables nonprofessionals and end users to design and write programs. 4GL help develop quick prototypes for applications. Most 4GL are interpreted rather than compiled, which means each line is checked for errors as it is written, rather than compile the whole program at once.

There is no standard in existence in the computer industry for a 4GL. There is a need for conversion schema from existing conventional languages to a 4GL for a huge inventory of software.

Merging 4GL with CASE tools has resulted in the development of fifth-generation languages.

FIFTH-GENERATION LANGUAGES

Fifth-generation languages (5GL) are *natural languages*, still in research form. These languages will closely resemble everyday human languages, and will include a very large vocabulary like most human languages. 5GL will also include the inconsistent syntax, idioms, and general ambiguity of human languages. Natural languages might be used to give instructions to a computer.

The research of natural languages is an important part of a larger field of research known as *Artificial Intelligence* (AI). There are many definitions of this field, but in general it may be thought of as the building of computer hardware and software systems that exhibit the same type of intelligence as humans. This intelligence includes listening, reading, speaking, solving problems, making inferences, and thinking.

17

Object-oriented design methods

This chapter covers the evolving object-oriented software methods: object-oriented programming and object-oriented design. The object-oriented software development method is receiving wide acceptance as standard technology within the software industry. This new technology changes the nature of software analysis and design as an industrial process. Software products can be developed similar to hardware products. Object-oriented programming changes from writing instructions to interconnecting reusable software components. In the future, a system engineer will be equipped with a component catalog. The components with which you interconnect can be reached for higher-level products—application products or other specialized components.

OBJECT-ORIENTED PROGRAMMING

Object-oriented thinking started with Simula 67 and SmallTalk efforts in the 1960's. Object-oriented programming was first discussed in Norway in the early 70's in connection with Simula language. In existence there are now object-oriented languages, operating systems, user interfaces, and databases. Covering the limited bases of Object-Oriented Programming is the scope of this book.

OOP method

Object-Oriented Programming (OOP) is a method for addressing difficult programming problems. OOP considers systems as independent objects that interact and operate on their components. Objects will be defined properly in OOD. Actions are made to objects and actions are taken by objects that communicate by messages. Actions taken within an object is hidden from the user. The only interface seen is the resulting message from the object.

OOP is a change of mindset. It considers the world as objects that can act. An object can take actions and have actions taken against them. Objects, from a very high-level view, are entities that exist uniquely in time and space. In other words, objects have a state, and are characterized by the actions they perform on other objects and by actions performed on them.

Objects can function as actors, agents, and servers, depending on their relationship to other objects. Actors operate on other objects, servers are only operated on, and agents perform operations on the behalf of other objects. Objects in OOP must communicate. The communication requirement helps with data hiding and gives an object-oriented language, such as C^{++}, SmallTalk, and Ada, the ability to treat objects as *black boxes*. In the application sense, objects are combinations of data and code.

Existing data structures are inherently part of an object. The attributes of one class might be inherited by any object or class and defined with the previously defined class, including any methods that are defined as part of the class.

Inheritance can form a change that gives the most recently defined class all the attributes of the previous classes. A class is defined as a type with various attributes that are used to define other classes and objects. Thus, a class is a general category of similar objects. An object created within a class also inherits the basic attributes that are common to that class. Methods defined for processing messages and data are also part of the class. A class is a passive defining construct. An object is the active instantiation of a class. Classes are used to relate to objects and their attributes. The existence of a class allows for the inheritance of attributes and actions, which in turn allows for new objects to inherit attributes from older objects. Functions and procedures exist in OOP, but are part of an object and are hidden from the user.

OOP strength

The strength of the approach is the way in which a complex system can be expressed in terms of its components and their relations, rather than addressing a system as one large process. Polymorphism is the key to OOP. Polymorphism is a Greek word that means ''many forms.'' It combines with dynamic binding and helps move OOP closer to the ideal of a truly generic code.

OOP helps to write code that specifies only generic instructions, which delegates implementation details to particular involved objects. The code can be reused on several different types of objects, which implies the object does what you want when you send the correct message, but the way the task is handled by the object is unimportant. A program can include an entire set of objects—all derived from different object classes—that respond to the same messages, even though their methods are different. OOP also includes multiple inheritance, which is another capability where an object inherits characteristics from more than one parent.

OOP vs. conventional approach

OOP is most suitable for problems that lack predictability. If all aspects of a problem are well understood and require control logic, then a more conventional approach is probably needed. Conversely, if you are sure what action should be performed next, then express the problem in terms of its constituents, states, and desired behaviors.

The advantages of using OOP are that the software should be modular, robust, extensible, portable, reusable, and easy to use. Experienced professionals are needed so these properties are achieved. There are some object-oriented software design methods and methodologies available that produce modular reusable code. Reusable codes will reduce the time required for producing complex software systems. Some of these methods are discussed in this chapter and in the following chapters.

OBJECT-ORIENTED DESIGN

Object-Oriented Design (OOD) focuses on the design and implementation aspects of the software process. Grady Booch is the developer of this method. OOD addresses these activities: preliminary design, simulation, prototyping, detailed design, coding, testing, and software maintenance.

OOD concept

OOD devises a model of a system that is based on real entities. A problem space is always rooted somewhere in the real world, and the solution space is implemented by a combination of software and hardware. H. Ledgard developed a model that describes a typical programming task. An example of this task is shown in FIG. 17-1.

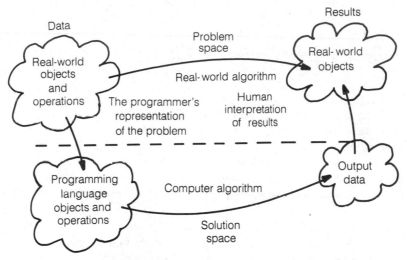

Fig. 17-1. Typical programming task model

In the problem space, there are some real-world objects, and each of which has a set of appropriate operations. These objects can be as simple as a checkbook ledger or as complex as an interplanetary spacecraft. Also in the problem space, there are some real-world algorithms that operate on objects and provide transformed objects as results. For example, a real-world result might be a balanced checkbook or a course for a spacecraft.

All things in the real world are abstractions. Almost all human languages consist of two primary components: noun phrases and verb phrases. A parallel structure exists in programming languages because they provide constructs for implementing objects (noun phrases) and operations (verb phrases). Object-oriented programming concentrates on defining:

- Abstractions from the problem space as objects
- Collections of abstractions as classes
- Relationships among objects and classes as inheritance

However, most languages developed prior to Ada are primarily imperative, which means they provide a rich set of constructs for implementing operations, but are generally weak when abstracting real-world objects. Conventional languages create a wider gap between the problem space and the solution space.

Similarly, most design methods avoid a reasonable implementation of the real-world object abstraction, where the notion of an object plays the central role. MacLennan suggests, "programming is object-oriented mathematics." Dijkstra was perhaps the first person who identified the importance of composing systems in levels of abstraction. The real world is neither flat structure nor sequential, but is multidimensional and often highly parallel. These methods are forced into a sequential way of thinking and do not provide any tools for identifying parallelism inherent in the problem space. A mental transformation from the solution space to the problem space is necessary.

OOD principles

In OOD, the system is designed around objects that exist in the model of reality. An object is defined as an entity that:

- Has state
- Is characterized by the actions that it suffers and that it requires of other objects
- Is a unique instance of some (possible anonymous) class
- Is denoted by a name
- Has restricted visibility of and by other objects
- Can be viewed either by its specification or by its implementation

The first two points show that an object is something that exists uniquely in time and space, and can be affected by the activity of other objects. The state of an object denotes its value and the objects denoted by this value. For any well structured object-oriented system, each object encapsulates some state and all states within the system are encapsulated in some object.

The concept of a method emerges from SmallTalk. A method denotes the response by an object to a message from another object. The activity of one method might pass messages that invoke the methods of other objects. Abstract data types deal with operations in a related way. Liskov and Zilles suggest that operations can be divided into two groups:

1. Groups that do not cause a change of state, but allow observation of some aspect of the state
2. Groups that cause a change of state

One other kind of operation is iteration, which permits visiting of all subcomponents of an object. These operations are:

- Constructor
- Selector
- Iterator

A *constructor* is an operation that alters the state of an object. A *selector* is an operation that evaluates the current object state. An *iterator* is an operation that permits visiting to all parts of an object.

The specification of an object or class of objects should define "the object, the whole object, and nothing but the object." An object can be classified as an actor, agent, or server. Classification depends on how it relates to surrounding objects. An actor object suffers no operations, but operates only on other objects. Thus, actors tend to be fairly autonomous entities. Whereas, a server only suffers operations and cannot operate on other objects. An agent is an object that performs an operation on behalf of another object.

An object exhibits both *static* as well as *dynamic* semantics. Static semantics are expressed by the existence of the operations it suffers or requires of other objects. Dynamic semantics are expressed by the effect that each operation has on the object. Dynamic semantics can include concurrency among objects.

If the state of an object is a function of time, then the object is implemented by using some multiprocessing construct, which is provided by the underlying language such as tasks in Ada. Another important characteristic of objects is that each object is a unique case of some class. Alternately, a class denotes a set of similar but unique objects.

A class is characterized by a set of values and a set of operations that are applicable to objects of the class. Thus, constructors, selectors, and iterators apply here as a way of categorizing the operations of a class. For example, your car is a class of items with applicable operations such as:

- Starting
- Turning
- Stopping

For all instances of this class, such as your car, my car, his car, etc., these same principles apply. Thus, the car class serves to factor all common car operations. In some cases, the class of an object might be anonymous.

The concept of inheritance from SmallTalk permits a hierarchy of classes. All objects of a class might be a subclass of another class. For example, the class of a given object, is a subclass of the general class, collection, which in turn is a subclass of another more general class, object. An object inherits the methods of this chain of classes. Thus, all objects of the class, bag, have the same operations that are defined by the class, collection, and for the bag subclass. More operations can be added to modify the existing operations from its superclass.

The rule is: objects are unique cases of a class and names that only serve to denote objects. Every object has two parts, and can be viewed in two different ways:

1. Outside
2. Inside

The outside view of an object serves for capturing abstract behavior. One object can interact with another by seeing only the outside view without knowing how the other is represented or implemented. The outside view of an object or class of objects is its specification. The specification captures all of the static and dynamic semantics of the object. In the specification of a class of objects, several resources are exported to the rest of the system by including the name of the class. Operations are defined for objects of the class. The outside view of an object is visible to other objects.

The inside view indicates how the behavior is implemented, and is not visible from the outside. In the body of an object or class, you choose one of many possible representations that implements the behavior of the specification. The benefits of separation interface and implementation should be clear. Not only does this separation enforce the abstractions and help manage the complexity of the problem space, but by localizing the design, decisions are made about an object and the scope of change in the system is reduced. A topology of a software system uses object-oriented techniques, shown in FIG. 17-2.

OOD method

The OOD method has been in use since 1981 and has been applied to a broad spectrum of problem domains. The method addresses:

- Logical and physical decomposition
- Static and dynamic behavior

The method also addresses the two dimensions of system structure that are peculiar to object-oriented systems:

- Parent child and seniority hierarchies
- Object and class decomposition

The fundamental criterion for decomposing a system that uses the object-oriented technique is: each module in the system denotes an object or a class of objects from the problem space. Abstraction and information hiding thus form the foundation of OOD. Actually, abstraction is employed daily and develops models of reality by identifying the objects and operations that exist at each level of interaction. Thus, when you are driving a car, you consider the accelerator, gauges, steering wheels, brakes, etc., as well as the operations you can perform on them and the effect of those operations. When you are repairing an automobile engine, you consider lower-level objects such as the fuel pump, carburetor, and distributor. Similarly, the major steps of OOD are given in the following list. These steps evolved from an approach that was first proposed by Abbott, and should

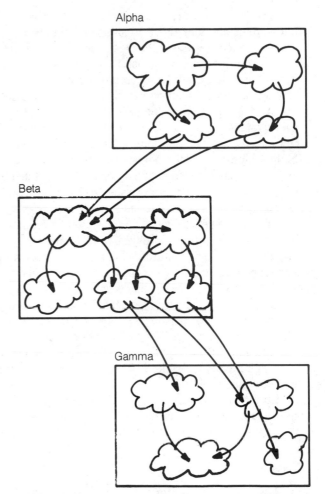

Fig. 17-2. Topology of a system using object-oriented techniques

be viewed as an approach that adds value to the identification of objects and classes, as well as the building blocks of complex systems.

1. Identify the objects and their attributes.
2. Identify the operations suffered by and required of each object.
3. Establish the visibility of each object in relation to other objects.
4. Establish the interface of each object.
5. Implement each object.

Step 1   This step identifies the objects and attributes and recognizes the major actors, agents, and servers in the problem space with their role in the reality model. The objects are identified from the nouns that describe the problem space. There can be several similar objects. If there are many similar objects, you need to establish a class of objects.

The attributes of an object can be characterized by its time and space behavior. The first step, establishing the abstraction of the problem space, is the hardest. The problem is simple to recognize, but finding the abstractions can be difficult. The fundamental challenge lies in drawing the boundaries of each abstraction so that you end up with a set of abstractions that accurately capture the model of reality, are resilient to change, and express interesting behavior. In short, abstractions satisfy the properties of an object.

Step 2   This step identifies the operations that are suffered and required of each object, and also serves the behavior characterization of each object or class of objects. This step draws concrete boundaries around the abstractions that have been identified in the first step. The static semantics of the object are established by determining which operations can be meaningfully performed on the object or by the object. Dynamic behavior of each object is established by identifying time and space constraints that must be observed for each operation.

Step 3   The visibility of each object in relation to other objects is established. Static dependencies among objects and classes of objects are identified. The purpose of this step is topology capturing of objects and classes from the reality model. You might begin seeing a pattern of objects in this step. At that time, an engineering decision must be made to create all these objects or to continue managing individual yet similar objects.

Step 4   The interface's establishment of each object (or class) produces the outside view of each object (or class) by the use of some suitable notation. This step captures the static semantics of each object or class of objects that were established in the previous step. This specification also serves as a contract between the clients of an object and the object itself. The interface forms the boundary between the object's outside view and inside view.

Step 5   The final step is the implementation of each object, which involves choosing suitable representation for each object or class of objects. Implementing the interface forms the previous step, which can involve either decomposition or composition.

OOD notation

A notation must be represented clearly, so all relevant details of the design are visible. The visibility includes logical and physical design decisions, static and dynamic semantics, and the aspects of both dimensions of systems structure. Also, the notation must be simple enough so that you can study the design, reason about its implications, visualize alternatives, and accurately communicate these decisions to other team members.

A notation consists of four parts. Generating a set of these parts constitutes the products of OOD. The four parts are:

1. Hardware diagram
2. Class structure
3. Object diagram
4. Architecture diagram

These diagrams are produced in order. Depending on the complexity of the system, production of only one diagram might be necessary, or production of more than one of each diagram might be necessary. These artifacts constitute a *project model*. For any given system under consideration, there can be many versions of a project model that represents the design of a released version, version in test, and version under development. The important requirement is a self-sufficient model.

Hardware diagram   The hardware diagram asserts the existence of processors, devices, networks, and connections. A processor can run x number of programs. A device is a resource used by processors. A network connects processors. And a connection connects processors and devices, processors and processors, and processors and networks. The symbols that appear in a hardware diagram are shown in FIG. 17-3. A hardware diagram appears as a graph, whereas processors, devices, and networks are vertices of the graph, and connections are directed arcs. For each of these symbols, a name, its semantics, and design notes are provided.

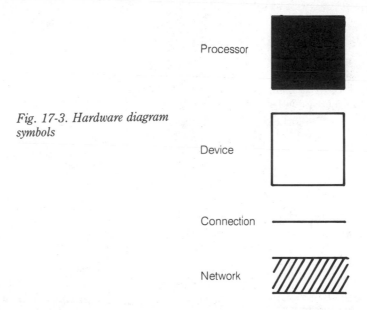

Fig. 17-3. Hardware diagram symbols

Hardware diagrams outline the underlying target hardware system. After a target hardware architecture is selected, a hardware diagram can be produced. In the simplest of systems, there might be a single hardware diagram that contains exactly one processor symbol and no other. However, sometimes complex hardware systems development proceeds in parallel with, or even lags, software development. Thus, generating a hardware diagram might not be possible until implementation of the objects, when you begin making hardware/software tradeoffs in the physical design of the system. At this time, you can make intelligent decisions for allocating processes. The needed capacity of computational resources and load balancing among processors is typically based on empirical evidence from prototypes.

Class structure   The class structure forms the logical design of the software system. It denotes the first dimension of the logical model of the system. From a static-semantics class perspective, structures are used to denote relationships among class objects. In addition, these diagrams can be used to capture the dynamic behavior of individual classes. A project model might contain one or more class structures. Multiple class structures can be used to group meaningful collections of classes. Each class structure can contain symbols that denote classes and relationships among the classes. The symbols that appear in a class structure are shown in FIG. 17-4. A class structure takes the form of a graph, where classes are vertices of the graph and relationships are directed arcs.

Class

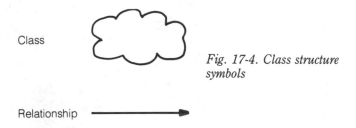

Fig. 17-4. Class structure symbols

Relationship

For each class, a name, its semantics, and design notes are provided. In addition, the static behavior of a class is stored by recording certain items. Each item contains a list of some textual information. These items express the resources and are exported by a class. In other words, the abstraction constitutes its outside view:

- Constants
- Types
- Variables
- Constructors
- Selectors
- Iterators
- Exceptions

When completing a graph of the static semantics for a class, the forms of the class should be denoted with any constraints on the class that might be relevant. The number of cases that make the classes might also be relevant. A *finite state machine*, which is another graph-like diagram, can be introduced so that the dynamic semantics can capture a class.

With this diagram, you can express any allowable time that orders operations, and the alteration of the state of any cases that are due to interactions among operations. For each relationship, the kind of relationship that exists between two classes is described. The following five relationships are typical among classes of a system:

1. Inherited
2. Instantiated
3. Subtype
4. Derived
5. Synthesis

Inherited means there is a superclass to subclass relationship. *Instantiation* means that one class is a parametrized instance of another class. *Subtype* means that one class is a constrained copy of another class, which means the two classes are interchangeable. *Derived* means that one class is a constrained copy of another class, which means the two classes are not interchangeable, but are treated as distinct classes. *Synthesized* means that one class is a composite of several classes.

Class structures are generally produced during steps 2-4 of the OOD process. Classes offer a powerful vehicle for reuse of abstractions.

Object diagram   Object diagrams represent the second dimension of the logical design of a system. Statically, object diagrams are used for expressing the visibility of each object in relation to other objects. Dynamically, object diagrams are used to express time and space constraints on interobject communication, and to express the parallelism that might exist among a given collection of objects.

A project model contains one or more object diagrams. Multiple object diagrams are used to group meaningful collections of objects. Each object diagram can contain symbols that denote objects and visibility. These objects represent distinct objects and visibility represents the visibility between two objects. Figure 17-5 shows the symbols that might appear in an object diagram. An object diagram takes the form of a graph, which represents the seniority hierarchy where objects are vertices of the graph and visibilities are directed arcs. For each object, a name, its semantics, design notes, and any relevant constraints on the object are provided. A single object expression of the parent child hierarchy can be exploded into another complete diagram, which represents the structure of all its children.

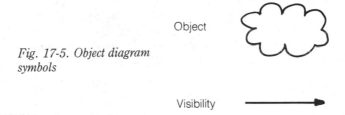

Object

Fig. 17-5. Object diagram symbols

Visibility

Visibility, as a directed arc, denotes an asymmetric relationship between two objects: object A might see object B, but is not seen by object B. For each visibility, a list of items is supplied that denotes data or control. The objects can flow between two objects or operations, which might invoke one object on another.

Each flow has its own set of design decisions. For example, the invoked operation must match with an appropriate operation and be exported by the class of the designated object. The class travels along the flow, either with or against the direction of the visibility and performance information such as the frequency of the flow and manner of synchronization.

Object diagrams are generally produced during steps 2-4 of the OOD process. In fact, the production of such diagrams are incrementally common. As objects are identified, they are included in an object diagram. Later, visibility decisions are made and then the graph is decorated with arcs that denote visibility relationships. As with class structures, an iterative element exists in the design process: you can choose to alter the boundaries of objects for a variety of technical and nontechnical reasons.

Architecture diagram   Architecture diagrams represent the physical design of a system. Thus, they primarily capture static information. A project model contains one or more architecture diagrams. Multiple architecture diagrams are used to group meaningful collections of objects. Each architecture diagram contains symbols that denote components and dependencies. The components represent structural elements that are provided by the underlying implementation language. Dependencies represent compilation dependencies among components. The symbols for an architecture diagram are somewhat language specific because not all languages provide the same packaging mechanisms, generic units, and tasks. The symbols for Ada are provided in FIG. 17-6.

An architecture diagram takes the form of a graph where components are vertices of the graph, dependencies are directed arcs, and the topology of the graph satisfies the rules of separate compilation for the programming language.

For each component, a name, its semantics, and relevant design notes are provided. Static design decisions are captured by recording the kind of components that use the vocabulary of the underlying implementation language. Each component references a set of classes from class structures of the same project model, or objects from object diagrams of the same project model. This set of entities registers the design decisions with regard to packaging the implementation of individual classes and objects. Typically, there is a one-to-one mapping of classes to components and many one-to-one mappings of objects to components.

If the rules of the underlying implementation language allow, some components explode and reveal the unveiling of another complete architecture diagram. Dependencies denote asymmetric relationships among components.

Architecture diagrams are generally produced during step 5 of the OOD process. Production of a diagram motivates changes in corresponding class structures and object diagrams as the logical design is molded to the physical constraints of the system. These diagrams facilitate the representation and sharing of components among programs, even when such programs execute in a distributed environment.

OOD and the software development life cycle

The OOD is a partial life-cycle method. It focuses on the design and implementation phases of software development. Coupling is therefore necessary with appropriate requirements and analysis methods. This approach will assist you to develop an efficient model of the problem space.

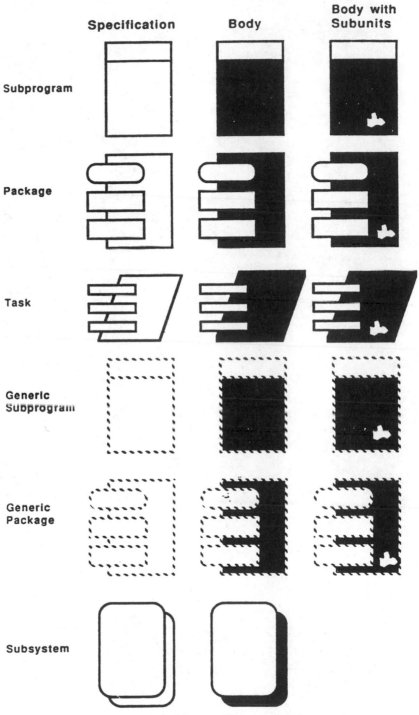

Fig. 17-6. Architecture diagram symbols

7

18

More object-oriented design methods

Two more object-oriented design methods will be discussed in this chapter. These methods are Object-Oriented Structured Design (OOSD) and Hierarchical Object-Oriented Design (HOOD).

OBJECT-ORIENTED STRUCTURED DESIGN

Object-Oriented Structured Design (OOSD) is a notation for the architectural design of software systems. It was developed by Anthony Wasserman, Peter Pircher, and Bob Muller at Interactive Development Environment (IDE), and builds on ideas from Constantine's Structured Design and Booch's Object-Oriented Design. The OOSD synthesizes traditional top-down design with modern concepts of object-oriented design that yields a comprehensive approach for models of software designs.

OOSD goals

The major goal of OOSD is to support system partitioning into a software architecture, which provides a visual representation that shows the interfaces among design components. OOSD supports automated generation of code for multiple programming languages, but remains independent of any single language.

Support of object-oriented concepts, class, hierarchies, and inheritance is another goal of OOSD. This method facilitates reuse of designs and design components. OOSD also provides a clear and simple notation that is suitable for automation and easy communication among designers and reviewers.

OOSD concepts

OOSD is fundamentally built on the following design concepts:

- Abstraction
- Modularity
- Concurrency

Abstraction is the ability to concentrate on the essential qualities of something while hiding some of its details. Thus, the description of a sorting routine can specify its behavior, while hiding details of the algorithm it uses.

Modularity refers to partitioning a system by areas of responsibility. A module is responsible for physical objects, data structures, or program actions. Modules provide a level of abstraction by hiding details and showing a well-defined set of interfaces to other modules. The fundamental ideas of modularity come from the pioneering work of David Parnas and structured design, where particular attention is given to the function that is performed by a module, or program unit, and the ways that modules are connected to one another.

Concurrency refers to the ability for asynchronous activities to share resources dynamically. For example, different programs frequently need to share access to a database. The support for concurrency is based on Hoare's concept of monitors.

OOSD approach

OOSD synthesizes top-down and bottom-up approaches to software design and various mixed approaches. The top-down design uses a process of functional decomposition to partition a system into modules. Structured design supports functional decomposition that uses structure charts as a design representation. A structure chart includes symbols for different module types and module connections, including calls and parameters.

Object-oriented approaches are based on the identification of the classes of *objects* in a system. Classes are described as behavior and structure. Each object models a real-world entity. For example, in a banking system there could be a class of checking accounts where each account is an object.

Object-oriented design identifies classes that are appropriate for a given system. These classes are often derived from classes that have used previous designs, and thereby support reuse. The object-oriented design is effectively a *bottom-up* design approach.

Classes serve as building blocks in the overall design structure. Figure 18-1 illustrates the OOSD approach. The foundation of OOSD is structured design. It has been augmented by features for object orientation and concurrency. This approach permits designers to add to their experience with SD and evolve toward OOSD.

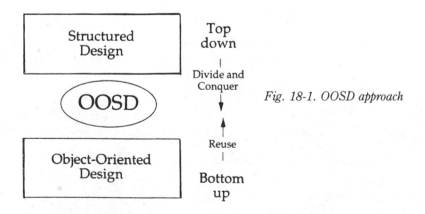

Fig. 18-1. OOSD approach

OOSD notation

OOSD emphasizes a standard design notation that can be used and understood by all software designers, managers, and developers. The symbols used in OOSD also build on those from SD by adding the notation for exception handling, parallel processing, and the extension of Booch's OOD notation. The notation consists of the following parts:

- Classes
- Exceptions
- Instantiation of objects
- Generic classes
- Instantiation of classes
- Inheritance
- Concurrency

Classes   Dynamic allocation and deallocation of storage is useful in many applications. In the definition of the class *storage*, shown in FIG. 18-2, the operations are *allocate*, *free*, and *reset*. Each of these operations has a visible part and a hidden part. The visible part shows the interface to the operation, and the hidden part contains private information about the implementation details. Representation information is hidden in the data module's *storage pool*. In the figure, allocate accepts a single input data parameter, called size, and returns a single output data parameter, called addr. Both of these items are used as inputs to the free operation.

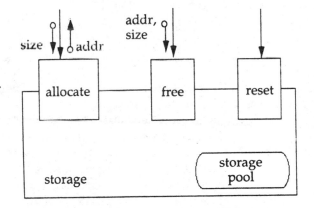

Fig. 18-2. OOSD notation: Dynamic allocation and deallocation of storage

Exceptions   Operations on a class can raise exceptional conditions that indicate a failure of the operation. The exceptional handling features control these conditions as shown in FIG. 18-3. The defined operations are *push* and *pop*. The defined exceptions are *over* and *under*, which are represented by the diamonds on the class definition for stack. The push operation, accepts *item* as an input data parameter, accepts an object of the class (stack) as an input/output parameter, and can raise the *over* exception.

Instantiation of objects   Objects are defined as instances of a class and are normally defined in a module that uses the class. In FIG. 18-4, the module *Parse Expression* instantiates an object *evalstak* of the class stack, as shown by the return value on the

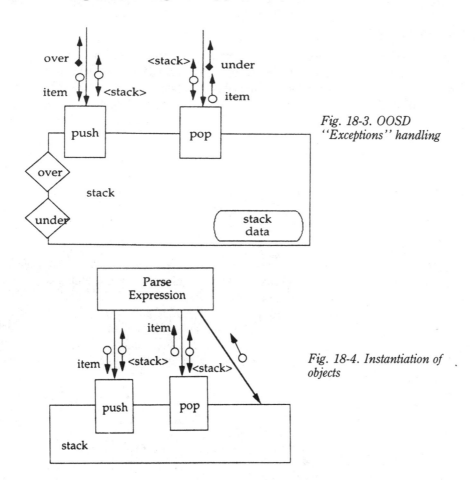

Fig. 18-3. OOSD "Exceptions" handling

Fig. 18-4. Instantiation of objects

thick arrow, which denotes instantiation or visibility. Multiple parameters can be used to show the instantiation of multiple objects.

Generic classes   A generic class definition is shown with a dashed box in FIG. 18-5. It has the same characteristics as a class definition with the added ability to denote parameters. The generic class creates specific classes and provides values for the parameters. For example, the generic classes, *Table*, *size*, and *rectype*, are generic parameters that allow the creation of different classes of tables. The parameter, *size*, defines the size of the table, and the parameter *rectype* defines the type of the records that comprise the table. The insert operation uses an input data parameter named *item* and an input/output data parameter of the class *Table*.

Instantiation of classes   The generic class definition can be used in the instantiation of classes by providing values for the generic parameters. In FIG. 18-6, the class, *Symbol Table*, is derived from the generic class, *Table*, which could also be used for other class definitions. The class, *Symbol Table*, inherits the operations *insert*, *delete*, and *search* from the *Table* so that they are defined on objects of the class, *Symbol Table*.

Inheritance   The object-oriented design requires a hierarchy of classes where a class can inherit operations and structure from other classes. For example, the definition of a class, *polygon*, can contain a subclass, *rectangle*, which in turn has a subclass, *square*.

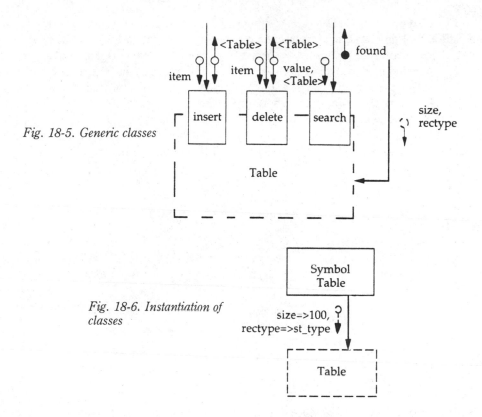

Fig. 18-5. Generic classes

Fig. 18-6. Instantiation of classes

The class, *polygon*, has a superclass, *shape*. A subclass by default inherits all of the operations of its parent class, which is redefined. The subclass is extended with new operations and structure. Figure 18-7 shows that *polygon* is a subclass of *shape*; the dashed connection between the two lines indicates inheritance. The *area* operation is defined on the class, *shape*, and is automatically defined on the class, *polygon*, which also contains the *sides* operation.

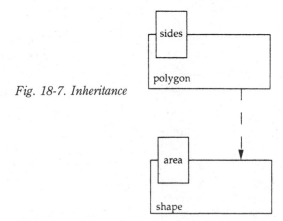

Fig. 18-7. Inheritance

Concurrency   OOSD provides support for the design of concurrent systems, as needed in real-time systems, transaction processing systems, and many other applications. The concurrency mechanism is very general and is based on Hoare's monitors. A monitor, denoted by a parallelogram, is similar to a class except that the monitor encapsulates data that is shared among various operations of the monitor. Figure 18-8 shows that in the buffering of data, one or more processes deposit data in a buffer, *put*, while one or more processes remove data from the buffer, *get*. These operations require exclusive access to the shared data in *buffer data*. The need for shared access cannot be represented by a class, so a monitor is used to show this requirement.

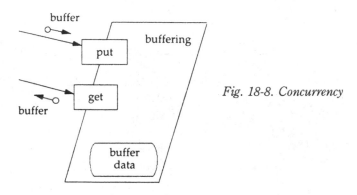

Fig. 18-8. Concurrency

OOSD benefits

The benefits of OOSD increase design quality, improve productivity, and have better communication among designers and reviewers. The method can be used for many different types of software designs and architectures. The method supports numerous programming languages, including Ada, object-oriented languages such as C^{++}, Eiffel, and SmallTalk, as well as traditional programming languages such as FORTRAN and C.

OOSD supports modern object-oriented approaches more effectively than other design notation, and allows object-oriented design components to be gradually added to existing designs. The method also provides a well-defined visual interface to modules, classes, and monitors, which reduces design errors that are caused by improper interface specifications.

OOSD also supports the reuse of designs because the definition of classes and monitors is separated from the use. Thus, a generic class definition, such as *Table*, can be used in the derivation of many class definitions for many systems and applications.

OOSD application

An example for the design of the automobile cruise control is discussed here at very high level.

Problem definition   In normal operation, the driver of an automobile monitors the actual speed of the vehicle by watching the speedometer and moving the accelerator pedal to keep actual speed close to desired speed. The cruise control system relieves the driver of this responsibility by automatically maintaining the speed requested.

The cruise control system can operate only when the driver has started the engine successfully. When the driver activates the system, the system stores the current speed as the desired cruising speed and maintains that speed by monitoring actual speed, computing the required throttle position, and setting the throttle actuator to that value. While cruising, the driver can request the system to gradually accelerate, then stop acceleration and use the current speed as the new desired cruising speed; this is done with two buttons on the cruise control panel. Pressing the brake pedal stops the acceleration and suspends cruising; pressing the "Resume" button on the cruise control panel resumes cruising.

The driver may deactivate the system at any time by pressing the "Off" button on the cruise control panel. Turning off the engine also deactivates the cruise control; the hardware implements this by initiating a "Deactivate" event when the engine is turned off. If the driver wants to temporarily slow down, he or she can press the brake pedal; the driver can then instruct the system to resume cruising by pressing the "Resume" button.

Tire size and wear affect the speed measurements. Therefore, the system requires calibration of these measurements. When the cruise control is deactivated, the driver can start measuring a mile, then stop measuring a mile, both of which are buttons on the cruise control panel. The system will reset its internal speed conversion factor to reflect this calibration. In order to protect the driver, this feature is limited by factory-preset ranges so that only reasonable values for the conversion factor can be set by the driver.

Overall design of the cruise control software   The overall object-oriented design strategy for the system, which is to be implemented in Ada, is to build active packages that monitor, actuate, and sense events and values in the hardware, then to interface these active packages to controlling procedures that implement the finite state machines derivable from the requirements statement. The structure of the system hides all hardware interface details within logical packages that represent the specified features of the cruise control system. The structure also directly reflects the control structure required for each object.

The cruise controller   The Cruise_Controller diagram, shown in FIG. 18-9, shows the top level of the cruise control design, which consists of the Cruise_Control procedure and the Cruise_Controller task that is lexically included within the procedure. The body of the procedure contains an entry call to enable entry of the controller task. That task monitors engine events and cruise control events, activating cruising or calibration as requested. The two procedures, activate_cruising and calibrate, are lexically included in the task, making them completely private. The task must have the engine and cruise control monitors visible. These monitors manage event handling for the appropriate set of events specified from the Events package. In this context, the task waits for an Engine_On event, then waits for any cruise_control event (indicated by passing Null_ Event to the monitor wait_event interface). The task clears the events after processing them.

The activate_cruising procedure, shown in FIG. 18-10, is the largest component of the cruise control design and the most complex. This procedure monitors cruise control and brake pedal events in order to test for an acceleration or braking request and to wait for some cruise control request. This procedure controls the actual cruising behavior of the system by setting cruising speed, cruising, maintaining acceleration of cruising

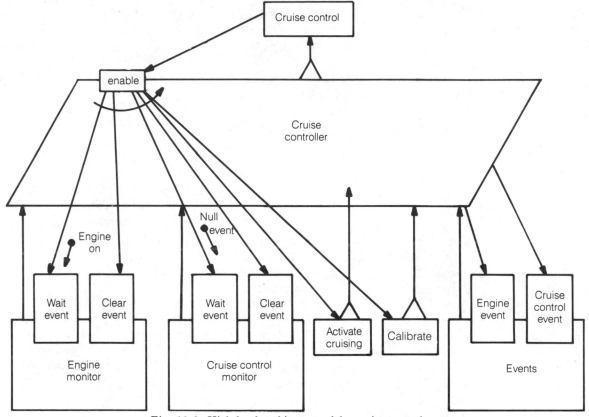

Fig. 18-9. High-level architecture of the cruise control system

speed, resuming cruising after braking, and exiting or deactivating the cruise control when the driver turns off the engine or presses the "Deactivate" button.

The Speed package need only be visible to the set_speed_and_cruise procedure in this diagram. The cruise and maintain_acceleration procedures implement mutually exclusive processes and are developed further below.

The design logic for representing the relationship between setting speed, cruising, and resuming cruising requires division of the process into three procedures: cruise, set_speed_and_cruise, and resume_cruising. The latter two procedures call the first; the difference is that set_speed_and_cruise sets the desired speed, which is declared within the activate_cruising procedure, while the resume_cruising procedure calls cruise without changing the desired speed. The choice as to which routine to call depends on the flag value of the resume_cruise_request variable, declared within the activate_cruising procedure. The decompositions for the calibrate, cruise, and maintain_acceleration procedures are not shown.

Note that the rules for visibility in conjunction with lexical inclusion in Ada imply that all visibility really takes effect at the level of the top procedure in the inclusion hierarchy. In this case, all visibility is global to all of the parts of the Cruise_Control procedure, despite the limited visibility shown in the diagrams. The design specifies lexical inclusion

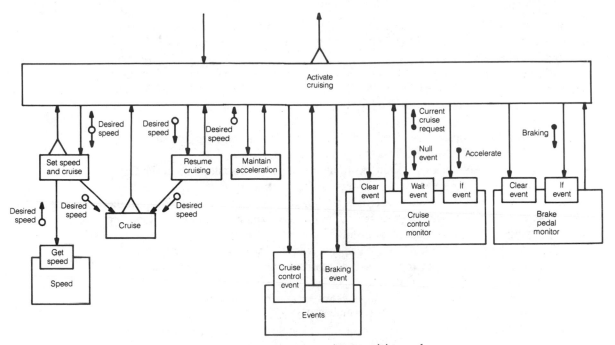

Fig. 18-10. OOSD chart for activate-cruising package

instead of breaking up the procedures into separate library units because the procedures have no meaning outside of the Cruise Control system, cannot be reused, and should not be accessible to other procedures in order to guarantee effective concurrent processing. This does mean, however, that visibility relations are somewhat less useful in controlling reference errors within the Cruise_Controller task.

Events   The Events package packages the various data types used to represent the several events that occur in the Cruise Control system. The Event type can represent any event in the system. The Braking_Event type can represent the Braking event. The Engine_Event type can represent the starting and stopping of the engine. The Cruise_Control_Event type can represent any of the several starting and stopping of the engine. The Cruise_Control_Event type can represent any of the several Cruise Control events such as Activate, Stop Mile, or Accelerate. Any unit that must test a type or deal with an event must make this package visible. The Events package is shown in FIG. 18-11.

The monitor   The Monitor is a generic package that represents an active package that monitors some type of event in the system. The type of event is a generic parameter, as is the interrupt that indicates the event occurrence and the object that represents

Fig. 18-11. OOSD chart for events package

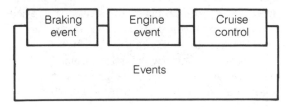

the null event, which indicates that no event of the given type has occurred. The interrupt sets a value at a specific location in memory that indicates the event, which allows for multiple events at one interrupt.

A Monitor consists of two tasks, both of which handle the same asynchronous interrupt. The Monitor Task waits for the interrupt, then sets a data value in the Monitor package to hold the current event. The Monitor Task can also clear the event by setting the current event to the null event. The Wait Task waits for a specific event to occur. This enables a calling procedure to wait for a particular event, then to access the current event maintained by the Monitor Task when that event occurs.

The entries in the tasks are sequenced, as indicated by the numerals in the upper right-hand corner of the entry. In the Monitor Task, the monitor first receives an interrupt, then waits for a clear request before being able to receive another interrupt. In the Wait Task, the task first waits for a request to wait, then waits for the interrupt, looping until receiving the requested interrupt event.

The package must have the System package with its Address type made visible, as it uses a memory address to represent the interrupt parameter. No assumptions are made as to the nature of the Event type.

The interface for the Monitor package allows for several operations on the Monitor: getting an event (if one has occurred), testing for the occurrence of some event, testing for the occurrence of a particular event, clearing an event, and waiting for a particular (or any, if the parameter is the null_event) event.

The Monitor package illustrates the variable specification techniques used in OOSD. If a variable is global to several procedures, it can be shown as an explicit data module, as is current_event. If a variable is simply passed to another module or is returned from a module, it can be shown as a parameter on the call. Other variables that exist only locally and that are not passed to other modules are not shown. Such variables must be specified in annotations to the diagram or in the PDL associated with a module. The Monitor generic package is shown in FIG. 18-12.

The actuator The Actuator, shown in use in FIG. 18-13, is a generic package that represents an active package that actuates some hardware device external to the system. An Actuator gives the software system the ability to control the hardware. The type of actuator assumed here simply accepts a value at a given memory location and sets itself to that value. It is up to the software to set the value type to correspond correctly to the type of actuator. Thus, the generic package has two parameters, the Value type and the location address.

An Actuator consists of a single task that has a single entry, allowing the set_value interface to the package to activate the task, setting a particular value in memory. This in turn activates the actuator.

The sensor The Sensor, also shown in FIG. 18-13, is a generic package that provides an interface to a particular address in memory. This corresponds to an area maintained by an external hardware sensor that places a value into that area of memory, allowing the software system access to the value. This value is updated as often as the sensor hardware interrupts the system.

The package has two generic parameters, the Value type and the location address. The Value type allows the package to get access to any type of value stored by a sensor, the location address specifies the address of that value and allows the package to declare

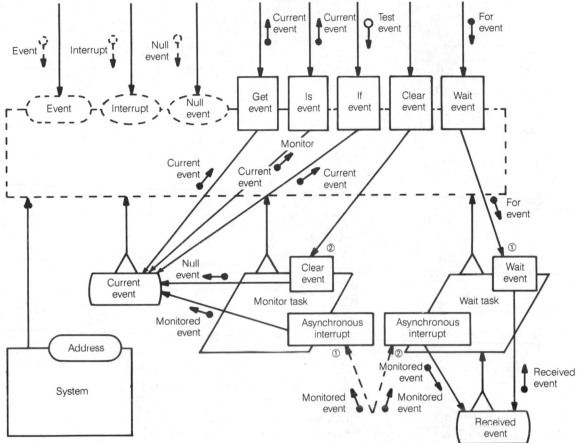

Fig. 18-12. OOSD chart for the monitor generic package

the reading variable at that address using a representation clause. Whenever a caller calls the read_value function, it reads the value currently stored in the reading variable, which is at the location specified by the location parameter.

The auto parts The Auto Parts diagram, shown in FIG. 18-13, shows the generic instantiations that represent the various Monitors, Actuators, and Sensors used in the Cruise Control System.

The three monitors (Cruise Control, Engine, and Brake Pedal) are instantiations of the Monitor package. Each of these monitors is instantiated with one of the three Event types (Cruise_Control_Event, Engine_Event, and Braking_Event, respectively) and with a specific address as the interrupt. The Throttle Actuator and the Driveshaft Sensor are instantiations of the Actuator and Sensor packages using the Float type to represent the value types and specific addresses to represent locations of the values.

The instantiation specifications appear as parameters to the calls from the packages to the generics. The generic Monitor appears twice in order to simplify the diagram, which would otherwise have too many lines crossing over one another. Each instantiation must have its respective generic package visible, as indicated by the visibility connections.

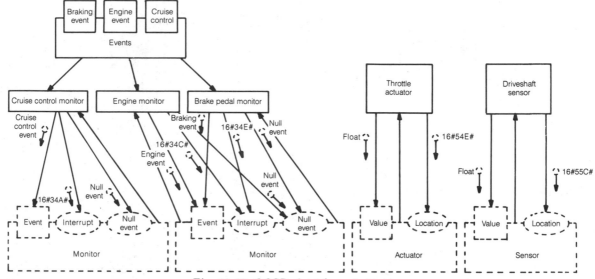

Fig. 18-13. OOSD chart for auto-parts

The Monitor instantiations must have the Events package accessible, as specific event types are used in the instantiation.

The instantiations do not show the exported subprograms that are inherited from the generic package and thus there is no need for the generic reference to include those either. When a procedure calls the instantiation, the subprograms will appear there.

The speed package   The Speed package, shown in FIG. 18-14, implements various procedures and a task that enables the cruise control system to monitor the speed of the automobile continuously. This package allows the system to get the current speed, get the current acceleration, and set the rotation factor.

The Speedometer is an independent, or entryless, task that constantly reads the number of rotations from the Driveshaft Sensor and computes from the rotations and the rotation factor the current speed, which it places in a variable that is global to the package. When a caller calls the get_speed function, it returns the value that is currently in the variable. When a caller calls the get_acceleration function, the function calls the current speed twice to compute the rate of change of speed. When a caller calls the set_rotation_factor procedure, it puts the value passed into the internally global rotation factor variable after checking to make sure the value is between the factory-preset minimum and maximum values.

This package hides the implementation details surrounding speed from the rest of the system. This package could also be used in other areas of the automobile to implement a Speedometer display or to run the Odometer.

HIERARCHICAL OBJECT-ORIENTED DESIGN

The Hierarchical Object-Oriented Design (HOOD) is an architectural design method for developing Ada projects. The identification of target architecture is supported and

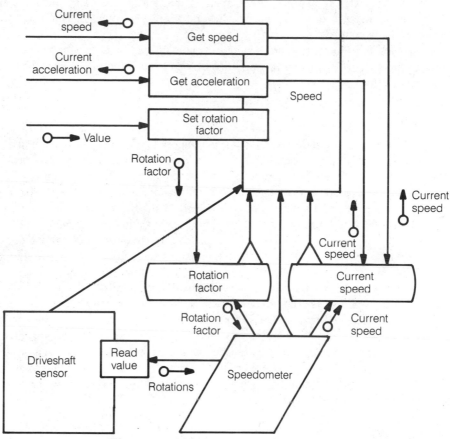

Fig. 18-14. OOSD chart for the speed package

leads to the detailed design where objects are further designed with Ada. The method is applied primarily to the preliminary and detailed design phases of the software process. HOOD is derived from combining Matra's work on abstract machines with Cisi-Inge-niere's work on OOD. HOOD was developed by the European Space Agency Technical Directorate as an Architectural Design Method for software programming.

HOOD concepts

The concept of HOOD is the resultant approach of the methods—Abstract Machine and OOD. An important goal of HOOD is the mapping of its features directly to Ada concepts. HOOD includes a *uses hierarchy*, which shows the use of abstract objects by one another, and also supports active and passive objects, where active objects interact directly with a control flow. There are two hierarchies established in the method:

1. Seniority hierarchy
2. Parent-child hierarchy

The seniority hierarchy presents the abstract machine method and permits senior objects control and use of junior objects. Layers of objects are established with high cohesion and low coupling.

The parent-child hierarchy allows an object the composition of other objects, which is basic to the concept of subcontracting software objects to different organizations. The method distinguishes between active and passive objects.

HOOD method

HOOD asserts a set of design rules that are enforced on users. The productivity is improved by means of a consistent, top-down method of decomposition. The problem domain is successively mapped into design and implementation by modeling real-world entities as a set of objects. These objects can in turn be decomposed further into objects that become more software-oriented objects, called Abstract Data Types.

HOOD supports the software engineering principles of Abstraction and Data Hiding. Thus, Ada packages are built that encapsulate the data (state of the objects) and provide access only through operations or functions. This access leads to an inherently more maintainable system with considerable benefits in the software integration stage. The consistency checks that are built into the decomposition and interface-definition process result in quality benefits. The method emphasizes the early and clear definition of inter-faces, which are checked by the HOOD Toolset.

The method has prescribed steps for handling timing constraints, spatial con-straints, and special features of the target hardware architecture and operating system. These steps are accomplished by describing nonfunctional constraints as informal com-ments in a field of the document template for each object. Concurrency and fault-toler-ance issues are treated the same way.

HOOD notation

HOOD notation simply lists all of the operations associated with an object. Textual modes of representation include narrative overviews of modules and a program design language, both of which are required. The required iconographical modes are data flow diagrams and control flow diagrams. The method facilitates the transformation across phases of the software process by using informal text description in a natural language before going to formal descriptions, PDL, and code.

19

Object-oriented
software methodologies

This chapter covers the evolution of an object-oriented software methodology: Object-Ory.

OBJECTORY

ObjectOry is an object-oriented software development methodology. It covers the analysis, design, and test phases of the software development cycle. It supports object-oriented features such as objects, classes, and inheritance during both analysis and design. The development steps are unified in a seamless way. A process is considered as a factory, which is installed in a systems development department where the analysts, designers, and programmers become the mechanisms for operating the process.

System development

The scenario assumed when building a system is similar to the construction that is carried out in many other disciplines such as housing or designing electronic systems. In a simplified form, a system is built of a set of application modules that will be called *blocks*, as shown in FIG. 19-1. A block may be made up of other lower-level blocks, or *components*. Components are standard modules that can be used for many different applications. The lowest level blocks are made up of components only. Blocks and components are implemented as classes, which use object-oriented programming.

The input to ObjectOry is the customer requirements, and the output is a system description that includes the complete program code, as shown in FIG. 19-2. The customer requirements and the system description are two different, yet related, models of the behavior of a system. The requirements should be met by the system description. The program code, included in the system description, has a formal meaning and can be interpreted unambiguously.

In between these two end-points, a number of other models are designed. The objective is to partition the complex work on a large system into steps, and allow more developers participation in the work. Each new model gives the developers an abstrac-

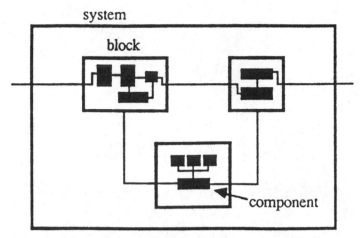

Fig. 19-1. A system is composed of blocks. Blocks are designed with components.

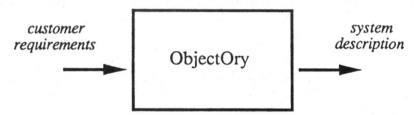

Fig. 19-2. The system development process ObjectOry, its input and output.

tion of the system. Developers make proper decisions for getting closer to the final model—a well-formed system. Every new model gives more formal structure to the system than the previous model did.

In order for transferring the different models as simple and error free as possible, one model of the system must easily relate to the next. The models are seamlessly related to one other if concepts introduced in one of the models can be found in the other model by simple mapping.

Most of the systems in the industry must live a long life. During this lifetime, they undergo constant changes. System development is an activity that changes a system from one thing to another different thing. The first development cycle is a special case: a change from nothing to something. Software development is done incrementally, rather than concurrently. The main items in the system are modeled first and then the items of less importance and so on. Work on different models can be described as sequential. Normal modeling is in parallel.

Because the modeling process is viewed as a changing process, this technique also is useful for rapid prototyping. A particularly interesting part or feature can be studied in advance. A prototype of the system is made that can easily be changed.

ObjectOry consists of two processes, system analysis and design, shown in FIG. 19-3.

These processes correspond to the real-world oriented analysis phase and implement the oriented design phase of system development. These processes encapsulate

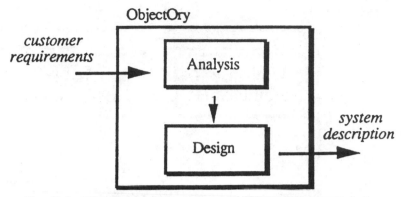

Fig. 19-3. ObjectOry consists of two subprocesses: analysis and design.

the activities as well as the objects manipulated by the activities. Processes can be concurrent. They communicate with one another by messages. A process is also an object, but an object as an enterprise model and not a computational object.

System analysis

System Analysis (SA) uses the customer's requirements and produces a specification of the requested system in cooperation with the customer. It consists of five subprocesses, which are shown in FIG. 19-4. There is only one instance of a specification process created for each identified object in the system. The main concepts of SA are:

- Use cases
- Entities
- Interface objects
- Services

Use cases A *use case* is a special sequence of transactions performed by the system interacting with a user in dialogue. A user can be an object representing anyone that is external to the system and interacting with it in some way, i.e., by exchanging information with it. A user can be another system, another computer that communicates with your system via a network, or a human. A transaction is initiated by a stimulus, which in turn can create new stimuli or transactions. When no more stimuli can be generated, the transactions will end and the use case is finished. A use case is always initiated by a user. In general, there can be several use cases that perform in parallel in the system.

The basic idea of ObjectOry is designing for the users. The system is described as a blackbox by the description of a number of aspects of the system. Each aspect corresponds to a behaviorally related sequence.

In order for the users to be guaranteed the system they want and need, the system's total behavior is structured so each aspect corresponds to a use case. The collected description of the set of use cases then constitutes the total behavior of the system, which is the main part of the input that is designed. The guarantee then becomes a matter for the designers, so requested ways to use the system are implemented. Tracing a given use case is possible throughout the entire design.

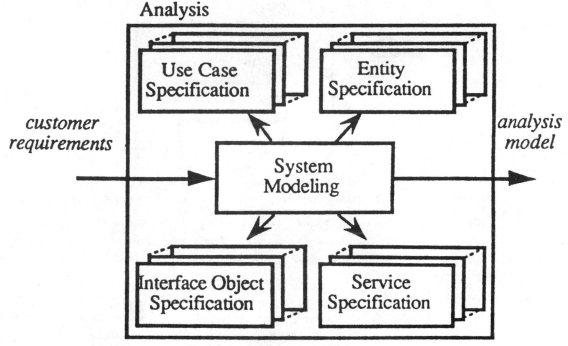

Fig. 19-4. Analysis with its subprocesses

The use cases are illustrated in FIG. 19-5. It consists of nodes and arcs. The nodes correspond to use cases, and the arcs represent associations between the use cases. Dotted arrows indicate that they associate classes of objects rather than instances. The figure contains two types of associations:

1. "isA" associations mean that the associating use case inherits all of the behavior, which is defined in the other use case. It also contains more behavior that is added to the inherited parts. Therefore, this use case can be seen as a specialization of the inherited one. Multiple inheritances are common.

2. "builtOn" associations indicate that the associated use might be extended by the behavior in the associating use case. In this manner, only the extending part has to be specified in the associating use case. The behavior of the associating use case will be added and also will be specified.

Each use case is described in a semiformal manner, by using structured English or by using graphics—data flow diagram or a state transition diagram. The use cases are handled during a great number of activities. Therefore, they have a unique identity that follows them through these different activities.

Entities In ObjectOry, data is modeled as entities with operations. Entities are things, often close to reality, about which you make assertions and from which you want information. A specific piece of information that is being modeled as an entity is a use case that has been identified. Because entities mirror objects in reality, entities should

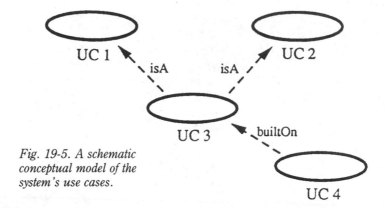

Fig. 19-5. A schematic
conceptual model of the
system's use cases.

be reflected in the developed system. Then the system can follow reality. Changes in reality can be transferred in a simple manner to changes in the system.

A use case that needs to inspect or manipulate data that is stored in an entity, also has an *access association* to the entity. Access associations correspond to operations on the information in the entity. Operations are defined in the entity. An example of entities and access associations is shown in FIG. 19-6. Access associations are represented by a full-drawn arrow, which is an indication that they associate instances of the objects and are unlike the "isA" association.

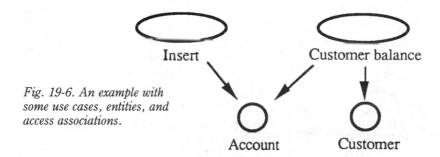

Fig. 19-6. An example with
some use cases, entities, and
access associations.

Entities are associated to one another in many different ways. Like use cases, entities can inherit each other and model an "isA" association as well. There are two or more associations that associate instances of entities. The *acquaintance association* is used to describe how different entities depend on each other and show their relations to each other.

An entity can have access associations to other entities as well as use cases. As with a use case, access associations represent a permission for an instance of the associating entity to access data stored in the associated entity. In this way a lot of the intelligence in the system is located in the entities. Behavior that is closely related to the entities is attached to the entities directly.

Information is never used independently by the use cases, but is always used via an entity and is modeled as an attribute. The total amount of information of an entity is made up of its attributes and its acquaintance associations. The entities with their "isA" and acquaintance associations are shown in FIG. 19-7.

Interface objects   Complete descriptions of the interaction between the users and the system are called *interface objects*. All communication between a user and the system goes through interface objects, even for automated users. Examples of interface objects are a terminal and a communication protocol.

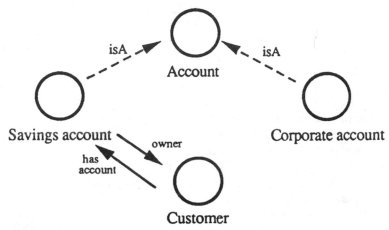

Fig. 19-7. A schematic conceptual diagram modeling some entities and their associations.

All use cases that a user needs for communication with a specific interface object are connected to the interface object via *communication associations*. Therefore, several use cases can be reached via one interface object. On the other hand, one use case can communicate with the outside of the system by more than one interface object. Also, several users can communicate with the system by the same interface object. Two interface objects can have a communication association.

Interface objects serve as a translator of stimuli that is sent from users to the use cases and vice versa. The stimuli is transformed into information that the receiver can understand. The demands on this transformation can be found in the *presentation objects*, which define the communication between the outside and the inside of the system.

Presentation objects can be specified by finite automatons, which define the possible states of the communication. Automatons show how information is to be presented for the user at each state. One important property for defining the user interface separately from the deeper structure of the system: if the system is moved to another outer environment, only the interface objects might be changed.

Services   A conceptual model consists of use cases, entities, and interface objects, and is a complete functional specification of a system in a semiformal form. The collective behavior of the system is described so that both the customer and the designer can be satisfied. The system is presented to the customer in terms of use cases that correspond to the requirements of the system. Those entities correspond to the objects in the system in terms of interface objects that define the system from the outside.

Through the entities and the interface objects, the designers have obtained a source for structuring their model of the system into suitable modules. By letting each entity and each interface object correspond to a block, a system is obtained that seamlessly reflects its surroundings. Changes in the surroundings are frequently local in real objects, and will also be local in the system.

Unfortunately, use cases are not easy to modularize. A use case cuts right through the system and normally means that many mutually dependent system functions are used. By looking at the modeling of service, the objects that are identified will be put together into packets that contain objects that correspond functionally. These packets are called *services*.

Services have two important tasks during system development:

1. The identification of the packets that contain behaviorally related functions.
2. The identification of different packets of functions that shall be offered to the buyers of the system. A specific set of packets corresponds to each customer.

These two functions of services motivate an analysis activity, not a design activity. The services are identified with use cases. The use cases that are related functionally are put together in a service. However, the behavior encapsulated in the use cases must be used uniquely, which means the same piece of behavior must not be found at more than one place in the service model, not even as a part of larger use cases. Therefore, behavior that is common to two or more use cases is identified and separated from these use cases and constitute a use case of its own. This new abstract use case is inherited by the use cases that share it, and it is allocated to a service independently. When all the unique behavior in the use cases has been mapped into the services, then the rest of the identified objects, that is the entities and the interface objects, will be distributed among the services. The criterion of functional dependency will be used to distribute the objects.

The services are related to the use cases in the following manner:

*   A use case employs a specific set of services.
*   A service can participate in many use cases.
*   The set of use cases for a specific customer determines the mixture of services that are to be ordered.

The conceptual model of the services is the input to the design activities. The conceptual model provides support in selecting the architecture for the design.

System design

Input to design is the analysis model with four conceptual diagrams—use cases, entities, interface objects, and services. The analysis model will not be seamlessly mapped into a design model, which includes the final implementation in the form of the program code. Design is partitioned into subprocesses, shown in FIG. 19-8. The system level design transforms the entities and services into a model of the system as a set of communicating physical blocks. Within this model, use cases are transformed into test cases that will show how the use is implemented by the blocks. The block design breaks down each block into components and components design uses a library or specifies what modules are ready for programming.

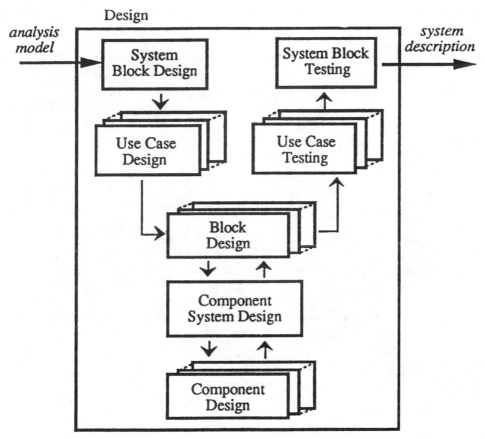

Fig. 19-8. Design with its subprocesses

The system block design identifies the system structure. The services and the objects are used to identify the blocks of the system in a seamless fashion. A new model of the system is formed: the system is a set of communicating blocks.

Use case design creates many processes as there are use cases. The use cases are translated seamlessly into a new model, which shows how each use case is implemented by means of the identified blocks.

A block design creates one process for each block in the system.

A component system design identifies the system components. The component system design is responsible for the component library and consequently approves specifications and descriptions of new components. For very extensive system development activities, this process should be common to the design of several types of systems.

In a component design, one process is created for each component in the library.

The blocks that implement a use case are combined, and the use case is tested. Each use case is tested separately so that the system requirements are met. The use cases constitute the key aspect through the entire development activities.

System block testing utilizes integration tests to make up the total set of use cases.

OBJECTORY METHODOLOGY DISCUSSION

The design model of a system is a statical set of interconnected blocks. These blocks communicate dynamically over well-defined interfaces by sending stimuli to one another. These stimuli can have different semantics that rely on how the blocks are implemented. The selection of a block is a compromise between the satisfaction of the requirements and the procurement of a system with good performance attributes.

The ideal structure is achieved if each service is implemented as a block, a so-called *function block*, and each object in all of the services is implemented as an *object block*. In many cases, every object can be translated and identified in the analysis directly into a block. When the block is structured, however, the language, tools, and implementation environment should be considered. Other behavioral requirements, such as response times, reliability, and efficiency, will also influence the structure. A set of blocks is identified with each structure containing a set of object blocks that originates from the objects in the services, as is shown in FIG. 19-9.

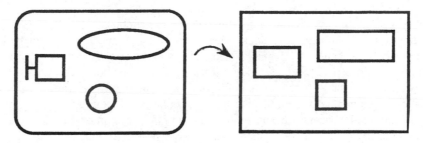

Fig. 19-9. The services and the objects contained in them correspond to blocks in the system block.

For large systems, these blocks should be grouped in large blocks and called subsystems. A system block contains subsystems blocks, which in turn contains function blocks. Object blocks exist at the lowest level in the block hierarchy.

Blocks are shown in a block diagram, which presents the blocks and the communication paths among the blocks, shown in FIG. 19-10. The figure only shows the blocks that correspond to the object at the bottom of the "isA" structure. Blocks that correspond to objects higher up in the structure will be shown in an inheritance diagram. This diagram shows the "isA" associations between the blocks. The semantics in these associations are determined by the selected programming language.

When the blocks have been identified, the design work continues as each specified use case is implemented and described in a subset of the blocks. This subset compromises the blocks that participate in the use case. This work is shown as an interaction diagram in FIG. 19-11, and shows the interactions among the blocks when carrying out the use case on a vertical time axis. The exact semantics of the diagram is specified by the selected programming language. A skeleton of an interaction diagram with the permitted communication paths can be generated mechanically from the block diagram.

Blocks are application objects that are created in order so they can be combined with other blocks to form a system. The blocks communicate with one another and fulfill the

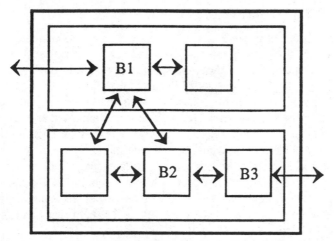

Fig. 19-10. A schematic block diagram

requested use cases. For example, a telephone system contains blocks that handle the communication with subscribers, blocks that handle the communication on junction lines that surround telephone exchanges, blocks that interconnect subscribers with other subscribers or lines, and blocks that keep track of all the telephone calls.

Blocks are reusable for customer adaption of a specific application. There is an unambiguous relation between a service and a set of blocks. Blocks are equipment units that are sequentially ordered and assemble a system for a customer. Services are units that can be ordered. In FIG. 19-11, block B1 can receive two stimuli, m1 and m2. Other stimuli to block B1 can be extracted from other use case interaction diagrams.

Blocks are implemented as classes in an object-oriented programming language. When designing a class that corresponds to a block, properly interconnected components are used. The resulting source code of the block is tested by the designer and

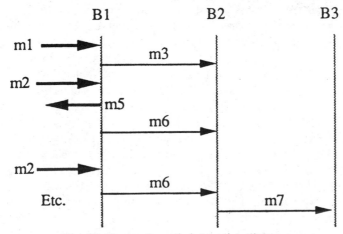

Fig. 19-11. A schematic interaction diagram

verified that it behaves as intended. If the source code passes the test, then the block is output with other blocks for use in case testing.

Components must be powerful, have simple well-defined interfaces, be easy to learn and use, and have a wide area of use. In other words, components are highly reusable program elements. Some examples of components in the software field are buffer, queue, list, and tree, which are suitable for use in normal programming. Other examples are window, icon, and scroll area, which are suitable for developing graphical man-machine interfaces. Components are defined on top of each other (or on top of the primitives), and they are designed bottom-up.

During the implementation of a block, you might recognize the need for a module for use in several other blocks. If the module will be useful for many other blocks, then you can propose that the identified module will be standardized and classified as a component. Each component is implemented as a class in an object-oriented programming language.

ObjectOry has different types of objects:

- Use cases
- Entities
- Interface objects
- Services
- Blocks
- Components

These objects have a lot of individual properties, but they also have many properties in common. For example, there are instances of them. These instances belong to classes and classes can inherit one another. All these common properties are found in a general type of object call *object*, and all object types inherit Object. The reason for all these different types of objects is that the criteria for identifying objects with different duties in the system are very different, as shown in FIG. 19-12.

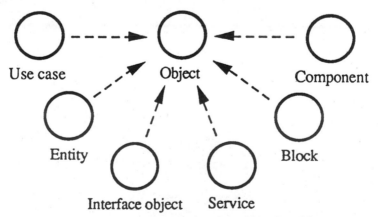

Fig. 19-12. The common properties of the ObjectOry object types.

Thus, ObjectOry has combined a well-proven technique for large systems design that is called block design with conceptual modeling and object-oriented programming. These three techniques are very natural in unification because they rely on similar paradigms that aim at reusable software products.

ADVANTAGES OF OBJECTORY

- Descriptions of system requirements as real-world models are easily understood by both analyst and client.
- Significant reduction of mistakes during requirements analysis reduces errors that are expensive to correct when detected later in the life cycle.
- Objects provide a natural way that models the description of concurrent activities.
- Encapsulation of data and operations in objects localizes the effects of change, and hence reduces the cost of systems modification.
- Because developers can understand the system quickly and there is no discontinuity in the design process, improved productivity results from the paradigm shift between conventional design methods and object-oriented programming languages.
- Changes in the development staff are easier because new staff can understand the design and purpose of the system.
- The major benefits of object-oriented concepts can be combined with languages that do not fully support these concepts, such as Ada, FORTRAN, and COBOL.
- When combined with object-oriented programming languages, the maximum benefits of these languages are realized.

The ObjectOry methodology was developed by the Swedish company, Objective Systems.

20

Object-oriented methodology

In this chapter, the Object-Oriented Methodology (OOM) for software engineering is discussed. OOM covers all phases of the software development life cycle, but is still in evolution.

OBJECT-ORIENTED METHODOLOGY FOR SOFTWARE ENGINEERING

The Object-Oriented Methodology (OOM) is the combination of an object-oriented approach, a data structure approach with entity-relationship modeling, and a functional process approach. It provides a systematic methodology for problem analysis of real-time, scientific, and business systems. Changes are propagated through all relevant steps and reviewed at each phase of software development, in accordance with DOD-STD-2167A.

OOM simplifies transitions between various phases of software development. It enhances communication among the software engineers, management, and users at all stages of the life cycle. OOM supports analysis and understanding of the requirements, and the methodology is supported by many CASE tools. OOM makes the evolving software a quality product that is visible and controllable at all stages of software engineering. OOM is an open-ended, teachable, and easily transferable methodology.

OOM goals

The goals of OOM capture in detail the domain-specific knowledge of the application in a form that lends itself to careful point-by-point verification by domain experts. The methodology provides a detailed and well-documented foundation by formal models of the problem domain. With this foundation, requirements decisions can be made. The methodology transfers the domain knowledge accurately to the software engineers and communicates the requirements analysis in a form that is easily understood and mapped into an object-oriented design.

OOM concepts

The concepts of OOM understand the customer's requirements, and graphically show the logic to the customer. Then OOM determines objects, establishes relationships among objects, determines instantiation criteria for objects and their relationships, and develops functional processes.

This methodology uses concepts from object-oriented and structured approaches, including abstract data types, inheritance, and module coupling and cohesion. It uses graphical models, with proper documentation, that transfer requirements from one phase to another for implementation. OOM couples its analysis into OOD, which is implemented in a suitable object-oriented language, such as Ada.

This concept maintains the traceability of the requirements for embedded systems; providing the project controls and communication tools for management, quality assurance, and documentation formats. Such systems can be developed cost effectively and efficiently, and they can be effectively maintained for a longer period of time.

OOM is centered around the notion of an object. An object can be recognized by the data it carries, its behavior, and the processing it performs. The point of view of the problem determines objects and their attributes. For example, a car is an object; average speed and fuel consumption are attributes of the car object.

The models that comprise OOM are:

- Object Analysis Model (OAM)
- Object Information Model (OIM)
- Object Behavior Model (OBM)
- Object Process Model (OPM)
- Requirements Definition Model (RDM)
- Object-Oriented Design (OOD)

Object Analysis Model   The Object Analysis Model (OAM) consists of all the analysis needed so the customer's requirements can be understood. It also contains information regarding all the identified external interfaces, which is especially important for embedded systems. These interfaces are linked with external systems, shown in FIG. 20-1. The graphic is drawn so the customer's requirements are understood in an unambiguous way. Material about requirements analysis has been discussed in the previous chapters. The model can be extended by identifying processes, data storages, and data flows.

The goal for OAM is that the requirements are mutually understood and recorded in the proper document before proceeding to further analysis or design activities. The definition of the notations used in the graphic should be clearly defined and properly recorded in the document. The object data dictionary can be initiated at this level by recording the essential information.

Object information model   The Object Information Model (OIM) identifies the conceptual entities of the problem, and formalizes the entities as objects and attributes. Complete and unambiguous understanding of the problem is the goal.

OIM is the beginning of the analysis phase. It identifies things about the problem and their relationships. Objects and associations are modeled here. The model is simple

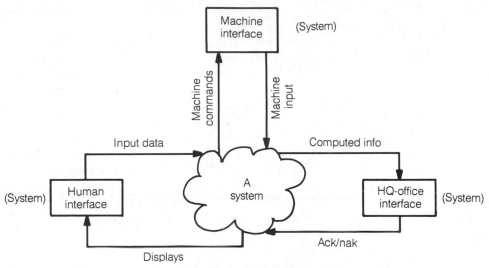

Fig. 20-1. OAM diagram

enough to be easily read and understood. Significant emphasis is placed on formalizing relationships between objects. A model is developed and depicted graphically, and is shown in FIG. 20-2. Textual descriptions are used in the definition of the model's semantics.

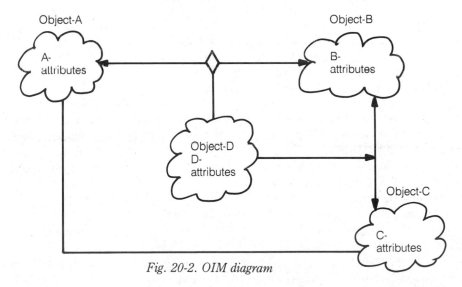

Fig. 20-2. OIM diagram

In the figure, abstractions of like items are grouped into sets. Items are alike if they behave in the same way and can be described by the same characteristics. This is first cut by naming an object. Characteristics that all elements of the set have in common are called attributes of the object. An attribute is the abstraction of a single characteristic from an object that is possessed by all entities. The set of attributes must be complete, fully factored, and mutually independent. There is a dot notation for attributes. For example, "Object.Attribute."

The types of attributes are descriptive, naming, and referential. Descriptive attributes provide facts that are intrinsic to each object. The naming attribute provides a fact about the arbitrary name carried by each object. The referential attribute links one object to another object.

Tables are used to define the types of questions that can be answered by inspection of the objects. The table name is the name of the object. Each column of the table is an attribute of the object, and each row is an instance of the object. The instance is the specific element of the set and is denoted by that object name. As illustrated in FIG. 20-3, every box in a table contains exactly one value. Attributes of an object should not contain internal structure. Tables are the basic formal structure of the OIM because they are simple and adequate. The object representation by a table assists to identify the objects and attributes. The table also helps to represent instances of objects.

Object-A

Attribute-A1	Attribute-A2	Attribute-A3	
Instance-A			

Fig. 20-3. OIM table

Associations between items exist in the real world. These associations must be formalized in this model, which can be recognized by verb phrases in the descriptions. For example, "The car *has* tires." Thus a relationship is named by a verb phrase. It can be phrased in both directions of the relation. For example, "A class *is composed* of students," and "Students *compose* a class."

Two objects can have more than one relationship between them, depending on their type of relationship. An object might be related to itself. There can also be a relationship between multiple objects. For example, "Floppy disk *was formatted* on the disk drive," "Floppy disk *is owned* by a student," or "Floppy disk *contains* disk files."

This type of relationship involving two objects can be classified into three fundamental forms and called *multiplicity* as listed in TABLE 20-1.

A graphical notation is necessary for the replacement of a table for complex objects, as shown in FIG. 20-4. The graphical notation eases the handling of complex systems. This graphical notation represents spatial compression of a model. OIM notation representations are shown in FIG. 20-5. Supertype and subtype constructs are shown in FIG. 20-6. The correlation table is illustrated in FIG. 20-7.

Table 20-1. Multiplicity Forms

Multiplicity	Notation	Example
one-to-one	(1:1)	Husband <u>has</u> a wife
one-to-many	(1:M)	Student <u>owns</u> books
many-to-many	(M:M)	Capacitor <u>is</u> a component of a computer

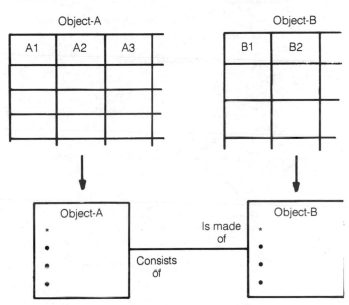

Fig. 20-4. OIM table and object relationship

Fig. 20-5. OIM notations

Object data dictionary The object, attributes, and their relationships are documented in an object data dictionary (ODD). This document consists of a written description of objects, formalizes the identification of objects, forms part of the formal system specification, and separates descriptions that are written for each object. This live docu-

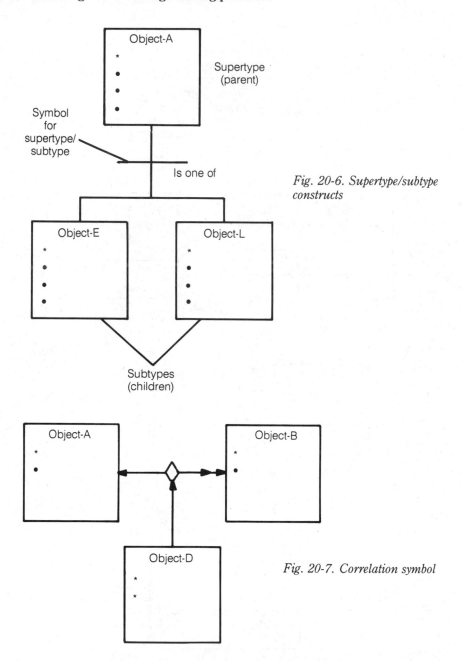

Fig. 20-6. Supertype/subtype constructs

Fig. 20-7. Correlation symbol

ment should be started at the beginning of the software engineering phase, and be enhanced throughout the software development and maintenance phases.

Selection criteria for a correct object   There are four major tests that help to avoid accepting false objects, which are:

1. Uniformity test
2. More-than-a-name test

3. OR test
4. More-than-a-list test

The Uniformity test is based on the definition of an object. Each instance of the object must have the same set of characteristics and be subject to the same rules.

The more-than-a-name test is applicable to objects that cannot be described by attributes. These objects have no characteristics other than a name. Usually, the attribute is of another object.

The OR test is conducted on the object description. If the inclusion criteria in the object description uses the word "or" in a significant manner, then you probably have a set of diverse items rather than an object.

The more-than-a-list test is also conducted on the object description. If the inclusion criteria is in the object description, then it is simply a list of all specific instances of the object, and is probably not a true object.

Object behavior model   The Object Behavior Model (OBM) formalizes the life or event histories of objects and relationships. Items go through various stages during their lifetime in the real world. The life cycle of an object is then the behavior of an object during its lifetime. An example of the object lifetime diagram is presented in FIG. 20-8.

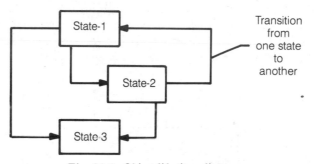

Fig. 20-8. Object life-time diagram

An object might be in *only* one stage at a time. The stages are mutually exclusive. These stages are discrete. Transitions can occur instantaneously. Transitions from one stage to another stage are not always allowed. Incidents cause transition of items between stages. Some incidents cause a progression only when the item is in certain stages of its life cycle. Similar characteristics of real-world items have a common life cycle. Thus the OBM is a formalization of the life cycle of an object in regard to the following parts:

- States
- Events
- Transitions
- Actions

The state of OBM corresponds to the state of an object's life cycle. An event is an incident or action that causes a progression to another state or within the same state. The transition is the new state of an object if a particular event occurs while the object is in a particular state. The action is the function that is performed immediately when entering a new state. Each state can have only one action, but that action might consist of many processes.

A sample OBM is shown in FIG. 20-9. The boxes represent the states, and lines represent the events. The event causes the transition to the new state.

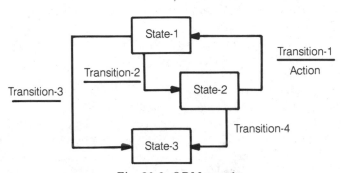

Fig. 20-9. OBM sample

Figure 20-10 represents an alternative version of a State Transition Diagram (STD), which is a kind of OBM. An alternate form of state model representation is the State Transition Table (STT) shown in the figure. In STT, rows represent states, columns represent events, and cells represent the effect of each event in each state.

	Event-1	Event-2	Event-3
State-1	Effects of event-1 in state-1		
State-2		Effects of event-2 in state-2	
State-3	Effects of event-1 in state-3		

Fig. 20-10. State transition table sample

When a particular event cannot happen for a particular state of the object, then the cell entry cannot occur. The event can be prevented from happening for many reasons, such as physical impossibility, definition of the object, any constraints, etc. If a particular event can happen for a specific state of the object, but the object does not respond to the

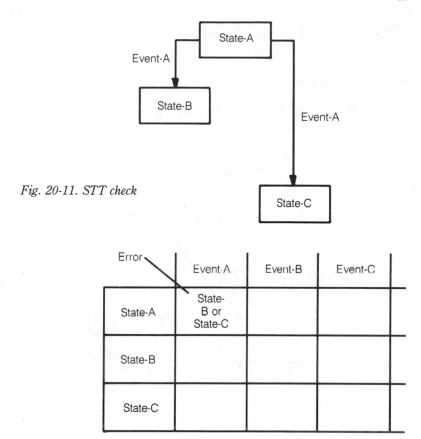

Fig. 20-11. STT check

event, then an "event ignored" entry is made in that cell. If the event is ignored then the object stays in the same state.

The advantage of STT is that it can be extended by adding an additional column for action, which is associated with entering each state. The information contained in the STT or STD is the same. But the development of the STT from STD will catch one of the most common errors in developing OBM, which is illustrated in FIG. 20-11.

OBM is built for each dynamic object in the OIM. The following list contains suggestive guidelines for constructing an OBM.

- Take one instance of the model. Analyze and record the life cycle of that instance.
- Write down the various states for that instance.
- Find the states that consider all relationships of the object.
- Build an STT.
- Check the table for new or additional states.
- Define the action that will be executed when entering into a state.
- Identify nonfinal states.
- Identify events that the object must generate so it can exit nonfinal states.

- Expand actions that generate these events.
- Add the new events to the STT.
- Complete the STT.
- Complete the STD.

Object process model   The Object Process Model (OPM) makes use of data flow diagrams and develops the required processes that drive the objects through their event chains. Only a few concerns with objects will be discussed in this section.

The following list contains the processes for developing a data flow diagram for a single object.

- Develop an OBM that formalizes the behavior of an object over time.
- Analyze the action that is performed when the state is entered.
- Break the action down into a sequence of processes.
- Depict each process as a data flow diagram.
- Place each action data flow diagram on a separate page.

The data of an object is represented as a data store in the data flow diagram. The data store will be recorded in the Object Data Dictionary, and contains all data and attributes of the object. The instances of the object are created and stored in the data store. The data store is shared by all action data flow diagrams.

Requirements definitions model   The Requirements Definition Model determines what information and processes will be used within the automated system, as opposed to those processes that will be carried out by operators or other external agents. This model describes the boundary statements and clarifies the system specification.

Object-oriented design   Material for OOD has been covered in previous chapters.

OOM and DOD-STD-2167A

OOM fits in DOD-STD-2167A requirements for software development. A set of formal reviews and audits are necessary at different phases of software development and testing. The standard should be tailored to produce necessary documentations. Some OOM notations should be identified with respect to the standard.

The object and its life cycle should be considered as a capability. Each capability should be correlated to match requirements in the system specification. Its purpose should be stated clearly and its performance should be described in measurable terms. The data item description specifically refers to an established relationship of the capability to the state and modes of the system.

The external interfaces are established and the internal interfaces are further identified by OOM models. Data elements of the standard can be recognized by organizing objects and attributes. A computer software configuration item corresponds to system/ problem domain of the OIM. The computer software components correspond to the identified objects, and the computer software units relate to the processes.

OOM benefits

The OOM is stable with changing requirements. It does not require system boundary, and notations used are simple and understandable. This method aids in minimizing code.

OOM weaknesses

Although OOM is evolving and not yet matured, there is a lack of standardization. External stimulus and responses are not yet apparent.

IV

CASE Tools

21

CASE technology

Computer-Aided Software Engineering (CASE) encompasses a collection of automated tools and methods that assist software engineering in the phases of the software development life cycle. CASE tools are not a replacement for any method of the software development, but are supplements for the methods and are enhancements for generating quality products.

CASE tools demand a new and disciplined engineering approach to software engineering. The right CASE tools must be found for the right applications, and the professionals who use the tools must be properly trained.

DEFINITION OF CASE TOOLS

CASE tools apply rigorous engineering principles in the development of software throughout the life cycle. This approach saves cost and time of software engineering, and achieves efficiency and quality in the final products. CASE tools have the potential to automate all phases of the software life cycle.

CASE tools are only devices that aid the work of software engineering. The tools by themselves have little value. The effectiveness of the tools depends on the persons who are using them and how good the tools are. Thus, a CASE tool can be defined as a computer program used that aids in the development, testing, analyzing, or maintaining another computer program or its documentation. A CASE tool links the software and requirements engineering with a central database. The database eases the retrograde steps and moves forward with the waterfall process model, as is shown in FIG. 21-1.

CASE tools are rapidly becoming the standard for developing software. A CASE workbench implements a complete software development environment. It supports the entire life-cycle process by: customizing each workstation, creating powerful graphics, coordinating project levels, and ensuring intelligent operation. A CASE tool has five basic components:

1. Data dictionary repository
2. Software engineering
3. Project management support
4. Quality assurance support
5. Software life-cycle support

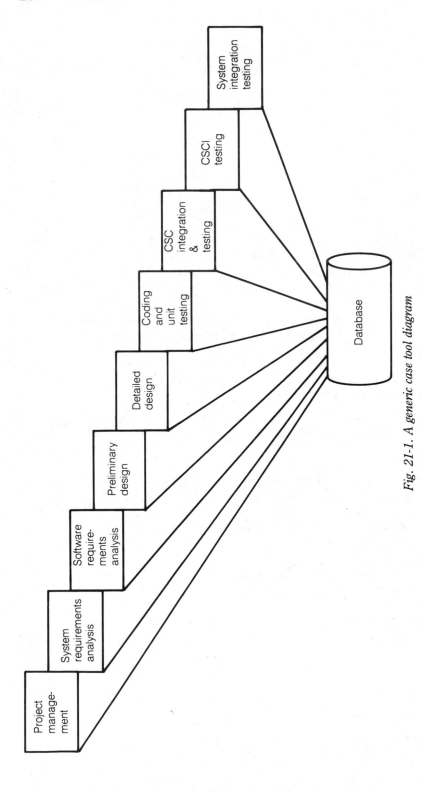

Fig. 21-1. A generic case tool diagram

Integrated CASE tools provide separate workbench components for each aspect of the life cycle. The front-end planning components (analysis and design products) are closely integrated with the back-end components (code, database and documentation generation facilities).

Integrated CASE tools are capable of generating highly efficient code that can be used without a performance penalty in a heavily loaded transaction processing. The present tools are not completely integrated, and the inclusion of all these features would lead us to the next generation of CASE tools.

The main features of advanced CASE tools are:

- Graphical design aid
- Automated design analyzers
- Expert systems
- Integrated code generators
- Reverse software engineering
- Resoftware engineering

CHARACTERISTICS OF A GOOD CASE TOOL

The characteristics of a good CASE tool should meet the requirements of various phases of software development and be in accordance with DOD-STD-2167A. These phases provide a model of the software development process that covers a broad range of activities. Divisions in the phases are not disjointed, overlapping occurs throughout the phases as well as an interactive feedback loop between the phases.

The CASE tools that are used during these phases generally support technical software engineering activities. The characteristics of a good CASE tool further rely on its value in a specific situation, which include:

- The tool does something relevant to the situation.
- The tool assists human labor by automating aspects of useful methods and techniques.

Tools that support the activities of project management should also be included. The objectives, activities, and created objects of the following phases will be discussed.

1. Project management
2. System requirements analysis
3. Software requirements analysis
4. Preliminary design
5. Detailed design
6. Coding and unit testing
7. Software component integration and testing
8. Software configuration item testing
9. System integration and testing

Project management

Project management is not a phase of the software development life cycle, but it is a set of activities that span all phases. The software development life cycle represents a process. Like all processes, it should be managed effectively. The configuration management activities are included in project management. The following activities are involved with project management:

- Project estimation (staffing and cost)
- Project planning (scheduling, critical path analysis, and resource allocation)
- Status reporting and progress tracking
- Resources used and cost tracking
- Information collection and data management
- Communications (within and between projects)
- Quality assurance (reviews and audits)
- Configuration management (configuration control and version control)
- Risk analysis
- Standards verification
- Productivity measurement

The tools generally used in this phase are:

- Pert Chart
- Gantt chart
- Documentation
  - spread sheets
  - tables
  - statistics diagrams
  - graphs
  - text

System requirements analysis phase

During this phase system requirements are refined through studies, system engineering activities, analysis, and development of prototype hardware and software. Requirements are allocated to equipment. Software and interfaces are defined. The major activities of this phase are:

- System requirements definition analysis
- Partitioning of requirements to hardware and software
- Prototyping of hardware and software
- System timing and sizing analysis
- Walk-throughs

Objects that are created during this phase include system/segment specifications, prime-item development specifications, preliminary interface requirements specifications, and preliminary software requirements specifications for each major software component. The tools that can be used in this phase are:

- Graphic model
  - context diagram
  - high-level data flow diagrams

- System simulation
- Prototype model
- Data dictionary and database (high level)

Software requirements analysis phase

The system needs are studied and arrive at a refined definition of software requirements. The software requirements, functional, performance, and interface, are top-level defined. The detailed requirements are developed with active coordination, analysis, review, and planning. The analysis of any implementation language is accomplished independently. The major activities of this phase are:

- Requirements definition—analysis and decomposition
- Trade-off studies
- Rapid prototyping—for algorithm analysis and man-machine interfaces analysis
- System performance simulation
- Timing/sizing analysis
- Test software requirements definition
- Software quality standards and measure definitions
- Software development planning.

For the object-oriented approach, there are information, behavior, and process models that are created in this phase. The objects that are created, analyzed, and refined are generally textual and graphical. The CASE tools that can be used during this phase of the life cycle are:

- Data flow diagramming and analyzing
- State transition diagramming and analyzing
- Time and size analyzing
- Object-oriented models and analyzers
- Enhance data dictionary and database

Preliminary design phase

The allocation of the requirements for top-level components is the primary objective of this phase. The processes that take place in these functional components are described, as are the interface relationships that include data flows and control flows between the components. For the object-oriented approach, graphical symbols for the

OOD are drawn and mapped into the analysis. The deliverables in this phase include specification documents that prescribe in a complete, precise, and verifiable manner the requirements, architecture, design, behavior, and other characteristics of a system or system component. This phase generally terminates with the successful completion of a preliminary design review. Other, more general activities are:

- Software test plan description
- Software requirements and interface requirements specifications
- Software requirements traceability (tracing/tracking)
- Top-level software design document creation and analysis

The suggested tools for use during this phase, beside the ones which have been mentioned in the previous phases, are:

- Specify and verify requirements specification language with protocols and document requirements
- Support structured analysis methods
- Support object-oriented methods
- Enhance data dictionary and database

Detailed design phase

The objectives of this phase are to refine the design approach by the development of a detailed design for the software solution. This development includes a more detailed definition of the interfaces among units and a detailed procedural flow. The functions that are performed meet the requirements of the specifications. The detailed definitions of the components, modules, interfaces, test approach, and data for the software systems are created and reviewed.

This process is iterative, resulting in changes to the specification and the design. For the object-oriented approach, the objects, object classes, and packages are more refined in detail and then documented. This phase generally terminates with the successful completion of a critical design review. Other activities of this phase are:

- Design analysis and further partitioning/differentiating
- Walk-throughs
- Prototyping
- Completion of:
  - detailed software design document
  - interface design document
  - database design document

- Test procedures completion

The tools and objects that can be used in this phase of the life cycle are:

- Program design language
- Prototyping

- Structured design
- Data flow diagrams
- Control flow diagrams
- Detailed data dictionaries and database
- Design analyzers and tools
  - module hierarchy diagrams
  - graphical representations of control and data structure
  - lists of access data blocks

Coding and unit testing phase

The objective of this phase is to implement the design generated in the previous phase. The software product is created from design documentation, is unit tested, and then debugged. The necessary tools that support this phase of the life cycle are:

- Language support software
  - compilers
  - linkers
  - assemblers

- Symbolic debuggers
- Context editors
- Instruction set simulators
- Module test case generators

The products of these tools are source code, object code, and executable code.

Software component integration and testing phase

The main objectives of this phase are: check the execution of aggregates of software against the requirements and determine whether all modules function together as specified in the requirements. Emphasis should be placed on the interaction between software units and their interfaces. Software units demonstrate complete processing functions and validate performance requirements. The main activities of this phase are listed as follows:

- Reviewing
- Inspecting
- Testing
- Checking
- Auditing

A list of these activities should also include the establishment and documentation of whether or not items, services, or documents conform to the requirements.

Testing is usually performed in increments as more and more of the software units are completed and integrated with additional modules. Integration testing should be performed by an independent organization that is both technically and managerially separate from the organization that is developing the product. Activities of this phase are:

- Preparing and evaluating integration test procedures
- Conducting formal quality tests
- Producing test reports

The tools that support this phase are:

- Symbolic debuggers
- Emulators
- Test analyzers
- Test report generators
- Test scenario generators

Software configuration-item testing phase

The software configuration-item testing phase ensures the proper operation of a major software component. The objectives and activities are the same as the software component integration and testing phase except that the activities are performed on major components rather than small aggregates of software modules.

System integration and testing phase

The system integration and testing phase is a period in the software development life cycle where major software components are integrated with each other. All software is integrated into its operational environment. Testing of the entire system is performed to ensure that it satisfies the requirements. The following activities take place in this phase.

- Requirements verification and validation
- Review of:
  - test plan
  - procedures
  - results for compliance to standards

- System integration testing
- System integration problem identification and test reporting
- Documentation verification

The recommended tools for this phase are:

- Environment simulators
- Scenario generators
- Test data analyzers
- Requirements traceability (trackers/tracers)

TYPES OF CASE TOOLS

Three major types of CASE tools are identified in this section.

1. Forward Software Engineering
2. Reverse Software Engineering
3. Resoftware Engineering

Forward software engineering

Forward Software Engineering (FSE) is the traditional process of moving from high-level abstractions and logical implementation independent designs to the physical implementation of a system. FSE follows a sequence that goes from requirements through design of the implementation. It leads forward to new development of software throughout the life-cycle phases. It starts from the initial phase of analysis of the new requirements and forward to the development of all phases until completion of the project.

FSE consists of front-end CASE tools, for analysis and design phases of software engineering. These tools draw diagrams that analyze requirements and graphically map the design. These tools also assist with the creation of appropriate system specifications. The front-end tools assist in the development of a data dictionary and the generation of proper documentation. FSE also includes back-end tools for software implementation.

Reverse software engineering

Reverse Software Engineering (RSE) extracts design artifacts and building or synthesizing abstractions that are less implementation dependent. RSE implements changes made in later phases of the existing software, and automatically brings back the early phases. RSE starts from any level of abstraction or at any stage of the life cycle, which consists of back-end CASE tools. These tools produce code by a combination of screen painters, report generators, and code generators.

RSE includes data and process-reverse engineering, interfaces to data dictionary, and CASE tools and repositories. In spanning the life-cycle stages, RSE covers a broad range that starts from the existing implementation, recaptures or recreates the design, and deciphers the requirements that are actually implemented by the system. RSE also includes modifications of documentations.

Resoftware engineering

Resoftware Engineering (RE) is the renovation, reclamation, examination, and alteration of the existing system software for the changing requirements. RE will reconstitute the existing system software into a new form and the subsequent implementation of the new form. RE dominates during the software maintenance life cycle. RE helps to identify and separate those systems that are worth maintaining from those that should be replaced. Many embedded systems must be maintained much longer than their development duration. During the maintenance phase, requirements will continuously change. The change might be one or a combination of the following types.

- Corrective
- Adaptive
- Perfective
- Preventive

RE also improves the future maintainability of existing systems. RE assists in correcting problems and implies that new changes are more efficient and cost effective, which includes full life-cycle support. RE includes software maintenance, forward and reverse software engineering, software restructuring, and process logic and data restructuring. RE generally includes some form of RSE and FSE. The relationship between them is shown in FIG. 21-2.

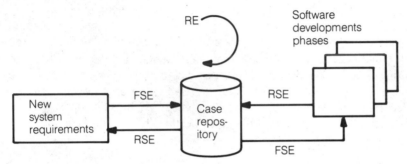

Fig. 21-2. FSE, RSE, RE relationship

CASE TOOLS EVALUATION GUIDELINES

Evaluation of a CASE tool depends on a particular requirement, environment, and ideas about how the tool should work. No industry standard exists for evaluating a CASE tool. There is a variety of CASE tools available that cover many areas of software development. The six guidelines for evaluating a CASE tool are:

1. Ease of use
2. Capability
3. Robustness
4. Functionality
5. Ease of insertion
6. Quality of support

Ease of use

The ease of use is a measure of a tool's effectiveness for interaction by a user. The functionality or completeness of a tool does not matter. If the user spends most of his time thinking about how the tool should be used or how the tool works, then the tool is a hindrance and is not helping with the task.

A CASE tool should be user-friendly and easily used. The tool should be capable of tailoring to the needs of a particular user. The tools should be helpful to the user and perform particular functions. The more intelligent a tool is, then the more functions it will perform without direct specification by the user. The tool should anticipate user interaction and provide a simple and efficient means for executing functions.

Unpredicted responses from the tool usually result in unhappy users and unwanted output. Command names should have a function. The user should rarely be surprised by a tool's response. Also, the tool should check the user's errors and check and correct these errors whenever possible. A good tool will accommodate interaction with many users or other tools.

Capability

The capability of a CASE tool is the extent that it understands the product it is manipulating, and also the extent that simple commands can cause major effects. The capability is also demonstrated by reasonable performance, which is achieved with efficient use of the computing resources. A good tool can give the impression of greater power capability, which keeps more knowledge about its internal state.

The performance of a CASE tool greatly affects the ease that it is used, and can ultimately determine the success of a tool within an organization.

Robustness

The robustness of a CASE tool is a combination of the following factors:

- Reliability of the tool
- Performance of the tool under failure conditions
- Criticality of the consequences of tool failures
- Consistency of the tool operations
- Way that the tool is integrated into the environment

The consistency of operation of the tool confirms its degree of robustness. Consistency relates to well-defined syntax and semantics. A CASE tool evolves over time and accommodates the changing requirements, changing environment, correction of detected flaws, and performance enhancement. A good tool should be built, evolve, and retain compatibility between versions.

After all, a CASE tool is a piece of software that performs a function, and might not be free of bugs. A tool should be self-instrumented and assist in determining the cause of a problem. The tool should contain a self-test mechanism that ensures it is working properly.

Functionality

The functionality of a CASE tool is not only driven by the task for which it is designed, but also by the methods used in the accomplishment of that task. Many tools support methodologies. The accuracy and efficiency that the tool supports a method can directly affect the understandibility and performance of the tool, as well as determine the quality and usefulness of tool outputs.

A CASE tool integrates methods and ties a methodology together. The tool supports all aspects of the methodology and transports the results from one phase to another phase. The tool should support the communication mechanisms of the methodology, such as a textual or graphical representation, without any alterations. The tool provides an adequate scheme for storing, organizing, and manipulating the products of the application. The tool should also provide guidance and ensure that the concepts of the methodology are followed when the tool is used.

During the CASE tool evaluation, guidelines should be established and observed so the tool operates correctly and produces correct outputs. The tool should generate output that is consistent with what is dictated by the methodology. The tools should also check to see if the methodology is being executed correctly.

Ease of insertion

Ease of insertion is the ease with which a tool can be incorporated into the target environment. Management and users need to be aware of how well the tool fits within the existing environment, and they must accept changes that the tool might inflict on their environment. When evaluating a CASE tool, you should know how much effort is necessary to effectively learn the tool and put it into practice. The tool's command set should be consistent and understandable. The tool interacts with the user and helps learn proper use of the tool. The tool should have templates or other aids that guide interaction.

A good CASE tool should run on the existing system. A tool should also be easy to install. A good tool should use file structures and databases that are similar to what is currently used. The data should be able to interchange between the tool and other tools that are currently employed by the organization.

Quality of support

The quality of support refers to the ranges from cost maintenance agreements to the level of required training provided. When evaluating a tool, consider the track record of past performance of the vendor and the product. The tool should be sound and mature. The product should be from a well-reputed vendor. The purchase/rental agreement should reflect the following items.

- Explicitly specify what is or is not being acquired.
- Cost reduction for the purchase of multiple copies.
- Corporate site license available.
- Can the tool be leased?
- Any warranty time that a CASE tool can be returned for full refund.
- Can a customer acquire full rights and access the source code.
- Is the user free of all vendor's obligations?
- Is a maintenance agreement available?
- Can the user receive future updates free?
- Does the vendor provide a responsive helpful hot-line service, and what is the turn-around time for a problem reports?
- What is the delivery time of the tool?

- Does vendor have effective training program available? Are examples and exercises available for self-study courses? How much free training is attached with the purchase of the CASE tool?
- Are vendor representatives knowledgeable and well-trained?

The CASE tool should be supported with ample documentation manuals for installation, use, maintenance, and interfacing. Documentation provides a big picture of the tool and what it does. The documentation should be simple to read, understandable, complete, accurate, and affordable.

ASSESSING CASE TOOLS FOR SELECTION

The process of assessing a CASE tool for selection is carried out by the organization that wishes acquisition of the tool. Each organization has its own needs and requirements for the procurement of a tool. The assessment process involves the following steps:

- Perform needs and requirements analysis
- Perform analysis of the existing environment
- Develop a list of candidate CASE tools
- Apply assessment criteria and select a tool for use

Perform needs and requirements analysis

The needs and requirements must be established for the procurement of a CASE tool. The organization has to outline the relevancy and the justification for procurement of a particular CASE tool. The organization should consider the relevant model of the software development and major technical and managerial tasks. The organization defines what tasks should be performed or assisted by automated tools. The organization estimates the benefits that are obtained from specific new tools. The organization should be crystal clear about its software development process, methods and management, and the needs to make a decision for the acquisition of a CASE tool.

Perform analysis of the existing environment

Performance of analysis of the existing environment is conducted in conjunction with the previous step. A tool should successfully fit the environment of your organization. There might be some constraints involved in this analysis, such as economics, time, personnel skill level, vendor relations, and current practices. Your environment should be understood and the constraints of the environment should be made within the organization. Environmental analysis should not only identify constraints, but it should also identify constraints that can realistically be removed or changed, which includes tradeoffs involving the relaxing of some constraints.

Develop a list of candidate CASE tools

After an organization identifies its needs and requirements, then a list of candidate tools that will meet those needs and requirements is developed. Presently there are many CASE tools available, and many more are cropping up every day.

Trade shows, trade publications, and technical journals provide ample information for available products. Appendix B also will assist you to select an appropriate CASE tool.

Apply assessment criteria and select a tool for use

The application of assessment criteria and the selection of a suitable tool for use is the most important step. The assessment criteria applies each of the candidate tools and analyzes the results. The criteria should be established and evaluated for the best selection of a CASE tool. Cost and time are main factors in this assessment. If time permits, visit the selected vendors and assess their tools. The few selected tools should be thoroughly experimented with hands-on tests.

Finally, the analysis of the data collected from these experiments and tests should be studied, which will result in a determination of how well the tool satisfies each of the criteria. Special attention should be paid to criteria that is ranked highest by the organization. The final decision should be based on the judgement of the people in the organization who will receive the most benefits from the tool.

USE CASE TOOLS EFFECTIVELY

Tools, if effectively used, can improve the quality of software engineering. CASE tools are valuable because they perform a function, save time, save labor, save money, or make something possible that is otherwise difficult or not possible. The productivity of an organization is enhanced, and software errors are reduced considerably. If a CASE tool is used effectively, the benefits gained are plenty:

- Graphical aids that model the system
- Interactive prototyping
- Reverse engineering
- Generate automatic documentations
- Better control over timetable
- Detection of errors
- Correction of inconsistencies
- Identification of reusable software components
- Better control over budget
- Effective management

22

CASE tools

Various CASE tools have been selected for discussion in this chapter. The methodologies that are related to these CASE tools have been covered in the previous chapters.

CASE TOOLS FOR INFORMATION SYSTEMS
BY McDONNELL DOUGLAS

The CASE Tools for Information Systems by McDonnell Douglas is called Pro-Kit*WORKBENCH (PKWB). Version 2.0 was released in 1989. This tool is a set of advanced integrated development tools that are used during the analysis and design phases of the software development life cycle. PKWB provides graphics support for data modeling, prototyping, and the creation of data flow diagrams and structure charts. These graphic models are integrated with a data dictionary that serves as a central repository of information, which was collected during analysis and design. Output from the CASE tool satisfies project documentation requirements and fosters communication between the developer and end user.

PKWB is a project support tool that runs on the IBM family of Personal Computers and most compatible clones under PC/MS-DOS.

Corporate data dictionary interface support is provided as well as a facility for transporting information between different ProKit workstations. The primary use of this product is for development projects, but it can also be used or strategic information analysis, gathering product acquisition requirements, work-flow analysis, and post-development documentation.

Figure 22-1 illustrates the steps in transferring the information from PKWB to PRO-IV, which includes ProKit*WORKBENCH definitions, creation of the Import file, transportation of the Import file to the PRO-IV environment, and completion of the PRO-IV functions. The design units, database/files, and images (both on-line and batch) are created in ProKit*WORKBENCH with the complete data element definitions. PKWB functions define the following objects:

- Analyzer
- Prototyper

Interface Process

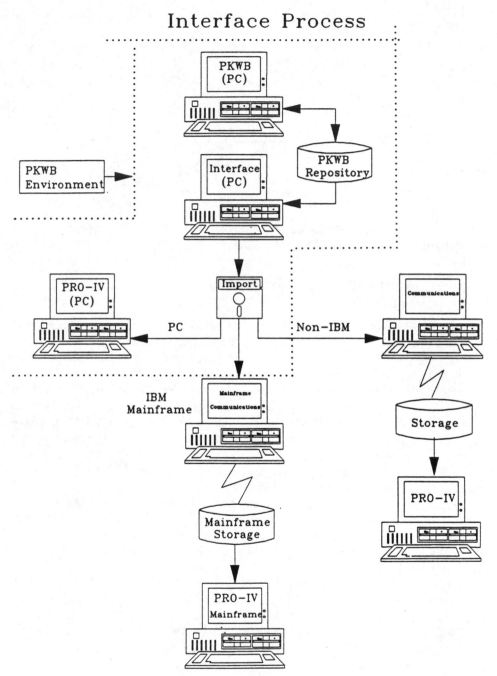

Fig. 22-1. Steps from PKWB to PRO-1V

- Data modeler
- Designer

The analyzer provides both graphic and data dictionary support that is related to the widely used Gane and Sarson data flow diagramming techniques. Figure 22-2 shows the main menu with a submenu. The Analyzer assists with the analysis phase of the software development life cycle. This tool, along with Data Modeler and Prototyper, provides the necessary tools for translating strategic business objectives into a logical model of the current or proposed system. Analyzer carries a model through progressive stages of analysis, until the system is ready for tactical design. Information that is collected during early analysis is refined. Additional detail is added as more is known about the system requirements.

This logical model, along with supporting information in the underlying data dictionary, becomes the central repository of what is known about the project. The logical model is developed by PKWB's diagram editor, and produces data flow diagrams that are based on Gane-Sarson graphic conventions. An example of this model is shown in FIG. 22-3.

The data flow diagram progresses from a high-level "system view" to lower-level diagrams that represent decomposition of process detail. PKWB supports a system level diagram from which three additional levels of process detail can be exploded. The number of diagrams that can be produced is essentially limited to disk space. Up to 800 sym-

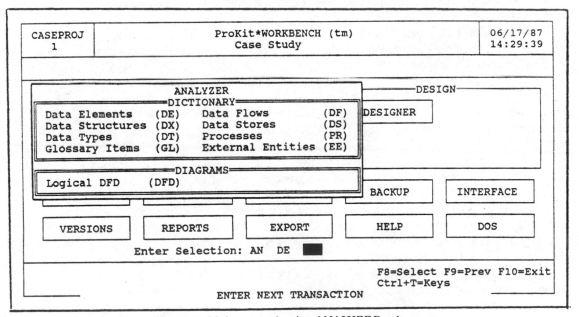

Fig. 22-2. Main menu showing ANALYZER submenu

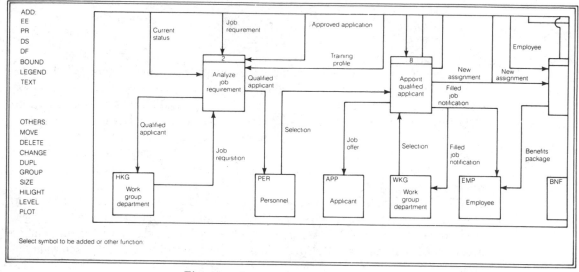

Fig. 22-3. Data flow diagram editor screen

bols can be displayed on each diagram. The size of the diagram can be dynamically adjusted for the accommodation variability in project size and scope. Drawings can be routed to output devices, ranging from 80 column graphics printers to large E-size (36 by 48 inches) plotters.

PKWB validates each data flow diagram against proven diagramming techniques as they are drawn. Improper source/destinations for data flows, mixing of global and local relationships, and invalid process identification are just a few of the integrity checks that are made as symbols are being drawn and labeled. In addition, special reports are designed to ensure that data, flowing through a diagram, is in balance horizontally as well as vertically between diagrams levels. This special editing helps to ensure the validity of the model and assists in catching errors as quickly as possible without a lot of time spent in "manual checking."

As the diagrams are drawn, pertinent information is automatically placed in the data dictionary, which is integrated with all PKWB's graphics tools. A sample of a data element attribute report is shown in FIG. 22-4. A sample of a data store contents report is shown in FIG. 22-5. Conversely, diagram symbol labels will be supplied by the data dictionary, if the information has been previously recorded. In addition, a *hot key* is provided for switching between the diagram editor and the data dictionary. This key allows you to obtain directory lists by object, and to perform direct dictionary maintenance for the capture of nongraphic facts about graphic symbols. Any related changes made to a dictionary object are automatically reflected in the corresponding symbol on all diagram surfaces. Data dictionary objects are also updated automatically when changes are made to the corresponding data flow diagrams.

Prototyper provides a screen, menu and report, image painting, and execution capability that can function independently or be tightly linked to data dictionary contents.

```
VERSION        :1                          ProKit*WORKBENCH CASE STUDY                        PAGE        2
USER ID        :USER                         DATA ELEMENT ATTRIBUTES                        DATE:06/30/87
WORKSTATION ID:MASTER                            SAMPLE REPORT                              TIME:07:40:04
MACRO NAME     :CS.ATTRIBUTE.DE


======================================================================================================
                             SHORT                                    WORKSTATION                ---LAST---
                           --NAME--                                  ----ID-----   --OWNER-  ACCESS  --UPDATE--
-----DATA ELEMENT NAME-----   ADD-BENE                                MASTER       SYSTEM     W      06/29/1987
ADDITIONAL-BENEFIT-CODE                                                             USED TO          ORIGIN  ORIGIN
 LENGTH/      PHYSICAL
PRECISION  --SIZE--  CLASS UNIQUE NULL ENCRYPTED -----UOM-----  --RESOLUTION--  FORK DISTRIBUTE  --FROM---  --DATE---
 00000003      3      C     Y        N                                          N      N       DICT-DIRECT 05/28/1987
------------------------ALIASES-----------------------          ------------------------COMMENTS------------------------
BENEFIT-CODE

RESPONSIBLE INDIVIDUAL :BENEFIT COORDINATOR            PHONE  : (314)555-5555

DESCRIPTION:     CODE NAME OF BENEFIT EMPLOYEE CAN ADD TO THEIR EXISTING
                 BENEFITS.

EDIT RULES:      CODE MUST BE ONE OF THE VALUES IN THE SET OF DISCRETE
                 VALUES.

------------------------------BOUNDED BY DOMAIN VALUE SET---------------------------------------------
 -------VALUE---------                        ------------------MEANING------------------
    DEN                                        DENTAL PLAN
    HLT                                        HEALTH PLAN
    HOS                                        HOSPITALIZATION PLAN
    VAC                                        VACATION PLAN

TOTAL ITEMS :     4
======================================================================================================
```

Fig. 22-4. Data element attributes report

```
VERSION        :1                          ProKit*WORKBENCH CASE STUDY                        PAGE        1
USER ID        :USER                           DATA STORE CONTENTS                          DATE:06/30/87
WORKSTATION ID:MASTER                            SAMPLE REPORT                              TIME:08:55:06
MACRO NAME     :CD.CONTENTS.DS


======================================================================================================
----ID----   ----SIMPLE DATA STORE NAME----
D1           APPLICANT

------------------------------SIMPLE DATA STORE CONTENTS (\DX,DE)------------------------------------
                                              --DATA--   LENGTH/   PHYSICAL            MAXIMUM
 -----\DATA STRUCTURE, ELEMENT NAME------  OPT  ALT  DISCR  --TYPE--  PRECISION   SIZE   ITER  ITERATION
    SOCIAL-SECURITY-NUMBER                          NUMERIC      9          9
 \PERSON-NAME
    LAST-NAME                                       CHARACTE    25         25
    FIRST-NAME                                      CHARACTE    20         20
    MIDDLE-INITIAL                                  CHARACTE     1          1
    TELEPHONE-NUMBER                                NUMERIC     10         10     Y        2
 \JOB-HISTORY-INFORMATION
 \EDUCATION-INFORMATION
    COLLEGE-DEGREE-NAME                             CHARACTE     3          3
    APPLYING-POSITION-NAME                          CHARACTE    20         20
    AVAILABLE-DATE                                  JULIANL      7          7
    EXPECTED-SALARY-AMOUNT                          NUMERIC      8          8
    CURRENT-SALARY-AMOUNT                           NUMERIC      8          8
    PERSONNEL-APPROVAL-CODE                         UNDEFINE                8
 \ADDRESS-INFORMATION
    STREET-NAME                                     CHARACTE    45         45
    CITY-NAME                                       CHARACTE    20         20
    STATE-NAME                                      CHARACTE    20         20
    ZIP-CODE                                        NUMERIC      5          5

TOTAL ITEMS IN DATA STORE:     19          TOTAL DATA STORE SIZE - MIN:    201   MAX:    211
======================================================================================================
```

Fig. 22-5. Data store contents report

The Prototyper function of ProKit*WORKBENCH has been designed to assist the software engineer in defining, documenting, and simulating a proposed system prior to its actual development. Through the use of Prototyper, user input and feedback can easily be obtained. This feedback helps to ensure the acceptance of the final system and to meet man/machine interface requirements, and to meet business and system objectives. The very fact that the user can "see" and "touch" how he or she will interface with the system greatly improves the quantity and quality of their input. Changes can be identified and made early in the project prior to a significant investment of effort and money. In addition to uncovering system requirements, Prototyper is an excellent tool for refining, validating, and documenting these requirements as analysis progresses into design.

Prototyper accomplishes its objectives assisting in rapid definition (painting) of screens, menus, reports, and forms. On-line application help panels can also be defined for these prototype images. In addition, navigation paths and rules between images can be defined. After image navigation has been defined, the prototype system can be executed to simulate the actual system or modification being proposed.

Image painting of screens, menus, reports, and forms is the main function of Prototyper. These images reflect data or control flows in or out of the system under development. Each image can be associated with an existing data flow already defined in the data dictionary, or the Image Painter can be used to create and define a data flow and its contents. If the data flow has been previously defined, the "painting" of the associated image is a simple task. The data elements (contents of the associated data flow) and their size attributes are made available in a pop-up work window from which they can be selected for placement on one or more image surfaces. Known information about data type and size are used to ensure that adequate image space is reserved. If a new data flow is being defined, the data type and size information is automatically captured in the data dictionary as the data element is being added to the image surface. A directory list of existing data elements and/or data structures can be obtained to assist in the definition of this new data flow. Image and field labels along with the line (and box) graphics complete the set of variables necessary for image painting. Of course, all of these variables can be moved, copied, deleted, or modified after placement on the image surface. Display attributes can be modified for image variables, rules concerning permissible data entry can be defined, and image level help text can be documented.

To assist in making the images "life like," ProKit*WORKBENCH's default keyboard behavior configuration and global screen display attributes can be modified to satisfy unique requirements. Keys that address screen navigation, field editing, access to help, cursor movement, and many other functions can be redefined. Display modifications can be made to support both color and monochrome monitors. In addition, global display attributes can be assigned to the screen border, background, and image variables. Multiple keyboard and display configurations can be defined and recalled by name for prototyping execution.

The second major Prototyper function is defining the path and rules for navigating between images or system *states* being prototyped. The term used to describe this function is *state specification*. Each state represents a specific snapshot or user's view of the system and is associated with an image created by the Image Painter.

State specification allows for:

- Naming and defining system states to be portrayed by the prototype system
- Identifying (coupling) the image to be associated with each system state (the ability to couple an image to a state), at will, provides a mechanism that permits multiple prototypes of a system to be built reusing existing painted images
- Defining the proper image initialization for each system state
- Defining the start and termination state for the prototype system
- Defining permissible transition paths between system states
- Defining complex edit rules involving multiple fields on an image to determine status of a state transition request
- Storing the above information in the main dictionary for reuse, review, and modification

The final major function is execution of the prototype system that has been defined through the Image Painter and State Specification functions. The starting state is defined, which gives the reviewer the capability of "breaking in" at various points within the prototype system. In addition, the appropriate keyboard and display configuration can be specified to give the prototype session a "custom touch" and to permit various "what if" scenarios to be experienced.

Complementing the three major Prototyper functions are several utility functions that provide additional support to the prototype builder. The utilities permit:

- Modification of the cursor visitation sequence on data entry screens
- Generation of copy libraries in one of seven different languages to assist in the actual development of the "painted" prototype images (the seven languages are Ada, Assembler, Basic, C, COBOL, FORTRAN, and Pascal)
- Creation of special reports that provide information concerning image, keyboard, and display configuration specifications
- Creation of prototype image *hardcopy* for review and documentation
- Linking of help text together to form a help panel (on-line help) for a prototype image

In summary, the Prototyper bridges the gap between a logical "paper" model of a system and its physical representation, which users will experience in the actual system. Crossing this bridge can be a major contributor to ensuring that the system being developed will satisfy both business and user requirements.

Data Modeler includes graphic and dictionary functionality that is required for data model development. Data Modeler uses either Chen or Bachman graphic conventions.

The objective of ProKit*WORKBENCH's data modeling facility is to enable organizations to understand, document, and integrate their data resources. It supports planning and controlling of an integrated data environment, and facilitates physical database design and implementation.

Data Modeler uses an extended version of Bachman or Chen entity relationship (E/R) diagrams to produce strategic and detailed data models. Each model is fully supported by a project data dictionary. Four user selectable data model views are available:

1. Basic Entity Relationship (E/R)
2. Keyed Entity Relationship
3. Fully Attributed Entity Relationship
4. Fully Characterized Entity Relationship

Each displays extensive attribute and relationship information for the data analyst, data administrator, and physical database designer. Key and nonkey attributes are explicitly shown and foreign-key attributes are automatically detected and indicated. All relationships can be named and directed, providing explicit graphic semantic integrity.

Binary relationships (one to one, one to many, and many to many) and N-ary relationships (forked one to one, one to many, and many to many) are supported, as well as recursion, system applications, and full or sparse relationships.

A unique feature, data store to data entity synchronization, accommodates the flexible work environment needed to support analyst as well as data administrators. Each work independently at discovering and documenting data requirements (storage + relationships and accessibility), and yet come together incrementally as both of their activities begin to stabilize.

ProKit*WORKBENCH solves many "leveling" problems that plague data flow diagrammers and data modelers by supporting *composite* objects (data entities and data stores). Each composite can contain many simple data stores or data entities, allowing information system modelers to reduce graphic complexity, but maintain integrity with respect to balancing and usage.

Business rules associated with each data entity and relationship are also captured, acting as an additional check and balance against the story depicted by the graphic data model.

The Data Modeler assists all project personnel involved with data analysis in more quickly completing their assigned activities. Every major deliverable and most working documents needed to understand data and relationships can be produced with this tool. Some of the deliverables that can be produced are:

- Conceptual data model and supporting schema
- Internal data model and supporting schema
- External data model and supporting schema
- Data entity attributes (contents)
- Data entity integrity rules
- Data entity characteristics
- Relationships among data entities
- Relationship integrity rules
- Relationship characteristics
- Conceptual data model views—partial static models to support design units and coding

- Dynamic models reflecting expected usage—immediacy, volume, and response
- Create/delete rules
- Data entity to data store analysis and synchronization

Symbols used by Data Modeler are: simple and composite data entities, access profiles, subset data entities, relationships, boundary definitions, text, on-page connectors, and a system-generated diagram legend. A user-defined, global profile functions allows for easy modification of display behavior. What is displayed, what is prompted for, what colors are used, how symbols are aligned on the diagram, and how large the text default should be are under the control of the profile function.

As with all of ProKit*WORKBENCH's diagram editors, dictionary object information is captured as the data model is being drawn. Also, a hot key exists for viewing and directly updating dictionary objects from the diagram editor. The main menu showing Data Modeler submenu is presented in FIG. 22-6.

Designer couples graphic support for Constantine-based structure charts with full dictionary support for preparation of design deliverables, such as program specifications and test plans.

The ProKit*WORKBENCH Designer facility assists the software engineer to transform the results of analysis into a blueprint for computer system implementation. Beginning with the requirements statement from analysis, the designer develops a detailed physical model using the tools in Designer. The output from Designer completes the deliverables required for full system specifications, which pass to the system developers.

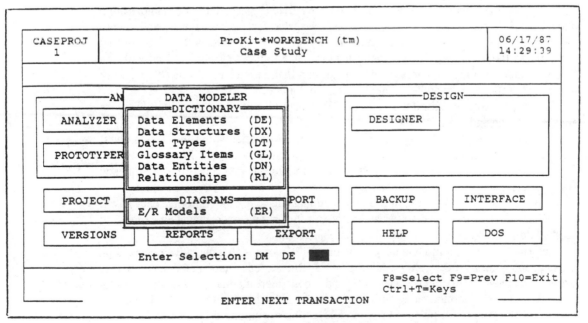

Fig. 22-6. Main menu showing DATA MODELER submenu

Designer can be used for both strategic and tactical design. In strategic design, questions concerning response time, growth, reliability, volatility, and importance are addressed. Based on this information, the designer can group processes that have similar time and function attributes into design units. Choices can be made concerning manual/automation boundaries, on-line batch, language selection, and many other decisions that help bridge the gap between the logical model and the physical solution.

Designer provides a data flow diagram editor for the development of design data flow diagrams to support the transition from the logical model of analysis to the tactical model of design. The design data flow diagram contributes another level of physical detail to the design unit by adding additional processes for reads, writes, and other machine-level activities. These processes correspond to the worker modules that will be placed on structure charts, which will accurately represent the physical design unit characteristics.

Designer's structure chart diagram editor allows the designer great flexibility in producing and maintaining structure charts. Seven module type designations are provided to align with needs of program logic and language requirements. (The seven module types are computing resource, function, load module, paragraph, program, subprogram, and undefined.) Linkage between these modules can be fully characterized with linkage variables symbolized as control for data, public or private. Recursion loops, and decision points can also be represented. In addition, the ability to explode high-level modules into separate structure charts increases the flexibility of design modeling.

A special structure chart symbol shows modules lexically included in others. It also provides a boundary function for grouping modules as a subset, allowing the software designer to emphasize functional or organizational unity.

As with other graphic tools, information displayed on the diagram surface is automatically captured and stored in ProKit*WORKBENCH data dictionary. Information documented during the analysis phase is also available for review, reuse, and refinement. For example, a process and its narrative can be associated with a module that implements the solution. This process narrative can be automatically included with the module's logic specification area. The designer can then extend and refine the narrative to properly reflect the module's complete logic definition.

To support the design effort, four specific design objects are supported. They are subsystems, design units, modules, and database/files.

For subsystems, ProKit*WORKBENCH stores information about the design units, structure charts, design data flow diagrams, and modules with which it is associated. Preliminary input for a user guide can also be documented. Notes concerning a proposed test plan can also be recorded for the subsystem.

Design unit documentation in the data dictionary includes its contents: data flows, processes, data stores, and external entities. Information concerning test notes and user guide text can also be entered for this object type.

Information about a module's logic can be stored along with a narrative description. Linkage information between modules can also be stored. Lists maintained include "modules called," "modules called by," and "contained modules." Associated database/files can be identified along with access intent of each reference. As with the previous two objects, a test plan for each module can be documented.

Database/file objects constitute the storage requirements of the system and can be

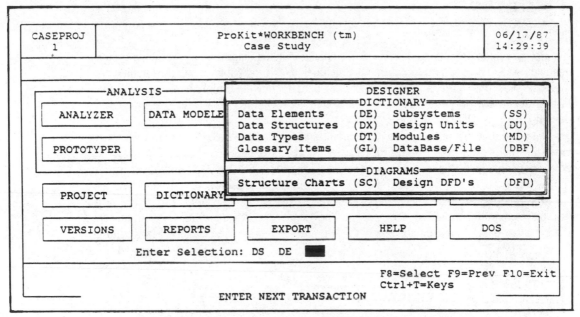

Fig. 22-7. Main menu showing DESIGNER submenu

either simple or composite. The data stores implemented by the physical database/file can be identified. Input/Output relationships with modules with access intentions can be documented.

The main menu showing Designer submenu is presented in FIG. 22-7.

SOFTWARE THROUGH PICTURES
BY INTERACTIVE DEVELOPMENT ENVIRONMENTS

Since 1985, Software through Pictures (StP)is the product of Interactive Development Environments (IDE). The CASE tool was developed by Anthony Wasserman. Its open architecture allows the linking of StP to other tools and applications. All file formats, database definitions, messages, and other system attributes are accessible for modification. StP supports many analysis and design methodologies with a family of graphical editors, the template-driven Object Annotation Editor, and Document Preparation system. All graphical editors display a consistent user interface when diagrams are being created and edited. Extensive programs for checking design rules verify the completeness and consistency of diagrams. StP supports the following methodologies:

- Structured System Analysis (DeMarco/Yourdon and Gane/Sarson)
- Real-Time Requirements Specifications (Hatley/Pirbhai)
- Hierarchical Data Structures (Jackson)
- Entity-Relationship Modeling (Chen)
- Structured Design (Constantine/Yourdon)
- User Software Engineering (Wasserman)

- SERA
- SED

StP provides open and published interfaces, including diagram file formats and database schema. The open architecture also includes user-modifiable configuration files and message files. The open architecture includes user-modifiable templates for object annotation, document preparation, code generation, SQL schema generation, and program design language (PDL).

The architecture of the StP environment is shown in FIG. 22-8. The main menu provides a "mouse-and-menu" interface to the entire set of StP tools, including graphical editors, checking routines, code generation programs, and the document preparation tools. The mouse has three buttons. The buttons are pressed separately and selects, cancels, deletes, or pulls down a menu or window. StP provides windows that view several pages simultaneously on the screen. The graphical editors and tools communicate with a shared relational database via the StP Tools Library and Object Management Library (OML).

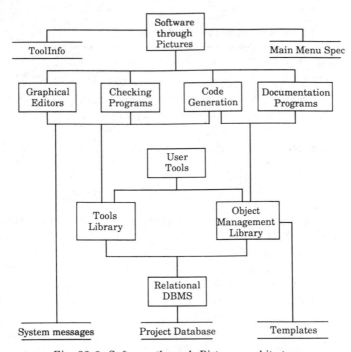

Fig. 22-8. Software through Pictures architecture

StP uses standard symbols for creating the diagrams and allows the user his/her own symbols definitions. PICture is an object-oriented drawing program that is used for creating free-form system drawings, and is shown in FIG. 22-9.

StP provides a series of static checks that ensure consistency between levels and within a level. For example, the lower-level bubble (children) must be associated with an upper-level bubble (parent). Arrows must be labeled with a data item. A data item must

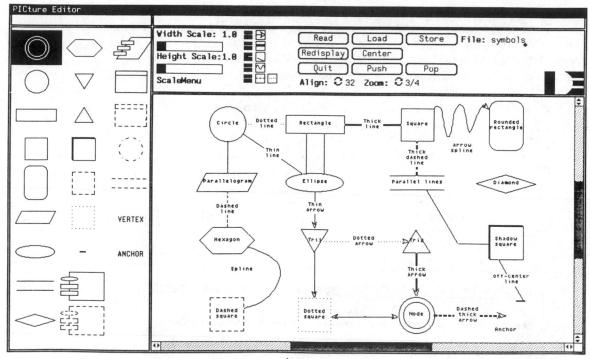

Fig. 22-9. PICture editor symbols

be defined in the data dictionary. Failure to conform to these rules will cause StP to flag the errors. These errors are summarized in a diagnostic listing. The checking capabilities of StP include:

- Diagram/table checking
  - unconnected nodes
  - undefined data items
  - improperly labeled nodes and flows
  - prohibited connections
  - individual control specification (c-spec) table checking
  - unique initial states and events in c-spec tables

- Decomposition checking
  - balancing of data flows, processes, and data stores
  - balancing of a control flow in a c-spec with the associated control flow diagram

- Data dictionary checking
  - consistent name usage between editors
  - consistency between state transition diagrams and c-specs
  - consistency among c-spec tables
  - control inflows that are required for use in c-spec tables
  - control outflows that are required to generate in c-spec tables

StP runs on Apollo, DEC Vaxstation (VMS and Ultrix), HP 9000, and Sun workstations. The Sun and Apollo workstations provide a large high resolution screen. StP functions well in both a stand alone and multiuser mode in UNIX. Password security is also provided by the UNIX operating system. StP allows and encourages third party integration through its open-architecture approach. You can call StP routines to access its data dictionary.

Version control is provided through the normal UNIX file management utilities. StP integrates with many third party configuration-management products. IDE provides interfaces to desktop publishing systems. StP also integrates with Interleaf, as shown in FIG. 22-10. Interleaf integration offers considerable flexibility because users can manipulate StP symbols and text in Interleaf. StP includes a growing set of applications, which are:

- Automatic documentation
- Requirements traceability
- Data dictionary analysis
- DOD-STD-2167A support

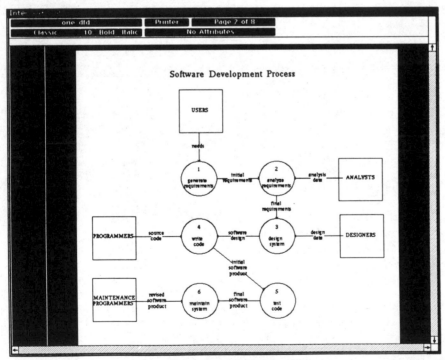

Fig. 22-10. Interleaf integration

Automatic documentation includes predefined templates that can print graphical editor diagrams and associated object annotations at any time in the software development life cycle. For example, a user can print all data flow diagrams or a single data flow diagram during the analysis phase. Documentation is always available with only a few clicks of the mouse button, which improves communications and keeps projects on track.

Requirements traceability enables software developers to track original customer requirements throughout early phases of the software development life cycle. It includes predefined document preparation system templates and user-modifiable object annotation templates. The tracing of customer requirements enhances management control and improves communications between software developers and their customers.

Data dictionary analysis uses predefined templates for reporting data dictionary contents. Data dictionary reports improve software quality by ensuring completeness and consistency of the system model.

DOD-STD-2167 support provides DOD contractors automation that aids the analysis and design phases of the software development life cycle. The support includes object annotation templates and predefined document preparation system templates that produce six Data Item Descriptions (DID). Graphics and tables are always up-to-date when generating DID's. Thus, they increase the productivity of software developers.

IDE offers a broad range of support, educational, and consulting services to ensure the success of its customer's project development. IDE provides comprehensive support for its products through a technical support hotline, product warranty program, annual maintenance contracts, and ongoing product development activities.

PROMOD BY PROMOD INC.

ProMod toolset is the product of Promod, Inc. The ProMod methodology and CASE tools graphics have been discussed in chapter 12. A project library is the central database. The data is checked for each analyst and also for the entire model to ensure the whole project model is consistent. This CASE tool tracks software functional requirements. The user inputs are natural language descriptions of requirements that are tied to functions in the data flow diagram, called *miniature specifications* (mini-specs). The components of ProMod CASE tool are:

- ProMod/SA
- ProMod/RT
- ProMod/TMS
- ProMod/DC
- ProMod/Source
- ProMod/MD
- ProCap
- Re/Source
- ProMod/CM

ProMod/SA automates the structured analysis methodology, which creates a graphical specification of a system during the project requirements analysis phase. Global analysis checks for multiple definitions, data list errors, invalid parameters, and inconsistent interfaces. ProMod/SA provides drawing support for data flow diagrams. It also checks data flows for consistency and completeness. Short descriptions can be stored with each function in the data flow diagram.

ProMod/RT, structured analysis for real time, automates the structured analysis with real-time extensions methodology. It supports control flow diagrams and control specifications. Real-time extensions, such as control flow diagrams, control specifications, state transition diagrams, and requirement dictionary entries. Real-time extensions provide visibility and control of complex real-time elements. ProMod/RT provides balancing and leveling checks on all graphic diagram relations.

ProMod/TMS, traceability matrix system, automatically traces requirements that are identified in the requirements analysis phase through the architectural and detailed design phases. User-definable trace items give designers visibility and control of critical requirements or milestones. Reports can show where each trace item is found, referenced, missing, or duplicated in documents.

ProMod/DC, design charts, provides a module hierarchy chart that is a graphical picture of the total system structure, and shows the major system components. Structure charts are also provided that include detailed parameter names, processing directional arrows, iterative calls, multiple calls, and import/export functions identification in the system's structure. ProMod/DC provides a function network chart that shows all the functional interconnections over any portion of the design model.

ProMod/Source provides a template for the final programming activity. The design data collected in ProMod/MD also contains all the structures needed to create source code. Pro/Source inserts the syntactically correct control structures for Ada, C, or Pascal.

ProMod/MD has created subsystems, modules, functions, hidden data, internal functions, data types structures, I/O parameters, and import/export relationships.

ProCap couples source code in Ada, C, or Pascal with corresponding pseudocode and documentation that provides high-level program design in the target language pseudocode. ProCap provides a language syntax-directed editor that prompts for correct syntax of the language, checks for errors, preprocesses the code into a structured format, and provides early detection of coding errors. ProCap supports the full VAX series with the VMS 4.x operating system, which includes the VAX workstation. Part of the product line can be run on IBM PCs with 640Kb memory, 10Mb hard disk, 1 floppy disk, and EGA or Hercules graphics.

Re/Source examines existing Ada, C, or Pascal source code and prepares the code that goes into modular design. This function produces structure charts and design documentation of the module structure. ReSource becomes a reverse engineering tool when combined with ProMod/MD, Pro/Source, and ProCap. Re/Source provides a textual and graphic picture of the overall structure of existing programs, identification of reusable elements, and visibility of the impact of proposed changes.

ProMod/CM, configuration management, is designed for interfacing with current VAX-based configuration management tools, such as DEC's CM or simply the DEC VMS directory system. Reports include summaries of items that have been added, deleted, or changed since the baseline version was established.

PROBLEM STATEMENT LANGUAGE/
PROBLEM STATEMENT ANALYZER BY META SYSTEMS

Problem Statement Language/Problem Statement Analyzer (PSL/PSA) is Meta System's core product that automates CASE tasks for the system professional. The PSL/PSA CASE tool assists in the description, analysis, and design of information processing systems. It consists of a formal language used to define information, containing

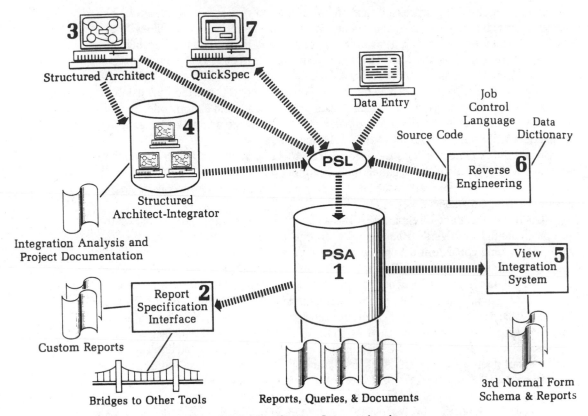

Fig. 22-11. Meta Systems Integrated tool set

the system description and requirements, in machine processible form. PSL/PSA has an analyzer that maintains the information in a central (Meta) repository, monitors design activities, responds to ad hoc queries, performs analyses, and generates reports.

PSL/PSA can be used for each phase of the development life cycle and can assist project members in describing, analyzing, and designing the target system. It can also be used after the completion of the project to assist testing and maintenance. A Meta system integrated tool set is illustrated in FIG. 22-11, and is tabulated as follows:

1. PSL/PSA Repository Database
2. Report Specification Interface
3. Structured Architect
4. Structured Architect-Integrator
5. View Integration System
6. Reverse Engineering
7. QuickSpec

PSL/PSA automates the requirements specification, analysis, and design of information systems. PSL is a structured English-like language that has been adapted to the formulation of statements, and is used to describe information processing systems. PSL statements are checked, processed, and stored in a Meta repository by the PSA. The Analyzer provides repository editing, query, and report generation capabilities. PSL/PSA provides extensive modeling, analysis, reporting, and documentation capabilities.

Report Specification Interface (RSI) is a companion to PSL/PSA, customizing reports and documentation in accordance with standards like DOD-STD-2167A. RSI also automates system implementation by the translation of the contents of the PSA database into database management system checks, data dictionaries, or skeleton code. In addition, RSI can be a rules processor for complex quality assurance analyses, design transformations, and other operations on the PSA database.

Structured Architect is the PC-based analysis tool that allows data flow diagrams to be drawn while automatically updating the system encyclopedia. You can edit the encyclopedia directly or generate analyses, reports, and documentation according to the rules of Structured Analysis.

Structured Architect-Integrator (SA-I) is a mainframe integration tool that allows the efforts of multiple analysts to be merged into one project-wide system specification, while maintaining consistent definitions of shared data.

View Integration System (VIS) automates data modeling tasks by integrating and normalizing data view specifications that were previously entered into the PSA database.

Reverse Engineering enables you redocumentation of existing code, improves maintenance, validates top-down analysis efforts, converts hardware, and/or facilitates language conversions or extensions to 4GL, COBOL, FORTRAN, and data dictionaries.

QuickSpec is the front-end PC tool that works with MS-Windows and entering information about your system is easy without learning PSL. You can upload the description entered on your PC to PSL/PSA, or transfer the contents of your PSA database to a PC for further editing with QuickSpec.

PSL/PSA supports IBM VM/CMS mainframes and Digital VAX and Micro VAX under VMS.

CASE TOOLS FOR TAGS BY TELEDYNE BROWN ENGINEERING

The Technology for the Automated Generation of Systems (TAGS) is a CASE tool that provides for automated definition, design, documentation, simulation, testing, and maintenance of complex real-time embedded systems, and is shown in FIG. 22-12. All system representation, that is, data flow, functional flow, control flow, and timing, is tightly connected in the database and checked for consistency by its Diagnostic Analyzer. The Simulation Compiler models the system, validates the design, and supports alternative designs or trade studies.

TAGS consists of a graphical, executable system design language called the Input/Output Requirements Language (IORL), which is supported by a series of interactive and fully integrated software packages in a distributed workstation environment. The IORL that TAGS implements was developed by Teledyne Brown Engineering in the early 1970's. The automation of this language, (i.e., the TAGS Toolset) was started in the late 1970's. IROL has been successfully used as a system engineering tool for ten years. Teledyne Brown claims that TAGS has been used on programs with the U.S. Army, Air Force, Navy, Strategic Defense Initiative Office and NASA.

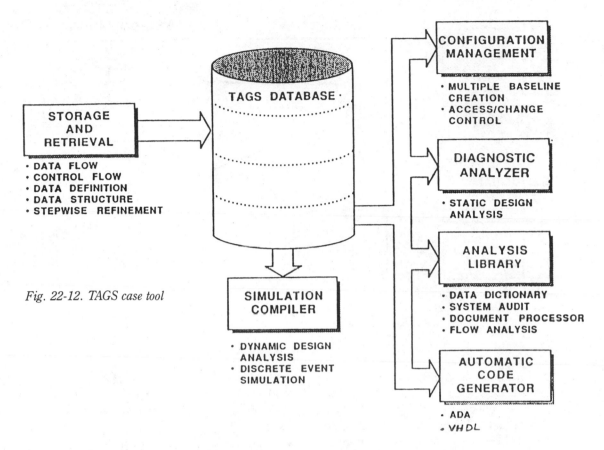

Fig. 22-12. TAGS case tool

TAGS is operated with a mouse, icons, and full pop-up, pull-down menus. Menus are only used for initializing the software tools. Icons, a mouse, and paint-and-click screens are used after the user is in the drawing mode.

The IORL uses a variety of design symbols that are used in the diagrams. These symbols are shown in FIG. 22-13. These diagrams are:

- Schematic Block Diagram (SBD)
- Input/Output Relationships and Timing Diagram (IORTD)
- Predefined Process Diagram (PPD)
- Input/Output Parameter Table (IOPT)
- Data Structure Diagram (DSD)
- Internal Parameter Table (IPT)

SBD is the highest level of definition in IORL, and identifies "black box" system components. The SBD "black boxes" represent the principal system components or functions with connecting arrows that show the data interfaces that flow among them. The elements of a schematic block diagram are called components. Each component on the top-level SBD is decomposed and produces a lower-level SBD. This SBD is given

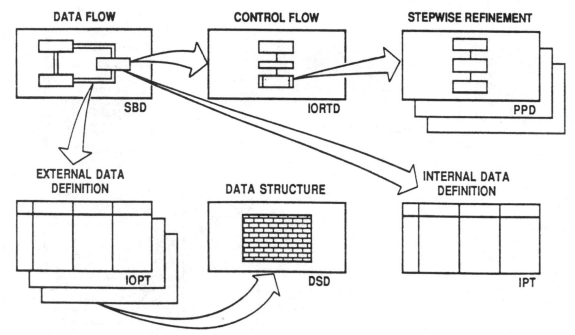

Fig. 22-13. TAGS computer-aided software environment

the name of the top-level SBD as its reference identification (ID) and its interfaces are then defined. Interfaces that are carried forward from the parent schematic appear as dashed arrow connectors. This decomposition process is continued until the components can no longer be divided or until the desired level of detail is reached.

The IORTD expresses the control flow within the components or ''glass box'' perspective. Each IORTD is associated with the SBD component whose control flow it defines. Timing requirements can be precisely specified as start, duration, tolerance, probability, and other details for input and output event symbols that appear on IORTD's.

An IORTD is a collection of symbols that are logically organized and specify the mathematical, logical, and timing relationships between the inputs and outputs of the system components. The diagrams can specify the occurrence of an event during a relative time frame. For example, a process might occur after the last time-dependent event, but before the next time-dependent event on the logical path.

PPD's depict detailed logic flow and are connected to IORTD's or the PPD's. PPD's either describe the detailed logic of IORTD processes or define the logic of previously defined PPD's. Stepwise refinement is applied by the continual breaking down of an algorithm into lower PPD levels.

IOPT contains the definitions of interfaces. Interfaces are defined in either an IOPT, IPT, or a PPT. Interfaces are dependent on how the data passes over an interface between two components if the data is not local to an individual IORTD or PPD. An IOPT is required for each SBD interface and identifies, defines, organizes, and quantifies information that is transferred across the interface. Data is organized into parameter groups. Each group is transferred as a unit in a continuous operation.

A DSD is a graphic representation of system data, such as interface messages bit positions. The tabular DSD describes data physical organization and storage allocation. Data structures are defined in a DSD. The DSD form specifies a menu or report format. The DSD picture displays a drawing as a reflection of data functions.

An IPT defines variables that are internal to one IORTD and associated PPD's. An IPT contains internal data definitions.

TAGS CASE tool provides standard symbols and creates the system representation with a graphic-editing capability. The system representation is read by TAGS as an intelligent image, which can be checked syntactically by the Diagnostic Analyzer (DA) according to the Backus-Naur-Form (BNF) of the IORL language. The DA package has three processing options: analysis, compilation, and integration. Each of these processes performs a different kind of construction-error diagnosis.

The analysis process detects basic errors in the actual structure of a TAGS system design, such as missing symbols, invalid symbols, and unconnected symbols. The compilation process ensures correct data definition with parameter tables, and proper use of that data within diagrams, such as missing parameter information, invalid parameter information, and invalid parameter use. The analysis and compilation processes can be run on an incomplete system design, which gives the user intermediate checks on the design.

After each process is completed, a display or printed copy of errors that are detected within the TAGS system design can be requested. Design problems can be identified because each error condition is explicitly coded according to type and location.

Accuracy and completeness of the system's logic dynamic representation is first checked by the DA and then by design simulation. Simulation permits you to review the expected behavior of the system in operation. TAGS provides a dynamic testing or simulation of the system with the simulation compiler.

TAGS detects dynamic errors of the system such as timing faults, race conditions, and other queuing-theory problems. Simulation can be done for any system that passes the static diagnostic, and as long as there is interface closure, missing components are "graphically stubbed."

TAGS software is written in Ada and runs on the Unix-based workstation, such as Sun Sparc, IBM RS6000, and DEC Station 3100. The current hardware configuration consists of the following:

- 19-inch monitor with 1024 by 800 pixel resolution
- 4Mb to 8Mb main memory
- 140Mb Winchester drive
- 60Mb tape backup

TAGS uses the Unix operating system, Windows, and POSTSCRIPT standards. Password and identification are required for using the TAGS system.

TAGS provides a configuration management package that controls and documents changes to the system baseline. The package will support multiple revisions of individual TAGS system design pages. TAGS interfaces with document processors, such as Context or INTERLEAF. These processors hold the templates for all documentation that is required by CALS or DOD-STD-2167A, and provide automated "cut and paste" for

TAGS graphics with the POSTSCRIPT interface. Additional documentation templates can be user defined.

Teledyne Brown Engineering (TBE) provides adequate user documentation in a set of eight manuals. TBE offers a training program at their Huntsville, Alabama facility as well as at customer sites. Teledyne Brown is continually upgrading TAGS through regularly scheduled maintenance and software revisions. These releases are shipped to all TAGS customers that have purchased TAGS maintenance.

ARTIFEX BY ARTIS

Artifex is the CASE environment that ARTIS created for the production of event-driven systems. Their tool does analysis, simulation, design, prototyping, and implementation. The PROTOB methodology is supported by Artifex. Artifex provides computer-aided software modeling. Artifex allows you to build specification, design, and implementation models that are automatically translated into code. Models are tested on-line with their development. The same model is refined from system analysis to implementation. This model refinement is shown in FIG. 22-14.

Rapid prototyping allows for system testing to be performed incrementally: errors are detected early, variants can be tested, and components are more understandable. The whole implementation code is generated automatically from models of software by Total Code Generation.

The major benefit of Artifex is that the software development and maintenance costs are cut dramatically, as is shown in FIG. 22-15. System quality is increased at all levels. Know-how is formalized in components that are easy to understand and reuse.

The key features of Artifex are:

- Visual models
- Object orientation
- Rapid prototyping
- Incremental system testing
- Virtualization of Ada and C
- Total code generation

Artifex supports system engineering. It allows you to analyze, specify, and simulate the hardware shown in FIG. 22-16. It models and emulates the environment that the system must interact. It analyzes, designs, and implements the whole software. System

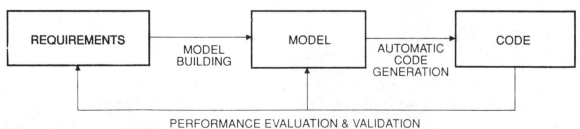

PERFORMANCE EVALUATION & VALIDATION

Fig. 22-14. Model refinement

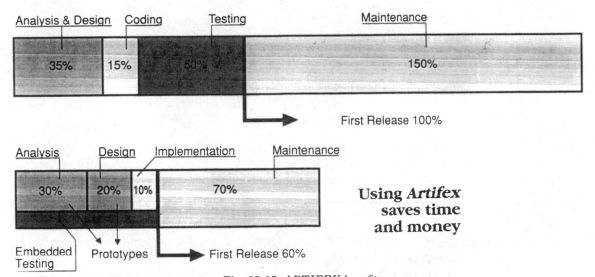

First Release 100%

Using *Artifex*
saves time
and money

First Release 60%

Fig. 22-15. ARTIFEX benefits

Systems Engineering

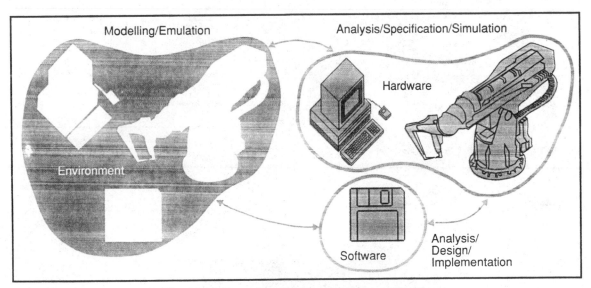

Fig. 22-16. Incremental system simulation and testing

simulation allows evaluation and improvement of the performances of the system by modifying and correcting the hardware layout and software definition. You do not need to change from formulizing the environment by stepping from analysis to implementation.

During the specification phase, you build a model of your system and of the external environment. You then study its behavior by means of interactive simulation with the animation of the graphical model.

During the design phase, the specification model is refined and the actual system architecture is taken into account. Refining the model eventually results in a hierarchical conceptual definition of the system implementation. The implementation model is detailed, and is automatically translated into the implementation code, as is shown in FIG. 22-17. The generated code is object oriented and handles multitasking automatically. It can be embedded on dedicated hardware or distributed over a LAN of nodes with different operating systems. The internode and interprocess communication is handled automatically.

The hardware culture is based on components that can be reused. Whereas, the software culture is based on languages and algorithms. Large systems must be decomposed according to the object-oriented paradigms. Artifex does this decomposition and allows you to build ''software chip'' models, as is shown in FIG. 22-18. Software chips interact with the rest of the world with input and output *pins*, which are shown in FIG. 22-19.

Artifex supports Ada and C and runs on DEC, HP, SONY, SUN, and 286/386 PC's. The operating systems are VMS, ULTRIX, UNIX, and DOS.

Documentation is integrated in the models. A report generator automatically combines texts and graphics in high-quality documents that are always up to date.

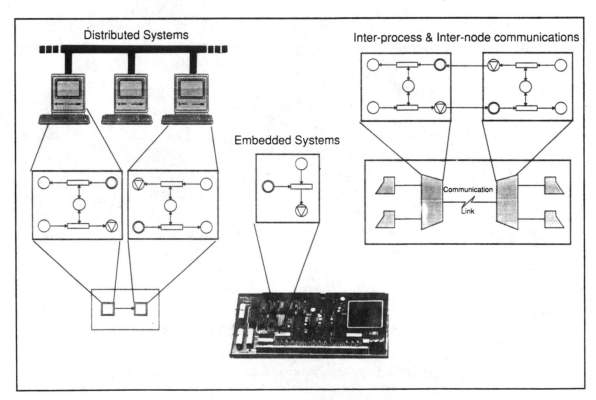

Fig. 22-17. Turning models into code

The *Artifex* software chip

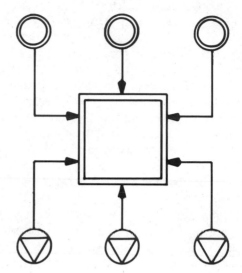

Fig. 22-18. The Artifex "Software Chip"

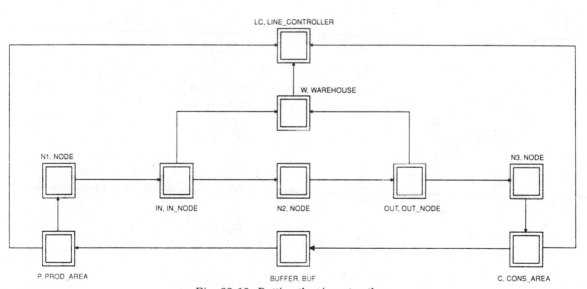

Fig. 22-19. Putting the pieces together

TEAMWORK BY CADRE TECHNOLOGIES

Teamwork is the product of Cadre Technologies. It consists of six CASE tools:

1. Teamwork/IM—Information Modeling
2. Teamwork/SA—Structured Analysis
3. Teamwork/RT—Structured Analysis with Real-Time Extensions

4. Teamwork/SD—Structured Design
5. Teamwork/ACCESS—Utility to Access its Data Dictionary
6. Teamwork/DPI—Document Production Interface

The Teamwork approach to software design provides consistency and early detection of errors. It substantially boosts overall quality and productivity by eliminating many software errors that are typically generated in the analysis and design phase. Teamwork also minimizes development costs because it prevents errors from slipping into the coding, testing, and maintenance phases. During the coding and debug phases, SA/SD documentation can be used to trace the ripple effect of changes to the software, before those changes are incorporated within a design. Another Teamwork advantage is that Designs can be done independent of target hardware or programming language considerations and result in a transportable design. The Teamwork CASE environment is shown in FIG. 22-20.

Teamwork/IM provides an environment of information modeling, which permits modeling of entities, relationships, and attributes of complex information and information flows. This modeling supports the creation and checking of Chen-entity relationship diagrams for database definition. Although no specific schema generation capability is provided by Teamwork/IM, you could employ Teamwork's ACCESS package that is combined with user-written C programs to implement this capability. With Teamwork/IM, analysts build, revise, store, review, and maintain complex data models quickly and accurately. A sample of Teamwork/IM is shown in FIG. 22-21.

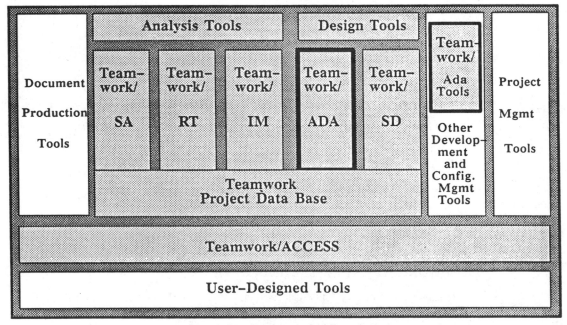

Fig. 22-20. The Teamwork CASE environment

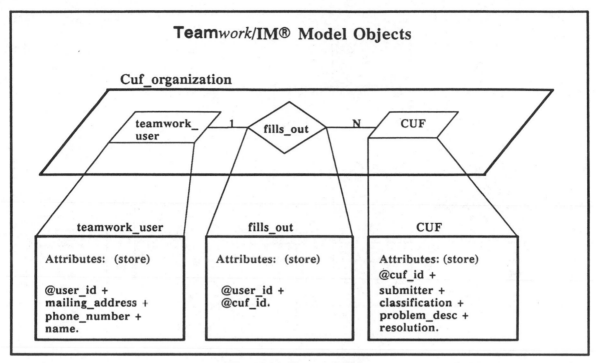

Fig. 22-21. Teamwork/IM

Teamwork/SA includes necessary baseline capabilities to perform system analysis. This capability allows you to easily create, store, and update the elements of the Yourdon/DeMarco structured method:

- Data Flow Diagram (DFD)
- Process Specification (P-Spec)
- Data Dictionary (DD)

With Teamwork/SA, you can rapidly construct the DFD's shown in FIG. 22-22. Elements such as data flows, processes, and files are easily assembled and describe the system. Starting at the highest level, each process is partitioned into its child diagram. After partitioning to the lowest level, each process is described by a simple textual description, called a process specification (P-Spec). Data elements are described throughout the model in the Data Dictionary Entries (DDE's). P-Specs and DDE's are attached to diagrams for easy retrieval and updating.

All elements of DFD's, P-Spec's and DDE's are stored in a project database. The database serves as the base for effective communication within the project team. The database can be printed easily and can create specification documents. The leveling form context diagram to DFD is shown in FIG. 22-23.

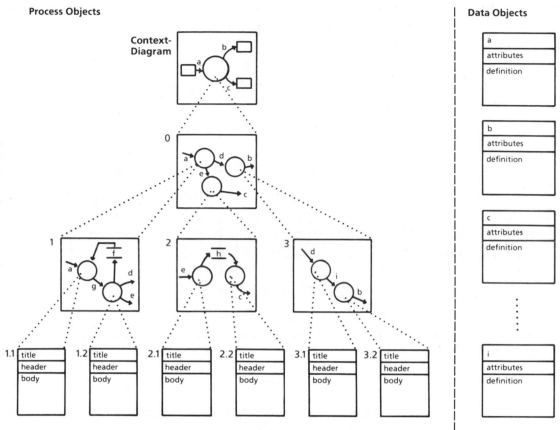

Fig. 22-22. Teamwork/SA DFD's

Teamwork/RT is structured analysis with real-time extensions, which includes capabilities that address the needs of real-time system designers. Teamwork/RT includes:

- Control flow diagrams
- State transition diagrams
- Process activation tables
- Decision tables
- State/event matrices

Teamwork/SD is an environment for system design that works in conjunction with Teamwork/SA or Teamwork/RT. It implements the Constantine/DeMarco structured design approach. The key concept of structured design is the decomposition of a large complex system into a hierarchy of smaller more manageable pieces. The elements used to describe a structured design are structure chart, data dictionary, and module specifications (M-Spec's). Figure 22-24 depicts a structure chart that consists of boxes representing modules, arrows (called invocations) connecting the modules, and short arrows with circular tails (called couples) representing data passed from one module to another.

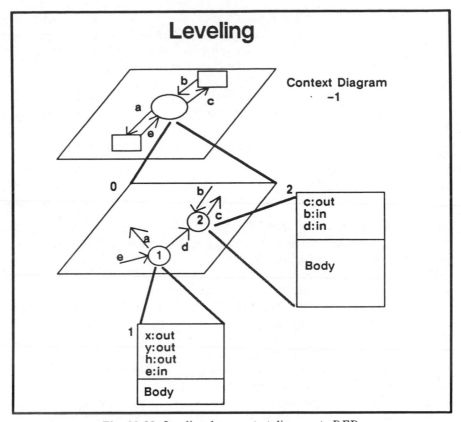

Fig. 22-23. Leveling from context diagram to DFD

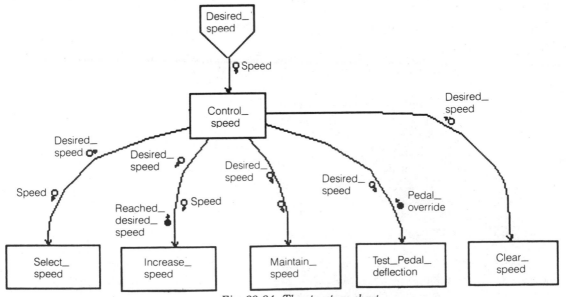

Fig. 22-24. The structure chart

Teamwork/ACCESS is a software package that gives you read (and write in version 2.3) access to Teamwork's data dictionary with routines written in a higher-level language. This open architecture provides you with ability to add on and extend the product. Teamwork/ACCESS can be used for the following scenarios.

- Transfer dictionary information between the project dictionary and specialized project management tools (cost and schedule tracking tools, cost estimation tools, etc.)
- Create custom reports that are not provided by the normal reporting or document production facilities
- Develop custom add on applications like simulation facilities, code generation facilities, or specialized-design metrics

An important feature of Teamwork/ACCESS is its use of read and read/write locking, so that custom extension work can be used in a multiuser environment.

Teamwork/DPI is a package that automatically produces first-cut documents and conforms to user-specified templates or DOD-STD-2167A data item descriptor templates. The package works in conjunction with Teamwork/SD, but allows any picture or text in the Teamwork database or other ASCII text files on the host platform to be automatically pulled into the template format. The resulting first-cut documents can then be refined with the Interleaf, Context, or Scribe publishing software. These packages include editing and page formatting capabilities.

The Teamwork CASE tool set is easy to use. It provides a consistent user interface across a variety of hardware platforms and network capabilities. It is an integrated product and has multiuser, multiwindow, and multitasking applications. It runs on Apollo workstations, Sun-2 and Sun-3 workstations, Hewlett Packard 9000-300, DEC VAX station II, and IBM PC. Teamwork also supports various available networks.

AISLE BY SOFTWARE SYSTEM DESIGN

AISLE is the Ada/ADADL Integrated Software Lifecycle Environment of Software Systems Design, and is shown in FIG. 22-25. It consists of the following nine components:

1. ADADL—Ada-based program design language
2. DocGen—automatic MIL/DOD-STD document generator
3. TestGen—Ada design and code testing tools
4. GraftGen—graphical Ada design system
5. ASE—Ada/ADADL syntax-directed editor
6. ARIS—Ada/ADADL RTSA requirements interface system
7. AIEM—on-line design debugging and analysis tools
8. QualGen—quality metrics generator
9. RETT—requirements traceability

ADADL is the Ada-based program design language (PDL) toolset. It provides an understandable description of the design. It improves productivity, and analyzes the pseudocode to find design logic errors before they become code errors. It supports rapid

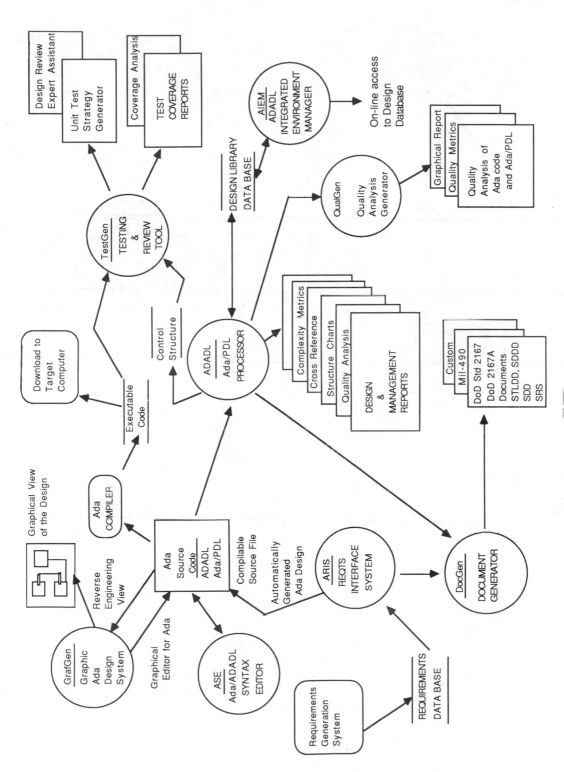

Fig. 22-25. Ada/ADADL Integrated Software Life-cycle Environment (AISLE)

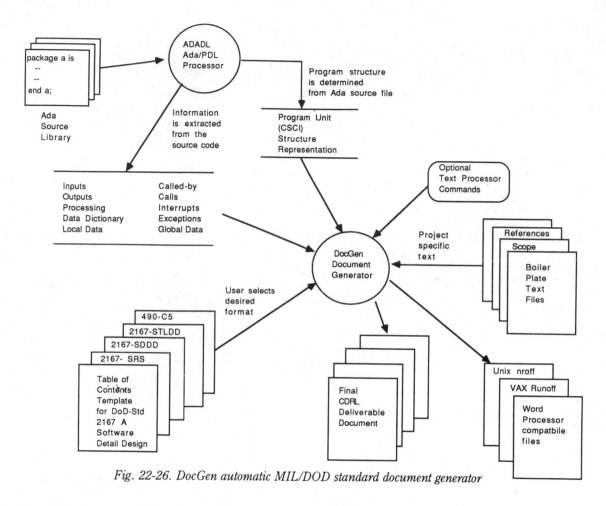

Fig. 22-26. DocGen automatic MIL/DOD standard document generator

prototyping and reusability, and provides detailed cross reference of all Ada entities in both pseudocode and executable code. It also evaluates the McCabe complexity of the pseudocode algorithm.

DocGen is an automatic document generator. It supports available word processor and automatically produces the required MIL/DOD/NASA documentation. It improves documentation productivity, and ensures that the documentation and design are consistent. Figure 22-26 shows a sample DocGen.

TestGen is an Ada design and code testing tool. It aids in the reduction of design review and software testing costs. A sample of TestGen is shown in FIG. 22-27. TestGen helps detect design flaws, and helps prepare unit test procedures for complete path coverage, total branch coverage, and structured (McCabe) testing. It also determines the conditions that will be set at each branch point and will ensure complete testing. It assists to estimate that the effort is needed and tests each program unit. It also determines the number of paths, number of branches, and structured testing metric for each program unit. It supports functional testing and unit testing.

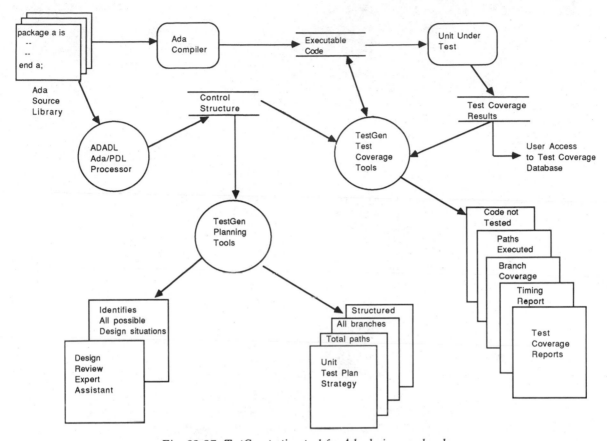

Fig. 22-27. TestGen testing tool for Ada designs and code

GraftGen is the graphical Ada design system tool. It displays graphic output for Ada program and interfaces. Reverse engineering in the Ada design capability displays Ada package structures, invocation structure trees, and Ada dependencies. It also shows visible objects and types, and allows the user to create and modify Ada programs graphically. GraftGen supports both Booch and Buhr diagrams, as shown in FIG. 22-28.

ASE is the Ada/ADADL syntax-directed editor. It helps Ada programmers produce well-documented Ada programs and Ada design. It improves productivity by eliminating syntax errors. ASE is a useful tool for both pseudocode and executable code.

ARIS is a tool for Ada/ADADL requirements interface system. It automatically converts requirements to an object-oriented top-level Ada design. It uses the (OOD) method for constructing a preliminary Ada design directly from the RTSA database. ARIS eliminates errors by automatically converting requirements to the starting point for design refinement, and provides requirements traceability to the design and code. ARIS also automatically produces consistent objects and definitions between RTSA database and Ada code.

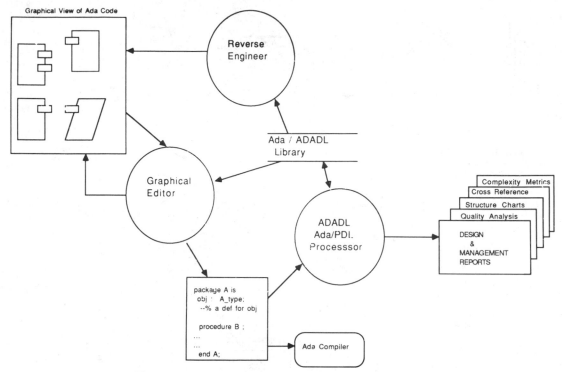

Fig. 22-28. GrafGen: Graphical Ada/ADADL design tool

AIEM is an integrated environment manager. It is a comprehensive set of design database analysis tools, and is an on-line documentation of the entire Ada design. It provides the user with instant knowledge about any aspect of design.

QualGen is an Ada quality analysis and metrics generator. It analyzes designs and codes for calculation of quality metrics. It also provides quality analysis between program units. The metrics can be viewed graphically and numerically.

RETT is the requirements evaluation and traceability tool. It traces requirements throughout the development life cycle. You can instantly see where requirements are satisfied and not satisfied. RETT helps assess impact of proposed changes to any portion of the documentation or design.

23

Emerging CASE tools

The following CASE tools are discussed in this chapter.

- Object Plus by EasySpec
- CASEWorks Tool Set by CASEWorks
- Digital CASE Environment by Digital

OBJECT PLUS BY EASYSPEC

Object Plus is the product of EasySpec. It supports the object-oriented approach. It is a Windows-based integrated CASE tool set. This is supplemented with code generation, and an array of report generation functions that aid in system documentation. The Object Plus Object-Oriented Environment is shown in FIG. 23-1.

Object Plus is an evolutionary approach for software engineering. The life cycle is divided into two phases. Software engineers and designers can partake of portions of these phases as they see fit, and eventually arrive at a comprehensive system specification that is replete with generated code. The two phases are:

1. User requirements
2. Object-oriented analysis, design, and code generation

User requirements are the *CORE* phase that systematically identifies the users, their requirements, and the data elements. You can bypass this phase and proceed directly with the second phase. After identifying the users and their requirements, you need to develop a detailed interface document that uses a word processing package for each requirement. In addition, you must specify the input and output elements that appear on the interfaces to the application, as is shown in FIG. 23-2. These data elements are defined in Object Plus's Element Dictionary, which is shown in FIG. 23-3.

Object-oriented analysis, design, and code generation phases identify the objects and the C^{++}, Ada, and C complete object-code generation, along with the corresponding database schema structure. Object Plus uses the object-oriented methods, which

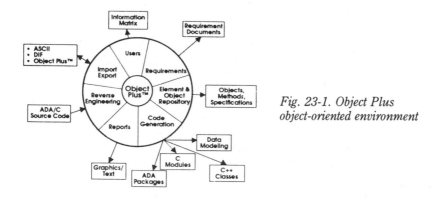

Fig. 23-1. Object Plus object-oriented environment

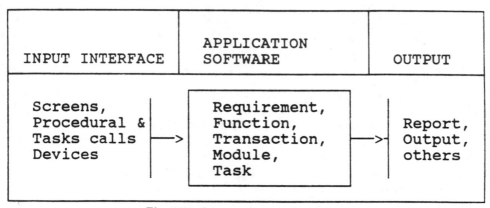

Fig. 23-2. Input and output interfaces

designs and generates the code for the objects. The object menu identifies and designs objects. Designing objects involves four steps:

1. Identify the objects
2. Define the methods associated with each object
3. Specify the connections among the objects
4. Specify the objects by using the Object Specification Template

An object is identified by the use of either the top-down or the bottom-up process. The top-down process considers the problem space and tries to identify the most obvious top-level objects. Organizational structures or reports should be used as a means for identifying objects. The bottom-up process uses the set of elements or objects that have already been identified to compose higher-level objects. The methods associated with each object are create, copy, get, and set.

An object can contain other objects that form nested objects. Object Plus generates the proper code and links objects according to their structure. An object may be defined as the child of another object (ancestor object). During code generation, this object will statically inherit all the properties of its ancestor(s) attributes and methods.

Element Name	Type	Size
OR_ID	CHARACTER	16
SEN_TYPE	CHARACTER	10
SAMPLE_RATE	CHARACTER	10
SENSOR_VALUE	INTEGER	3
CONVERSION_SLOPE	FLOAT	3
OR_HEALTH	CHARACTER	8
SENSOR_HEALTH	CHARACTER	6
SUBSYSTEM	CHARACTER	16
SEN_DESCRIPTION	CHARACTER	32
SUBSYSTEM_DESCRIPTION	CHARACTER	32
SENSOR_COUNT	INTEGER	3
DELTA_TOLERANCE	INTEGER	5
LOW_LIMIT	INTEGER	5
HIGH_LIMIT	INTEGER	5
MSID	CHARACTER	16
UNITS	CHARACTER	10
RATE_HI_LIMIT	FLOAT	5
RATE_LO_LIMIT	FLOAT	5

Fig. 23-3. Object Plus's element dictionary

Object Plus is still evolving. The documentation comes in a standard three-ring binder. The operation of the software is straightforward. Object Plus provides an Analysis and Design methodology, which is based on an object-oriented style developed by Dr. Anthony Lekkos. The major steps of the Lekkos methodology are as follows:

1. Develop an application requirement document with the application requirement proposed outline
2. Identify application users
   User Categories:
   - Human
   - Software
   - Hardware
   - Communication

3. Identify individual functional requirements per user
4. Document the purpose of the function and design its interface
5. Identify the elements or objects that appear in the interface and build an elementary dictionary
6. Use the set of elements and objects from the interface and identify some of the problem space objects
   - Nested objects
   - Hierarchical objects

7. Identify operations for every object
8. Build a C^{++} class, C object-based module, or an Ada package for every identified object and do some unit testing
9. Repeat steps 2 through 8 in any order so that you can be somewhat specific (assume sequential processing)
10. Build the following driver modules:
   - Main module
   - Class/package for every user
   - Procedure for every functional requirement

11. Proceed with functional requirement-specified detailed logic design and implementation (parallel distribution)

The major goal of Object Plus, as stated by the developer, is to shorten the time and cost of development by generating code for reusable software components in the form of objects. This tool lowers the cost of maintenance and generates object-oriented modules that conform to modularity and information-hiding concepts. It also supports the full software life cycle and provides facilities to support the life cycle.

CASEWORKS TOOL SET BY CASEWORKS

CASEWORKS is an integrated tool set that consists of CASE:W for Microsoft Windows and CASE:PM for OS/2 Presentation Manager. CASE:W and CASE:PM are productivity tools for prototyping, developing, testing, and maintaining Microsoft Windows and OS/2 Presentation Managers applications.

CASE:W is a tool for constructing skeletal Windows applications. It is a kind of expert system. An expert system assists the programmer by performing the Windows part of an application, which permits the developer to focus on the application-specific segments. CASE:W is also a Windows application that manages menus, script files, icons, and dialog boxes in a "What You See Is What You Get" (WYSIWYG) context.

CASE:W is a CASE tool that automatically generates Microsoft Windows graphical interfaces and their controls. CASE:W processes are centered around the expert system. The application-development processes for CASE:W are:

- Design
- Tools
- Generate
- Edit
- Make
- Run

The Design facility specifies program configuration and memory management parameters for the C compiler and linker. The developer can also design the main window's characteristics, design the menu bar and pull-down menu system, and specify dialog boxes, as is shown in FIG. 23-4. The result of the design phase is stored and retrieved

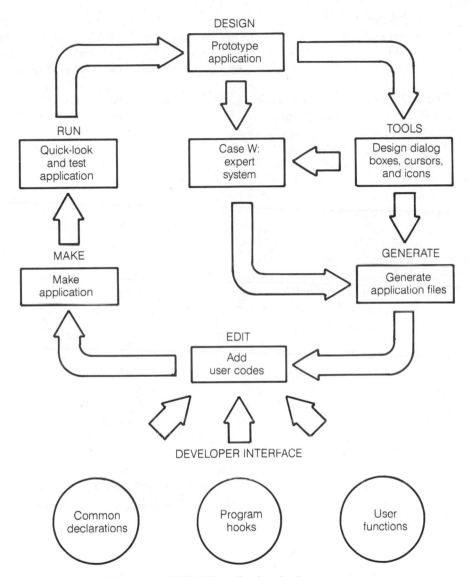

Fig. 23-4. CASE: W application development process

by use of the File facility. The format of the CASEWORKS.APP files is consistent between the CASE:W Windows product and the CASE:PM Presentation Manager product.

The Tools facility modifies the CASE:W environment for up to 15 different tools. The first 4 tools are the Software Development Kit components, the Dialog Editor, the Icon Editor, and the Font Editor.

The Generate facility activates the Interface Engine of the Expert system, which generates all the files that are used to make the Windows application. Code management is also performed by the Generate facility.

The Edit facility is a user-configured interface with a character-based or Windows-compatible text editor program. This principal facility is used for the developer's interface. Application-specific declaration, processing functions, and message handling routines are entered in this facility. The user-added codes are generated each time the Generate facility is used.

The Make facility is a Windows/386 facility only. It operates the character-based Make utility in a DOS virtual window. The Make utility processes the generated Make file that runs the resource compiler, C compiler, and linker programs.

The Run facility is provided to "quick-look" and to test all of the finished Windows application. Run lets you view the Windows interface and operate the menu items, pop-up menus, and dialog boxes. Run will then verify their operation. After the application codes are added, Run lets you test the entire program.

Besides these processes, there are Options and Help facilities. The Option menu item is used to view and select various options that CASE:W makes available for each of its Design modes. The Help facility is a context-sensitive mode of the CASE:W system. When in Help mode, operation of the CASE:W menu bar and popup menu items presents a help window with an explanation of the selected facility.

The software is easily installed. The manual is not lengthy and is easily used. CASE:W requires an IBM AT, PS/2, or compatible with an Intel 80286 or 80386 microprocessor with a minimum of 2Mb of RAM, a hard disk drive that has at least 40Mb of free space, EGA or VGA graphics with a monitor, and a Windows-compatible mouse.

CASE:PM is a CASE productivity tool. It helps with prototyping, generating, testing, and maintaining the OS/2 Presentation manager applications. With this expert system created from CASEWORKS, a specialized knowledge base of Presentation Manager code sets and production rules is created.

CASE:PM supports the full cycle of PM application development. CASE:PM generates concise well-structured and pretested code. It provides a code management facility that automatically carries forward programmer code from one generation of an application to the next. CASE:PM also generates Presentation Manager code from its stored application description files that were developed with CASE:W. CASE:PM's prototyper allows dialog boxes or user-defined code to be added as menu bar items or pull-down menu items.

DIGITAL CASE ENVIRONMENT BY DIGITAL

The Digital CASE Environment (DCE) is a comprehensive solution to the problem of creating and maintaining quality software in today's diverse computing environment. DCE ties together tools that support the entire software life cycle, as well as tools that coordinate your development team. DCE includes tools that are developed by independent software vendors and by the Digital, and provides these tools in an environment that allows you to concentrate on development energies. The DCE supports all kinds of application development and is shown in FIG. 23-5. There are four fundamental elements to DCE.

1. Adherence to architectural standards
2. A CASE integration framework

3. Comprehensive tools that address all aspects of software development and maintenance
4. Support that provides all levels of consulting, training, and service

This CASE strategy, in its adherence to architectural and industry standards, promotes Digital's Network Application Support (NAS). In the NAS model, complex applications can be built in a single development environment, and executed in whole or in part on a range of multivendor hardware and operating system platforms. For example, VMS, ULTRIX, MS-DOS, Macintosh, and IBM mainframes are distributed and networked environments. In short, NAS makes the vision of a unified software environment a reality. A unified software environment allows concentration of your development efforts to value-added aspects of your application and lets you create that application faster.

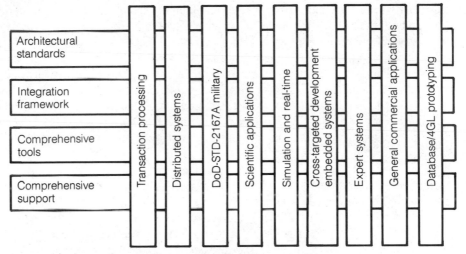

Fig. 23-5. Digital CASE environment

DECwindows, Digital's Environment software that implements the X Window System, is one such NAS service. DECdesign is Digital's analysis and design tool and a key application in the Digital CASE Environment and is built on two NAS services: DEC windows and Compound Document Architecture (CDA). DECdesign helps you to develop software and databases by using industry-standard techniques. DECwrite helps to unify the software environment by synthesizing, organizing, and updating project documentation from multiple sources.

Three other environment-unifying NAS services exist in the DCE that help with the efficient creation of terminal- and device-independent applications: DECforms (based on the ISO Forms Interface Management Standard[FIMS]), DECPHIG (implementation of the ANSI standard for three-dimensional graphics), and DEC GKS (implementation of the ISO and ANSI GKS standard). These services free the developers from the need to be conversant with each machine where forms or graphics software will run. Digital's adherence to well-conceived standards, as exemplified by NAS, fosters a consistent, cohesive computing environment where you can practice CASE most efficiently.

Digital provides a comprehensive CASE integration framework that eliminates redundancy, enhances communication, and promotes sharing of common data. The DCE addresses three types of integration needs:

1. Presentation integration
2. Data integration
3. Control integration

Presentation integration allows interaction with different tools. With use of the DECwindows user interface, multiple tools in DCE have the same look and feel. Future third-party tools will likely have the same user interface as DECwindows because it has been adopted by the Open Software Foundation (OSF) as the application program interface for the OSF/Motif user environment.

Data integration allows tools in the CASE environment to share data. Its capabilities are particularly critical to information system development, where multiple applications must be built around a series of common databases. The DCE promotes data integration through its open, published interfaces and its distributed, active repository. Use of the repository accelerates the development process, provides a tracking mechanism when application modification is required, reduces the opportunity for error, and ensures consistent treatment of data for reliable business analysis by end users.

Today's implementation of the Digital distributed CASE repository is based on the VAX Common Data Dictionary (CDD)/Plus on VMS. VAX CDD/Plus provides a single, logical storage point for data and data definitions when used in multiple applications and tools.

CASE productivity tools, that are joined through the repository, are tightly integrated for more efficient and effective application development and maintenance. The more tools that are integrated, the greater the savings in development time and energy. The more error-free the source code produced by the repository-connected development process is, then there is a greater quality assurance in the end product.

Among the Digital-designed CASE tools that are integrated with the repository are: DECdesign, a new window-based analysis and design tool: the VAX COBOL Generator, a program generator that provides error-free source code directly from a top-down application design; and VAX RALLY, a powerful fourth-generation language environment. These tools enable you to utilize automatic application generation technology with repository-shared data. Development speed is increased while product quality is retained.

The DCE operates across the network with a common user interface and a distributed repository. The repository facilitates data integration. Separate tools share actual data and information about data, as shown in FIG. 23-6. Data and data definitions, that are stored in the repository, can be accessed by information-system building blocks, such as Digital's relational database management system, SQL (a powerful fourth-generation language), CODASYL-compliant database management system, and a database interconnect system for access to IDMS/R, IMS, DB2, and VSAM files.

In addition, the nature of the Digital development environment enables distributed applications in a modular fashion. You can separate an application's data access modules, processing component, and user interface. Later, you can decide where in the network each module should be deployed. No redesign of your system is required. This flexibility allows for maximum growth without redevelopment expenses.

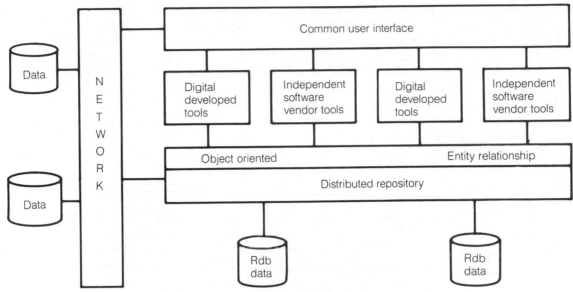

Fig. 23-6. Data integration network

Control integration, provided by DCE, regulates how tools interact with each other. It manages and defines procedures for the software development process. The control integration capabilities are particularly important in defense and technical system development where modification of a complex system after deployment must result in rebuilt software that is identical to the original.

Current configuration management features ensure access to the original configuration of all the deliverables for your software: analysis and design diagrams, source code, object code, documentation, test files, etc. With this access, you can modify your software system as it is required regardless of the point in time where the modification is mandated.

In addition to retroactive system reconstruction, version control and change control are inherent in configuration management in the Digital environment, which permits freezing your developing system for periodic evaluation. Meanwhile, work on a new version of the deliverable can continue. Furthermore, several development streams can work from a common base of software. This approach is useful when newer versions of software are prepared and are being released.

Configuration management in the DCE tracks variant streams of development. This tracking enables a change that is made to a module in one stream of development to be merged with the same module in another stream.

Another common problem in complex technical systems is discrepancy among the deliverables. Because manual tracing of affected components is difficult when requirements change, the source code is often all that is updated. Deciphering resultant software is difficult when maintenance is required. This problem is avoided in the DCE. Requirements traceability features allow a system requirement to be traced in the diagrams, code, and documentation that address the requirement. Also, documentation, code, and diagrams can be traced back to their system requirement.

The DCE provides you with a rich set of automated tools for the entire life cycle, shown in FIG. 23-7. It provides tools for system analysis and specification, system design, coding and debugging, integration and testing, and maintenance and support. These automated tools begin with analysis and design tools that help create a sound design for your application. The tools continue with coding aids and implementation tools, and spiral up and out through every stage of the development cycle. You can efficiently and reliably modify an application long after its initial creation.

Many of these third-party analysis and design tools are included in the DCE and were presented in the preceding chapters. Among these tools are Teamwork from Cadre Technologies, Inc. and Software through Pictures from Interactive Development Environments, Inc. Also included is Digital's new analysis and design tool, DECdesign. DECdesign is a key component with the VAX COBOL Generator and fourth-generation languages.

The DCE also provides a wealth of third-generation languages and compilers, including Ada, Basic, C, COBOL, FORTRAN, and Pascal implementations. Powerful editors, debuggers, and analyzers are available, which accelerate development and minimize errors during the complex coding phase of the development cycle.

Automated librarians and system builders keep track of project files during development. The librarians connect those files and build an up-to-date version of the application. Testing and verifying tools enable you to thoroughly test your application during the implementation phase without getting bogged down in time-consuming and labor-intensive tasks.

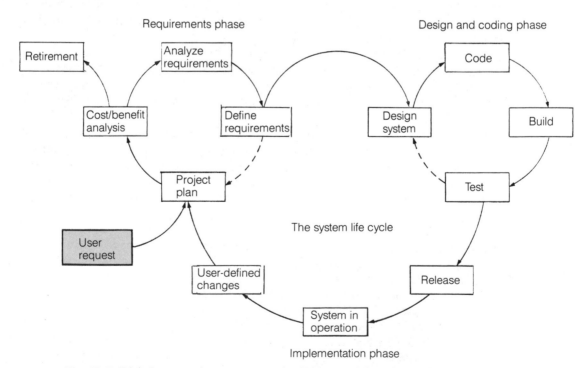

Fig. 23-7. Digital case environment supports all phases of the software development life cycle

Many of these core productivity tools include a DECwindows graphical interface, which simplifies use. Programmers can concentrate their energies on the task at hand. The DCE supplements its core productivity tools with specialized products that are needed by advanced technologies, such as artificial intelligence (AI) and object-oriented programming. Expert system, OPS5, and LISP implementations are among the additional CASE products of special importance to AI developers.

Applications built with the DCE tools are well documented and recorded. Blueprints of the original application are available, as well as information on how it existed at subsequent intervals. In addition, software reengineering tools can reverse the development process and work backward to a design from an existing application.

The Digital Ada programming support environment also includes the VAXELN Ada runtime execution system for dedicated real-time programs that run on VAX targets and the XD-Ada cross-compilation system. Ada developers can have targeting applications for non-VMS systems. You can benefit from the productivity advantages of development with VAX Ada and the Digital CASE Environment.

Digital provides a comprehensive range of CASE and software engineering training events and services that help you successfully implement CASE technologies in your particular organization. Digital consultants will assist you and conduct a technology assessment audit that evaluates your software engineering environment and related upper management issues.

Digital CASE education includes examination of different aspects of CASE automation and what they will mean to your organization. Instruction on specific CASE products is available. The depth of these product courses is tailored for either management or practitioner levels. Courses that are complimentary to traditional CASE disciplines are also available, including courses in database technologies, artificial intelligence, networking, and both Digital's hardware and software operating systems. Digital CASE software is backed by ongoing maintenance support and a staff of service professionals.

24

CASE future trends

CASE tools hold promise for the future by addressing many of today's software engineering needs. Some of these needs will be establishing a uniform standard, creating a generic template, and using understandable English instructions. Standardized CASE tools must accommodate many formal methods, standards, and countless parties with a strategic interest in information technology. Tools will not be effective without the appropriate levels of documentation and training. Software engineering, which will include a good methodology and CASE tool, will help manage system software development and enhance maintainability.

One of the major problems in the computer industry is that of cost overruns and delaying schedules. Proper use of CASE tools will help control costs, reduce development time, and achieve quality products. In this chapter, three types of CASE tools are discussed:

1. Intelligent CASE tools
2. Software prototyping/simulation CASE tools
3. Supporting CASE tools

INTELLIGENT CASE TOOLS

Intelligent CASE Tools (ICT) will develop software for complex computer systems with a minimum of human interface. ICT will be cost effective and efficient. These systems will include software engineering goals and principles. The ICT will assist to automatically select a suitable method and to complete the requirement. They will keep track of details so that no inconsistencies will arise or prevent the various parts of the program from working together as an integrated whole. An intelligent CASE tool will consist of the following components:

- Function modules that will be the tasks embodying the analysis and design of a software system.
- Prepare necessary documentations that will let engineers understand the progress of requirements during various phases of the software development.
- A simulation feature that will show the engineer how the models will behave.

- Matrices that will flag missing inputs or outputs and will help keep the software free of logic errors.
- A data dictionary that will serve as a repository for function modules, documentation, and matrices.
- A programming language that will be tailored to the task of describing each function in terms of states, conditions, and transitions.

ICT will help you understand the requirement graphically by making a system model. It will assist in designing modules for each program function, establishing hierarchical links between modules, determining whether the program will perform as intended, and testing a design before coding.

End users will be able to review various phases of the software development. Necessary documentations will automatically be produced in accordance with the established standard. These documentations can then be reviewed and accepted by the end users.

ICT will assist in selecting a suitable coding language. Coded modules will be automatically tested and integrated. The result will be produced to the satisfaction of the end users. ICT will be an integrated part of the computer system.

Some of the major features of ICT include:

- Software engineering life cycle coverage
- Information and system planning
- Software integration environments
- Knowledge-based tools
- Automation coding, testing, and documenting
- Software reusability
- Reverse engineering
- Resoftware engineering
- Reusable software engineering
- Requirements implementation traceability

An ideal ICT will include a generic template for common applications. The template will be made so that plain English can be understood. Such an ICT will be built as a computer within a computer. This CASE tool will bring results more than you can imagine.

Knowledge-Based CASE Tools (KBCT) are intelligent tools still in evolution. Research is being conducted and development of such tools is beginning that will integrate the whole automation process of the software life cycle.

SOFTWARE PROTOTYPING/SIMULATION TOOLS

Software prototyping/simulation tools will assist in effective communication between end users and engineers. The explorative prototyping will emphasize clarification of requirements and features for future development, which will help to select from alternative solutions.

Experimental prototyping will assist to determine if the proposed solution will be adequate before a large investment in development will be made. Input screens and menus will be developed. Output screens and reports demonstrate what the end user will see. Parts of the software will be written for use in the final product. The functional prototypes will concentrate on specific capabilities that will be required in the deliverable system. The development will illustrate and analyze the logical flow of the software functions.

The simulation will be used for estimating metrics such as response times, database access time, throughput rates, and other performance characteristics that might be required in the system.

This prototyping method will also illustrate data flow/information model and changing data values as the system is simulated. Simulations will demonstrate the input and dynamically changing output that the end user will see during execution. Some of the available CASE tools that are geared towards prototyping are:

- Foresight by Athena Systems
- STATEMATE by i-Logic Inc.
- LUIS by Lockheed
- PAWS/GPSM by Information Research Associates

SUPPORTING CASE TOOLS

There are many stand alone CASE tools available for evaluating project management, quality performance, and test cases generator.

ADAMAT is the product of Dynamics Research Corporation. ADAMAT analyzes Ada source code and reports on how effectively engineers are using features of Ada. It also assesses whether the developers are adhering to established software quality principles. These reports are based on the percentage of time that those quality principles are being adhered to. The tool uses a metrics hierarchy for reporting on software quality. The top level of the hierarchy addresses the three quality goals of reliability, maintainability, and portability.

The "T" tool is the product of Programming Environments Inc. This tool describes an automatic test case input generator. End users requirements are entered into a standard format by the use of structured English statements. Each requirement in the system specification is identified so the requirements can be traced for testability. All requirements must be defined, verified, and completed before using "T" for tracking the requirements. The tool generates test cases before coding begins with a knowledge-based approach that identifies the most probable errors. Rules are enforced that combine functional tests, boundary value testing, and partitioning of tests. "T" supports queries of the requirements database, and runs on the IBM PC/AT and compatibles.

Future supporting CASE tools should be integrated with intelligent CASE tools and software prototyping/simulation tools.

Appendix A

List of
acronyms and abbreviations

ADL	Ada Design Language
ANSI	American National Standards Institute
APSE	Ada Programming Support Environment
ASSM	Abstract System Semantic Model
CAIS	Common APSE Interface Set
CASE	Computer-Aided Software Engineering
CCB	Configuration Control Board
CDR	Critical Design Review
CDRL	Contract Data Requirements List
CFD	Control Flow Diagram
CIDS	Critical Item Development Specification
CM	Configuration Management
COCOMO	Constructive Cost Model
COTS	Commercial Off-The-Shelf
CPM	Critical Path Method
CRISD	Computer Resources Integrated Support Document
CSC	Computer Software Component
CSCI	Computer Software Configuration Item
CSDM	Computer Software Development Methodology
CSOM	Computer System Operator's Manual
CSP	Control Specification
CSU	Computer Software Unit
DBMS	DataBase Management System
DCE	Digital CASE Environment
DD	Data Dictionary
DEC	Digital Equipment Corporation
DFD	Data Flow Diagram
DID	Data Item Description
DOD	Department Of Defense
DSD	Data Structure Diagram

EC	Estimated Cost
ECP	Engineering Change Proposal
ELOC	Estimated Line Of Code
ER	Entity Relationship
ESA	Essential System Analysis
ESD	Essential System Design
EV	Earned Value
FCA	Functional Configuration Audit
FIMS	Forms Interface Management Standard
FQT	Formal Qualification Testing
FSE	Forward Software Engineering
GFS	Government Furnished Software
HIPO	Hierarchy, Input, Process, Output
	High-Order Language
HOOD	Hierarchical Object-Oriented Design
HWCI	Hardware Configuration Item
ICT	Intelligent CASE Tools
IDD	Interface Design Document
IDE	Interactive Development Environments
IEEE	Institute of Electrical and Electronics Engineers
I/O	Input/Output
IOPT	Input/Output Parameter Table
IORL	Input/Output Requirements Language
IORTD	Input/Output Relationships and Timing Diagram
IPT	Internal Parameter Table
IRS	Interface Requirements Specification
ISO	International Standards Organization
IV&V	Independent Verification and Validation
JSD	Jackson Structured Development
JSP	Jackson Structured Programming
KAPSE	Kernel Ada Programming Support Environment
LOE	Labor Of Efforts
LRM	Language Reference Manual
MANPRINT	Manpower and Personnel Integration
MAPSE	Minimal Ada Programming Support Environment
NAS	Network Application Support
NDS	NonDevelopment Software
OAM	Object Analysis Model
OBM	Object Behavior Model
OIM	Object Information Model
OML	Object Management Library
OOD	Object-Oriented Design
OODB	Object-Oriented DataBase
OODM	Object-Oriented Design Method
OOM	Object-Oriented Methodology
OOP	Object-Oriented Programming

OOSD	Object-Oriented Structured Design
OPM	Object Process Model
OSF	Open Software Foundation
OSI	Open System Interconnection
OTS	Off-The-Shelf
P-Spec	Process Specification
PAMELA	Process Abstraction Method for Embedded Large Applications
PCA	Physical Configuration Audit
PDL	Program Design Language
PDR	Preliminary Design Review
PERT	Program Evaluation and Review Technique
PKWB	ProKit*WORKBENCH
PPD	Predefined Process Diagram
PSA	Program Statement Analyzer
PSL	Program Statement Language
QA	Quality Assurance
QSA	Quintessential System Analysis
RDM	Requirements Definition Model
RE	Resoftware Engineering
REVS	Requirements Engineering and Validation System
RFP	Request For Proposal
ROM	Read-Only Memory
RM	Refinement Method
RSE	Reverse Software Engineering
RSI	Report Specification Interface
RSL	Requirements Statement Language
RTL	Run Time Library
SA	Structured Analysis
SADT	Structured Analysis and Design Technique
SBD	Schematic Block Diagram
SCR	Software Cost Reduction
SD	Structured Design
SDD	Software Design Document
SDF	Software Development File
SDL	Software Development Library
SDP	Software Development Plan
SDR	System Design Review
SECP	Software Engineering Conversion Plan
SED	Software Engineering Design
SEDP	Software Engineering Development Plan
SEI	Software Engineering Institute
SEMP	Software Engineering Maintenance Plan
SERA	Software Engineering Requirements Analysis
SOW	Statement Of Work
SPM	Software Programmer's Manual
SPS	Software Product Specification

SREM	Software Requirements Engineering Methodology
SRR	System Requirements Review
SRS	Software Requirements Specification
SSA	Structured System Analysis
SSD	Strategies for System Development
SSDD	System/Segment Design Document
SSPM	Software Standards and Procedures Manual
SSR	Software Specification Review
SSS	System/Segment Specification
STD	Software Test Description
STP	Software Test Plan
STR	Software Test Report
STRADIS	Structured Analysis, Design and Implementation of Information System
STT	State Transition Table
SUM	Software User's Manual
TAGS	Technology for the Automated Generation of Systems
TRR	Test Readiness Review
UCRA	User-Centered Requirements Analysis
UI	User Interface
UC	User Cases
VDD	Version Description Document
VDM	Vienna Development Methodology
WBS	Work Breakdown Structure

Appendix B

List of vendors
CASE tools and software
engineering methodologies

CASE TOOLS

VENDORS	PRODUCTS
ADA GRAPH 1700 N Moore St., Suite 1220 Arlington, VA 22209 (703) 558-7400	PAMELA Ada Graph
ADVANCED LOGICAL SOFTWARE 9903 Santa Monica Blvd. Beverly Hills, CA 90212 (213) 653-5786	ANATOOL
ADVANCED MICROSOLUTIONS (415) 365-9880	ATS
ADVANCED TECHNOLOGY INTERNATIONAL, INC. 350 Fifth Ave., 19th Floor New York, NY 10118 (212) 947-4755	Ada PDL Super PDL Super CASE
ANALYSTS INTERNATIONAL CORP. (212) 465-1660	Corvet

VENDORS	PRODUCTS
ARTIS s.r.l Advanced Research Tools for Information System Via Morgari 35-10125 Torino, Italy +39 11 669.09.33	Artifex
ATHENA SYSTEMS INC. 139 Kifer Ct. Sunnyvale, CA 94086 (408) 730-2100	Foresight
BACHMAN INFORMATION SYSTEMS, INC. (617) 354-1414	IDMS DB2
BOOLE & BABBAGE, INC. (408) 735-9550	Team-Errico
BYTEL CORP. (415) 527-1157	Cogen Genifer
CADRE TECH 222 Richmond St. Providence, RI 02903 (401) 351-5950	Teamwork
CADSYS SOFTWARE TOOLS 5833 Humblebee Rd. Columbia, MD 21045 (301) 997-4330	cadSYS
CADWARE, INC. 800-223-9273	Sylva Picture Programmer
CASE CONSULTING, INC. 1701 N Collins Blvd. Richardson, TX 75080 (214) 644-0008	Dynomod
CASEWORKS, INC. 800-635-1577	CASE:PM CASE:W

VENDORS	PRODUCTS
CGI SYSTEMS, INC. 800-722-1866	Pacbase
CINCOM SOFTWARE, INC. 800-543-3010	Mantis M/Text CPCS
CLEAR SOFTWARE, INC. 637 Washington St. Brookline, MA 02146 (617) 232-4720	Clear
COMPUTER COMMAND & CONTROL CO. 2401 Walnut St. Philadelphia, PA 19103 (215) 854-0555	Model
CONTEXT CORP. 8285 SW Nimbus Ave. Beaverton, OR 97005	TekCASE
CODING (THE) FACTORY, INC. (201) 981-0100	Cofac
COGNOS, INC. (613) 738-1440	PHLEX
CONTROL DATA CORP. 8100 34th Ave., S Bloomington, MN 55420 (612) 853-6628	PRECISE
CORTEX CORP. (617) 894-7000	Corvision
CULLINET SOFTWARE, INC. (617) 329-7700	Enterprise: Generator
DAVID R. BLACK & ASSOCIATES (216) 688-2741	Cobol Program Generator

VENDORS	PRODUCTS
DEC 3 Results Way Marlboro, MA 01752 (617) 467-7043	VAXset, VAX Rally, VAX Cobol Generator, VAX Code Management System, VAX Module Management System, VAX DEC/Test manager, Vax Performance and Coverage Analyzer, VAX Language Sensitive Editor, VAX Source Code Analyzer, VAX Document, VAX Software Engineering Tool, CASE for Information Systems
DIVERSIFIED SOFTWARE SYSTEMS, INC. 18630 Sutter Blvd. Morgan Hill, CA 95037 (215) 692-9687	Docu/TEXT
DYNAMICS RESEARCH CORP. 60 Frontage St. Andover, MA 01810 (508) 475-9090	AdaMAT
EASYSPEC INC. 17629 El Camino Real Suite 202 Houston, TX 77058 (713) 480-3233	Object Plus
EVANSVILLE DATA PROCESSING CORP. (812) 479-6951	Gen81
E-Z GEN, INC. (609) 428-0211	E-ZCOB
GENERAL DATA SYSTEMS, INC. (215) 985-1780	GDX
HELP/SYSTEMS, INC. (612) 933-0609	Genesis V
HEWLETT-PACKARD CO.	HP64000 AxCASE
IBM	Cross System Product

VENDORS	PRODUCTS
ICONIX SOFTWARE ENGINEERING, INC. 2800 28th St., Suite 320 Santa Monica, CA 90405 (213) 458-0092	AdaFlow Power Tools
I-LOGIX INC. 22 Third Ave. Burlington, MA 01803 (617) 332-8678	STATEMATE
INDEX TECHNOLOGY INC. One Main St. Cambridge, MA 01719 (617) 494-8200	Excelerator/RTS
INTEGRATED SYSTEMS INC. 2500 Mission College Blvd. Santa Clara, CA 95054 (203) 722-1722	Autocode
INTELLIGENT ENVIRONMENTS OF TEWKSBURY Tewksbury, MA 01876	Application Manager CASE, 4GL, 3GL Expert system tools
INTERACTIVE DEVELOPMENT ENVIRONMENTS 595 Market Street, 12th Floor San Francisco, CA 94105 (201) 368-8383	Software through Pictures
INTERACTIVE SOFTWARE ENGINEERING, INC. (805) 685-1006	Eiffel
LANGUAGE TECHNOLOGY, INC. (508) 741-1507	Recorder Recorder/CICS Inspector
MAGEC SOFTWARE 800-336-2432	Magec
MAGNA SOFTWARE CORP. (212) 691-0300	Magna 8

VENDORS	PRODUCTS
MANAGER SOFTWARE PRODUCTS, INC. (617) 863-5800	Source manager
MENTOR GRAPHICS CORP. 8500 SW Creekside Pl. Beaverton, OR 97005 (503) 626-7000	CASE Station and Codelink
MARK JEFFERY KOCH & ASSOCIATES, INC. (609) 596-0808	ACT/1
MARK V SYSTEMS 16400 Ventura Blvd., Ste. 303 Encino, CA 93063 800-666-6232	Adagen
MATRIX SOFTWARE TECHNOLOGY CORP. (617) 567-0037	Layout
MATTERHORN, INC. 800-634-4255	Hibol
MCDONNELL DOUGLAS INFORMATION SYSTEMS Box 516, St. Louis, MO 63166 800-325-1087	ProKit* WORKBENCH
MENLO BUSINESS SYSTEMS, CO. (415) 948-7920	Foundation
MENTOR GRAPHICS CORP. 8500 SW Creekside Pl. Beaverton, OR 97005 (202) 845-7767	Mentor Graphics CASE
META SYSTEMS, LTD. 315 E. Eisenhower Pkwy. Ann Arbor, MI 48108 (313) 663-6027	PSL/PSA

VENDORS	PRODUCTS
MICHAEL ROSS & COLE LTD. (312) 916-0662	MRC-productivity series
MICRO FOCUS, INC. 800-872-6265	Micro Focus Cobol/2 Workbench
NASTEC 24681 NW Hwy. Southfield, MI 48075 800-872-8296	CASE 2000, RTrace
NETRON, INC. (416) 636-8333	Netron/CAP Development Center
ONLINE SOFTWARE INTERNATIONAL, INC. (201) 592-0009	Intelagen
OPTIMA, INC. 800-633-6303	Brackets Plus
PANSOPHIC SYSTEMS, INC. (312) 505-6000	Telon
PEAT MARWICK ADVANCED TECHNOLOGY (312) 938-1000	Pathvu, Retrofit, Goldrun
PHOENIX TECHNOLOGIES, LTD. 800-843-3787	Pfinish
POLYTRON CORP. 800-547-4000	PVCS, Poly DOC, Poly Make
PROGRAMMING CONCEPTS, INC. (516) 467-5200	Clist
PROMOD INC. 23685 Birtcher Dr. Lake Forest, CA 92630 (301) 571-9313	Pro/Source, Pro Cap
QUALITY CONSULTANTS, INC. 800-338-3772	Artessa

VENDORS	PRODUCTS
QUANTITATIVE TECHNOLOGY CORP. (508) 626-3081	Software Foundary
READY SYSTEMS CORP. 449 Sherman Ave. Palo Alto, CA 94306 (415) 326-2950	CARDtools
REALIA, INC. (312) 346-0642	Realia Cobol, Real DL/1, Real CICS
REASONING SYSTEMS, INC. 1801 Page Mill Rd. Palo Alto, CA 94304 (415) 494-6201	REFINE
SAGE SOFTWARE INC. 1700 NW 167th Pl. Beaverton, OR 97006 (503) 645-1150	vsDesigner
SCANDURA INTELLIGENT SYSTEMS (215) 664-1207	Prodoc
SOFTLAB, INC. (415) 957-9175	Maestro
SOFTWARE AG OF NORTH AMERICA, INC. (703) 860-5050	Natural Construct/ Natural/Predict
SOFTWARE BUSINESS APPLICATIONS (312) 863-4020	Vssearch
THE SOFTWARE CONSORTIUM (213) 822-8634	The Programmer's Helper
SOFTWARE INTELLIGENT SYSTEMS (A div. of Galeo Corp.) (805) 499-7206	Protool/Online
SOFTWARE RESEARCH, INC. (216) 871-3135	micro-CAPS

VENDORS	PRODUCTS
SPS SOFTWARE PRODUCTS & SERVICES, INC. 14 East 38th St. 14th Floor New York, NY 10016 (212) 686-3790	EPOS
STERLING CASTLE 800-722-7853	Logic Gem
SYNOPTIC CONSULTING, INC. (212) 779-1588	R.A.P.
SYSCORP INTERNATIONAL 800-727-7837	Micro Step
TELEDYNE BROWN ENGINEERING Cummings Research Park 300 Sparkman Dr. NW P.O. Box 070007 Huntsville, AL 35807 800-633-4675	TAGS
TEXAS INSTRUMENTS, INC. (214) 575-4404	Information Engineering Facility (IEF)
THE ANALYTIC SCIENCES CORP. 55 Walkers Brook Dr. Reading, MA 01867 (617) 942-2000	Ada GRAPH
TRANSFORM LOGIC CORP. 24681 Northwestern Hwy. Southfield, MI 48075 800-872-8296	DesignAid
TRAVTECH, INC. (203) 277-9595	Analyzer, Traps, Scoreboard
VERILOG USA 800-347-0371	Geode, Logiscope

VENDORS	PRODUCTS
VESTRONIX, INC. 800-265-2682	Pro-C
VIASOFT, INC. 800-622-6682	Via/Center
WANG LABORATORIES, INC. (508) 459-5000	Pace
WORLDWIDE DATA 17 Battery Pl. New York, NY 10004 800-451-8424	CHARM
XANALOG CORP. (617) 938-8722	Xanalog Graphics to Fortran Generator
YOURDON 1501 Broadway New York, NY 10036 (212) 391-2828	Analyst/Designer Toolkit, Cradle

SOFTWARE ENGINEERING METHODOLOGIES

VENDORS	PRODUCTS
ADA GRAPH 1700 N Moore St. Suite 1220 Arlington, VA 22207 (703) 558-7400	PAMELA
ADVANCED SOFTWARE TECHNOLOGY SPECIALISTS 3418 Broadway Fort Wayne, IN 46807 (219) 456-9260	ADM
ADVANCED SYSTEM ARCHITECTURES Johnson House 73-79 Park St. Camberely, Surrey UK	AUTO-G
AGS MANAGEMENT SYSTEMS, INC. 880 First Ave. King of Prussia, PA 19406 (215) 265-1550	MULTI/CAM

VENDORS	PRODUCTS
ASCENT LOGIC CORPORATION Suite 200, 180 Rose Orchard Way San Jose, CA 95037 (408) 943-0630	DCDS
ASYST TECHNOLOGY, INC. 1080 Beaver Hall Hill, Suite 1400 Montreal, Quebec Canada H2Z 1S8 (514) 871-0108	MINI-ASYST
CAINE, FARBER, & GORDON, INC. 1010 E Union St. Pasadena, CA 91106 (818) 449-3070	PDL/81
CISI-INGENIERIE 2, rue Jules Vedrine 31400 Toulouse France (33) 6120 4324	HOOD
COLON KNIGHT 23 Carlton Rd. Caversham, Reading R447Nt England 0734 470440	DSSAD
CONTROL DATA CORPORATION 511 11th Ave. South Minneapolis, MN 55401 (612) 853-6628	NIAM
COMPUTATIONAL LOGIC, INC. 1717 West Sixth, Suite 290 Austin, TX 78703 (512) 322-9951	GYPSY
DANSK DATAMATIK CENTER Lundtoftevej 1 C DK-2800 Lyngby Denmark	VDM

VENDORS	PRODUCTS
GEORGE MASON UNIVERSITY School of Information Technology & Engineering 4400 University Dr. Fairfax, Virginia 22030-4444 (703) 323-3530	DARTS
GEORGE W. CHERRY THOUGHT ** TOOLS, INC. P.O. Box 2429 Reston, VA 22090 (703) 437-4450	PAMELA-2
GODDARD SPACE FLIGHT CENTER Greenbelt, MD 20771 (301) 286-7631	GOOD
Grady Booch c/o RATIONAL 835 S Moore St. Lakewood, CO 80226 (303) 986-2405	OOD
Hannu Kangassalo University of Tampere P.O. Box 60SF-33101 Tampere Finland	COMIC
HARRIS CORPORATION P.O. Box 98000 Melbourne, FL 32902 (407) 984-6006	InnovAda
HUGHES AIRCRAFT COMPANY Information Systems Division P.O. Box 92919 Los Angeles, CA 90009	UOSE
IBM CORPORATION P.O. Box 700 Suffern, NY 10901 (914) 578-3535	S-JAD

VENDORS	PRODUCTS
IBM SYSTEM INTEGRATION DIVISION 6600 Rockledge Dr. Bethesda, MD 20817 (301) 493-1463	IBM/4LDM
IMPERIAL SOFTWARE TECHNOLOGY 60 Albert Court Prince Consort Road London SW7 2BH England 01 581 8155	IStar
Imtiaz A. Pirbhai SYSTEMS METHODS 2026 Yale Ave., E Seattle, WA 98102 (206) 324-4137	SSD
INFORMATION SYSTEMS INSTITUTE 2770 Indian River Blvd. Vero Beach, FL 32960 (407) 569-3722	BOX STRUCTURES
INSTITUTE V Box 6501 S-113 83 Stockholm Sweden +46-8-23 39 90	ISAC
INTERACTIVE DEVELOPMENT ENVIRONMENTS, INC. 595 Market St. 12th Floor San Francisco, CA 94105 (415) 543-0900	StP
INTERMETRICS 733 Concord Avenue Cambridge, MA 02140 (617) 661-1840	BYRON
JAMES MARTIN ASSOCIATES, INC. 1850 Centennial Park Dr. Reston, VA 22180 (703) 620-9504	IEM

VENDORS	PRODUCTS
JOHN E. STOCKENBERG 30 East St. Newport, RI 02840 (401) 847-8875	SEM
Ken Jackson SD-SCICON PLC Pembroke House, Pembroke Broadway Camberely, Surrey GU15 3XD England	MASCOT
KEN ORR AND ASSOCIATES, INC. 1725 Gage Blvd. Topeka, KS 66604 (913) 273-0653	DSSD
LOCKHEED MISSILES AND SPACE CO. P.O. Box 3504 Sunnyvale, CA 94089	SSPM
McDONNELL DOUGLAS P.O. Box 516, Dept. L860 St. Louis, MO 63166 800-325-1087	STRADIS
META SYSTEMS, LTD. 315 E. Eisenhower, Suite 200 Ann Arbor, MI 48108 (313) 663-6027	PSL/PSA
MICHAEL JACKSON SYSTEMS LTD. 22 Little Portland St. London WIN 5AF United Kingdom (01) 499 6655	JSD
OBJECTIVE SYSTEMS SF AB Torshamnsgatan 39 Sweden +46 8 730 45 30	ObjectOry
PHILIPS RESEARCH LABORATORY 2, av. Van Becelaere B-1170 Brussels Belgium	ERAE

VENDORS	PRODUCTS
PRAGMATIC, INC.	MBOOD

PRAGMATIC, INC.
P.O. Box 3429
Waikoloa, HI 96743
(808) 883-9011

PROJECT TECHNOLOGY, INC.   OOA
2560 Ninth St., Suite 214
Berkeley, CA 94710
(415) 845-1484

RAMTECK INC.   ABDLSLCM
727 Eastern Lane
Bricktown, NJ 08723
(201) 477-8248

SD-SCICON PLC   CORE
Pembroke House, Pembroke Broadway
Camberley, Surrey GU15 3XD, England
0276 686 200

SEMA.METRA   MERISE
16 Rue Barbe's
92126 Montrouge Cedex, France

SOFTECH INC.   SADT
460 Totten Pond Rd.
Waltham, MA 02254
(617) 890-6900

SOFTWARE DEVELOPMENT CONCEPTS   WARD/MELLOR
424 West End Ave., 11 E
New York, NY 10024

SOFTWARE SYSTEMS DESIGN, INC.   AISLE
3627 Padua Ave.
Claremont, CA 91711
(714) 625-6147

TELEDYNE BROWN ENGINEERING   TAGS
Cummings Research Park
Huntsville, AL 35807
800-633-4675

VENDORS	PRODUCTS
THE ATLANTIC SYSTEMS GUILD, INC. 353 W 12th St. New York, NY 10014 (212) 620-4282	E-DEV/ESA
Vaclav Rajlich DEPARTMENT OF COMPUTER SCIENCE Wayne State University Detroit, MI 48202 (313) 577-2477	RM
WAYNE STEVENS 11 Myron St. Fairfield, CT 06430 (203) 259-2781	SD

Appendix C

List of software development standards

ANSI/IEEE Std 729-1983	IEEE Standard Glossary of Software Engineering Terminology
ANSI/IEEE Std 730-1984	IEEE Standard for Software Quality Assurance Plans
ANSI/IEEE Std 828-1983	IEEE Standard for Software Configuration Management Plans
ANSI/IEEE Std 829-1983	IEEE Standard for Software Test Documentation
ANSI/IEEE STD 830-1984	IEEE Guide to Software Requirements Specifications
ANSI/IEEE Std 983-1986	IEEE Guide for Software Quality Assurance Planning
ANSI/IEEE Std 990-1986	IEEE Recommended Practices for Ada as a Program Design Language
ANSI/IEEE Std 1002-1987	IEEE Standard Taxonomy for Software Engineering Standards
ANSI/IEEE Std 1008-1987	IEEE Standard for Software Unit Testing
ANSI/IEEE Std 1012-1986	IEEE Standard for Software Verification and Validation Plans
ANSI/IEEE Std 1016-1987	IEEE Recommended Practices for Software Design Descriptions
ANSI/IEEE Std 1042-1988	IEEE Guide to Software Configuration Management
ANSI/IEEE Std 1058.1-1987	IEEE Standard for Software Project Management Plans
ANSI/IEEE Std 1063-1987	IEEE Standard for Software User Documentation
DOD-STD-2167A	U.S. Defense System Software Development
DOD-STD-2168	U.S. Defense System Software Quality Program
DOD-STD-7935	Automated Data Systems Documentation Standards

GOSIP	U.S. Government Open System Interconnection Profile
IEEE Std 982.1-1988	IEEE Standard Dictionary of Measures to Produce Reliable Software
IEEE Std 982.2-1988	IEEE Guide for the Use of IEEE Standard Dictionary of Measures to Produce Reliable Software (IEEE Std 982.1-1988)
IEEE Std 1028-1988	IEEE Standard for Software Reviews and Audits
IEEE Standards	To provide recommendations reflecting the application of software engineering principles to the development and maintenance of software
MIL-STD-286	Tailoring Guide for DOD-STD-2168
MIL-STD-287	Tailoring Guide for DOD-STD-2167A
MIL-STD-480A	Configuration Management Practices for Systems, etc.
MIL-STD-480B	Configuration Control Engineering Changes, Deviations, and Waivers
MIL-STD-483A	Configuration Management Practices for Systems, Equipment, Munition, and Computer Software
MIL-STD-490A	Specification Practices
MIL-STD-499A	Engineering Management
MIL-STD-882B	System Safety Program Requirements
MIL-STD-1521B	Technical Reviews and Audits for Systems, Equipments, and Computer Programs
MIL-STD-1750A	U.S. Military Standard for Microprocessors
MIL-STD-1803	Software Development Integrity Program
MIL-STD-1815A	Ada Programming Language
NIST Standards	U.S. National Institute of Standards and Technology

Bibliography

Allworth, S. T., and R. N. Zobel. *Introduction to Real-Time Software Design*. New York: Springer-Verlag, 1987.

Agresti, W. W. *Tutorial: New Paradigms for Software Development*, Los Angeles, Calif.: The Computer Society Press, 1986.

Balzer, R. "A 15 Year Perspective on Automatic Programming," *IEEE Trans. Software Engineering*. SE-11,1 (Nov 1985): 157–167.

Balzer, R., T. Cheathm, and C. Green. "Software Technology in the 1990's: Using a New Paradigms." *Computer* 16, 11 (Nov 1983): 39–46.

Bauer, F. L. "Programming as an Evolutionary Process." Proc. 2nd International Conference Software Engineering, IEEE Computer Society, Jan 1976, 222–234.

Bergland, G. D., and R. D. Gordon. *Software Design Strategies*. Washington, D.C.: IEEE Computer Society Press, 1981.

Birrell, N. D., and M. A. Ould. *A Practical Handbook for Software Development*. New York: Cambridge University Press, 1985.

Bjorner, D., and C. B. Jones. *Formal Specifications and Software Development*. Englewood Cliffs, N.J.: Prentice-Hall, 1982.

Blank J., and M. J. Krijger. *Software Engineering: Methods and Techniques*. New York: Wiley Interscience, 1983.

Boehm, B. "Software Engineering." IEEE Trans. Computers C-25, 12 (Dec 1976), 1226–1241.

_____. *Software Engineering Economics*. Englewood Cliffs, N.J.: Prentice-Hall Inc., 1981.

_____. "A Spiral Model of Software Development and Enhancement." IEEE Computer, Vol. 21, No. 5, May 1988.

Bohm, C., and G. Jacopini. "Flow Diagrams, Turing Machines and Languages with only Two Formation Rules." Communications of the ACM, Vol. 9, No. 4, May 1966.

Booch, G. *Software Engineering with Ada*. Menlo Park, Calif.: Benjamin/Cummings Publishing Co., 1982.

_____. "Object-Oriented development." IEEE Transactions on Software Development, Vol. SE-12, No. 2, Feb 1986, 211-221.

Brackett, John W. "Software Requirements." SEI Curriculum Module SEI-CM-19-1.0, Dec 1988.

Budde, R., K. Kuhlenkamp, L. Mathiassen, and H. Zullighoven. *Approaches to Prototyping*, New York: Springer-Verlag, 1984.

Budgen, David, and Richard Sincovec. "Introduction to Software Design." SEI Curriculum Module SEI-CM-2-1.2 (Preliminary), July 1987.

Buhr, R.J.A. *System Design with Ada*. Englewood Cliffs, N.J.: Prentice-Hall, 1984.

Cameron, John. JSP & JSD: The Jackson Approach to Software Development. Washington, D.C.: IEEE Computer Society Press, 1989.

Case, A. *Team System Analysis*. Englewood Cliffs, N.J.: Prentice-Hall.

Chen, P. P. "The Entity-Relationship Model—Toward a Unified View of Data." ACM Transactions on Database Systems, Vol. 1, March 1976, 9 – 36.

Clement, P.C., R.A. Parker, D.L. Parnas, J.E. Shore, and K.H. Brit. "A Standard Organization for Specifying Abstract Interfaces," Washington, D.C.: Naval Research Laboratory.

Collofello, James S. *The Software Technical Review Process*. SEI Curriculum Module SEI-CM-3-1.2 (Preliminary), July 1987.

Connor, M. F. "Structured Analysis and Design Technique (SADT) Introduction." Engineering Management Conference Record, IEEE, May 1980, 138 – 143.

Cross, N. *Development in Design Methodology*. New York: John Wiley, 1984.

Davis, C. G., S. Jajodia, P. A. Ng, and R. T. Yeh. *Entity-Relationship Approach to Software Engineering*. New York: North Holland, 1983.

DeMarco, T. *Structured Analysis and System Specification*. Englewood Cliffs, N.J.: Prentice-Hall, 1979.

Dijkstra, E. W., F. Dahl, and C. A. R. Hoare. *Structured Programming*. New York: Academic Press, 1972.

DOD Ada Joint Office. "Ada Methodologies: Concepts and Requirements," (Methodman Doct.), Nov 1982.

Druffel, L. "Software technology for Adaptable, reliable systems—program Strategy." SIGSOFT Software Engineering Notes, Vol. 8, April 1983.

Fairly, R. *Software Engineering Concepts*. New York: McGraw-Hill, 1985.

Firth, Robert, Bill Wood, Rich Pethia, Lauren Roberts, Vickey Mosley, Tom Doice. *A Classification Scheme for Software Development Methods*. Carnegie-Mellon University, Pittsburgh, Pa.: Technical Report, Software Engineering Institute, November 1987.

Fox, J. M. *Software and Its Development*. Englewood Cliffs, N.J.: Prentice-Hall, 1982.

Freeman, Peter, and Anthony Wasserman. "Tutorial on Software Design Techniques," Washington, D.C.: IEEE Computer Society, 1983.

Gane C., and T. Sarson. *Structured Systems Analysis: Tools and Techniques*. Computer, July 1977.

Gommaa, H. "Software Development of Real-Time Systems," Communications of the ACM 29, July 1986, 657 – 668.

Harel, D., A. Pnueli, and R. Sherman. "On the Formal Semantics of Statecharts," Proceedings of the 2nd IEEE Symposium on Logic in Computer Science, Ithaca, N.Y., June 22 – 24, 1987.

_____. "STATEMATE: A Working Environment for the Development of Complex Reactive Systems," New York: IEEE Press, 1988, 396 – 406.

Hatley, D. and I. Pirbhai. *Strategies for Real-Time System Specifications*. New York: Dorset House, 1987.

Heitz, M. *HOOD: Hierarchical Object Oriented Design for development of large technical and realtime software*. CISI Ingenierie, Direction Midi Pyrenees, November 1987.

Hori, S. *CAM-I Long Range Planning Final Report for 1972*. Chicago: Illinois Institute of Technology Research, 1972.

Husa, J.D. "Stimulating software Engineering process—A report of the software engineering planning group," ACM SIGSOFT software engineering notes, Vol. 8, No. 2, April 1983.

Humphrey, Watts. "CASE Planning and the Software Process." Technical Report, CMU/SEI-89-TR-26.

IEEE, Software Engineering Standards: 3rd Edition, N.J., 1989.

Jackson, M. *The Jackson Design Methodology, Infotec State of the Art Report, Structured Programming*. 1978.

Johnson, A. L. "Software Engineering Combines Management and Technical Skills." SEI Bridge, Aug/Sep 1986.

Jorgensen, Paul C. *Requirements Specification Overview*. SEI Curriculum Module SEI-CM-1-1.2 (Preliminary), July 1987.

Katzan, Harry. *Systems Design and Documentation*. New York: Van Nostrand Reinhold Company, 1976.

Liskov, B. and S.N. Zilles. "Programming with Abstract Data Types." ACM SIGPLAN Notices 9(4) April, 1974, 50 – 60.

Martin, Charles F. *User-Centered Requirements Analysis*. Englewood Cliffs, N.J.: Prentice-Hall.

McMenamin S. M., and J.F. Palmer. *Essential Systems Analysis*. New York: Yourdon Press, 1984.

Mills, Everald E. *Software Metrics*. SEI Curriculum Module SEI-CM-12-1.0, October 1987.

Mills, H. D. "Stepwise Refinement and Verification in Box-Structured Systems." IEEE Computer, Vol. 21, No. 6, June 1988, 23 – 36.

Palmer, J.F. "Integrating the Structured Techniques with JAD: Leveled Systems development." A working paper presented at 12th Structured Methods Conference, Aug 1987.

Parnas, D. "On the Criteria to be used in Decomposing Systems into Modules." Communication of the ACM, Vol. 15, Dec 1972.

Parnas, D. L., P.C. Clements, and D.M. Weiss. "The Modular Structure of Complex Systems." IEEE Transactions on Software Engineering, Vol. SE-11, No. 3, March 1985.

Partsch, H., and R. Steinbruggen. "Program Transaction Systems." Computing Surveys, Vol. 15, No. 3, Sept 1983, 199 – 236.

Pedersen, J. S. *Software Development Using VDM Curriculum Module SEI-CM-16-1.0*. Carnegie-Mellon University, Pittsburgh, Pa.: Software Engineering Institute, 1988.

Peters, L. J. *Software design: Methods and Techniques*. New York: Yourdon Press, 1981.

Rombach, H. Dieter. "Software Specification: A Framework." SEI Curriculum Module SEI-CM-11-1.0, Oct 1987.

Ross, D. T. "Applications and Extensions of SADT." IEEE Computer, Vol. 18, No. 4, April 1985, 25 – 34.

———. "Douglas Ross Talks about Structured Analysis." IEEE Computer, Vol. 18, No. 7, July 1985, 80 – 88.

Royce, W. W. "Managing the Development of Large Software Systems." Proc. 9th International Conference Software Engineering, IEEE Computer Society, 1987, 328 – 338.

Rush, G. "A Fast Way to Define System Requirements." *Computerworld*, Oct 7, 1985.

Sathi, A., T. Morton, and S. Roth. "Callisto: An Intelligent Project Management System," AI Magazine 7, 5 (1986), 34 – 52.

Scacchi, W. *Model of Software Evolution: Life Cycle and Process*. SEI Curriculum Module SEI-CM-10-1.0, Oct 1987.

Scacchi, Walt. *Models of Software Evolution: Life Cycle and Process*. SEI Curriculum Module SEI-CM-10-1.0, October 1987.

Shlaer, Sally and Stephen J. Mellor. *Object Oriented Systems Analysis, Modelling the world in Data*. Englewood Cliffs, N.J.: Yourdon Press, 1988.

Sodhi, Jag. *Computer Systems Techniques: Development, Implementation, and Software Maintenance*. Blue Ridge Summit, Pa.: TAB Professional and Reference, TAB Books Inc., 1990.

_____. *Managing Ada Projects using Software Engineering*. Blue Ridge Summit, Pa.: TAB Professional and Reference, TAB Books Inc., 1990.

_____. "Evaluation of Teaching SERA." Seventh Annual National Conference for Ada Technology, 1989.

_____. "Overview of Ada Features for Real-Time Systems," Defense Science, November 1988.

Sodhi, Jag, and K.M. George. "Objects with Multiple Representations in Ada." Seventh Annual National Conference for Ada Technology, 1989.

STARS Joint Services Team. *Stars Software Environment (SEE) Operational Concept Document (OCD)*. Proposed Version 001.0, Dep. Defense, Oct 1985.

Stevens, W. P., G. J. Myers, and L. L. Constantine. "Structured Design." IBM Systems Journal, Vol. 13, No. 2, May 1974, 115 – 139.

Teichrow, D. "PSL/PSA: A Computer Aided Technique for Structured Documentation and Analysis of Information Processing Systems." IEEE Transition Software Engineering, SE-3, 1 (Jan 1977), 41 – 48.

U.S. Air Force. *ESD Implementation Guide for DOD-STD-2167A System Software Development Standard*. Mass.: Jan 30, 1989.

U.S. CECOM. *Software Engineering for Managers*. M101, Teacher's Guide, 1986.

_____. *Software Methodology Catalog*, 1989.

U.S. Department of Defense, Military Standard. *Defense System Software Development, DOD-STD-2167A*. Washington, D.C.

Ward, T. Paul, and Stephen J. Mellor. *Structured Development for Real-Time Systems*. Volumes I, II, III, Englewood Cliffs, N.J.: Prentice-Hall, 1985.

Warnier, J.D., and Kenneth T. Orr. *Structured Systems Development*, New York: Yourdon Press, 1977.

Wasserman, A. I., P. A. Pircher, and R. J. Muller. "An Object-Oriented Structured Design Method for Code Generation." SIGSOFT Software Engineering Notes, Vol. 14, No. 1, Jan 1989, 32 – 55.

Wirth, N. "Program development by Stepwise refinement." Communications of the ACM, Vol. 14, No. 4, April 1971, 221 – 227.

Wood, William G., John P. Long, and David P. Wood. "Classifying Software Design Methods." Technical Report, CMU/SEI-89-TR-25.

Yourdon, Edward, and Constantine L. Larry. *Structured Design*, New York: Yourdon Press, 1978.

Yourdon, E., ed. *Classics in Software Engineering.* New York: Yourdon Press, 1979.

Zave, P. "An Organizational Approach to Requirements Specification for Embedded Systems." IEEE Transaction on Software Engineering, Vol. 8, No. 3, May 1982, 250–269.

Index

A

abbreviations and acronyms, 349-352

abstraction, 5, 68, 175-176

access association, ObjectOry, 263

acronyms and abbreviations, 349-352

activity chart languages, 122

ADAMAT CASE-supporting tools, 347

adaptability, 5, 8

adoptability
  methodology selection, 59
  STRADIS, 69-70

afferent, 40

AISLE CASE tools, 328-332

Alford, 153

analysis, 3, 4

analysis library, TAGS, 191-193

approaches to software development, 39-50

architectural configuration, 19, 97

architecture diagrams, object-oriented design (OOD), 242-243

Artifex CASE tools, 320-323

artificial intelligence, 230

B

Bachman, 88

Bachman diagrams, 167-168

backlog interface, refinement method (RD), 101

Baldassari, Marco, 127

batch systems, 7

Bauer, Fritz, 3

Bjorner, 175

black box, 111-113

blueprinting, system (see SADT)

Boehm, B., 24, 25

Booch, G., 47, 48, 149, 245

bottom-up approach to design, 246

box structure methodology for information system development, 111-113

Britton, Kathryn, 109

Bruno, Giorgio, 127

bubble charts (see also data flow diagrams (DFD)), 87

Buhr, 149

Byron language, 225-229

C

Caine, 149

CASE tools, 5, 6, 8, 285-298
  AISLE, 328-332
  Artifex, 320-323
  assessment of CASE tools for selection, 297-298
  basic components, 285

candidate list, 298

capability assessment, 295

CASEWORKS, 336-338

coding and unit testing, 291

detailed design phase, 290

Digital CASE Environment (DCE), 338-343

DOD-STD-2167A, 287

ease of use assessment, 294-295

effective use guidelines, 298

environmental analysis, 297

evaluation guidelines, 294-297

forward software engineering (FSE), 293

functionality assessment, 295

generic CASE tool diagram, 286

good design characteristics, 287-292

insertion ease assessment, 296

intelligent CASE tools (ICT), 345-346

knowledge-based (KBCT), 346

needs and requirements analysis, 297

Object Plus, 333-336

preliminary design phase, 289

problem statement language/problem statement analyzer (PSL/PSA), 314

project managment, 288

ProKit WORKBENCH, 299-309

CASE tools (*con't*)
  ProMod, 313-314
  resoftware engineering (RE), 293
  reverse software engineering (RSE), 293
  robustness assessment, 295
  SERA, 95
  software component integration and testing, 291
  software configuration-item testing phase, 292
  software engineering design (S, 106
  software prototyping/simulation, 346-347
  software requirements analysis phase, 289
  Software through Pictures (StP), 309-313
  structured design (SD), 100
  supporting tools, 347
  system integration and testing phase, 292
  system requirements analysis phase, 288
  Teamwork, 323-328
  Technology for automated generation of systems (TAGS), 316-320
  types of CASE tools, 293-294
  UCRA, 90
  vendor support, 296
CASEWORKS CASE tools, 336-338
cell model theory, 83
central transforms, 41
characteristics of software engineering, 5-8
charateristics of systems, 5
Chen, 48, 88, 119
class structure, object-oriented design (OOD), 239-241
classes, OOSD, 247
clear box, 111-113
Clements, Paul, 109
closed objects, PROTOB, 128, 130, 137
coding, 3, 4, 16, 291
cohesion, 43-44, 98
coincidental cohesion, 44
common data coupling, 43
communication association, ObjecTory, 264
communicational cohesion, 44

completeness, 5
component design, 19
computer languages, 175
  artificial intelligence, 230
  Byron, 225-229
  fifth-generation, 230
  fourth-generation, 229-230
  input/output requirements language (IORL), 182-184
  language-dependent methods, 223-230
  object-oriented programming (OOP), 231-233
  program design language (PDL), 223-224
  SADT, 84-85
  structured design (SD), 99
computer-aided programming, ProMod, 155
concurrency, OOSD, 250
concurrent systems, 7
configuration management, 3, 4
  SADT, 86
  TAGS, 185-187
confirmability, 5
Constantine, 97, 101, 119, 245
constraints, 13, 54
constructors, object-oriented design (OOD), 235
content coupling, 43
control coupling, 43
control flows, software through pictures (StP), 117-118
controls, 3, 15, 44-45, 98
cost analysis, 6, 7, 54, 109-111
coupling, 42-43, 98
Cox, 128
cross validation, 68

D

data coupling, 43
data dictionaries, 88, 275-276
data flow diagrams (DFD), 89
  SADT, 84
  SERA, 93
  software engineering design (SED), 101-103, 107
  SSA, 87
  STRADIS, 68, 71-76, 78
  structured design (SD), 98, 99
  Yourdon DFD, 88
data item descriptions (DID), 27, 32-34
data management, 4
data-based methods, 171-178

data-item tasking standards, 37
data/entity-oriented methodologies, 161-170
database management systems
  Vienna development method (VDM), 177-178
databases, 4, 68, 90
Davis, 48
debugging, 19
decision trees, STRADIS, 79-80
Defense Department (DOD) standards, 28-35
DeMarco, 40, 87, 88, 91, 97, 119, 149
Department of Defense (DOD) standards, 28-35
derivation, object-oriented design (OOD), 241
descriptive characterization, modeling, 21
design approach for real-time systems (DARTS), 123-125
design processes, 3, 4, 13-15
design unit packaging, 82
detailed design phase, CASE tools, 290
development process, 9-16
  delivery scheduling, 31
  design processes, 13-15
  implementation process, 16
  maintenance process, 16
  reviews, 30
  study processes, 10-13
diagnostic analyzer, TAGS, 188-190
diagrams (*see* data flow diagrams (DFDs))
Digital CASE Environment (DCE) CASE tools, 338-343
Dijkstra, 234
distributed computer design system (DCDS), 153
distributed processing systems, STRADIS, 68
document processor, TAGS, 193-194
documentation, 4, 8, 19, 98
DOD-STD-2167A, 28-32, 92, 152
  CASE tools, 287
  object-oriented method (OOM), 280
dynamic animation, SADT, 85

E

effect, scope, 44, 98

efferent, 41
efficiency, 5
entities, ObjectOry, 262-264
entity diagrams, 166-167
entity-relationship approach to
    design, 48
environmental objects, PROTOB,
    142-143
error handling, 5
essential systems analysis (ESA),
    113-115
essential systems develpment (E-
    DEV), 113-115
estimation, 4
evaluation criteria, structured
    design (SD), 98
event-oriented approach to design,
    48
exceptions, OOSD, 247-248
external coupling, 43

F

fan-ins/outs, 42
Farber, 149
Faulk, Stuart, 109
feasibility study, 12
fifth-generation languages, 230
finite state machines, object-ori-
    ented design (OOD), 240
firmware standards, 37
Foresight, 347
forward software engineering
    (FSE) CASE tools, 293
fourth-generation languages, 229-
    230
functional cohesion, 44
functional requirements, 13, 17,
    102
functionality, 7

G

Gane, C., 63, 88, 119, 122
general project plans (GPP),
    STRADIS, 66, 69
generic classes, 248, 249
goals and objectives of software
    engineering, 5
Gommaa, Hassan, 123
Gordon, 149
Gotvald, G.J., 181-182

H

hardware diagrams, object-oriented
    design (OOD), 239
Harel, 122

Hatley, Derek, 119, 125
heuristic design, 44-45, 98
Hevner, A., 112
hierarchical decomposition, SSA,
    87
hierarchical object-oriented design
    (HOOD), 134, 256-258
HIPO chart, structured design
    (SD), 99
Hoare, 246
Hori, 83
human subsystem (HSS), STRA-
    DIS, 66

I

IEEE standards, 28
implementation process, 16, 98
incremental development
    SADT, 85
    SERA, 91
    software cost reduction (SCR),
        109
incremental modeling, 23
information hiding, 5, 15
inheritance
    OOSD, 248, 249
    object-oriented design (OOD),
        241
input/output requirements lan-
    guage (IORL), TAGS, 182-184
instance trees, PROTOB, 135
instances, PROTOB, 128
instantiation of classes/objects,
    OOSD, 247-248
Institute of Electrical and Electron-
    ics Engineers (IEEE), 28
integration, 3, 4, 19, 291-292
intelligent CASE tools (ICT), 345-
    346
interface objects, ObjectOry, 264
interfaces, 8, 15
iteration, 14
iterators, object-oriented design
    (OOD), 235

J

Jackson, 119
Jackson Structured Programming
    (JSP), 161-163
Jackson system development
    (JSD), 167-170

K

knowledge-based CASE tools
    (KBCT), 346

L

Labaw, Bruce, 109
language-dependent methods, 223-
    230
Ledgard, H., 233
life cycles, 8, 17-26
life-cycle modeling, 21
Linger,R., 112
Liskov, 234
localization, 5
logical cohesion, 44
LUIS, 347

M

MacLennan, 234
maintainability, 5
maintenance process, 3, 16, 19
management, methodology selec-
    tion, 56
*Managing Ada Projects Using
    Software Engineering*, 57
Martin, 88
McMenamin, 114
Mellor, 91, 101
MESH, 94
Meta-IV specification language,
    175
metalanguages, 175
methodologies/methods, 6, 7, 51-
    59
metrics, 58-59
MIL-STD-1521B, 35
MIL-STD-483A, 32
MIL-STD-490A, 34-35
Mills, H., 112, 113
miniature specifications, SERA, 91
modeling, 4, 20-26, 68
    PROTOB, 144-148
    SADT, 83-84
    UCRA, 88
    Vienna development method
        (VDM, 176-177
modifiability, 5
modularity, 5, 98
module chart languages, 122
modules, 42, 45, 90
Muller, Bob, 245
multiplicity, object-oriented method
    (OOM), 274-275
multitasking, DARTS, 123-125
Myers, 97

N

natural languages, 230

network design, STRADIS, 68
nondeliverable software, standards, 37
nonfunctional requirements, 13

O

object analysis model (OAM), object-oriented method (OOM), 272
object behavior model (OBM), object-oriented method (OOM), 277-280
object data dictionary, object-oriented method (OOM), 275-276
object diagrams, object-oriented design (OOD), 241
object information model (OIM), object-oriented method (OOM), 272-275
Object Plus CASE tools, 333-336
object process model (OPM), object-oriented method (OOM), 280
object-oriented approach to design, 46-48
object-oriented design (OOD), 233-243
  architecture diagram, 242-243
  class structure, 239-241
  concepts, 233-234
  constructors, 235
  derivation, 241
  finite state machines, 240
  hardware diagram, 239
  inheritance, 241
  iterators, 235
  method, 236-238
  notation, 238-243
  object diagram, 241
  principles, 234
  project models, 239
  selectors, 235
  software development life cycle vs., 243
  static vs. dynamic sematics, 235
  system topology, 237
object-oriented design methods, 91, 231-243
object-oriented method (OOM), 271-281
  concepts, 272
  correlation symbol, 276
  DOD-STD-2167A, 280
  goals and objectives, 271

multiplicity, 274-275
notations, 275
object analysis model (OAM), 272
object behavior model (OBM), 277-280
object data dictionary, 275-276
object information model (OIM), 272-275
object process model (OPM), 280
pros and cons, 281
requirements definition model, 280
selection criteria for correct object, 276
state transition table, 278
supertype/subtype constructs, 276
object-oriented programming (OOP), 231-233
object-oriented software methodologies, 259-270
object-oriented structured design (OOSD), 245-256
  actuator package, 254
  benefits of use, 250
  bottom-up approach, 246
  chart of process, 253
  classes, 247
  concepts, 245-246
  concurrency, 250
  events package, 253
  exceptions, 247-248
  generic classes, 248, 249
  goals, 245
  high-level architecture example, 252
  inheritance, 248, 249
  instantiation of classes, 248, 249
  instantiation of objects, 247-248
  monitor package, 253, 255
  notation, 247
  sensor package, 254
  speeds package, 256
  use and application example, 250-256
ObjectOry, 259-270
  access association, 263
  advantages of use, 270
  block diagrams, 267
  blocks and components, 259
  communication association, 264
  entities, 262-264
  interface objects, 264

methodology discussion, 267-270
objects, object types and properties, 269
presentation objects, 264
schematic interaction diagram, 268
services, 264
system analysis (SA), 261-265
system design, 265-266
system development, 259-261
use cases, 261-262
objects, PROTOB, 128
operational modeling, 26
Orr, Ken, 163

P

PACKAGE objects, PROTOB, 134-135
packaging, 98
Parnas, David, 109, 149, 246
partitioning, 19
Partsch, H., 26
PAWS/GPSM, 347
performance, 7
Peters, L., 45, 97
Petri nets, PROTOB, 127, 130
pins, PROTOB, 128
Pirbhai, Imtiaz, 119, 125
Pircher, Peter, 117, 245
planning, 3, 4
Pnueli, 122
polymorphism, 47
portability, 5
preliminary design phase, CASE tools, 289
prescriptive characterization, modeling, 21
presentation objects, ObjectOry, 264
problem assessment, 12
problem domains, 6
problem statement language/problem statement analyzer (PSL/PSA) 171-175, 314-316
procedures, 3
productivity, 58-59
program design language (PDL), 45, 223-224
project control (*see* controls)
project management, 4, 6, 288
project models, object-oriented design (OOD), 239

project tracking (*see* tracking)
ProKit WORKBENCH CASE
   tools, 299-309
ProMod, 149-153, 313-314
   automated tools, 150
   computer-aided programming,
      155
   design charts, 151-153
   DOD STD-2167A, 152
   major components, 149-150
   modular design, 151-152
   report generators, 156
   source code generators, 154
   structured analysis (SA), 150-151
   traceability, 157
PROT nets, PROTOB, 127, 130-134
PROTOB,   127-148
   closed objects, 128, 130, 137
   connecting objects, 143-144
   environmental objects, 142-143
   example of use, 140-142
   hierarchies of structure/intercon-
      nect, 129
   HOOD methodology, 134
   instance trees, 135
   instances, 128
   interconnection of instances,
      135-138
   objects, 128
   PACKAGE objects, 134-135
   parent/child relationships, 129
   pins, 128
   PROT nets, 130-134
   selective routing and broadcast-
      ing, 138-140
   senior/junior relationships, 129
   stack operations, 134-135
   superports/superlinks, 136
   system behavior modeling, 144-
      148
   systems, 129
   user and device instances, 129
   user and device objects, 139
   views, 140
prototyping, 4, 17, 23-24
   CASE tools, 347
   SADT, 85
   SERA, 91
   software cost reduction (SCR),
      109
   tools, 346-347

Q

quality assurance, 3, 4, 54, 86

R

R-nets,   SREM, 159
Rajlich, Vaclav, 100
reactive systems, 7
real-time systems methods, 117-
   148
reference materials/reading list,
   371-375
refinement method (RM), 100-101
reliability, 5
report generators, ProMod, 156
requestor, STRADIS, 63
requirements determination and
      analysis, 6, 10-13, 17
   CASE tools, 288
   object-oriented method (OOM),
      280
   software engineering require-
      ments analysis (SERA), 90-95
   standards tailored to needs, 35-
      37
   user-centered requirements
      analysis (UCRA), 88-90
resoftware engineering (RE) CASE
   tools, 293
retained state information, 15
retirement of obsolete software,
   19-20
reusability, 5
reuse of components, 8, 24
reverse software engineering
   (RSE) CASE tools, 293
reviews, 30
risk assessment, 12, 86
robustness, 7, 14
Ross, 12
Royce, W., 21
runtime issues, 15

S

Sarson, P., 63, 88, 119, 122
Sayani, Hasan, 171
scheduling, 4, 6, 31
scope of control, 44, 98
scope of effect, 44, 98
selectors, object-oriented design
   (OOD), 235
semantics, static vs. dynamic,
   object-oriented design (OOD),
   235
separation, 14
sequential cohesion, 44
services, ObjectOry, 264

simplicity, 14
Simula, 231
simulation, 4, 17, 23-24
   CASE tools, 347
   SADT, 85
   SERA, 91
   simulation compiler, TAGS, 189-
      191
   tools, 346-347
simulation compiler, TAGS, 189-
   191
SmallTalk, 231
software cost reduction (SCR),
   109-111
software development files standards, 36
software engineering design
      (SED), 101-106
   case study in design, 106-108
   context diagram, 106
   data flow diagram, 101-103, 107
   functional requirements list, 102
   SERA usage, 101
   state transition diagram (STD),
      103, 105, 108
   system hierarchy chart, 104, 107
software engineering requirements
      analysis (SERA), 90-95
   data flow diagrams, 93
   major components, 91
   MESH, 94
   miniature specifications, 91
   object-oriented design methods,
      91
   software engineering design
      (SED), 101
   system context diagram, 93
software requirements engineering
      methodology (SREM), 153-159
   architecture, 159
   concepts, 158
   goals and objectives, 156-157
   overview of system, 158
   principles, 155-156
   R-net notations, 159
   software support tools, 154
Software through Pictures (StP),
   117-121, 309-313
source code generators
   ProMod, 154
   TAGS, 194-195
span of control, 98
specifications, 5, 85
   miniature, 91
spiral modeling, 24-26

stacks, PROTOB, 134-135
standards, 27-37, 92
    software development, 369-370
    tailoring to needs, 35-37
state box, 111-113
state transition diagrams (STD),
    103-105, 108
state transition table, object-ori-
    ented method (OOM), 278
statechart languages, 122
STATEMATE, 122-123, 347
Steinbrueggen, R., 26
stepwise refinement modeling, 48-
    49, 68, 178
Stevens, 43, 97, 100
strategies for system development
    (SSD), 125-127, 125
structured analysis, 40, 83-95
    ProMod, 150-151
    STRADIS, 70
structured analysis and design
    technique (SADT), 83-86
    concept model, 85
    data flow diagram, 84
    languages used with SADT, 84-
    85
structured analysis/design/imple-
    ment of information systems
    (STRADIS), 63-82
    access model, 79
    adoptability ease, 69-70
    case study, 70-82
    computer languages, 68
    data flow diagrams (DFD), 68,
    71-76, 78
    decision trees, 79-80
    diagram of process, 64-65
    error detection schemes, 68
    general project plan (GPP), 66,
    69
    hardware, 68
    human subsystem (HSS), 66
    logical model of system, 81
    management aspects, 69
    requestor, 63
    structured analysis, 70
    structured design, 82
    structured English, 79-82
    technical description, 67-69
structured approach, 39-46
structured charts, 41
structured design (SD), 40, 97-100
    coupling, 98
    data flow diagram, 98, 99
    design strategies, 98

documentation, 98
evaluation criteria/heuristics, 98
groups, 98
HIPO chart, 99
implementation strategies, 98
languages, 99
structure chart, 99
uses and applications, 99, 100
structured English, 79-82
structured methodology, 3, 109-
    115
structured programming, 45-46
structured programming design
    language (PDL), 45
structured programming Jackson
    structured programming (JSP),
    161-163
structured system analysis (SSA),
    87-88
structured walk-throughs, 57, 91
study process, 10-13
superports/superlinks, PROTOB,
    136
support environments (see also
    tools), 4
system blueprinting (see SADT)
system development, ObjectOry,
    259
system engineering standards, 37
systems classifications, 6-7

T

T CASE-supporting tools, 347
task model, object-oriented design
    (OOD), 233
Teamwork CASE tools, 323-328
technology for automated genera-
    tion of systems (TAGS),
    181-221, 316-320
    adoptability, 197
    analysis library, 191-193
    code generator, 194-195
    components, 184
    configuration management, 185-
    187
    diagnostic analyzer, 188-190
    document processor, 193-194
    examples of coding/performance,
    198-221
    greatest common denominator
    (GCD) system coding, 213-221
    input/output requirements lan-
    gauge (IORL), 182-184
    IORL hierarchy, 184

management aspects, 196-197
methodology charted, 183
simulation compiler, 189-191
storage and retrieval, 184-186
technical descriptions, 194-196
Teicherow, Daniel, 171
temporal cohesion, 44
testing, 3, 4, 16, 19, 291, 292
tools, 4-5
    CASE-supporting, 347
    intelligent CASE tools (ICT),
    345-346
    knowledge-based CASE
    (KBCT), 346
    prototyping/simulation, 346-347
    SADT, 86
    software prototyping/simulation,
    346-347
top-down design, 98
traceability, 5, 8
tracking, 3
training needs, 6, 19
transaction analysis, 98
transform-centered design, 98
transformation schema, 122
transformational modeling, 26

U

U.S. Department of Defense
    (DOD) Standards, 28-35
understandability, 5
uniformity, 5
URL/URA (see problem statement
    language)
use cases, ObjectOry, 261-262
user-centered requirements analy-
    sis (UCRA), 88-90
user-friendliness, 8

V

vendor support, 59
vendors, 353-368
Vienna development method
    (VDM), 175-178
    abstraction, 175-176
    blocks, 177
    data models/database manage-
    ment systems, 177-178
    modeling techniques, 176-177
    specification language, 175
    stepwise development, 178
    subprograms and macros, 177
    types and values, 176

variables, storage, locations, 177
views, PROTOB, 140

W

walk-throughs, structured, 57, 91
Ward, 91, 101
Ward/Mellor Real-Time method, 121-122

Warnier, Jean, 163
Warnier-Orr methodology, 163-166
Wasserman, Anthony, 117, 245, 309
waterfall modeling, 109
wide-spectrum languages, 175
Wirth, N., 48, 49, 149
waterfall modeling, 21-23

Y

Yourdon, 87, 88, 91, 97, 101, 119, 149

Z

Zilles, 234

Other Bestsellers of Related Interest

MANAGING ADA PROJECTS USING SOFTWARE ENGINEERING—Jag Sodhi

The Ada programming language was developed to produce high-quality software for embedded computer applications. This book examines the structured methods, tools, documents, standards, and procedures you need to help in the systematic development, production, and maintenance of your quality software. Sodhi lays down guidelines that managers, software engineers, systems analysts, and programmers can use to set up secure, cost-effective Ada projects. 260 pages, 87 illustrations. Book No. 3373, $34.95 hardcover only

CONFIGURATION MANAGEMENT HANDBOOK
—W.V. Eggerman

Now, for the first time under one cover, this handbook lays out field-tested plans that will help your firm achieve high performance on government-contracted jobs without struggling through years of trial-and-error experience. Here's in-depth information on the scope and application of all DoD and military standards and specifications for the management, change control, and status reporting of contractor specifications, engineering drawings, and related technical documentation. 210 pages, Illustrated. Book No. 3375, $29.95 hardcover only

STRATEGY, SYSTEMS, AND INTEGRATION:
A Handbook for Information Managers
—George M. Hall

Now you can successfully plan new data processing systems and integrate existing systems. Hall shows you how you can get beyond basic strategic problems and concentrate on mastering the techniques that will meet the increasing demands of your system. From an in-depth analysis of database requirements to key management issues, you'll follow the logical order in which systems should be designed and developed. 384 pages, 118 illustrations. Book No. 3614, $39.95 hardcover only

COMPUTER TOOLS, MODELS, AND TECHNIQUES FOR PROJECT MANAGEMENT
—Dr. Adedeji B. Badiru and Dr. Gary E. Whitehouse

Badiru and Whitehouse provide you with practical, down-to-earth guidance on the use of project management tools, models, and techniques. You'll find this book filled with helpful tips and advice. You'll also discover ways to use your current computer hardware and software resources to more effectively enhance project management functions. 320 pages, 112 illustrations. Book No. 3200, $32.95 hardcover only

THE C4 HANDBOOK: CAD, CAM, CAE, CIM
—Carl Machover

Increase your productivity and diversity with this collection of articles by international industry experts, detailing what you can expect from the latest advances in computer aided design and manufacturing technology. Machover has created an invaluable guide to identifying equipment requirements, justifying investments, defining and selecting systems, and training staff to use the systems. 448 pages, 166 illustrations. Book No. 3098, $44.50 hardcover only

BUILDING C LIBRARIES—Len Dorfman

Improve the quality of your programs while drastically reducing development time with this new guide from expert Len Dorfman. He shows you how to use the library manager to create your own professional window, screen, and keyboard handling libraries. *Building C Libraries* emphasizes interfaces and library development. You get line after line of well-documented source code for menus, pop-up windows, Macintosh-style pull-downs, bounce bars, and more. 432 pages, 198 illustrations. Book No. 3418, $26.95 paperback, $34.95 hardcover

Look for These and Other TAB Books at Your Local Bookstore

To Order Call Toll Free 1-800-822-8158
(in PA, AK, and Canada call 717-794-2191)

or write to TAB BOOKS, Blue Ridge Summit, PA 17294-0840.

Title	Product No.	Quantity	Price

☐ Check or money order made payable to TAB BOOKS

Charge my ☐ VISA ☐ MasterCard ☐ American Express

Acct. No. _____ Exp. _____

Signature: _____

Name: _____

Address: _____

City: _____

State: _____ Zip: _____

Subtotal $ _____

Postage and Handling
($3.00 in U.S., $5.00 outside U.S.) $ _____

Add applicable state and local
sales tax $ _____

TOTAL $ _____

TAB BOOKS catalog free with purchase; otherwise send $1.00 in check or money order and receive $1.00 credit on your next purchase.

Orders outside U.S. must pay with international money order in U.S. dollars.

TAB Guarantee: If for any reason you are not satisfied with the book(s) you order, simply return it (them) within 15 days and receive a full refund.   **BC**